The opening book in Cambridge's new **Cultural Margins** series is a ground-breaking study of racism and homophobia in British politics, which demonstrates the demonization of blacks, lesbians and gays in New Right discourse. Anna Marie Smith develops theoretical insights from literary and cultural critics, including Nietzsche, Foucault, Derrida, Hall and Gilroy, to produce detailed readings of two key moments in New Right discourse: the speeches of Enoch Powell on black immigration (1968–72) and the legislative campaign of the late 1980s to prohibit the promotion of homosexuality. Her analysis challenges the silence on racism and homophobia in previous studies of Thatcherism and the New Right, and shows how marginalization of lesbians and gays depends on previous demonizations of black immigrant and criminal figures. Overall this book offers a devastating critique of racism and homophobia in late twentieth-century Britain.

Cultural Margins 1

New Right discourse on race and sexuality

Cultural Margins

General editor

Abdul JanMohamed

Department of English, University of California, Berkeley

The series **Cultural Margins** originates in response to the rapidly increasing interest in postcolonial and minority discourses among literary and humanist scholars in the US, Europe, and elsewhere. The aim of the series is to present books (both contributory and by single authors) which investigate the complex cultural zone within and through which dominant and minority societies interact and negotiate their differences.

Studies published in the series will range from examinations of the debilitating effects of cultural marginalization, to analyses of the forms of power found at the margins of culture, to books which map the varied and complex components involved in the relations of domination and subversion. The books will engage with expressions of cultural marginalization which might be literary (e.g. the novels of African or Caribbean or Native American writers within a postcolonial context); or textual in a broader sense (e.g. legal or cultural documents relating to the subordination of groups under categories such as race and gender); or dramatic (e.g. subversive performance art by minority groups such as gays and lesbians); or in the sphere of popular culture (e.g. film, video, TV).

This is an international series, addressing questions crucial to the deconstruction and reconstruction of cultural identity in the late twentieth-century world.

Series titles to be published in 1995

Masks of difference: Cultural representations in literature, anthropology and art
by David Richards

Joyce, race, and empire
by Vincent J. Cheng

New Right discourse on race and sexuality

Britain, 1968–1990

Anna Marie Smith
Cornell University

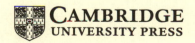
CAMBRIDGE
UNIVERSITY PRESS

Published by the Press Syndicate of the University of Cambridge
The Pitt Building, Trumpington Street, Cambridge CB2 1RP
40 West 20th Street, New York, NY 10011–4211, USA
10 Stamford Road, Oakleigh, Victoria 3166, Australia

© Cambridge University Press 1994

First published 1994

Printed in Great Britain at the University Press, Cambridge

A catalogue record for this book is available from the British Library

Library of Congress cataloguing in publication data
Smith, Anna Marie.
New Right discourse on race and sexuality: Britain, 1968–1990 /
Anna Marie Smith.
    p.   cm. – (Cultural margins: 1)
Includes index.
ISBN 0 521 45297 X (hardback)   ISBN 0 521 45921 4 (paperback)
1. Great Britain – Race relations – Public opinion.
2. Great Britain – Politics and government – 1979–   .
3. Sexual orientation – Public opinion – Great Britain.
4. Homosexuality – Public opinion – Great Britain.
5. Public opinion – Great Britain – History – 20th century.
6. Conservatism – Great Britain – History – 20th century.
I. Title.   II. Series.
DA125.A1S597 1994
305.8'00941'09045 – dc20   93–42801   CIP

ISBN 0 521 45297 X hardback
ISBN 0 521 45921 4 paperback

for Roxi

Contents

Acknowledgements

It is my pleasure to acknowledge the many colleagues and friends who made this project possible. I would especially like to thank Juan Maiguashca, York University, Toronto, Bob Gallagher, University of Toronto, Sue Golding, University of Greenwich and *The Body Politic*, a Canadian lesbian and gay publication, for introducing me to discourse theory; Ernesto Laclau and Chantal Mouffe for intellectual inspiration and academic support; and Aletta Norval for her contributions to our doctoral seminar in Ideology and Discourse Analysis at Essex. Parveen Adams, Erica Carter, Tessa Boffin, Martin Jacques and Ken Plummer all provided me with valuable comments on earlier versions of my research. Angela Eagle submitted many of my ideas to a vigorous critique and generously supplied me with parliamentary documents. Jeffrey Weeks, Simon Watney, George Chauncey, Renata Salecl and Slavoj Zizek made encouraging remarks about my work at crucial moments. Susan Buck-Morss, Stuart Hall, Alan Sinfield, Judith Butler and Abdul JanMohamed offered detailed comments on the manuscript. Kevin Taylor at Cambridge University Press guided me through the final stages of manuscript preparation.

Although I have been teaching for only a short while, my students have already had an enormous impact on my work. The theoretical research for this book was incorporated in my lectures for the Ideology and Discourse Analysis MA seminar in the Department of Government at Essex, between October 1990 and February 1991. I have also attempted to clarify various points following my discussions with students in two courses which I taught in the Department of Government at Cornell during the 1993 spring semester, 'Modern Social Theory' and 'Concepts of Race and Racism'.

Acknowledgements

I completed the major revisions to the text during a post-doctoral appointment at the Society for the Humanities at Cornell. I would like to thank Jonathan Culler, Dominick LaCapra, Mary Ahl, Aggie Sirrine and Linda Allen for making my stay at the Society a very pleasant experience. Mandy Merck and Judith Butler generously allowed me to participate in their Society seminars. Susan Buck-Morss, Biddy Martin, Mary Katzenstein, Nancy Hirschmann, Brett de Bary and Lois Brown gave me a warm welcome to Cornell and, through various discussions, challenged me to refine my arguments further. Martin Bernal, Elizabeth Sanders and Peter Katzenstein offered suggestions, criticisms and encouragement. Ben Anderson questioned my interpretation of Thatcherism; dissatisfied with my own response, I returned to the documents on the Falklands/Malvinas War and re-wrote a section of the Introduction. Walter Mebane cautioned me against over-interpreting the statistical data which I present in chapter 1. Nancy Hirschmann commented on the final draft of chapter 2 and shared some of her ideas about Rousseau with me. Sander Gilman and Dominick LaCapra helped me to navigate my way through a storm of Nietzschean criticism. My thanks also to Dominick for bringing the work of Cathy Caruth to my attention. Zillah Eisenstein offered excellent advice and friendship; she firmly believes that political theory really ought to be political and I have tried to follow her example. Finally, I would like to thank my queer allies whose support and spirit sustained me throughout this project: Ruthann, Sue, Cathy, Ros D., Louise, Sheridan, Sharon, Sarah, Roz K., Tessa, Jean, Cherry, Della, Joanne, Roxi, K. Lee, the members of OutRage! and the *Quim* women. I happily accept full responsibility for the errors and weaknesses which remain in the text.

I received financial assistance for my research at the University of Toronto (1986–7) and at the University of Essex (1987–91) from the following sources: the Province of Ontario (Ontario Graduate Scholarship, 1986–7), the Social Sciences and Humanities Research Council of Canada (Doctoral Fellowship, 1987–8), the Commonwealth Foundation (United Kingdom Commonwealth Doctoral Scholarship, 1988–9, 1989–90), the Canadian Centennial Scholarship Fund (Doctoral Award, 1990), and the Imperial Order of the Daughters of the Empire (Doctoral Scholarship, 1990–1). The Social Sciences and Humanities Research Council of Canada also provided a generous two-year post-doctoral fellowship which allowed me to continue my research at Cornell University (1991–3).

xi

Acknowledgements

Chapter 4 on Powellism is a re-written version of an essay which was published by the Department of Government at Essex in its *Essex Papers in Politics and Government* series in 1989. Different versions of some of the sections in chapter 5 have appeared in the following articles: 'A Symptomology of an Authoritarian Discourse: The Parliamentary Debates on the Prohibition of Homosexuality', *New Formations*, no. 10, summer 1990, 41–65; '"Which One's the Pretender?" Section 28 and Lesbian Representation' in Tessa Boffin and Jean Fraser, eds., *Stolen Glances: Lesbians Take Photographs*, London, Pandora 1991, 128–39; and 'Resisting the Erasure of Lesbian Sexuality: A Challenge for Queer Activism', in Ken Plummer, ed., *Fragments of Lesbian and Gay Experiences*, London, Routledge, 1992, 200–13. Kobena Mercer kindly granted me permission to quote from his doctoral dissertation on Powellism.

Introduction

People with other faiths and cultures have always been welcomed in this land, assured of equality under the law, of proper respect and of open friends. There is absolutely nothing incompatible between this and our desire to maintain the essence of our own identity.

Margaret Thatcher, address to the General Assembly
of the Church of Scotland, 22 May 1988

AIDS starts with and comes mainly from homosexuals [and] spreads to others.

Dame Jill Knight, House of Commons, 8 May 1987

Every political era is remembered in terms of its defining myth, and Thatcherism is no exception. Both leftist critics and right-wing supporters tend to agree that Thatcherism made its mark in British history in terms of its economic policies. They point to the fact that both the Labour and Conservative Parties had more or less accepted a Keynesian approach to managing the economy in the post-war period. The mixed-economy model which juxtaposed private enterprise with the public ownership of key industries and welfare state programmes became the dominant framework for political debates and policy initiatives. Private capital and the labour movement were brought together in various capital-labour-state social contracts which secured labour discipline in exchange for a stable economy and full employment. There were of course some deviations from the pure consensus approach in actual government policies. After Labour experimented unsuccessfully with National Plans in the 1960s, the Conservatives made various 'U-turns' between free market and managed economy policies between 1970 and 1974.

Although Labour returned to government with a strong interventionary and corporatist programme in October 1974, it introduced the first dramatic cuts to the welfare state and presided over a complete breakdown in state–trade union relations. The post-war 'consensus' model nevertheless obtained a bi-partisan hegemonic status to the extent that these policy shifts can be described as variations on a theme. From the economistic perspective which dominates the academic literature on British politics, Thatcherism's radical departure from previous political regimes consists in its total rejection of the consensus model for an individualist, monetarist and free market approach to the economy.

Standard accounts of the Thatcher governments (1979–90) therefore focus almost exclusively on economic policies: the massive cuts in government expenditure as a whole and public investment in roads, housing and the nationalized industries in particular; the privatization of nationalized industries, the de-regulation of business and the promotion of the sale of council housing; the shift to the management of the money supply rather than the management of aggregate demand; the weakening of the trade unions; the reduction in entitlements to social security benefits; and the introduction of taxation-cutting schemes.[1] Some analysts do insist on the importance of Margaret Thatcher's own personal leadership style and 'statecraft'.[2] Her views on social and moral issues, however, are generally regarded as less important than her positions on the economy. Thatcherite references to racist immigration controls, the British identity, the family, multiculturalism and morality – when they are noted at all by political analysts – are generally understood as marketing ploys which were used to sell the new economic policies. These references – so the story goes – amounted merely to superficial packaging: 'bitter-tasting market economics [were] sweetened and rendered palatable by great creamy dollops of nationalistic custard'.[3] Political analysts sometimes admit that Thatcher did have a utopian vision of the social, a vision of 'a world in which *small* businesses could compete freely for the favours of the individual *family* consumer; [in which] the State keeps law and order, including the elements of a moral order to protect family decency, and provide succour for the genuinely unfortunate who cannot help themselves'.[4] A distance, however, is usually introduced between this vision and her actual policies; she is seen as a pragmatic and 'shrewd' politician who 'zigzag[ged] towards her goals'.[5]

It is of course true that there are many important differences between Thatcherism and other neo-conservative discourses such as Reaganism. Although both political projects were based on a pro-free market platform, there was a much closer articulation – although never a total fusion – between economic and moral positions in Reaganite discourse. British pro-family and anti-abortion lobbies have a complex relationship with the Conservative Party; not all prominent Conservatives are morally conservative, and not all members of these lobbies are Conservative voters. Whereas right-wing religious groups have had at most an ambiguous effect on British politics, they have become a key movement in the United States. It is now widely recognized in the United States that contestations around sexuality play an important role at all levels of the official political system. Debates around sexuality have become fundamental sites for the establishment of an American politician's true conservative or progressive credentials. The official American political agenda – from the local government level to Presidential initiatives – includes struggles around access to abortion; sex education curricula in the schools; sexual harassment in the workplace; the censorship of pornography and lesbian and gay culture; the right to privacy; legislation which recognizes violence against lesbians, bisexuals and gays as 'hate crimes'; the funding of AIDS research, the treatment of people with AIDS, and the regulation of HIV testing procedures; the restriction of sexist, racist and homophobic[6] discourse on university campuses; the presence and conduct of lesbians, bisexuals and gays in the military; and legislation which protects sexual minorities from discrimination.

In contemporary British politics, sexuality appears to be a much less prominent issue. In the 1980s, political analysts emphasized only those aspects of the Thatcherite moral code which were explicitly linked with the legitimation of economic policies. Thatcher did, of course, make many statements on the relevance of Victorian family values to the construction of a free-market society. She often compared government expenditure to a well-managed household budget. For Thatcher, the welfare state's promotion of a dependency culture and the interference in the free market on the part of the nationalized industries and trade union movement constituted the most serious threats to moral standards. Economic renewal, therefore, entailed a moral revolution: a return to individual responsibility, free market entrepreneurialism and British nationalism. She laid out her government's economic policies in these terms in a 1979 post-election speech.

> The extent of our decline compared with other countries may show up most clearly in economic statistics. But that does not mean that the remedy lies only in economics. The mission of this Government is much more than the promotion of economic progress. It is to renew the spirit and solidarity of the nation ... At the heart of a new mood in the nation must be a recovery of our self-confidence and our self-respect.[7]

Thatcher explicitly recognized that Britain's decline had taken place in a post-colonial context. She phrased her conception of the national 'mission' in suitably neo-imperial terms.

> It will not be given to this generation of our countrymen to create a great Empire. But it is given to us to demand an end to decline and to make a stand against what Churchill described as the 'long dismal drawling tides of drift and surrender, of wrong measurements and feeble impulses'. Though less powerful than once we were, we have friends in every quarter of the globe, who will rejoice at our recovery, welcome the revival of our influence, and benefit from the message and from the example of our renewal.[8]

Taking the Thatcherite discourse at its word – rather than examining its coded demonizations and the tremendous political effects of those demonizations – political analysts tend to view the moral agenda of the Thatcherites only in terms of this nationalistic economic 'mission' of recovery. Issues around sexuality were supposedly absent from the Thatcherite agenda. In his review of the Thatcherite policies dealing with the family, Willetts comments that it is 'striking' that the Thatcherites 'avoid[ed] those areas of sexual behaviour which are the subject of so much prurient interest wherever people talk about morality or family values'. He notes that Thatcher and her Cabinet certainly did attack the 'permissiveness' of the 1960s, and recognizes that they linked the rise in criminality to socialist policies and the national decline. For Willetts, however, the Thatcherite attack on permissiveness remained a broad sweeping discourse which never dealt with the 'prurient' issue of homosexuality. He points out that the Thatcherites did not attempt to reverse the Labour Party's liberalization of abortion legislation and de-criminalization of homosexuality – as if this fact constituted sufficient evidence that the Thatcherites had nothing to say about sexuality. He dismisses Section 28 of the Local Government Act 1987–8, which prohibited the promotion of homosexuality, as a 'modest legal change'.[9] Willetts' failure to examine the role of right-wing discourse on homosexuality is typical of virtually the entire literature on

Thatcherism. Barring the odd scandal about cabinet ministers' indiscretions and the break-up of royal marriages, sexuality is supposed to be totally irrelevant to official British political discourse.

With racism, the story is somewhat different, but ultimately arrives at the same conclusion. British political scientists readily admit that Enoch Powell's racist campaign against black[10] immigration played an important role in British politics in the late 1960s and early 1970s. But it is generally assumed that as the last major crisis around a new 'wave' of black immigration wound down in 1972 – the crisis about the entry of the Ugandan Asians – black immigration and race more or less disappeared from the political agenda. Thatcher herself made a notorious speech on black immigration in 1978, in which she pledged to respond to the natural concerns of the British about the 'swamping' of their country by people from the 'New Commonwealth' – a code phrase for blacks. The Conservative Party's position in the opinion polls rose nine points directly after her speech.[11] Her 'swamping' comments, however, are typically dismissed as an exceptional moment. Powell's brand of nationalist racism is therefore quarantined in the political science literature in that it is represented as an isolated moment in the history of the Conservative Party. Racism, in short, is treated as if it were a very minor issue within Thatcherism.

I want to offer a radically different story. I do not promise to give an absolutely full account of all the socio-economic and cultural moments of British New Right discourse. Thatcherism, the most important variant of New Right discourse, is a particularly complex mixture of imagery, rhetoric and policies which was constantly re-defined in response to strategic circumstances throughout the three Thatcher governments. By focusing on race and sexuality, I am not claiming that racism and homophobia constitute the essence of Thatcherism and the British New Right in general, and that other socio-economic elements were irrelevant. To do so would be merely to reverse the essentialist erasures of the economistic account. I aim instead to re-construct two strategic moments which were central to the legitimation of Thatcherism, and to show the ways in which discourse on race and sexuality were absolutely central to them. First, a historical moment: the right-wing populist break with the consensus tradition. The success of Thatcherism's right-wing populist attack on collectivist and statist values cannot be explained purely in terms of the failures of the Wilson-Callaghan Labour government (1974–9). Hegemonic projects never emerge out of thin air; they always build on partially organized social groupings and popular ways of thinking. They especially target the social elements which have not been adequately represented within other political projects. Hegemonic strategies attempt to link or to articulate these elements together to form a new political bloc. The effectiveness of new articulations depends on two basic factors: the extent to which traditional articulations have become increasingly weakened so that social elements have entered a 'crisis' state of unfixity, and the extent to which the new articulations borrow from and re-work various traditional frameworks so that they already appear to be somewhat familiar.[12]

If we look back at the late 1960s, we can find substantial evidence that British voters had become increasingly likely to believe that they were not adequately represented within the existing two-party, consensus-oriented political system. (I shall discuss specific surveys and studies which deal with the rise of political alienation in the 1960s in chapter 4.) A right-wing populist movement did emerge at that time which spoke effectively to the concerns of many of the alienated and disenchanted. It offered a tremendously popular alternative to the consensus approach and, in this sense, laid some of the groundwork which was critical to the legitimation of Thatcherism's right-wing populist project. The key point is that this movement, Enoch Powell's anti-black immigration movement, was constructed around race and nationalism, rather than economic issues. Struggles around race – struggles around the very meaning of white-British-ness in a post-colonial world, struggles to protect the British borders against the black 'invader' from the former colonies – became the terrain for the most effective attack on the two major parties' 'business as usual' approach to socio-economic issues. It was in response to Powell's racist speeches that dock-workers and meat-porters marched on Parliament in an unprecedented show of solidarity with a Conservative MP. Thousands of people from virtually every part of the country – people who were unemployed, trade union members, teachers, managers and executives – wrote letters to Powell. They did not just say that they agreed with Powell on immigration. More importantly, they said that Powell was the only politician that they could trust. Powell spoke across class, partisan and regional divisions to bring the disenchanted together in a new populist bloc, and it was the specifically racist aspect of his movement's banner which united his followers.

Every imperial centre faces a national identity crisis after it undergoes the trauma of decolonization and the disintegration of an imperial system; European nations, the United States and the former Soviet Union are all dealing with this profound problem. Populist movements such as Powell's, which speak effectively to this post-colonial identity crisis, do not disappear overnight. While it is true that black immigration legislation never regained a prominent position on the British political agenda after the mid-1970s, and while it is true that Powell himself was confined to the parliamentary back benches after committing various strategic blunders in 1974, the Powellian legacy of guilt-free British nationalism – constructed through the exclusion of black otherness – became a powerful resource for Thatcherism.

However, Powell is usually regarded as a single-issue politician, and the impact of his racist movement tends to be narrowly measured in terms of actual immigration policies. There are a few notable exceptions to this tendency. Kavanagh, for example, describes Powell as an important right-wing challenger to the entire consensus tradition. He explicitly links economic policies to racial policies in his description of the 'core issues' in the consensus approach: 'public ownership, welfare benefits for the undeserving poor, abolition of capital punishment, some practices of trade unions, decolonization ... British membership [in] the European Community; and, *perhaps above all*, the belief that all British subjects (some 700 million) should have unrestricted entry to Britain'.[13] Kavanagh's central point is that opinion polls showed that there was no widespread support for the consensus; it constituted a 'top-down' discourse which was never successfully translated into a popular way of thinking. However, he privileges the *appearance* of a liberal immigration policy (let us, for a moment, put aside the fact that racial bias was introduced into British immigration legislation in 1962) as the most unpopular aspect of the consensus. He then proceeds to single out Powell's anti-black immigration discourse as one of the most effective critiques of the consensus approach.

> The importance of Enoch Powell's speech about immigration in 1968 was that a senior 'insider' broke out of the high-mindedness of the consensus. For a brief period he was the most popular politician in the land. Powell used mass fears to attack elite attitudes – the classic populist strategy – and in so doing he showed that parts of the consensus rested on unsteady foundations.[14]

Gamble takes a similar position on Powell's significance. 'Powell's speech [on race relations and immigration, 20 April 1968] was of decisive importance in launching a new politics of the nation, and in demonstrating the possibilities of a populist assault upon some of the central aspects of postwar social democracy.'[15]

Political analysts nevertheless tend to ignore this symbolic aspect of Powell's intervention. For the most part, they treat race like an 'issue' rather than a nodal point. In other words, they take up the race = immigration equivalence which had been established in the 1960s, trace the rise and fall of popular concerns around immigration, and note the enactment of specific immigration legislation, but they do not look any further. Gamble, for example, recognizes that the 'populist theme' of race may have been important to the legitimation of Thatcherism, but claims that it 'did not easily translate into positive government policies'. His test for the salience of race in official discourse is quite narrow: he points to the fact that although the Thatcher government did pass stricter immigration and citizenship laws, it did not respond to the right-wing calls for the 'repatriation' of black Britons to their countries of origin, and it did not attempt to repeal the existing race relations legislation.[16] Race, however, cannot be adequately dealt with in this narrow manner. Layton-Henry and Rich argue that racial antagonisms were highly relevant to a wide range of public policy areas for the Thatcher governments in the 1980s, including urban programmes, policing, youth unemployment, local government–central government relations, housing and education. Some local governments also deployed anti-racist campaigns and affirmative action initiatives in the 1980s.[17] Even at the level of public policy, race does not operate as an individual and isolated 'issue' in post-colonial Britain. Powell never treated black immigration as if it were a single 'issue' – and if he had done so, he probably never would have been such a prominent political figure. His campaign against immigration functioned as a 'new politics of the nation' precisely because he used racial antagonisms as a framework which could account for virtually every aspect of the national crisis. In Powellism, the relation between the white defenders of the true British nation and the anti-British black 'invader' became a nodal point: racial antagonism operated as the key which made the disintegration of the nation – and the inevitability of national recovery – intelligible.

Political scientists for the most part ignore interventions such as Layton-Henry's and Rich's text. However, this is not to say that they have not provided useful data on the role of race in the rise of Thatcherism. Kavanagh cites various surveys which show that in the late 1970s the electorate on average held positions well to the right of the two major parties on 'issues like immigration, law and order, discipline and standards in the schools, capital punishment and trade unions'.[18] It should, of course, be noted that by the late 1970s official discourse on immigration and law and order were structured extensively around racial antagonisms. The 1979 *British Election Study* included race relations as one of the eight key issues in the election. Crewe demonstrates that the Conservative Party's perceived position on six of these issues was much more representative of both the views of the electorate as a whole, and of working-class voters in particular, than the Labour Party's perceived position. These six issues were: unemployment policy, incomes policy, industrial relations law, social welfare benefits, nationalization and race relations. The 1979 *British Election Study* question on race relations asked the respondents to describe their responses to two alternative propositions: 'the first thing to do about race relations is to put a stop to all further immigration' and 'the first thing to do about race relations is to tackle the problem of jobs and housing in the large cities'. The respondents' answers were plotted on a seven-point continuum scale; full agreement with the first proposition would earn one point, indicating a far-right position, and full agreement with the second proposition would earn seven points, indicating a far-left position. The respondents' perceptions of the Conservative Party's and Labour Party's positions were rated at approximately 2.75 and 4.8 respectively; working-class voters' responses and the average response of the voters as a whole were rated at 3.1 and 3.5 respectively.[19] Although the racist immigration laws of the 1960s and 1970s had been introduced by *both* Conservative and Labour governments, the voters nevertheless continued to associate the Labour Party with excessively 'permissive' policies on race. The perception of a gap between the two parties was therefore an important factor in the 1979 election.

Racial discourse in British politics, however, did not remain confined to debates around immigration. Race was re-coded through the 1970s and 1980s, concealed within euphemisms and tensions around crime waves, law and order, inner-city unrest, the revival of British 'greatness' in its victory over the Argentinians in the Falklands/Malvinas War, local governments' affirmative action and contract compliance schemes, multiculturalism in local governments' programmes and education curricula, competing versions of British imperial history, freedom of speech in the Salman Rushdie affair, and the re-settlement of Hong Kong's elite in Britain. Indeed, the fact that race can be re-articulated at so many diverse sites of conflict is further evidence that race operates like a nodal point, rather than a single issue. Political scientists have for the most part failed to track these re-codings. Crewe, for example, notes the relative decline in popular concern around immigration in the 1980s. The respondents in a June 1983 BBC TV–Gallup survey were asked to list what they regarded as the most important issues in the 1983 election. Crewe comments, 'immigration, the hidden mover of votes in the 1960s and 1970s, dropped to the bottom of the political agenda (1 per cent)'. He also recognizes that the popular image of Thatcher's government as a 'no-nonsense, determined and firm' administration was a key element in its 1983 victory, and that its 'uncompromising nationalism' in the Falklands/Malvinas War contributed significantly to the creation of this image.[20] Crewe does not, however, search for the genealogical precedents for Thatcher's specific type of nationalist discourse which served her so well at the time of the Falklands/Malvinas War.

Riddell also argues that Thatcher's personal image as a leader of conviction earned her tremendous respect, and that her reputation as a competent and decisive leader won her many votes even when her policies were disliked. Her government, of course, benefited from the divisions within the Opposition and from its own stimulation of small economic recoveries at key political moments. Riddell nevertheless ranks Thatcher's own leadership style as a key factor in the Conservatives' electoral success through the 1980s. Like Crewe, Riddell directly links Thatcher's symbolic status as a decisive leader to the British Falklands/Malvinas War campaign. 'The Falklands War will be remembered for the single-minded leadership of Mrs. Thatcher, which made her international reputation.' In the sexist terms which are all too often used to describe extraordinary women leaders, Riddell comments that she is known internationally as the 'Boadicea with a handbag'.[21]

Thatcher's leadership symbolically represented the revival of Britain, and it makes sense that the Falklands/Malvinas War was the most important setting for this representation. The British handling of the dispute with the Argentinians over the Falklands/Malvinas actually constituted a moment of failed leadership and incompetence: the British had sold many arms to the Argentinian junta, a negotiated settlement in the form of a lease-back arrangement with the Argentinians was allowed to fail by Thatcher's cabinet, cost-cutting reductions in British naval strength in the South Atlantic were approved in spite of General Galtieri's numerous threats of invasion and neither the Defence Committee nor the full Cabinet discussed the Falklands/Malvinas between January 1981 and 25 March 1982.[22] This lack of foresight, indecisiveness and recklessness cost 259 British and more than 650 Argentinian lives.

It should be noted, however, that it was a post-colonial Britain which constructed the myth of the Falklands/Malvinas War – what might have struck another nation as ridiculous sabre-rattling from another age, an absolute bungling of diplomatic relations and an unacceptable loss of life, became an inspiring national victory. Nigel Lawson, who was Energy Secretary at the time of the Falklands/ Malvinas War and later became the Chancellor, explicitly links the 'Falklands factor' to the Conservatives' 1983 election victory. He also notes the post-colonial aspect of the Falklands mythology: this totally unnecessary skirmish had become a symbolic moment of triumph precisely because it released the British people from their repressed memories of national defeat around decolonization.

> In our first term came, out of the blue, the Falklands experience, which finally laid the ghost of Suez. It also showed the world – and, even more important, ourselves – that Britain still possessed a patriotism and a moral fibre that many thought had gone forever.[23]

The symbolic meaning of 'Suez' for the British can be compared to that of 'Vietnam' for the Americans. The Egyptians declared independence in 1922, but Britain retained a great deal of influence over Egyptian politics and continued to occupy the British base at Suez. In 1954, the British and Egyptians agreed a treaty which stipulated that British troops would be gradually evacuated from their positions within the Suez Canal Zone. Nasser, the Egyptian President, nevertheless followed an independent course in foreign affairs: he declined to join the British- and American-inspired Baghdad Pact and concluded an arms agreement with the Soviet Union in 1955. The United States and Britain retaliated by withholding funds which had been promised to Egypt for the construction of a dam at Aswan. In 1956, Nasser countered by unilaterally nationalizing the Suez Canal Company to pay for the Aswan dam and by creating an Egyptian authority to manage the Suez Canal. The Canal Company had previously had an international directorship and a mostly French administration. The British government had held seven-sixteenths of the Company's shares. A joint Israeli, British and French military campaign was launched against Egypt, and the

Egyptians blocked the canal. The Americans and Soviets ultimately persuaded the invaders to withdraw and the Egyptians obtained full sovereign and commercial rights over the canal. For the British in the post-colonial era, 'the Suez' marks a double defeat: the Americans and Soviets ultimately determined Europe's relations with Egypt, underlining their displacement of the British and the French as world powers, and the Egyptians, a former colonized people, asserted their independence over and against British interests.

The circumstances around the Falklands/Malvinas conflict were saturated with post-colonial references. The lease-back option was first considered by the Thatcher Cabinet in autumn 1979. Britain was at that time engaged in the final negotiations for the decolonization of Rhodesia (Zimbabwe). Anticipating a strong response from the Conservative right, Thatcher herself was 'appalled at the thought of giving the Falklands/Malvinas away, whatever the fancy terms'.[24] Both the Tory right and the Labour and Liberal front benches thoroughly rejected the negotiations around the Argentinians claims on the Falklands/Malvinas and the House was virtually unanimous in its support for the war. The symbolic character of Britain's defence of the islands lay in the fact that its opponent was a Latin American regime – when British forces met the Argentinians in the South Atlantic, they were fighting for nothing less than the Western tradition, and they were fighting against the entire memory of decolonization. Young comments that Thatcher saw the war as a battle between good and evil: 'It went far wider than the Falklands and their 1,800 British people. It was a challenge to the West.'[25] According to Secretary of State General Haig, Thatcher equated negotiations with the Argentinians with Britain's appeasement of Hitler in the 1930s. She claimed that a failure to defend the Falklands/Malvinas would 'send a signal round the world with devastating consequences'.[26] For Thatcher, the Argentinians were people 'of an alien creed', and the Falklanders – half of whom would have accepted a lease-back agreement with the Argentinians if it had gone through – were 'British in stock and tradition'.[27] Michael Foot, the leader of the Opposition, spoke in equally post-colonial terms during the Commons debate on the deployment of the British navy. Ignoring the un-democratic nature of Britain's colonial rule over the Islanders, he declared that Parliament had to act

> [to] uphold the rights of our country throughout the world, and the claim of our country to be a defender of people's freedom throughout the world, particularly those who look to

us for special protection, as do the people in the Falkland Islands.[28]

Sir Nigel Fisher, a Tory backbencher, described the bloodless Argentinian invasion as a 'humiliation', for the British people remained an imperial nation. 'We have failed – and failed lamentably – to defend the integrity of one of Britain's few remaining colonies.'[29] Powell himself spoke in the debate, and drew parallels between Britain's imperial duties in the South Atlantic and in Northern Ireland.

A Peruvian peace initiative emerged after the naval task force was sent to the Falklands/Malvinas. Referring to the dramatic explosion of patriotic spirit in Britain, *The Times* called for an unequivocal rejection of the Peruvian plan. 'This crisis has shaken the British people out of a sleep, and the people, once woken, will not lightly forgive those leaders who rang the alarm and then failed to fulfil their responsibility.'[30] The Peruvian peace proposals ultimately failed after a British submarine torpedoed the Argentinian cruiser, the *General Belgrano*, even though it was 30 miles outside the war zone and sailing away from the islands. The British submarine attacked without giving a warning. Its commander acted under direct orders from the fleet commander in Britain and with the approval of Thatcher herself. Altogether, 368 sailors on board the *Belgrano* drowned during the attack.[31]

Thatcher's popularity recovered from a dismal low to a 44 per cent approval rate following the Falklands/Malvinas campaign.[32] She exploited the victory at every partisan opportunity. At a party rally at Cheltenham on 3 July 1982, she stated that the Falklands/Malvinas victory marked a new era of national solidarity, and that the rail strike did not 'match the spirit of these times'. She triumphantly concluded,

> We have ceased to be a nation in retreat. We have instead a new-found confidence, born in the economic battles at home and tested and found true 8,000 miles away.[33]

At a 'Salute the Task Force' luncheon at Guildhall in October 1982, Thatcher declared,

> In those anxious months the spectacle of bold young Britons, fighting for great principles and a just cause, lifted the nation. Doubts and hesitation were replaced by confidence and pride that our younger generation too could write a glorious chapter in the history of liberty.[34]

It was in the afterglow of this mythical national victory that Thatcher was transformed from a radical right-winger with draconian policies and dubious leadership credentials into the very personification of the national recovery. Her defeat of the not-Western enemy centred her extremism: she became a leader who was always well respected, even when her policies were not well liked. Thatcher only emerged from the Falklands/Malvinas War as a triumphant warrior rather than an incompetent and belligerent diplomat because she was able to call upon a particularly jingoistic patriotic fervour which was, to a great extent, animated and defined in terms of the struggle against the not-Western colonial 'other'. Interpreted within this post-colonial framework, the South Atlantic crisis became an opportunity for the Thatcherites to re-write the story of decolonization and to liberate a revitalized guilt-free nationalism. The most important continuities between Powellism and Thatcherism therefore lie in their articulation of this post-colonial nationalism – and not solely in immigration policies. When Powell campaigned against black immigration in the late 1960s and early 1970s, and when Thatcher successfully translated an unnecessary and distant military skirmish into a legitimation for her domestic policies, both figures were addressing Britain's post-colonial condition.

Layton-Henry and Rich point out that political scientists have paid little attention to the complexities of popular nationalism in contemporary British politics. They argue that the fusion of race and nation in Britain has become so normalized that the differences between them have become almost imperceptible.

> *Race* has become so closely linked with this nationalistic rhetoric that it does not need to be formally stated, having been transformed in Britain from being a 'sign' of physical difference to a 'symbol' with a large store of implicit connotations which can be commonly understood without being actually stated.[35]

It is the task of political analysts to problematize normalized articulations. We should ask, in this particular case, within which tradition was Thatcher speaking when she mobilized a particularly post-colonial nationalistic spirit in 1982 with such a tremendous political effect? Powellian nationalism, which was constructed around the internal battle against a specifically post-colonial 'enemy within', the black immigrant, laid much of the groundwork for the jingoistic 'Falklands spirit'. If we were to investigate the relevance of 'race' in 1980s British politics, the Thatcherite deployment of nationalism would certainly be an important place to look, for post-colonial nationalist discourse has become one of the important sites for the re-coding of race. It makes sense that political scientists would tend to miss the re-codings of race, for we are trained to track explicit discourse rather than discursive reconstructions. In any event, I shall argue that race should not be excluded from our accounts of the legitimation of Thatcherism. Race played a crucial role in the formation of the Powellian movement, and Powellism was one of the most important precursors to Thatcherism.[36]

The second strategic moment which I want to deal with involves the Thatcherite attack on local government autonomy. Local governments had become important sites for resistance against Conservative central governments in the post-war era for two key reasons. The flight of the middle class from the inner cities into the suburbs from the turn of the century onwards had created large blocs of traditional Labour voters in urban centres, and the growth of the welfare state had led to an expansion in the role of local government in the delivery of the new services. With these developments, the 'municipal labourism' movement emerged as a force to be reckoned with in British politics. However, the Conservative and Labour central governments of the 1970s introduced reforms and cuts in the central government's grants to local government which sharply diminished local governments' autonomy. The Thatcher governments escalated this transformation in central government–local government relations through the imposition of much deeper cuts in grants; the strengthening of central government control over local government programmes, expenditures and local taxation levels; the abolition of the Greater London Council and the six metropolitan county authorities; the promotion of private contracting for local authority services, the sale of council housing and the 'opting out' of schools from local authority control; and the introduction of the community charge (the 'poll tax'). Again, the mere listing of these initiatives is insufficient. Political scientists also need to account for the legitimation of this drastic reduction in local democracy.

To approach the same problem from a different angle, it is quite striking that Section 28, the Thatcher governments' most important piece of legislation on homosexuality, was included in the Local Government Act, 1987–8. Virtually none of the commentators on Section 28, both in the lesbian and gay press and the mainstream media, paid attention to the precise location of this law. Section 28 specifically prohibited the promotion of homosexuality by *local governments*. I shall argue that the context of Section 28 is not accidental; the Local Government Bill, 1987–8 was not an arbitrarily chosen vehicle for an insignificant pet project from the parliamentary back benches. From the parliamentary speeches of the supporters of Section 28, and the Conservative Party's own campaign advertisements from the 1987 election, it is quite clear that Thatcherite discourse had fused local government autonomy and the promotion of homosexuality together. The MPs and members of the House of Lords who spoke passionately in favour of Section 28 in the parliamentary and committee debates certainly did not see the inclusion of legislation on homosexuality within local government legislation as an anomaly. They argued that homosexual militants had taken over local educational institutions, that lesbians and gays were being given special privileges in local government programmes and that overly permissive local government councillors were funding lesbian and gay political events. If heterosexual normalcy appeared to be threatened by an emerging lesbian and gay presence, this was not due to the efforts of independent activists, but to the treasonous linkages between the lesbian and gay movement and Labour local councillors. For the supporters of Section 28, the regulation of local government excesses was indeed all the more urgent because of the inextricability of local government autonomy and the promotion of homosexuality.

Given the saturation of the mainstream media with extremely homophobic representations of the AIDS phenomena at this time, this representation of local government autonomy through a homophobic framework became a highly charged strategy. Opinion polls found that homophobic attitudes both became more common and increased in severity in the late 1980s. When asked specifically about Section 28, huge majorities of the respondents approved of the measure. (Specific statistics will be given in chapters 1 and 5.) The MPs and members of the House of Lords devoted over 30 per cent of their debates on Local Government Bill, 1987–8 – a complicated bill dealing primarily with affirmative action in local government contracting – to Section 28.[37] There certainly was no outcry about the expenditure of valuable political time on this issue; there was no sign of popular confusion regarding the articulation between local government politics and homosexuality. We can assume, then, that this articulation was effective not only at an official level but at a popular level as well – that it made sense to the British people in the late 1980s that speaking about local government autonomy involved issues around homosexuality, and that restricting homosexual excesses necessitated the regulation of local government autonomy.

The demonization of homosexuality played a crucial role in the legitimation of the Thatcherite attack on local government autonomy. It would be meaningless to note that the Thatcher government just happened to be in power during a time in which homophobic attitudes and practices increased dramatically in Britain; such a coincidence could be dismissed as a pure accident of history. But when the official discourse which seeks to legitimate a key policy initiative, such as the centralist reduction of local government autonomy, is so thoroughly intertwined with homophobic arguments, we are no longer dealing with historical accidents. An analysis of the official deployment of homophobic demonizations therefore has to be included in the general account of Thatcherism.

My first objective, then, is to place racism and homophobia firmly on the agenda of all political scientists who are engaged in the study of contemporary British politics and to promote the treatment of racism and homophobia as symbolic nodal points rather than isolated 'issues'. My second and third objectives are more theoretical in nature. In the spring of 1988, I took part in several lesbian and gay demonstrations against Section 28, both in London and Manchester. I came to the official documents on this law as an activist and a journalist, not as an academic. I had already read some of the most offensive homophobic statements of the supporters of Section 28 in the reports in our community press. When I decided to have a look at the parliamentary debates as a whole, I was expecting to find more of the same – more bigoted declarations that homosexuals with AIDS constituted a threat to the rest of the population and deserved to die, that lesbian mothers were perverting their children, that nursery school children had to be protected from 'pornographic' sex education materials, and so on. I thought that the supporters' homophobia was a very simple discourse: they hated us and wanted to exclude us from society. I originally planned to skim the parliamentary reports and to take out a few of the more extremist quotations for a short article.

A simple discourse was certainly not what I found. The parliamentary debates were constructed around various complex figures of exclusion *and* inclusion; sophisticated and consistent differentiations between types of homosexuality; subtle distinctions between biological, behavioural and cultural forms of identity; a right-wing critique of left-wing essentialism; an obvious fascination with gay male sex practices; a sexist erasure of lesbian sexuality combined with a demonization of lesbian mothering; and debates on familial norms, gender roles and democratic values. Much to my surprise, my academic training in post-structuralist theories of identity and difference was actually quite useful in reading the Section 28 debates.

To say that this official homophobic discourse is much more subtle than I expected is not to say that it is less authoritarian. On the contrary, its complexity makes it all the more dangerous. I found that the very supporters of Section 28 – the law which prohibits the promotion of homosexuality – were themselves engaging in the promotion of a very particular type of homosexuality. They spoke again and again of a law-abiding, disease-free, self-closeting homosexual figure who knew her or his proper place on the secret fringes of mainstream society. They insisted that they fully accepted this imaginary figure as a wholly legitimate member of British society. (They did not, of course, recognize that no one could actually occupy this perfectly self-limiting position, that insofar as homosexuality conforms to their rules of normalcy, its subversive challenge to heterosexist norms is erased, and that their promise of inclusion therefore remained a purely imaginary promise.) They argued that they only aimed to restrict the activities of a completely different kind of homosexual, the promiscuous, diseased, angry, flaunting, self-promoting and militant homosexual – the kind of homosexual that we lesbians and gays ourselves call 'queer'. This distinction between the acceptable good homosexual and the dangerous queer ran through the entire discourse of the supporters.

Why should the more subtle aspects of an extremist discourse of bigotry be of any concern? If the supporters' promise of inclusion for the lesbian and gay community remains an imaginary promise which only supports their truly homophobic agenda, why should we not dismiss their differentiations of homosexualities as mere public relations exercises? I think they deserve our close attention for two reasons. First, even in this limit case, where there were huge majorities in favour of Section 28 and official homophobia in general, we find the supporters making every effort to occupy the position of the 'tolerant' middle ground. The supporters of Section 28 themselves documented the rise in discrimination and violent attacks against lesbians and gays – although they of course failed to consider the possibility that their 'tolerant' discourse had indeed normalized such behaviour in the first place. They agreed with lesbian and gay lobbyists that our community constituted an oppressed minority.

From their perspective, however, that oppression had developed because an otherwise peaceful, law-abiding and properly invisible social group was caught in the cross-fire between militant activists and the anti-homosexual backlash. The militants had inflamed the sentiments of the basically tolerant public by unnecessarily politicizing sexuality – by insisting on coming out, on demanding 'special' rights and 'special' services and so on. The problem was not the backlash itself, for the supporters argued that the response of the 'general public' to homosexual militancy was entirely natural. The supporters therefore argued that the best remedy for the persecution of lesbians and gays was in fact legislation which would stop local governments from promoting the cause of the militant queer.

Through these tactics, the supporters positioned themselves in the *centre* – they depicted themselves as standing with the heterosexual majority *and* the good homosexual in the centre, between the queer militants and out-of-control socialists on the one side, and the explicitly anti-homosexual extremists and queer-bashers on the other. In other words, their imaginary promise of inclusion, for all its impossibility, *centred* their discourse. Even though their sense of the 'centre' is, from a lesbian and gay rights point of view, located on the extreme right, the construction of the *appearance* of a centred position seemed to be an absolutely crucial priority in the supporters' discourse. Imaginary inclusions therefore have the effect of centring an extremist discourse, of re-coding an exclusion as a moment of 'tolerant' inclusion. If a political project is to obtain a hegemonic status, it must lose every trace of extremism. It must not appear to be just one alternative among many; it has to centre itself to the extent that there appears to be absolutely no other alternative. The intolerant always misrecognize themselves as 'tolerant'; they do so not only to legitimize their exclusions within a liberal-democratic framework, but also to transform their own violent exclusions into a reasonable discourse which would otherwise be unbearable to themselves.[38] It is perhaps the case that the imaginary 'average' voter generally prefers to support a pragmatic and moderate agenda rather than an extremist one. I would insist, however, that a political figure or political project only appears to occupy the 'tolerant' 'centre' thanks to the effects of strategic representations. From different vantage points, that same 'centre' position might connote either a right-wing or left-wing extremism.

The differentiation of homosexualities in the supporters' discourse therefore gave their right-wing extremism the kind of sober and 'tolerant' air which we usually expect from official discourse, and contributed to the legitimation of their strategies by centring their extremism. The supporters' differentiations are also important for a second reason. Homophobic heterosexuals who like to think of themselves as 'tolerant' were not the only receptive targets for the supporters' discourse. The good homosexual/dangerous queer differentiation is also performed within the lesbian, bisexual and gay communities as well. Although our communities have engaged in quite simply heroic resistances against right-wing extremism, the break-up of lesbian-led families by heterosexist legal officials, the AIDS epidemic and everyday discrimination, we have also witnessed a rise in exclusions from within our communities. Many lesbians and gay men agree with the Thatcherites that our communities have been subjected to surveillance and oppression because our militant activists have gone too far. Even more express concerns that our communities risk losing our fragile gains of equality whenever we fail to represent ourselves as the 'good citizens next door'. The good homosexual/dangerous queer differentiation is already a problem within our communities. When a similar differentiation is articulated at the level of official discourse, the already mobilized exclusions from within the communities can be accelerated even further, contributing to the further marginalization of those who do not fit the image of the 'good citizens next door'. Imaginary inclusions therefore can have a material effect on the identities of the social group which resembles the included figure; the promise of inclusion can be extremely seductive and can give rise to all sorts of strategies of self-correction and voluntary assimilation.

I was, in a sense, already prepared to see the Section 28 debates as a complex and productive discourse, rather than a simple exclusion. I had already participated in many different discussions on the effects of the official 'divide-and-rule' type of strategy as an activist in various projects ranging from anti-censorship resistance to the direct action lesbian and gay group, OutRage!. I doubt that I could ever recapture the nuances of these activist discussions with even the most sophisticated theoretical framework. I had been introduced to Foucauldian post-structuralism through the lesbian and gay media and lesbian and gay history projects in the early 1980s. I had already followed the Foucauldian insights of lesbian and gay historians such as Gayle Rubin and Jeffrey Weeks[39] back to Foucault's and Nietzsche's texts. From a Foucauldian and Nietzschean framework, Section 28 should be regarded like all other regulatory rules –

as a disciplinary strategy which promoted the domestication of difference by differentiating difference against itself and by inciting self-surveillance. Finally, I had already been exposed to the British cultural studies texts on race and racism, such as Stuart Hall *et al.*'s *Policing the Crisis* and Paul Gilroy's *'There Ain't No Black in the Union Jack'*, which bring some of the best aspects of post-structuralism and Gramscian post–Marxism together in politically inspired and *concrete* analyses. Paul Gilroy's analysis of the Conservative Party's invention and imaginary inclusion of the good black entrepreneur figure[40] was particularly useful for me in my construction of the good homosexual/dangerous queer distinction.

Homophobic discourse should not be depicted as an unusually sophisticated set of strategies; I certainly do not want to imply that it is inherently more complex than racist discourse. Like Section 28, Powell's speeches also appear to be nothing but a simple exclusionary discourse. He was, after all, demanding nothing less than the closure of Britain's borders against the black immigrant and the 'repatriation' of British blacks to their 'homelands' in the former colonies. This simple exclusionary appearance, however, conceals the richness of the Powellian interventions. As well as demonstrating the historical or genealogical location of Powellism, I shall emphasize the complexity of the Powellian claims around the British identity, the significance of the Empire for post-colonial Britons, the feminine gendering of the British nation in opposition to the masculinization of the black immigrant, the linkages between American black militancy and British racial antagonisms and the treasonous failure of mainstream British politicians and intellectuals to protect the British nation from the 'black invasion'. Powell himself did not issue an unequivocal promise of inclusion – even at the imaginary level – for any particular section of the black immigrant community. From his perspective, only a fully assimilated blackness could be safely added to the British nation, and the quantitative expansion of the black presence made assimilation increasingly unlikely. However, where Section 28 supporters claim to be acting in the name of the good homosexual, Powell also claims to be responding to the demands of his white *and* black constituents in promoting racially biased immigration laws. Powell may or may not have been lying about these demands; we'll probably never know exactly what happened in his private meetings with his black constituents. In any event, we can study the effects of his speeches – the ways in which he legitimated his extremist racist position by de-racializing and centring his discourse, and the ways in which his project was accepted in turn by many white Britons as a legitimate official course of action.

My second objective, in sum, is to insist on the complexity and productivity of these two discourses – Section 28 and Powellism – which appear to be nothing but strategies of simple and total exclusion. This aspect of my research could be described as the synchronic dimension: the analysis of these discourses at specific moments in time. My third objective relates to the genealogical relations between these two discourses. I was deeply impressed with the numerous continuities which I found between the arguments of the Section 28 supporters on the prohibition of the promotion of homosexuality and those of Powell on the regulation of black immigration. The demonization of homosexuality was framed not only in terms of AIDS-panic discourse, but also in terms of Powellian and Thatcherite racism. The Section 28 supporters explicitly linked the promotion of homosexuality with the promotion of multiculturalism. They drew extensively upon already normalized racist metaphors around disease, foreign invasions, unassimilable 'other' cultures, dangerous criminals, subversive intellectuals, excessive permissiveness and so on. Most of the commentators on Section 28 failed to note these important genealogical linkages. They did not recognize that Powellian and Thatcherite racism had become a hegemonic discourse – that it had become so normalized and so intertwined with political discourse that all other demonizations tended to be shaped in terms of its codes, tactics and metaphors. The theoretical point here is that populist demonizations do not emerge out of thin air. Although AIDS anxiety certainly did give the prohibition of the promotion of homosexuality project its force, racism provided some of its most important structures. If British voters were able to recognize the quite extraordinary obsession by various Conservative Party politicians with homosexuality as an acceptable expenditure of their political capital, it is because the radically new discourse on homosexuality was represented within already normalized racist structures. Lesbian and gay activists and AIDS activists are becoming increasingly aware that there are important linkages between homophobia and racism. However, if these linkages are only recognized at the level of empty slogans or vague conceptions of progressive solidarities, they will not be very effective. It is only when we do the work of showing the actual connections between particular forms of racism and homophobia in specific contexts that our recognition of these linkages will become a strategically effective resource.

The structures which are common to both Powellian/Thatcherite racism and Thatcherite homophobia are spatial structures. Powell constructed the entry into Britain of small numbers of peoples from the former colonies – often in years in which there was a net emigration *from* Britain – as a 'black invasion'. The imperial system had spanned the metropole/periphery divide; the colonized 'natives' had held the same British passports as the colonizers. There was no difference, *de jure*, between them. After decolonization, the British borders were re-invented through racially biased immigration laws. Because there were very few Indians, Pakistanis, Africans and Afro-Caribbeans who were permanently settled in Britain before decolonization, the British governments of the 1960s and 1970s were able to single out the specifically black holders of British passports through temporal and kinship distinctions. In 1962, holders of British passports whose documents had been issued outside Britain itself lost many of their rights to free immigration. The even more subtle patriality distinction was introduced in 1968 and 1971. Only those citizens of the former colonies who had been born in Britain, or whose father or grandfather had been born in Britain, continued to enjoy special immigration rights. The descendants of the former colonizers who wanted to return to Britain were guaranteed privileged access, while the British passports held by the majority of black Commonwealth citizens became meaningless pieces of paper.

These shifts in immigration laws re-defined the limits of the British nation. The racially coded immigration laws of the 1960s and 1970s should be regarded as spatial strategies which firmly placed the unwanted 'black invader' on the other side of the national frontier. Before the 1960s, the figure of the black immigrant did not exist. The threat of recapture had certainly haunted every African in Britain during the British involvement in the slave trade, and various waves of popular racisms had made Britain an inhospitable place for Asians, Africans and Afro-Caribbeans, but the movements of the colonized within the Empire had not been regulated on a legal basis.[41] The new laws of the 1960s invented the black immigrant because they legally constituted the Asian, African and Afro-Caribbean peoples from the former colonies as outsiders. By constructing these particular peoples as outsiders, the British legislators wrote into official discourse that which had been otherwise taken for granted: that Britain was, essentially, a white nation whose identity depended on its exclusion of black outsiders.

The Derridean conception of supplementarity offers several valuable insights for the analysis of texts which are structured around inside–outside metaphors. If it makes sense for us to consider an entity as a more or less unified space and as a relatively stable being, then it must be surrounded by a set of relatively fixed and impermeable frontiers. At its most basic level, the Derridean conception of supplementarity suggests that the enclosure of a space within a set of frontiers only comes about when an opposition has been established between that space and some sort of outsider figure. It is, in short, only against an outside that an inside is possible. In this sense, we could say that the inside space – such as the white nation in racist discourse – actually depends on its outsider figures – such as the black immigrant – for its constitution. The re-closure of the nation was indeed a particularly pressing problem in the 1960s; Britain's profound dependency on the imperial system for its identity meant that decolonization provoked an identity crisis, and internal antagonisms seemed to threaten the total disintegration of the nation from within. Powell's anti-black immigration campaign brought the nation together in a particularly effective manner because it drew upon the already normalized tradition of imperial racism and put that tradition to work in re-inscribing the national boundaries. The invention and demonization of the black immigrant are therefore performative strategies in the sense that they brought about a state of affairs which did not exist before their deployment: they were central to the re-closure of the broken British frontiers and, by implication, to the re-unification of the British nation.

No text can ever openly and fully confess the extent to which its closed spaces are dependent on their oppositions with outsider figures for their constitution. Supplementary relations are always hidden; inside–outside relations are always supported by various strategies which attempt to conceal the constitutivity of otherness. Powell, for example, argues that his patriotism only amounts to the recovery of an essentially unchanged Britishness. He claims that the colonies and the imperial periphery were absolutely irrelevant to the British people. He therefore plays both sides of decolonization at once. He speaks as if the British identity had remained absolutely intact throughout all the external accidents of imperial and post-colonial history. He acts, however, in a quite different manner. He acts as if Britain were indeed caught in the grips of an identity crisis,

24

as if decolonization had in fact involved the catastrophic loss of a constitutive outside. He devotes several speeches to the British national identity and constructs an entire political campaign around what he regards as the two greatest threats to the integrity of the British nation: black immigration and the European Economic Community. His racism is never just a domestic racism; it is always linked to questions around sovereignty and national identity.

The spatial location of blackness in Powellian racism as the *outsider* to a post-colonial nation – a nation which is struggling to recover its identity after the trauma of decolonization – is therefore profoundly important. Thatcherite homophobic discourse also locates homosexuality and heterosexuality in terms of a precise spatial structure. Deeply influenced by the homophobic media coverage of AIDS, the Section 28 supporters all accepted the dangerous myth of the high-risk group. This utterly fallacious theory suggests that an individual's risk of contracting the HIV virus depends on that individual's location within a socially and morally defined group. The Section 28 supporters therefore linked HIV transmission to identity, rather than to practices. Practices in fact never obey the spatial limits of identities. Many individuals who describe themselves as heterosexual regularly engage in unsafe sex and unsafe intravenous drug use. AIDS educators now insist that when it comes to an assessment of the risk of HIV transmission, it simply does not matter who you are – it only matters what you do. This privileging of practices which cannot be spatially fixed would have been incoherent for the Section 28 supporters. The high-risk-group theory allowed them to locate the AIDS threat to the British nation in a spatial manner, namely within the gay male community. To the extent that the Section 28 supporters recognized the presence of the HIV virus within heterosexual communities, they argued that the virus had originated in the gay male space and had subsequently spread to the heterosexual space. Their spatial distributions effectively equated the nation with the heterosexual 'normal' space. Gay male-ness and the HIV virus were so thoroughly equated that the Section 28 supporters' entire discourse can be described in terms of viral and bodily metaphors. They spoke about the heterosexual nation as if it were a body whose immune system had to ward off the dangerous homosexual virus which threatened to invade the nation from the immoral outside.[42]

The black immigrant had constituted one of the most dangerous 'invaders' for the British nation in the 1960s and 1970s, and, in the late 1980s, it was the diseased gay male who took the black immigrant's place. This is not, of course, the whole story. Racist white Britons are still haunted by the figure of the black immigrant, and the black enemy now 'invades' the nation at many frontiers. For the racist, blackness challenges the borders of the white nation in the form of criminals and rioters on the streets, anti-British teachers and anti-Christian pupils in the classroom, and 'loony-leftists' in local government. Homosexuality is represented in the Section 28 discourse not only as an 'invader' from an immoral outside, but also as a seducer who has already infiltrated the ranks of the heterosexual nation, a monster who must be captured and exhibited as a warning against deviation and a pretender who threatens to take the place of the male heterosexual as the head of the family. The 'invader' figure nevertheless remains the most prevalent form for the Thatcherite demonization of homosexuality. Thatcherite homophobia therefore borrows its structure from Powellian/Thatcherite racism in the sense that it re-constitutes the Powellian image of the nation under seige through the substitution of the dangerous queer for the black immigrant.

With these three objectives in mind, I have combined empirical investigations on race and sexuality – detailed analyses of speeches and legislation, critical summaries of opinion poll data, and genealogical surveys of historical trends – with theoretical discussions around the construction and deployment of identity games.[43] In chapter 1, I explore the most recent criticisms of Stuart Hall's analysis of Thatcherism as a hegemonic authoritarian populist formation.[44] Using a Lacanian-influenced conception of political identification, and drawing upon post-structuralist conceptions of power relations, I establish a distinction between hegemony-as-domination and hegemony-as-normalization. I argue that the latter approach to hegemony is best suited to contemporary political analysis. In chapter 2, I introduce my appropriation of the Derridean conception of supplementarity through critical readings of two texts, Powell's discourse on the Empire and Rousseau's discourse on the reconstitution of the 'natural' through socio-political intervention. Chapter 3 begins with an examination of the reproduction of racial differences in British official discourse on race. I argue that Nietzsche's and Foucault's theories of power can offer valuable insights for the analysis of authoritarian discourse which domesticates difference through the multiplication of difference. At the same time, however, I note that the texts of both these authors are highly problematic in their treatment of race. Chapters 4 and 5 bring these empirical and theoretical discussions together and put them to work in detailed analyses of Powellism and the Thatcherite discourse on the promotion of homosexuality. Finally, I offer some concluding remarks on the interconnectedness of racism and homophobia. I argue that where racism and homophobia flourish in countries such as Britain which have an imperial past, we should recognize that these two forms of authoritarianism share a common genealogical tradition, namely the colonial construction and regulation of racial and sexual hierarchies. Wherever that colonial tradition is re-invoked to fortify the national borders, we should expect even greater escalations of racist and homophobic discrimination and violence within these same countries.

Chapter 1

Thatcherism, the new racism and the British New Right: hegemonic imaginary or accidental mirage?

In the Introduction, I used the somewhat controversial term 'hegemonic project' to describe Thatcherism. I argued that the electoral success of the Conservatives under Thatcher's leadership cannot be explained entirely in terms of the failures of the previous Labour governments, or exclusively in terms of economic policies. Attention should also be given to a wide range of social, economic and cultural elements, including race and sexuality, which have emerged as nodal points in contemporary British politics. Instead of analysing Thatcherism as the mere sum of various policies, I emphasized the symbolic aspect of Thatcherite discourse. Its free market entre-preneurialism, for example, had a specifically moral dimension; its anti-statism took on a particularly anti-union, racist and homophobic character when it was applied to central government–local govern-ment relations; and its revival of nationalism was framed in terms of Britain's post-colonial condition. Instead of proposing an abstract model of British society, the Thatcherites responded directly to popular concerns – including anxieties around race and sexuality – and constructed a new and yet already partially normalized common sense. My analyses of Powellism and Section 28 discourse are therefore constructed within the post–Marxist framework of hegemony theory. Hegemony theory has of course been dismissed by several critics as theoretically inconsistent, misleading and wholly inappropriate. In this chapter, I shall clarify my own appropriation of hegemony theory through a discussion of these criticisms.

Hegemony: from a specific demand to a social imaginary

The conceptualization of Thatcherism as a hegemonic project is rightly associated with Hall's Gramscian analysis. For Hall, the Conservatives' victory in 1979 did not constitute just one more swing in the electoral pendulum. He coined the term 'Thatcherism' to refer to the profound re-definition of the Conservatives' discourse under Thatcher's leadership and the subsequent impact of this shift on British society. Although Hall recognizes that the British electorate never became, on the whole, enthusiastic supporters for specific Thatcherite policies, he argues that Thatcherism nevertheless became hegemonic: it exploited the weaknesses in leftist discourse, disorganized the opposition, re-organized the political terrain according to its own agenda and radically changed the balance of power in favour of right-wing political forces.[1]

In Hall's terms, Thatcherism took the form of an 'authoritarian populist' formation. Thatcherism articulated authoritarian policies and themes, such as the construction of a centralist 'strong state', law-and-order campaigns, anti-union initiatives and so on with populist strategies. Any analysis which dealt with the elements of the Thatcherite project as isolated 'issues' would fail to identify the operation of this articulation and would thereby fail to capture the specific force of Thatcherism's 'organization of consent'.

> Thatcherite populism is a particularly rich mix. It combines the resonant themes of organic Toryism – nation, family, duty, authority, standards, traditionalism – with the aggressive themes of a revived neo-liberalism – self-interest, competitive individualism, anti-statism ... 'Free market – strong state' : around this contradictory point, where neo-liberal political economy fused with organic Toryism, the authentic language of 'Toryism' has condensed ... The crisis has begun to be 'lived' in [Thatcherism's] terms. This is a new kind of taken-for-grantedness; a reactionary common sense, harnessed to the practices and solutions of the radical Right and the class forces it now aspires to represent.[2]

The Thatcherites invoked the themes which have been central to the entire Tory tradition, including 'nation' and 'family', but they did not simply impose an abstract Tory philosophy onto a contemporary political agenda. They re-shaped these traditional themes to respond to actual popular anxieties; Thatcherism's representations always worked within the partially developed frameworks of 'already-constituted social practices and lived ideologies'.[3]

Hall's argument regarding the articulation of moral conservatism with free market conservatism in Thatcherite discourse requires some qualification. As Durham[4] usefully insists, the terms 'British New Right', 'Thatcherism' and 'the Thatcher government' do not always have exactly the same political meanings. The New Right and Thatcherite movements have at times developed internal splits on moral issues. Some New Right and Thatcherite free-marketeers, for example, either ignored the debates on morality altogether or took a right-wing libertarian position on moral issues which placed them in quiet opposition against the pro-family, anti-homosexual and anti-abortion lobbies. Even where Thatcherite rhetoric has remained consistent on moral issues, the Thatcher government's legislative agenda has not always matched its rhetoric. The extra-parliamentary movements against abortion, embryo research, obscenity and safer sex education have been bitterly disappointed with the actual performance of the Thatcher government. Although several individual members of the Conservative Party are prominent members of the anti-abortion lobby, the Thatcher government did not give substantial support to the lobby's demands. While Thatcher herself expressed sympathy for the campaign to ban the prescription of contraceptives for teenagers aged under 16 without parental consent, her government ultimately refused to introduce any new laws in this area.

Feminist writers such as Lynne Segal, Beatrix Campbell and Elizabeth Wilson have also noted the relative absence of an explicit anti-feminist campaign on the part of the Thatcher government.[5] Thatcherism did attack many feminist gains through, for example, the reinforcement of the public–private division, the attacks on women's autonomy through the promotion of the rights of male breadwinners and fathers, the campaign against unionized workers in sectors such as the health service in which women are over-represented and the authoritarian closure of discourse on sexuality. The Thatcherites nevertheless avoided direct demonizations of individual feminists and feminism as a movement.[6]

For all her pro-family rhetoric, Thatcher often chose a cautious and moderate path when it came to implementing actual policies on moral issues. Homosexuality was the one area in the morality debates in which there was a much closer fit between the Thatcherite pro-family rhetoric and governmental initiatives. According to the opinion poll data which I shall present below, there was a strong consensus in favour of homophobic policies across the electorate in the late 1980s. Where such a consensus on moral conservatism emerged, the Thatcher government did not hesitate to realize the Thatcherite moral agenda. Clause 28 was given the full endorsement of Michael Howard, the Local Government Minister, when it was introduced as an amendment to the 1987–8 Local Government Act. When its passage in the House of Lords looked uncertain, government whips ensured its success. Government sources have acknowledged that Thatcher herself persuaded some of her reluctant Cabinet colleagues to support the measure.[7]

Hall's argument regarding the articulation of free market conservatism and moral conservatism in Thatcherite discourse only holds true – in terms of policies – on homosexuality. However, Hall is not just referring to actual policies. As I shall discuss below, he is also commenting on the Conservatives' construction of a new image of their party. Rhetoric does indeed matter when a political party is presenting itself to the voters, and when it is attempting to discredit its opponents, even if its rhetoric is not always matched by legislative initiatives. Thatcher may have even gained support because of the contradictions between some of her rhetoric and her policies. Thatcher's decision not to translate her entire moral agenda into actual policy allowed her to occupy an imaginary political 'centre' without paying a large price for the discrepancy. Because there was no credible political voice that was more right wing than her own leadership, she was relatively insulated from the charge that she had not completely realized her promised moral revolution.

The deployment within Thatcherite discourse of various coded and explicit representations around race and sexuality has to be understood in terms of Thatcherism's hegemonic project as a whole. The right-wing attacks on black immigrants, multiculturalism and queers played a crucial role in the legitimation of specific aspects of that project. Hall would of course agree that it is not enough to note that 'nation' and 'family' operated as two spaces which were central to the construction of the Thatcherite imaginary. We should look for the outsider figures against which these spaces were defined, for it is only against outsider figures that the boundaries of a social space are constructed. We should also look for the historical specificity of the relationship between the outsider figure and the social space. The outsider figure has to appear to personify some of the greatest threats to the social order. The social space has to appear to be deeply threatened by the outsider and yet, thanks to its apparent trans-historical permanence, ultimately recoverable. In the specific context of Powellian discourse on the 'nation', the black immigrant played the key role of the constitutive outsider figure while, in the case of the Thatcherite anti-local government discourse on the 'family', dangerous queerness was one of the most important outsider figures. Given the specific historical contexts of their representations, Powell and the Thatcherites were able to construct the black immigrant and dangerous queerness such that they operated as particularly credible figures of outsider-ness. These demonizations were central to the legitimations of specific authoritarian measures, such as the intensification of racially defined immigration policies and the reduction in local government autonomy, and to the more general re-orientation of the British right wing from the pragmatic 'consensus' approach to a radical right-wing populism.

This is not to say that all right-wing mobilizations have the same effect. In the United States, explicit attacks on lesbians and gays were made throughout the 1992 Bush–Quayle campaign. These attacks certainly did resonate with popular concerns around AIDS, sexuality and the family. American anti-lesbian and anti-gay organizations and initiatives have flourished in the early 1990s. A ballot initiative in Colorado was passed in 1992 which prevents the state from protecting lesbians and gay men from discrimination. In Oregon, a failed initiative would have banned the use of public properties and funds for the purposes of 'encouraging or facilitating' homosexuality, and would have directed state schools to recognize that homosexuality is 'abnormal, wrong, unnatural and perverse and ... to be discouraged and avoided' in their curricula. Similar initiatives were introduced and defeated in Florida and Maine. In Alabama, one recently passed law prevents state-supported colleges and schools from funding lesbian and gay groups, while another declares that 'from a public health perspective ... homosexuality is not a lifestyle acceptable to the general public and ... homosexual conduct is a criminal offence under the laws of this state'. Religious right-wing extremists have rallied against a public library in Mobile, Alabama, which rented space to a lesbian and gay film festival, a Gay Pride film festival in Tallahassee, Florida and the New York City Board of Education, whose multicultural curriculum supports lesbian and gay rights. Most of the local anti-lesbian and anti-gay groups are affiliated with Pat Robertson's Christian Coalition. Robertson's lobby sent 300 delegates to the 1992 Republican convention. Together with other religious right elements in the party, they promoted the passage of several extremist resolutions. One resolution committed the Republicans to forbid abortion in any circumstances, while another opposed anti-discrimination legislation which includes 'sexual preference as a protected minority'.[8]

Although the Bush–Quayle campaign's attacks on lesbians and gays were welcomed by the religious right, there is some initial evidence that they were counterproductive among the neo-conservative and libertarian Republicans and among the 'Reagan' Democrats. Bush and Quayle received only a temporary increase in support after the Republican convention and continued to trail Clinton and Gore by several points in the polls. Bush and Quayle incorporated the religious right's anti-lesbian and anti-gay position into their campaign discourse by emphasizing 'family values'. This strategy had three basic weaknesses. First, Bush and Quayle defined 'family values' so broadly that they virtually equated single-parent families with lesbian and gay relationships, and thereby alienated many voters from non-traditional families. Secondly, the anti-lesbian and anti-gay signifier was left floating as a specific demand which bore little relation to other concerns around the economy and unemployment. In their campaign speeches, Bush and Quayle made some attempts to link 'family values' to broader issues, such as education and inner-city crime, and sometimes depicted environmental protectionism as an effeminate attack on American masculinity, but these linkages largely failed. A CBS–*New York Times* poll taken after the Republican convention found that 90 per cent of the voters wanted to hear Bush's plans for an economic recovery and that only 23 per cent wanted to hear his position on gay rights.[9] Pat Robertson made virtually no attempt to link his extremist views with a credible economic platform. In a letter to his supporters in Iowa, he argued against the Equal Rights Amendment, stating, 'The feminist agenda is about a socialist, anti-family political movement that encourages women to leave their husbands, kill their children, practice witchcraft, destroy capitalism, and become lesbians.'[10]

Third, the religious right unequivocally excluded all forms of lesbianism and male homosexuality as illegitimate. Although other Republicans, such as Barbara Bush, attempted to 'soften' the 'family values' theme by blurring the definition of the 'acceptable' family, these attempts were widely regarded as superficial damage-limitation exercises which left the virulent anti-lesbian and anti-gay message of the religious right intact. Instead of using the anti-lesbian and anti-gay signifier as a nodal point which gave coherence to, summed up and offered a solution to a broad range of popular concerns, the religious right's position appeared as a diversionary ploy through which serious discussion of the Bush administration's economic record could be avoided. Instead of manufacturing an imaginary 'crisis' around homosexuality and emerging as a powerful statesman who could preside over the resolution to the 'crisis' – while of course maintaining a sanitary distance from the disinformation campaign which created the 'crisis' in the first place – Bush emerged as a hostage to an uncontrollable extremist faction within his own party.

In the right wing's attack on the Clinton administration, by contrast, the anti-lesbian and anti-gay signifier has not been left floating as an isolated concern which is presented solely in extremist terms. For example, Clinton's modest proposal to end discrimination against lesbians and gays in the military has been linked to his plans for cuts in military spending. It is highly probable that the homophobic American right will quickly learn from the errors of the Bush–Quayle campaign, and will begin to produce a much more subtle discourse which nevertheless preserves its basic authoritarian force.

The Thatcherite deployment of the anti-promotion of homosexuality signifier also took a different form from the Bush–Quayle strategy. The Thatcherites fused the mythical campaign to promote homosexuality together with disorder in local government, an issue of central concern to British voters. A study on voter participation shows that British voters are far more likely to act on local issues, such as planning and the environment, than on unemployment, the economy and foreign policy.[11] The 1987 *British Social Attitudes* study also shows that the survey respondents held local government in very low regard. They stated that the police, civil servants and national governments led by either the Conservatives, Labour and the SDP-Liberal Alliance were far more likely to serve the public interest than the local councillors of any party. Only the journalists on national newspapers fared worse than the local councillors in the respondents' estimation of their trustworthiness.[12] The respondents' confidence in local governments as a whole decreased through the 1980s. In 1983, 35 per cent agreed that local governments were 'well run', while only 29 per cent agreed in 1987. Confidence in the police and the National Health Service (NHS) also decreased significantly across this period. The 1986 and 1987 respondents nevertheless gave higher scores to almost all of the other private and public institutions. The only institutions which were ranked lower than local governments were the trade unions. It is significant that the respondents have the lowest levels of confidence in these two institutions, since they were prominent targets in Thatcherite rhetoric and reform legislation.[13]

For the Thatcherites, local government represented one of the few sites of effective leftist resistance. The Thatcherites responded to this resistance by reducing local government to a chaotic state through drastic cuts in funding and then proposed centralization as the best solution to the subsequent chaos. The relatively low levels of confidence in local government in 1983 and the further decline in confidence over the 1980s demonstrates that the electorate tended to agree with the Thatcherites that local governments were not well run. The centralization strategy, however, was not proposed in abstract terms. Thatcherite discourse on local government was so thoroughly intertwined with racial and sexual codes that local government autonomy became equated with subversive black activism and the homosexual abuse of children. The 'blackening' and 'homosexualization' of leftist local government forces was particularly effective because the divisions within the Labour Party on race and sexuality ensured an ineffective response from the Opposition. The deployment of these racial and sexual articulations also succeeded because they were constructed within already normalized traditions – the new racism, anti-feminist resistance, the law-and-order campaigns of the 1970s, the backlash against the 'permissiveness' of the 1960s and 1970s, the anti-black immigration campaign, Cold War rhetoric on communism, anti-Semitism, imperial and colonial discourse and so on.

The Thatcherites did not, therefore, speak about the defence of the family in abstraction. They grounded their defence of the family with reference to specific popular concerns and to effective demon figures. In this case, they argued that the British (read: white Christian) family could only be defended against extremist blacks, anti-Western Asians and diseased queers if central government were given more control over local government. They did not, in short, make the mistake committed by the Bush–Quayle 1992 campaign: instead of deploying the anti-lesbian and anti-gay signifier in an isolated and extremist manner, they linked their homophobia to a wide range of popular concerns.

This kind of symbolic transformation of a specific political demand

Table 1   *Question: From what you know or have heard about each (of these institutions), can you say whether, on the whole, it is well run or not well run? Possible answers: 1983: well run/not well run; 1987: very well run/well run/not very well run/not at all well run*

	1983 %	'Well run' 1986 %	1987 %
banks	90	92	91
the police	77	74	66
the civil service	42	47	46
the NHS	52	36	35
local government	35	35	29
trade unions	29	27	27
nationalized industries	21	31	33

into a much broader social imaginary is crucial to the operation of a hegemonic strategy. A credible political project is far more than the mere sum of its constituent policy elements. It has to function as a more or less coherent image of a whole new social order. To the extent that it becomes hegemonic, a political project will tend to be understood not just as one possible project among many alternatives, but as the only possible social order. Hegemony therefore involves a radical break with previously dominant discourses, and, at the same time, the concealment of extremism through the promotion of the sense that there is no alternative to the hegemonic project. The actual literal meanings of a hegemonic project's specific demands increasingly become less important than its general image. To the extent that a project achieves a hegemonic status, it appears that virtually any problem can be resolved within its framework.

In other words, a hegemonic political project operates as a social imaginary which establishes one single horizon of intelligibility. It maps out rules of coherence, tables of authorized subject positions and sets of legitimate demands, and only recognizes as coherent, authorized and legitimate that discourse which obeys its logic. It conceals its own partiality, historicity and contingency and normalizes itself as the only possible way of thinking about politics. It imposes itself as the universal framework for the interpretation of experience by ruthlessly eliminating alternative interpretations, but it conceals this violent ground in that it pretends to perform merely the a-political and innocent recognition of 'facts'. It claims that there is nothing beyond the boundaries of the hegemonic project except total political chaos. A hegemonic project does not dominate political subjects: it does not reduce political subjects to pure obedience and it does not even require their unequivocal support for its specific demands. It pursues, instead, a far more subtle goal, namely the naturalization of its specific vision of the social order as the social order itself.

To describe a political project as hegemonic, then, is not to say that a majority of the electorate explicitly supports its policies, but to say that there appears to be no other alternative to this project's vision of society. The Thatcherites actually used the slogan 'There is no alternative' to promote, in the first instance, monetarist policies, and later to denounce virtually every 'wet' Tory, centrist and leftist critique of Thatcherism.[14] The lack of an alternative is not, of course, an accident of history, but the product of strategic representations. A discourse can become hegemonic with or without 'the people's' belief in its specific claims; it achieves hegemonic status insofar as 'the people' believe that the cost of de-stabilizing its account of socio-political phenomena is too high. To the extent that their consent is hegemonically organized, 'the people' defend the stability of the hegemonic discourse's account. They protect the hegemonic account from disruption by participating in the erasure of alternative accounts, and they do so for the sake of stability itself.[15] David Gergen's contradictory discourse on the Clinton administration is a case in point. Gergen, who served in the Nixon, Reagan and Bush administrations, was quite critical of Clinton's lack of focus before he was appointed as Clinton's counsellor. Gergen nevertheless reminded other critics that Americans had a non-partisan interest in the stability of the presidency. 'America,' he stated, 'cannot afford the destruction of another presidency.'[16]

'The people's' views on the various details of the hegemonic account tend to have little effect on their increasing investment in its overall stability. Their defence of the hegemonic project's 'normal' status is therefore entirely consistent with *both* their like *and* dislike of its actual content. To argue that a social agent might disapprove of the content of a political project, while simultaneously supporting that project as the only possible solution to a national crisis, is not to re-introduce the highly problematic category of 'false consciousness'. Contradictory identifications with political discourses are not incoherent performances by inadequately rational individuals who require the intervention of a privileged knower – the intellectual, the party and so on – to straighten out their allegiance. No one fully escapes the constitutive processes of misrecognition; no one has access to the 'superior', 'coherent' and 'universal' rationality which Gramsci refers to in his analysis of the relation between the intellectuals and the masses.[17] With Zizek, I would argue that all political identifications are structured in terms of a fundamental cynicism: 'the cynical subject is quite aware of the distance between the ideological mask and the social reality, but [she] none the less still insists upon the mask'. Instead of the traditional Marxist formula, 'they do not know, but they are doing it', Zizek proposes the cynical formula of the fetishist, 'je sais bien, mais quand même . . .' (I know very well, but, nevertheless . . .). The cynical subject already knows the falsehood behind the truth claims and is already well aware that particular interests are being represented as universal interests, but she still refuses to renounce the claims.[18]

Zizek's Lacanian theory of political identification as cynical misrecognition has important consequences for the analysis of political discourse. Instead of proposing an elitist schema in which the privileged knower detects the contradictions within the masses' discourse, Zizek insists that we pay attention to the unconscious phantasmatic dimension of political discourse. The cynical subject's deep investment in hegemonic discourse cannot be weakened by a straightforward appeal to her conscious rationality. We might show her that certain racist and homophobic claims are utterly untrue; she might still respond, 'well, even so, I still think that affirmative action for blacks has gone too far, lesbians should not be allowed to be parents, gay men with AIDS ought to be quarantined' and so on. (I will give several examples of this type of racist and homophobic logic in chapters 4 and 5.) The force of a hegemonic discourse lies not in its actual content, but in its form. Zizek argues, for example, that the 'ideological power' of Mussolini's fascism 'lies precisely in the feature which was perceived by liberal or leftist critics as its greatest weakness: in the utterly void, formal character of its appeal, in the fact that it demands obedience and sacrifice for their own sake'.[19] Political subjects become cynical supporters of hegemonic projects because, at an unconscious level, they crave the order, or, at least, the 'minimum of consistency',[20] which the hegemonic project introduces into an otherwise chaotic political terrain. As long as alternative political projects remain stigmatized as incoherent and illegitimate, the subject's investment in the hegemonic project's order will stand firm regardless of her contradictory policy preferences.

Social fragments caught up in an organic crisis can be compared to

Lacan's infant; deeply troubled by the experience of dislocation, they search for some framework which offers them unity and permanence. Lacan's infant resolves the condition of dislocation through (mis-)identification with the *framed* and *stable* mirror image. Looking into a mirror, the infant (mis)takes itself as being the same as the reflected image. The radically uncoordinated infant finds compensation in the spatial coherence of the image, so that fragmentation is displaced by a sense of the self as a coherent totality. Although this (mis-)identification installs in the human subject a fundamental dependence upon external images which remain irreducibly 'other' – so that alienation, transitivism and paranoiac knowledge become 'essential' to subjectivity – it nevertheless plays an important strategic role. For Lacan, the process of in-form-ation provides the previously fragmented non-self with the basic condition of selfhood, namely constitutive self-enclosing boundaries or frontiers. He describes this fundamental enclosure as a rigid 'armour'. The 'armour' metaphor is of course ambiguous: the infant's new 'armour' restricts its spontaneous movement, but it may also provide it with a valuable defence mechanism.[21]

In socio-political terms, the relation between social fragments in an organic crisis to political discourses is analogous to the relation between the uncoordinated infant and the mirror image. The socio-political situation is of course more complicated. At any given moment, many different political discourses promise to 'in-form' the crisis-ruptured social. With discourse, as opposed to Lacan's mirror image, there is always some degree of contamination between form and content. The political discourse which appears to have the most coherent framework on offer wins that superior formal status through the stigmatization of various elements of alternative discourses. The developmental aspect of Lacan's account must be set aside, for (mis-)identification is of course a permanent condition rather than a single 'stage', and societies in 'organic crisis' are certainly not 'less mature' than stable societies. The Lacanian conception of (mis-)identification should not be read as a yet another type of false consciousness theory. The Lacanian point is that *all* identifications with political discourses are mis-identifications. Every political discourse holds out a false promise of resolving dislocation in favour of total coherence; in Lacanian terms, they catch social fragments up in the 'lure' of an orderly society when of course their perfect fantasies and totalistic imaginaries can never be fully realized.

There are, in short, two radically different approaches to hegemony. Hegemony can be understood as domination, which implies that because the subject performs an identification with the hegemonic project, she gives, by definition, her full and unequivocal support for the actual content of the hegemonic project. However, hegemony can also be understood as naturalization. In the latter case, the subject who performs a political (mis-)identification may actually disagree with the content of the hegemonic project. Although the form and content of a discourse can never be wholly separated, the promise of the hegemonic discourse operates as a formal promise, namely the promise to transform social fragmentation into an orderly totality. Because the hegemonic project strategically stigmatizes alternative projects so that it appears to offer the most coherent resolution to the organic crisis, the subject may consciously disagree with the content of the hegemonic project and yet, through (mis-) identification, give that same project her cynical consent. Critics of hegemony theory tend to conflate these two approaches. In his discussion of false consciousness, for example, Scott makes a sharp distinction between what he calls a 'thin theory of naturalization' and a 'fat theory of hegemony'.[22] This distinction might be valid for some aspects of Gramsci's original formulations, but it certainly cannot be applied to the more recent theories which I am appropriating.

Were the 1980s 'less conservative'? Hall versus Hirst and Crewe

Hall's conception of hegemony closely resembles the hegemony-as-naturalization approach which I have outlined above, but he is usually misread as a proponent of the hegemony-as-domination approach. He recognizes in his discussion of the Conservatives' 1987 election victory[23] that the Thatcher government was not a 'popular' government in the sense that its policies did not find widespread and unequivocal favour among the electorate. He states that between 1982 and 1987 'significant majorities consistently preferred Labour on unemployment, health, housing and education– the "welfare" issues'. A majority of Britons nevertheless said that the Conservative Party under Thatcher was '"doing a good job", "giving the country a lead", making people "feel good to be British again"'. Hall argues that in the 1980s people made choices between political parties not in terms of specific issues, but in terms of images; because they were well aware that a five-year mandate will be defined in terms of policies 'any way that the party in power likes', they simply expressed a 'broad, undefined "preference" for one scenario or another, this image or that'. For Hall, the failure of the Labour Party in the 1980s was principally due to its failure to engage in struggles over 'ideology and representation' when 'Thatcherism ha[d] been intervening ideologically with consummate skill ever since 1979'. Hall emphasizes that material interests are important factors in the choices between political projects, but that these interests are 'ideologically' defined.

> Even poverty and unemployment have to be ideologically defined. A young unemployed person may interpret this experience to mean that you should work and vote to change the system. But it could equally be defined as a sign that you should throw your fortune in with the winners, climb on the bandwagon, earn a fast buck and look after 'number one'.[24]

The sense of prosperity itself is managed through representations: if some people are 'doing well', and the 'alternative ways of measuring how "well" you are doing are effectively silenced or stigmatized', then a much larger number of people will be able to identify with the prospering group.

> Elections are not won or lost on so-called 'real' majorities, but on (equally real) 'symbolic majorities'. Mrs. Thatcher's 'symbolic majority' includes all who identify ideologically with the enterprise culture as the way of the future, who see themselves in their political imagination as likely to be lucky next time round. They form an 'imaginary community' around Thatcher's political project.[25]

Through its deployment of representational strategies which have organized and incited these identifications, Thatcherism constructed a new social bloc. Hall insists, however, that this bloc is complex and contradictory. 'It does not consist of one whole class or even part of one class. It has to be constructed out of groups which are very different in terms of their material interests and social positions.'[26] When Thatcherism pursued its privatization policy, for example, it attempted to include many new constituencies within this project by promoting the development of a new share-owning working class. When it attacked state education, it encouraged the formation of a newly 'empowered' bloc of parents from virtually every social sector.

Hall, writing in 1987, did not of course foresee the limitations of these complex strategies which came to the fore in 1990, namely that Thatcherism would fail to construct a broadly defined imaginary 'winners' bloc in the case of the poll tax and health service reforms, and that Thatcherism would be unable to produce an adequately complex representation of its policies *vis-à-vis* Europe. In the specific cases of its poll tax, health service and European policies, the Thatcherite position was left exposed as an extremist position rather than a 'common-sense' position. Hall is nevertheless right to insist on the complexity of the Thatcherite social bloc. There is no 'natural' group of Labour supporters; Thatcherism received the support of even those social elements which were identified by Thatcherism as the 'enemy'. The 'new' working class in the 'South' of England voted in a majority for Thatcherism. Many of the people in the 'under-classes', the 'unskilled, part-timers, young, unemployed, women living alone, black people, the homeless, inner-city casualties',[27] and, we might add, lesbians and gays, did not identify with the Labour Party's late-1980s image of its traditional working-class bloc of supporters: many of these people voted for Thatcher.

How did Thatcherism manage to speak effectively to those elements when in the very same moment it would identify them as the 'enemy'? Contradictory representational strategies, such as the juxtaposition of anti-union policies with home-ownership schemes for the working class, or the combination of racist exclusions with the de-racialization of racism, played key roles. Thatcherism constantly re-coded its exclusionary moments so that no single social element could be unequivocally defined as nothing but the 'enemy'. Again, it is in this respect important to analyse the most extreme moments of exclusion in British New Right discourse: Powellian racism and the Thatcherite attack on the lesbian and gay community. Even though these exclusions were extremely 'popular', the British New Right did not engage in a simple total war against these elements, but deployed a tremendously sophisticated complex of frontiers and differentiations.

Hall gives another example of the concealment of exclusions through representations in Thatcherite discourse: the deployment of the 'loony Left' figure. This representation was central to Thatcherism's attempt to legitimize its attack on local government autonomy from the mid-1980s to 1990. Through the 'loony Left' signifier, the Thatcherites equated progressive policies on race, sexuality and feminist issues with Labour-led local governments, high local taxes, political extremism, anti-democratic socialist 'social engineering' and so on. The myth of the 'loony Left' became hegemonic: it offered an explanation for the breakdown in local government–central government relations, it allowed Thatcherite centralism to be presented as the only possible alternative to this breakdown, it was taken up by *both* right-wing and leftist elements as a credible representation and, most importantly, it gave permission to the mobilization of racist, sexist and anti-lesbian and anti-gay discourse in the pursuit of centralism without ever mentioning the words 'black', 'women', 'lesbians' or 'gays'. Hall states:

> The discourse of the 'loony Left' is a code. In London it made it possible to expunge the legacy of the GLC [Greater London Council], and to bring into the election, race (the anti-anti-racism backlash) and sex (the anti-feminism, anti-gay, anti-permissive, post-AIDS backlash – Thatcherism's hidden 'moral agenda') without a word having to be explicitly spoken. So successful was it that the Labour leadership, the party machine, much of the traditional 'hard Left' and the slick *New Statesman* and all, could also make a heavy investment in it without having to reveal their hand about race, feminism or sexual politics.[28]

Hall's depiction of Thatcherism as a hegemonic formation has been criticized by several authors. The objections of Hirst and Crewe are especially relevant to this study. Hirst presents his criticism of Hall's position in a chapter which is entitled, 'The Mirage of Thatcherism'.[29] Hirst begins by making a *distinction* between hegemony and the sense that there is no alternative to an established political project. Against Hall, Hirst claims that '"Thatcherism" is a myth that tries to justify Conservative victory by ascribing it to fundamental social and attitudinal changes, rather than to the default of any credible alternative political force.'[30] Hirst argues that Britons widely believed that there was no alternative to Thatcherism because the Opposition parties produced inappropriate policies and remained disorganized. From his perspective, it is a matter of historical accident that this view was widely held: 'if Mrs. Thatcher has ruled by default, the Opposition cannot bank on the same *luck*'.[31] In other words, the representational strategies of the British New Right are supposed to have had virtually nothing to do with this sense that the Opposition was lacking, and that Thatcherism offered the only credible social order. Hirst states that there is 'very little evidence that the electorate wanted a partisan right-wing government', that Labour's health, education and welfare policies have been more popular than those of the Tories and that Labour's policies on economic management have not won the same support. He cites various opinion surveys which are supposed to show that no widespread conversion to Thatcherite attitudes took place in the 1980s. These 'facts' are supposed to 'make a mockery of Thatcherite "ideological hegemony"'. Hirst's basic argument is that the Labour Party should focus on defeating the Conservative Party only by changing its economic policies and by forming a coalition with the other Opposition parties.[32] The political issues which are raised by Hall, such as the Labour Party's position *vis-à-vis* the demands of black activists, feminists and lesbians and gays, are not addressed.

Hirst's criticism of Hall's position is based on an inaccurate caricature rather than a close reading. Hirst argues that the myth of Thatcherism implies that Thatcher is a 'monster' and a 'master politician'. Arguing as if he is opposed to Hall on this point, Hirst insists that Thatcher is not a genius, but has 'survived only because she has given enough of the voters enough of what they want', that she is much more of a 'political opportunist' than a politician who is driven by conviction and that she has 'repeatedly changed policy when that would win her support'. Although Thatcher emerged on the political scene with a 'partisan, doctrinaire and impossibly right-wing [programme] in 1976', the same programme was viewed as an entirely practical solution by 1979. Instead of analysing the complex and contradictory historical context in which the political centre was shifted towards the right in the late 1960s and 1970s, Hirst argues that this change in Thatcher's image was caused by Labour's failures alone: 'Conservative policy had become less unpopular because Labour policy had become very unpopular.' Hirst shows that the Conservatives' electoral victories in 1979, 1983 and 1987 depended to a great extent on the support of skilled and semi-skilled workers for Thatcher, but claims that this support was won not through 'ideological hegemony' but because Thatcher offered 'opportunistic prosperity-oriented policies' to them.[33] Here of course Hirst assumes that the practice of identifying with a political project is purely a matter of rational choice.

The weaknesses of Hirst's position become even more clear when he directly engages with Hall's analysis. Hirst distorts Hall's position in his caricature to the extent that Hall's basic arguments are entirely lost. Hirst claims that Hall argues that 'the new Conservatism had come to exert "hegemony" over people's attitudes and aspirations. Thatcherism had seized ideological hold of the affluent working class, which had become part of a "social bloc", an alliance of groups under Conservative leadership.' Hirst then asks why the voters who supported the Conservative Party should be considered as a social bloc, 'rather than a ramshackle coalition of instrumental interest groups, potentially highly unstable'.[34] Instrumentalism aside, this is of course *exactly* Hall's point, that there were no natural Thatcherites, that Thatcherism was structured so that it allowed even the most unlikely groups to identify with its enterprise culture and that these identifications were often contradictory and highly unstable.

As to the argument that Hall's analysis is based on an un-founded evaluation of Thatcher as a political genius, the theory of hegemony is not a theory of the distribution of manipulative skills. Hall does not claim that Thatcher was fully aware of the logic of her own arguments, and that Thatcherism was the mere expression of already fully developed intentions. In this study, I am not suggesting that the politicians who promoted the British New Right project were completely aware of the effects of their discourse. It would be absurd, for example, to claim that the supporters of Section 28 were aware that by differentiating between the good homosexual and subversive queerness in terms of gender, their discourse would mobilize the already entrenched gender divisions within the lesbian and gay community. This was, nevertheless, one of the effects of Section 28 and the criminalization of homosexuality. In any event, individual leaders never acquire a divine omniscience, since they themselves are produced within discursive contexts. British New Right discourse produced Powell, Thatcher, Tebbit, Ridley, Knight and so on, as much as it was produced by them.

Hirst leaves the most important questions unanswered. Why is it that there was such a widely held sense that there was 'no alternative' to Thatcherism, especially in 1987, when the Labour Party ran a highly organized campaign and the Conservative Party made many errors? If no majority bloc of support for *particular* policies of the Conservative Party existed, and yet the Conservative Party received enough support to form a majority government in 1987, why is Hirst so certain that a change in a *particular* Labour Party policy in itself would cause voters to switch to Labour? Most importantly, Hirst assumes that economic policies can be considered in abstraction from the terrain of non-economic representations, as if they had a meaning apart from the constant re-construction of political identities. Against substantial evidence that the links between class and voting behaviour have been significantly weakened,[35] Hirst insists on an extremely simplistic approach to class identifications. He states that 'workers judge politics and political parties apolitically, in terms of the expected benefits to themselves and their families', and uncritically uses categories such as 'affluent workers', 'manual workers' and 'middle classes' as if these categories corresponded to actual discrete interest groups. He recognizes that 'voters choose party images rather than detailed programmes', but assumes that we can still meaningfully analyse voting blocs in terms of rationally acting classes, and that politics is simply a game of cost-benefit analysis.[36]

This type of approach to class identities is particularly problematic with reference to Thatcherism, for many of the Thatcherite policies had the effect of radically re-shaping class identifications. Unemployment, anti-union policies, the weakening of the manufacturing sector and the global re-location of manufacturing production have contributed to the decline in the numbers of the traditional Labour supporters, the unionized manual workers. At the same time, the Thatcherite attacks on labour unions and the sales of local government housing to tenants have constituted invitations for the workers to re-identify as members of the amorphous 'middle class'. Class identifications have, in the context of these fluid re-identifications, become much weaker indicators of partisan allegiances.

Crewe also rejects Hall's approach and uses extensive opinion survey data to support his argument. He argues that the voters' electoral decisions in 1983 did not reflect their stated priorities and preferences in terms of the parties' actual policies and performances. The majority of voters said that unemployment was the most important issue, and that they preferred the Labour Party's approach to the problem. However, this preference for Labour's economic policies failed to translate itself into a majority vote for Labour, even though voters had already identified the economy as their prime concern.[37] Hall himself explicitly recognizes these facts, and explains the apparent contradiction between survey findings and election results in terms of imaginary identifications.

> Asked what policies they supported, significant majorities consistently preferred Labour on unemployment, health, housing and education – the 'welfare' issues. During the campaign, these remained the most important issues for the majority of voters polled. In fact, Labour actually had some success in pushing them up the agenda. However, both before and during the election, if asked about image – who was 'doing a good job', 'giving the country a lead', making people 'feel good to be British again' – a majority consistently said 'Maggie'.[38]

Like Hirst, Crewe focuses on the role of 'working class' voters, instead of the complex problem of identification. Through the 1980s, there was a 2.2 per cent total shift to the Conservatives, but this shift was concentrated in the 'working class': whereas the shift in the 'middle classes' was zero, it was 4 per cent in the 'working class'. Putting aside the difficulties of defining the 'working class' and of assuming its homogeneity, Crewe's findings are nevertheless remarkable; the advance of the Conservatives through the 1980s was won through the support of the 'working class' when it was the 'working class' which 'bore the brunt of the recession'.[39] Crewe also shows that the opinion poll data reveals that in terms of specific policies, the majority of voters preferred the Labour Party, and that their economic values were more 'social democratic' rather than Thatcherite.[40] Crewe concludes that the majority of voters nevertheless regarded the Labour Party as unfit to govern in 1983 and 1987, and therefore gave majority support to the Conservatives even though they preferred the content of Labour's policies.

Unlike Hirst, Crewe recognizes that the Conservative Party did contribute to the construction of this credibility gap between itself and the other two parties. Instead of representing the sense that there was 'no alternative' in terms of an historical accident, Crewe argues that Thatcher's 'statecraft' was central to Thatcherism's success. The Conservative Party effectively represented itself as a cohesive party with a sense of purpose which, under Thatcher's firm command, could offer decisive leadership. As Riddell puts it, 'Voters may have liked or often loathed her for being out of touch and divisive ... [but] her leadership style has won respect. It has conveyed an impression of conviction, competence and decisiveness – of being a convincing Prime Minister.' He cites an April 1989 survey which showed that 67 per cent of the respondents disliked her, and yet 63 per cent respected her.[41]

Like Hirst, however, Crewe leaves the most important questions unanswered: how was this representation of the 'statecraft' of Thatcher constructed? In what contexts, and through what strategies, was the Conservative Party able to represent itself as a unified party – when this was not, of course, actually the case – and in what way did Thatcher emerge as a 'decisive' leader? To explain these features in terms of individual skills is to ignore the extent to which 'cohesiveness', 'decisiveness' and 'leadership' are historical and strategic constructs. As Douglas argues, 'it is only by exaggerating the difference between within and without, above and below, male

47

and female, with and against, that a semblance of order is created'.[42] Thatcherism's complex campaigns against the 'enemies within' and Britain's 'foreign enemy' figures – especially the Argentinians in the context of the Falklands/Malvinas War – were central to the construction of Thatcher's extremist and divisive leadership as a successful form of 'statecraft'. Riddell explicitly links Thatcher's 'statecraft' to her management of crises, which featured three highly stigmatized 'enemies of the nation': the Argentinians, the miners and the IRA. 'A central factor sustaining the Conservatives' political dominance has been Mrs. Thatcher's leadership style – as demonstrated during the Falklands War and at other crises like the miners' strike and the Brighton bombing.'[43]

Crewe's argument is similar to Hirst's in that he claims that public opinion surveys show that there was no shift towards Thatcherite values over the 1980s. Crewe focuses on what he calls 'authoritarian populist' values in particular. Using data from the 1974 and 1979 *British Election Studies* and a 1987 Gallup poll, he argues that Britons did become increasingly 'conservative' between 1974 and 1979 about 'pornography, modern teaching methods, racial equality, sexual equality and the availability of welfare benefits', but that between 1979 and 1987, they became *less* 'conservative' in each of these areas. Compared to the studies on racism in Britain in the 1980s such as Gilroy's,[44] Crewe's findings are puzzling to say the least. How can the contradiction between cultural studies analyses, which show an increase in racism and a shift towards more complex racisms throughout the 1970s and 1980s, and this empirical data be explained?

One explanation is that Crewe was not working with a complete set of data for the latter half of the 1980s.[45] Anthony Heath *et al.* argue that the *British Election Studies* do not reveal a clear pattern in terms of popular opinions on pornography, abortion, equal rights for blacks, aid to the Third World, the death penalty and criminal sentencing through the 1980s. Respondents in the *British Election Studies* were asked in 1974 and 1979, 'And how do you feel about recent attempts to ensure equality for coloured people in Britain?' They were given five possible responses: 'gone much too far', 'gone a little too far', 'is about right', 'not quite far enough' and 'not gone nearly far enough'. In 1983 and 1987, respondents were asked, '[How about] attempts to give equal opportunities to black people and Asians in Britain?' They were offered three possible responses in 1983, 'gone too far', 'about right', and 'not gone far enough', and the five original options in 1987. The results for 1974 and 1979 were more or less the same: 26 per cent and 29 per cent agreed that equal opportunity policies for blacks had 'gone too far'. Although this figure declined to 18 per cent in 1983, it increased once again to 28 per cent in 1987.[46] The questions in these studies are of course highly unsatisfactory, for they do not indicate whether or not racist respondents had simply learned to say the 'right thing' to the questioners. These findings nevertheless weaken Crewe's claim that British voters had become less conservative on racial equality through the 1980s.

It should be noted that Crewe's entire critique of Hall's 'authoritarian populist' thesis ultimately rests on the empirical results from these inadequate tests of popular conservatism and racism. Even if these studies had included a more sophisticated test – designed to reveal far more than the respondents' desired self-image for the official surveyor – the usage of their data for mapping shifts in political positions over time would have been problematic. Just as Hirst assumes that signifiers such as 'prosperity' are neutral, Crewe takes the fixed meaning of key terms for granted. Crewe argues his comparisons in attitudes over fourteen years are legitimate because 'the identical questions [from the 1974 *British Election Study*] were repeated in 1979 and . . . in November 1987'.[47] This assumption of the perfectly fixed character of meanings is of course highly questionable. Theoretically, it would be quite surprising if the same question on racial equality – which is located on a highly politicized terrain – meant the same thing thirteen years later. The burden is on the empirical analysts to show that such an unusual continuity has obtained before comparisons of this nature can be accepted as valid. To defend their approach, they would have to show that studies such as Hall's and Gilroy's, which show tremendous shifts in discourse on race over this period, are fundamentally incorrect. To ask the same questions in 1974, 1979, 1983 and 1987, and to claim that the results adequately reflect popular opinion on 'authoritarian populism', is also to assume that authoritarian populism does not shift in terms of its demon figures. There is no reference to homosexuality in Crewe's list. It is probably true that lesbians and gays were not prominent figures in public discourse in 1974, but to omit any reference to homosexuality in an analysis of public opinions in the late 1980s is to ignore an issue which was central to Thatcherism's success.

Extraordinary polarizations: homosexuality and gender roles

The Social and Community Planning Research Institute (SCPR)'s 1987 and 1990 *British Social Attitudes* survey results sharply contradict Crewe's claims about the general shift towards less conservative views. Asked whether 'homosexual relations' were 'always' or 'mostly wrong', a greater proportion of the respondents agreed in 1987 and 1990 than in 1983. Their views on homosexuality were more conservative than those on pre-marital sex, and only slightly more 'permissive' than those on extra-marital sex. It should be noted, of course, that the popular media gave extensive coverage to the AIDS crisis in the latter half of the decade, and that AIDS was for the most part represented in terms of the fallacious equation, homosexuality = death = viral threat to the 'general population'.[48]

The 1987 study found that older people, people with the lowest levels of education, people outside London and people with strong commitments to religious beliefs were most likely to select the 'always wrong' and 'mostly wrong' categories for 'homosexual relations'.[49] The 1990 results indicated that the respondents who stated that 'revolutionaries' should not be allowed to publish pamphlets and to hold public meetings were more likely to choose the 'always' and 'mostly wrong' categories for homosexual relations. Analysts of the 1990 study as a whole also found that the respondents became polarized only in terms of their responses to moral questions, rather than economic questions. Their responses were extraordinarily divergent on gender roles and homosexuality in particular.[50] Heath and McMahon argue that this extraordinary polarization has a political connotation.

> While at present these sorts of moral issues [around gender and sexuality] do not constitute a major threat to social and political stability in Britain, they clearly seem to have the potential to grow in political significance alongside the more familiar class-based issues on which British politics continues to thrive.[51]

Large proportions of respondents in the 1987 study also stated that it was not 'acceptable for a homosexual person to be a teacher in school/to be a teacher in college or university/to hold a responsible position in public life': 50 per cent, 44 per cent and 39 per cent respectively. Eighty-six per cent of the respondents stated that lesbians should not be allowed to adopt a baby under the same circumstances as other couples, and 93 per cent opposed adoptions by gay

Table 2   *Questions:*
(a) If a man and a woman have sexual relations before marriage, what would your general opinion be?
(b) What about a married person having sexual relations with someone other than his or her partner?
(c) What about sexual relations between two adults of the same sex?
Possible answers: always wrong/mostly wrong/sometimes wrong/rarely wrong/not wrong at all/depends or varies/don't know

| | 'Always' or 'mostly wrong' | | | |
	1983 %	1985 %	1987 %	1990 %
pre-marital sexual relations	28	23	25	23
extra-marital sexual relations	83	82	88	85
homosexual relations	62	69	74	70

men.[52] Commenting on these findings, Lindsay Brook, Senior Researcher at the SCPR and co-director of this section of the survey, states, 'It is rare in the *British Social Attitudes* series to find such near-unanimity.'[53] The SCPR's questions are far more useful than the vague 'equal opportunities' questions in the *British Election Study*. The *British Social Attitudes* survey respondents were asked, in addition to their general views on 'homosexual relations', about specific scenarios relating to current political debates. The respondents' expression of intolerant attitudes towards lesbians and gays is especially significant in that we can assume that at least some of the respondents wanted to present themselves in the best possible light for the surveyors and that they erred on the side of a 'tolerant' response wherever they thought it appropriate.

The SCPR analysts grouped the 1987 survey respondents as either 'authoritarian' or 'libertarian' depending on their answers to questions on criminal sentencing, the death penalty, censorship, respect for 'traditional British values' and the law, the education of children on authority and the legitimacy of non-violent protests. Cross-tabulated with partisan identification, the survey found that as much as 24 per cent of the Labour 'identifiers' can be described as 'authoritarian', as compared to 49 per cent of the Conservative 'identifiers'. The results for a whole range of questions on sexuality, pornography, abortion, 'test-tube' fertilization and surrogate motherhood were then mapped onto the authoritarian/libertarian groupings. The authoritarians and libertarians differed least on abortion, 'test-tube' fertilization, artificial insemination by a husband and surrogate mothering. The respondents differed most, by contrast, on homosexuality: 24 per cent of the libertarians agreed that homosexual relations were 'always' or 'mostly wrong', 86 per cent of the authoritarians did so.[54] The survey results also suggest that there is some degree of positive correlation between conservative views on law-and-order issues – which, in Britain, are heavily racialized – and conservative views on homosexuality.

The authoritarians and libertarians also differed sharply on AIDS issues. 'Strong' authoritarians were four times as likely as the libertarians to agree that people-with-AIDS (PWAs) 'have only themselves to blame'. Eighty per cent of the strong authoritarians agreed with this statement, as compared to 63 per cent of the authoritarians, 42 per cent of the neither-authoritarian-nor-libertarian group, and 20 per cent of the libertarians/strong libertarians. Taken as a whole, 57 per cent of the respondents agreed that the PWAs are to blame for their condition. Authoritarians were also twice as likely as the libertarians to disagree with the statement that the NHS should devote more resources to care for 'people dying from AIDS': 32 per cent of the authoritarians disagreed, while 16 per cent of the libertarians disagreed. Sixty-six per cent of all the respondents agreed that 'official warnings about AIDS should say that some sexual practices are morally wrong' and 29 per cent agreed that 'AIDS is a way of punishing the world for its decline in moral standards'.[55]

It should be noted that the SCPR survey designers were extremely irresponsible in their phrasing of these questions. Even if they themselves knew that moral hierarchies have nothing to do with the transmission of viruses, their questions certainly did legitimize inappropriately moralistic views. The performative and educative function of 'neutral' research has to be taken into account, especially during an epidemic. If the surveyors did not want to avoid morally loaded questions, they should have at least weighted them in the opposite direction. Questions such as 'Would you agree with scientists, health officials and doctors that AIDS is a medical problem and has nothing to do with morality?' or 'Do you think that most people know that everyone can contract the HIV virus which is related to AIDS – that it depends on what you do rather than who you are?' or 'Do you think that most people are aware that un-protected intercourse – that is, penetration of the vagina or anus with a penis without the use of a condom – is a high-risk behaviour for all heterosexuals' would have been more responsible.

The SCPR survey instead dangerously reinforces the myth of high-risk groups. The respondents were given a list of groups and were asked to place them in the 'greatly at risk', 'quite a lot at risk' and 'not very much/not at all at risk' categories. It should be noted that they were not given the category 'insufficient information to estimate risk' as a possible response. The respondents were most likely to place 'people who inject themselves with drugs using shared needles', 'male homosexuals – that is, gays', and 'people who have sex with many different partners of the opposite sex' in the 'greatly at risk category': the figures for these three groups were 93 per cent, 87 per cent and 71 per cent respectively. Only the first group is correctly described – the needle-sharing group is associated with a neutral identity, 'people', and it is their practices which are relevant to HIV transmission that mark them as a group. The 'male homosexual' group is described inappropriately in terms of a social identity alone, with virtually no mention of the sexual and drug-use practices which are relevant to HIV transmission. The third group is somewhat better described but again there is no distinction between safe and unsafe practices among the promiscuous heterosexuals.

The respondents were less likely to place 'female homosexuals – that is, lesbians', 'married couples who occasionally have sex with someone other than their regular partner', 'people who have a blood transfusion' and 'doctors and nurses who treat people who have AIDS' in the 'greatly at risk' category: the figures for these four groups are 43 per cent, 12 per cent, 12 per cent and 5 per cent respectively. Again, the survey asks the respondents to compare radically different groups, and the definition of these groups is largely irrelevant to HIV transmission. There is no mention of the drug-use practices of any group except the needle drug-users; no indication of the sexual practices of the lesbians; and no reference to the use of condoms and other safe sex practices by the promiscuous married couples, blood transfusion recipients, doctors and nurses. The final group, 'married couples who have sex only with each other' is also not described in terms of drug-use practices, past sexual histories and current safer sex practices. Nevertheless, virtually none of the respondents located this group in the 'greatly at risk' category; 99 per cent chose the 'not very much/not at all at risk' category for this group. In terms of the general degree of concern around the AIDS phenomenon as a whole, 60 per cent of the respondents agreed that 'within the next five years, AIDS will cause more deaths in Britain than any other single disease' – a prediction which the

SCPR survey analysts themselves describe as 'deliberately extreme'.[56]

Homosexuality was the one area of moral issues in which the Thatcherites ultimately did match their conservative rhetoric with actual policies. One possible reason for this exception is that popular opinions on other moral issues were not polarized to the same extent as they were on homosexuality. Popular recognition of women's right to choose to have an abortion, for example, increased slightly through the 1980s. The SCPR analysts comment that the trend in opinions on abortion remained quite volatile, and that attitudes on other sexual issues such as pre-marital sex, extra-marital sex, pornography and the provision of contraception to persons under the age of 16 moved in a more conservative direction at the same time.[57]

Can racism be measured?

The 1987 and 1990 *British Social Attitudes* studies sharply contradict Crewe's argument that the British electorate became 'less conservative' through the 1980s. Intolerant attitudes towards homosexuality peaked at a high level in 1987 – the year in which the Thatcherites explicitly linked the promotion of homosexuality with the Labour Party in its election campaign and the year in which the Thatcherites added Section 28 to a local government bill. British voters became *more* conservative on a variety of issues related to homosexuality and AIDS, and the Thatcherites put this heightened intolerance to use in both their 1987 electoral campaign and their subsequent legislative agenda.

Crewe nevertheless may be right when he suggests that there was an increase in racial 'tolerance' through the 1980s if he simply means that more people identified themselves as supporters of 'racial equality'. These results are, however, wholly inconclusive on their own. Instead of disproving Hall's thesis, they may actually constitute 'evidence' which supports it. A profound shift took place in right-wing discourse on race in the late 1960s, as right-wing figures such as Powell and Thatcher re-framed their racial intolerance within discourse on cultural difference. Their fusion of race and national identity, and their appropriation of cultural relativism[58] constituted a radical break from previous discourses on race; in Martin Barker's terms, the British New Right embraced a 'new racism'.[59] 'Race' was defined by the New Right as a cultural category, with respect to language, rituals, traditions and values rather than physical features alone. New racism discourse claimed to recognize the legitimacy of the racially 'other' cultures of the Asian and Afro-Caribbean populations within Britain. Imperial racism, by contrast, had erected Eurocentric cultural standards such that the colonized was equated with a total lack of culture. For the colonizing 'settler', the 'native' did not have a different culture; she was, instead, the enemy of all culture. Fanon writes

> As if to show the totalitarian character of colonial exploitation the settler paints the native as a sort of quintessence of evil. Native society is not simply described as a society lacking in values. It is not enough for the colonist to affirm that those values have disappeared from, or still better never existed in, the colonial world. The native is declared insensitive to ethics; he represents not only the absence of values, but also the negation of values. He is, let us dare to admit, the enemy of values, and in this sense he is the absolute evil.[60]

The colonized 'native' during the imperial era could only obtain 'culture' by submitting to the assimilatory process of Europeanization – by adopting the customs, dress, language and value system of the white European 'settler', and, above all, by attending a European university.[61]

By the late 1960s, this imperial Eurocentrism had become taboo as white Europeans engaged in a collective repression of their violent and racist heritage. Racists such as Powell feigned a respect for the cultures of the Asians and Afro-Caribbeans within Britain, thereby erasing from view the power relations which had structured the exploitative colonization system for centuries. The new racists refused to claim that the racial 'others' were inferior; they were, quite simply, different. Powell himself, for example, consistently argued that he was not a racist because he did not claim 'that one race is inherently superior to another'.[62] By avoiding the superiority / inferiority argument, the new racists could conceal their occupation of a structurally empowered position over and against the racial 'others'. The British, or, more precisely, the white Christian English, constituted a 'race' just like the Asians, Africans and Afro-Caribbeans; each culturally defined group had a distinct way of life which was *equally* vulnerable to disruption by other cultures. The fusion of each race-culture with an imaginary nation contributed further to the de-racialization of the new racism. Each 'race' had a natural 'homeland' to which there corresponded an absolutely organic nationalist sentiment. With the fictitious concealment of the constitutive power relations between cultures, the erasure of differences within cultures, the naturalization of historical phenomena and the spatialization of mythical race-cultures, the new racism preserved the xenophobic intolerance of the imperial racism, but re-cast it in suitably 'tolerant' post-colonial terms. *Every* 'race' had an *equal* interest in erecting strict immigration controls which would preserve the spatial and cultural 'purity' of the race-nations. *Every* 'race' had a naturally exclusionary culture in which racial otherness was always, by definition, alien. If white Britons resented the presence of those who, by their cultural otherness, constituted threats to the vulnerable (white-)British nation, they should be allowed to express their naturally antagonistic sentiments. The new racism erects 'thresholds of tolerance': the racial 'others' could not be 'digested' by the host race-nation if they arrived in large numbers and retained their dangerous alien identities.

For the new racist, then, it is simple common sense to state that the essence of Britishness is white Christianity, and that it is the patriotic duty of every politician to protect that essence from contamination by racial invaders. The patriotic discourse of John Stokes MP is typical of the new racists. Stokes explained his motives for seeking election in the following racial and patriarchal terms.

> I came [to the House of Commons] to help my country. I have seen my task as that of trying to keep all that is best in England and to be able to hand on to my children, as my father handed on to me, a country to be proud of, a homogeneous nation sharing the same faith, history and background. I must make it clear that I do not blame the immigrants for coming – they came largely for the money – but I blame those who encouraged them and still encourage them.[63]

For new racists such as Stokes, consciousness of one's true identity translates directly into an awareness of one's race-culture and a natural interest in the fortification of that race-culture's national borders against racial aliens.

The new racism therefore transforms racist immigration policies into an entirely natural humanism. It re-codes 'intolerance' as a legitimate expression of natural beliefs; it liberates the racially intolerant from their post-colonial condition of guilt. Above all, the new racism promotes contradictory political identifications around racial intolerance. Within the new racism, it is perfectly consistent to state that a quite blatantly racist immigration law has nothing to do with racial intolerance and, indeed, ought to be passed in the interests of the racial minorities themselves, for greater restrictions on racial immigration will by definition prepare the way for better 'race relations'. Since the white backlash was inevitable – and had nothing to do with political leadership – the racial minorities themselves *needed* racist immigration laws to ameliorate their condition within Britain. I shall present several examples of this kind of logic in right- and left-wing discourse on immigration in chapter 5. For our purposes here, it should be noted that we cannot measure contemporary post-colonial racism in Europe with nineteenth-century ideas about racial intolerance. The new racism introduces a whole set of re-codings which de-racialize racism – the euphemisms in Britain's racist immigration laws are exemplary in this regard. The new racism teaches the racist that she has never been racist, that the racial minorities themselves would pursue exactly the same policies in their own 'homelands', and that the preservation of racial-cultural-national purity is the best defence against racial tensions.

Contradictory identifications around racial tolerance were prominent, for example, in the protests by white parents at a school in Dewsbury in 1988. They withdrew their children because the school's population was 85 per cent 'Asian-British'. They claimed that they did not object to the mere presence of these 'other' children, but that the quantitative 'imbalance' had a qualitative effect on their children's well-being. One parent commented, 'If it was 50:50, fair enough, I'd be happy. But 85 per cent, that just isn't on.'[64] Throughout the controversy, the parents maintained that they were not racist and consistently stated that they did not think that the Asian children were inferior. They nevertheless insisted that with the existing 'imbalance' between the two distinct populations, their children were not obtaining a proper Christian and British education. It is of course quite possible that these same parents, who were blatantly pursuing racial purification, may have given any number of different answers to the question, 'Do you think that the attempts to give equal opportunities to Asians and black people have gone too far?' Their explicit disavowal of racism is perfectly consistent with their cynical (mis-)identification with the hegemonic discourse of the new racism.

The mere fact that many respondents in the 1974, 1979, 1983 and 1987 *British Election Studies* claimed to be 'tolerant' around 'equal opportunities' for racial minorities should be interpreted in terms of the historical context of their responses – including the normalization of the new racism in Britain through the 1970s and 1980s. The

Table 3 *Question: Britain controls the numbers of people from abroad that are allowed to settle in this country. Please say, for 'each' of these groups ... whether you think Britain should allow more settlement, less settlement or about the same amount as now.*

	% saying more settlement		% saying less settlement		% saying about the same as now	
	1983	1990	1983	1990	1983	1990
Indians and Pakistanis	2	2	71	62	26	35
West Indians	2	2	67	58	28	39
Australians and New Zealanders	16	9	28	31	55	69
People from European Community countries	7	7	44	41	47	51

1990 *British Social Attitudes* survey questions on race are much more useful than the *British Election Study*'s question on 'equal opportunities' for blacks. The 1990 study once again includes imaginary scenarios in its testing of attitudes. From the respondents' answers to questions on job discrimination, the treatment of racial minorities in the courts and race relations legislation, it could be argued that a majority of them agree that racism exists in Britain, and that it should be opposed. Their responses to a question on immigration, however, reveal the persistent operation of racism underneath this appearance of racial 'tolerance'.[65]

Putting aside the fact that Britain's immigration laws are already racially constructed, and the fact that the 1960s and 1970s laws virtually ended primary black immigration, the results from this question are striking. The respondents were already quite intolerant towards immigration in 1983 for all four groups, and were even more intolerant towards black immigration. Support for the status quo in black immigration slightly increases in the 1990 study, and demands for less black immigration slightly decrease. However, even these statistics do not necessarily indicate a movement towards less racist attitudes. Lindsay Brook and Ed Cape comment that this shift 'surely reflects an awareness that controls *are* much stricter now', rather than a movement towards greater racial tolerance.[66] The gap between the proportion of respondents who demand less settlement

for black immigrants and the proportion who demand less settlement for white immigrants diminishes slightly between 1983 and
1990, but this decrease should be examined in relative terms. The last
large-scale panic around black immigration took place in the 1970s
over the Ugandan Asians' immigration, and racially biased immigration legislation has already been in operation since the early
1960s. The 'less-than-the-existing-rate-of-settlement' response for
Indians, Pakistanis and West Indians nevertheless amounts to a
demand for yet more legislation against black immigration. At a
continual rate of change, it would take between twenty and twenty-
five more years before equal proportions of the respondents
demanded new measures against black immigration and new
measures against European immigration. Even then, this would not
mean that the respondents would have become equally intolerant
towards black and European immigration; it would only mean that
their confidence in the racist operation of the existing immigration
system had increased. Equal proportions of the respondents might
select the 'less settlement' category for blacks and Europeans and, at
the same time, if they were asked, a much greater proportion of the
same respondents might state that black immigration was 'not good
for Britain' than the proportion which did so for European immigration. Because the question is phrased in terms of demands for
change within an already racist system, equal responses for the
different groups do not indicate a non-racist position.

In response to another question, 56 per cent of the 1990 respondents also favoured stricter controls for the dependent family
members of already settled immigrants, and about 47 per cent
opposed an 'unreserved welcome for political refugees'. The survey
analysts note that the Sri Lankan Tamil, Somali and Iraqi Kurdish
peoples were the most prominent refugees in the news before or
during the 1990 survey period. It can be suggested, then, that the
question on political refugees would have been viewed, either
consciously or unconsciously, by the respondents as a racial question.[67]

The disjuncture between self-description and behaviour has long
been a difficult problem for survey analysts. In the case of racial
discrimination, the tendency to disavow explicitly racist views and
yet to support racist policies is especially commonplace. Nicholas
Deakin, writing in the mid-1960s, states, 'One of the most curious
characteristics of the British, both individually and collectively, is
their capacity for considering themselves tolerant, even in the act of

displaying prejudice.'[68] In a 1969 survey of the white residents in Ilkeston, Derbyshire, 75 per cent replied that they were not racially prejudiced, and yet 75 per cent also said that they would not sell their house to a black person, 62 per cent would not take a black lodger, and 68 per cent disapproved of inter-racial marriage. The Institute of Race Relations conducted a survey in 1966–7 of white English adults' attitudes towards blacks. According to the survey report's original author, Mark Abrams, 35 per cent of the white respondents were 'tolerant', 38 per cent were 'tolerant-inclined', 17 per cent were 'prejudice-inclined', and only 10 per cent were 'prejudiced'. When Deakin examined Abrams' findings and re-interpreted the survey's results, he decided to change the labels of Abrams' categories. With the very same raw data, he reported that 35 per cent of the white respondents were 'tolerant', 38 per cent were 'mildly prejudiced', 17 per cent were 'prejudiced', and 10 per cent were 'intensely prejudiced'. In other words, Abrams could claim that 73 per cent of the white respondents were 'tolerant' to some degree, while Deakin could argue that 65 per cent were 'prejudiced' to some degree.

The results from the 1967 Political and Economic Planning (PEP) survey also contradicted Abrams' optimistic conclusions. The survey analysts concluded 'unequivocally that there was widespread discrimination against coloured citizens in employment, housing and personal service'. In the area of housing, the majority of Abrams' respondents, the 'tolerant' and 'tolerant-inclined', did state that they would not attempt to avoid having black neighbours, and that black tenants should not be refused council housing and privately rented accommodation. The actual tests of practices in the field, such as the ones in the 1967 PEP survey, are the most reliable indicators of social and political positions. The PEP survey found that three out of four accommodation agencies practised racial discrimination, two out of three estate agents discouraged black clients with false information, many council officials employed various means for detecting the race of their housing applicants and black tenants were usually offered the oldest council properties. In a discrimination test which involved actual housing applications from a white Englishman, a white Hungarian immigrant and a black West Indian immigrant, 75 per cent of the white landlords who did *not* specify a colour bar in their vacancy advertisements nevertheless discriminated against the black West Indian. The white Hungarian was discriminated against in 5 per cent of his applications, and the white Englishman was not discriminated against at all. The Milner-Holland Report found that only 11 per cent of housing advertisements did not specify a colour bar at this time; if these findings are combined with the PEP results, it could be argued that only 3 per cent of all landlords acted in a non-discriminatory manner.[69]

If opinion surveys on the 'tolerance' of white Britons towards blacks were already weak indicators of actual behaviour in the 1960s, then the *British Election Studies* need to be supplemented by much more detailed research. For the Asian, African and Afro-Caribbean Britons who have been the targets of racial discrimination, the institutionalization of racism in Britain is an everyday reality. Through the 1980s, the unemployment rate for black men and women has been twice as high as the rate for white men and women across all adult age ranges. On average, the period of unemployment is twice as long for blacks as that for whites.[70] For example, a 1985 governmental Labour Force Survey stated that the unemployment rate for whites was 10 per cent, while the rate was 21 per cent for West Indians, 17 per cent for Indians, 31 per cent for Pakistanis and Bangladeshis and 20 per cent for all racial minority groups together. Sixteen per cent of white youths aged from 16 to 24 were unemployed, in contrast to 34 per cent of West Indians and 48 per cent of Pakistanis and Bangladeshis in the same age group.[71]

Racial attacks have increased in Britain through the late 1980s and early 1990s. According to the Home Office, there were 4,383 of these attacks in 1988 and 7,780 in 1991. The Anti-Racist Alliance estimates that only one in ten of violent racial incidents are reported. They propose a much higher estimate of 70,000 violent racial attacks per year. Eight people were killed in racial violence in 1992 alone.[72] The meaning of these statistics can be grasped only through an examination of actual incidents of racist violence. The Runnymede Trust published the following list of typical racist incidents in 1986.

> Five Asians arrested following clashes between Asian and white youths in Spitalfields in London's East End. The fighting started after a white man was reported to have sprayed Bengali children with beer and called them 'Pakis'. Following disturbances, a number of shops in the area were damaged.
> Two white youths reported to have thrown a petrol bomb into an Asian family's home in Bradford. The youths, aged 16 and 15, told police that they had thrown the missile 'for fun' and admitted arson.
> Five families in Slough near London reported to have been forced to leave their homes following racial harassment.

School-children were said to have thrown missiles at the doors and windows of the Asians' homes while shouting racial abuse.

A gang of seven white youths were reported to have waged a campaign of racial violence against an Asian family in Ilford in London. The family's car had been overturned twice, bottles, bricks and stones have been thrown at their house and racist graffiti daubed on their front door.

Two Asian men selling kebabs from a van in Slough were sprayed in the face with a burning liquid by two young whites in an unprovoked attack.

Five Asian youths were reported to have been beaten in another unprovoked attack in Leicester, one being hit in the face with a glass and the other being badly injured.

An Asian man narrowly escaped death when he was pushed onto an underground railway line in Glasgow by two football hooligans. The court heard that the Asian had been racially abused before he was pushed towards the live electric track.[73]

It is perhaps the case that Le Pen's successes in France and the racist and anti-Semitic violence in Germany have strengthened the myth that unlike its Continental and American counterparts, Britain is a basically tolerant and non-racist society. Although some of the differences in unemployment rates for the various racial groups could have been explained in the 1950s and 1960s in terms of the different qualifications of the white Britons and the new immigrant populations, the persistence of these differences in the 1980s and 1990s cannot be dismissed in the same manner. Finally, the increase in racist violent incidents should be taken as further evidence that racism is indeed prevalent in Britain.

The stigmatization of the Labour Party: unions, blacks and queers

Crewe's claim that the British electorate had become less conservative under the Thatcher governments is no longer convincing once these other indicators of racist and homophobic attitudes and practices are taken into account. If cynical consent does not necessarily entail straightforward approval of the positions in a hegemonic discourse, the 'test' for the hegemonic status of Thatcherism should not take the form of a survey designed to measure explicit agreement with Thatcherite positions. Cynical consenters who perform various disavowals ('I'm in favour of equal opportunities for racial minorities, but ...', or 'I don't care who you sleep with in your own home, just don't bring your perversity into the workplace') may have voted for Thatcher, but would not have been counted as 'ideological Thatcherites' in Crewe's sample.

One of the ways in which the hegemonic status of a political project can be tracked is by studying the stigmatization of alternative political projects. It is of course not enough to note merely that the Labour Party lost the 1979, 1983 and 1987 elections; it might have done so because its policies were not well liked. Hall and Crewe both show, however, that this was not the case; on the issues which the voters themselves identified as the most important, majorities preferred Labour's policies. Thatcher's 'statecraft'– the product of various representational strategies – was of course an important factor in the Conservatives' election victories. Another important factor, however, was the stigmatization of the Labour Party through the strategic linkage of Labour with contemporary demon figures.

In the following analysis, I shall focus on three demon figures in particular, the trade unions, racial minorities and lesbians and gays. (There were, of course, many other demon figures who became central to right-wing political representations through the 1980s, such as the anti-nuclear peace movement, the IRA, the Argentinians, leftist teachers, progressive intellectuals and so on.) It is clear from the confidence ratings of public and private institutions cited above that the unions were not well respected in Thatcher's Britain. Through the 1980s they were ranked, with the nationalized industries and local government, as the most poorly run institutions, lagging far behind the police and the banks. The 1978–9 'winter of discontent' and the 1984–5 miners' strike were invoked by the Thatcherites as particularly disruptive moments of union-led anarchy. Young comments that the miners' strike was a 'disaster' for Labour: 'Unable or unwilling to denounce [Arthur Scargill, leader of the National Union of Mineworkers], they [the Labour leadership] became passively associated with every offence he gave to the opinions of middle England.'[74] With respect to racial minorities and lesbians and gays, Hall argues that the Labour Party was linked with these demon figures through the Conservatives' 'loony Left' smear. To what extent had these articulations actually taken hold at the common-sense level of the electorates' everyday discourse?

The 1987 *British Election Study* contains an interesting section which, to my knowledge, has not been discussed elsewhere. Even the raw data from this survey – which does not indicate the specific responses of Conservative voters alone – provides remarkable evi-

Table 4   *Question: How closely does 'party x' look after the interests of trade unions?*

	Conservatives %	Labour %	SDP/Liberal Alliance %
very closely	5	67	5
fairly closely	18	28	40
not very closely	38	4	46
not at all closely	38	1	4
don't know	1	1	5
(number of respondents)	(3,331)	(3,342)	(3,233)

dence that these articulations were indeed 'taken up' by many of the respondents.[75] The responses to this question suggest that the majority of the respondents did believe that the Labour Party was dedicated to the representation of the trade unions. The SDP/Liberal Alliance's relation to the unions was viewed in a more 'moderate' light. By contrast, most of the respondents saw the Conservatives as not serving the interests of the unions – 72 per cent described the Conservatives and unions relation as 'not very close' and 'not at all close', while only 5 per cent did so for Labour. The relatively small number of 'don't knows' also reveals that the respondents had an already developed sense of the three parties' relationships with the trade unions. In this case, then, the stigmatization of Labour as a party which was held hostage by the trade unions had in fact made its mark in everyday discourse. With data from only one moment in time, we cannot tell whether or not the stigmatization of Labour was increasing or decreasing in 1987, but it is clear that its relative stigmatization *vis-à-vis* the popular perceptions of the other parties' relations with the trade unions was quite strong.[76]

In the case of racial minorities, the differences between the various party associations are somewhat less striking. It is nevertheless significant that 30 per cent of the respondents stated that Labour 'very closely' serves the interests of racial minorities, while only 9 per cent and 7 per cent did so for the Conservatives and the SDP/Liberal Alliance. As Hall, Gilroy, Layton-Henry and Rich argue, race was thoroughly re-coded throughout the 1980s within discourse on national identity, multiculturalism, Western democratic values and law and order. In the 1960s and 1970s, by contrast, discourse on race was shaped almost inevitably by discourse on immigration. In

Table 5   *Question: How closely does 'party x' look after the interests of black people and Asians in Britain?*

	Conservatives %	Labour %	SDP/Liberal Alliance %
very closely	9	30	7
fairly closely	41	51	51
not very closely	39	16	33
not at all closely	11	2	4
don't know	1	1	5
(number of respondents)	(3,345)	(3,334)	(3,228)

chapter 4, I shall present substantial evidence that Labour was demonized as a pro-black immigration party at a time when black immigration was widely viewed as a major threat to the (white) British way of life. When Conservatives such as Peter Griffiths refused to condemn slogans such as, 'If you want a nigger for a neighbour, vote Labour', they capitalized upon, and further legitimated, rising waves of racial hatred. I shall argue that Powell's criticisms of Labour and the left in general for pursuing what he regarded as a treasonous policy on race relations played a central role in the 1970 election.

Labour's actual conservative policies on race from the mid-1960s to the present appear to have had very little effect on this right-wing stigmatization campaign. As Peele puts it,

> minorities constituted something of a problem for Labour. On the one hand it was clear that the ethnic minority population was an important constituency to which Labour could appeal successfully ... On the other hand there was a danger that too overt a solicitation of blacks would alienate white voters.[77]

Peele takes the reaction of white racist voters as an unchangeable factor, and makes no attempt to place the racial representation of Labour into its complex historical context. She argues that the 'minorities problem' for Labour was exacerbated when black activists within Labour demanded what she calls 'special provisions', namely a black section or caucus within the Party. When an amendment was passed at the 1983 Labour Party Conference in favour of a black section, the party set up a working group to 'defuse the issue'. Peele notes that the Labour leadership consistently frustrated grassroots efforts to establish a fully-fledged black caucus throughout the

1980s.[78] Jacobs, by contrast, does not represent the proposed black section as a 'special provision'. He rightly associates the demands for a black section with the frustration of minority and anti-racist party members around Labour's consistent under-representation of racial minorities. His descriptions of the sensationalistic press coverage of the anti-racist mobilizations within Labour nevertheless underline the fact that the black section demands were widely viewed not as a legitimate democratic development, but as one more extremist attack on the Labour leadership, and as one more failure by the leadership to discipline its radical members.[79]

The 'loony Left' smear of the 1980s had both racial and homosexual connotations. Although many of the forces behind these smears were not officially connected with the Conservative Party itself, the attacks on Labour were exploited by the Conservatives at every turn. The Conservatives took advantage of the rise in AIDS anxiety and homophobia in 1987 both in their legislative agenda and in their election campaign. Lord Halsbury introduced a private member's bill which would have prohibited local authorities from giving 'financial or other assistance to any person for the purpose of publishing or promoting homosexuality' and from representing homosexuality as a 'pretended family relationship'. Although the bill did not progress beyond the House of Commons Committee stage, it received substantial support. After the election, Lord Halsbury's bill was used as a prototype for Section 28 of the 1987–8 Local Government Bill. The Conservatives did not hesitate to deploy racist and homophobic codes in their 1987 election campaign. I shall present several examples of the Conservatives' construction of linkages between Labour and homosexuality in chapter 5. For my purposes here, however, it should be noted that the mere listing of homophobic elements in the Conservative Party's attack on Labour in 1987 is insufficient. Was this articulation, Labour = queer rights, taken up by the voters?

The extent to which the Conservatives had successfully linked leftist local government politicians to lesbian and gay rights became evident in the February 1987 by-election in Greenwich. The local Labour Party chose Deirdre Wood, a former member of the Greater London Council as its parliamentary candidate. After an intensive press campaign against Wood, she lost the by-election to the SDP candidate. Not only did Labour's share of the vote drop by 4 per cent from the 1983 election results, but a massive switch also took place: many Conservative voters switched to the SDP to block Wood's

Table 6   *Question: How closely does 'party x' look after the interests of homosexuals, that is, gays and lesbians?*

	Conservatives %	Labour %	SDP/Liberal Alliance %
very closely	4	25	5
fairly closely	23	39	34
not very closely	42	26	42
not at all closely	30	8	14
don't know	2	2	6
(number of respondents)	(3,310)	(3,310)	(3,203)

election. The aides to Neil Kinnock, the Leader of the Opposition and the Labour Party, specifically blamed what they called 'the London effect'. Patricia Hewitt wrote in a letter to Frank Dobson, chair of the London group of Labour MPs, 'The "loony Labour left" is taking its toll; the gays and lesbians issue is costing us dear among the pensioners.'[80] The following data indicate that the Greenwich pensioners were not the only ones who associated Labour with lesbian and gay rights.[81]

On average, the respondents saw Labour as more closely associated with the trade unions and racial minorities than with the lesbian and gay community. There is, nevertheless, a sharp contrast between the respondents' perception of Labour's relation with the lesbian and gay community and that of the Conservatives. Sixty-four per cent of the respondents stated that Labour very closely or fairly closely looked after the interests of the lesbian and gay community, while only 27 per cent did so for the Conservatives. Seventy-two per cent of the respondents stated that the Conservatives did not very closely or did not at all closely look after the interests of the lesbian and gay community, while only 34 per cent did so for Labour. The size of the 'don't knows' for this question is also significant. The official discourse on the parties' positions and images around AIDS and homosexuality either mirrored popular discourse or had made some impression upon it; the respondents were just as prepared to answer this question as they were for the previous questions on trade unions and racial minorities. If homosexuality had in fact been irrelevant to the representation of the three parties in 1987, we would expect that the 'don't know' option would have been selected by a much larger proportion of the respondents.

For Labour, these results indicate that the voters' perception of the party's close relationship with the trade unions constituted a costly stigmatization at the time of the 1987 election. The respondents also saw Labour as closely identified with the interests of racial minorities and the lesbian and gay community. It should be noted, again, that anti-lesbian and anti-gay bigotry peaked among British voters during the election year. Any extraordinary degree of association between the Labour Party and lesbians and gays at this time therefore amounted to further stigmatization. Efforts by the party leadership to distance itself from radical trade union leaders, black activists, demands for lesbian and gay rights and progressive local government councillors may have limited the negative effects of these articulations. Again, because we only have data from 1987, we cannot indicate the change in popular perceptions of Labour over time. In any event, the distancing strategies did not eliminate the differences between popular perceptions of Labour and that of the other two parties. Given the tremendous symbolic force of these linkages, no amount of distancing would have blocked the return of their stigmatizing effects at the level of the unconscious. It is worth reiterating Hall's argument that the Labour leadership actually risked the reinforcement of these stigmatizations through its refusal to engage in a vigorous defence of progressive positions on race and sexuality. These statistics should not be used to support Hewitt's position, namely that Labour should abandon progressive politics as a 'loony Left' mistake. Labour should instead recognize that the damaging effects of these articulations can only be effectively countered through direct and principled engagement with the voters' anxieties around unions, blacks and queers.

Empirical studies should continue to attempt to analyse popular positions on race and sexuality, but they should do so by looking at the respondents' contradictory statements and behaviour, rather than their self-descriptive opinions alone. Survey designers should also pay attention to the fact that popular and official discourses do not represent blacks and lesbians and gays as monolithic groups, and that complex linkages between leftist positions and racial and sexual signifiers have been naturalized as common sense. They should place their studies in specific historical contexts; where opinions on race and sexuality are concerned, they should take note of the fact that the New Right has radically re-defined important signifiers such as 'equality' and 'tolerance'.

Public opinion surveys and the 1979, 1983 and 1987 election results nevertheless tell us a great deal about Thatcherism. Many of the voters who cast their ballots for Thatcher preferred Labour's policies, even in the key policy area of the economy. For Hirst, this paradox results from the fact that Thatcher benefited from an accident of history, namely the lack of a credible Opposition. Against Hirst, Crewe points to Labour's actual success in promoting its policies. Crewe accounts for the gap between policy preferences and voting behaviour by citing Thatcher's strong statesman-like image. From Crewe's perspective, however, Thatcherism did not penetrate civil society; he argues that the electorate's shift towards 'less conservative' positions on authoritarian populism issues demonstrates the inorganic character of Thatcherite official discourse. Other empirical data on attitudes towards homosexuality and AIDS, however, sharply contradict Crewe's findings. Even the survey data which shows that opposition against 'equal opportunities' for blacks declined in the early 1980s was contradicted by further evidence which shows virtually no overall shift across the 1970s and 1980s on this issue. In any event, this type of empirical data does not indicate the extent to which popular racist discourse actually retains its fundamentally racist logic while simply re-coding 'intolerance' as 'tolerance'.

Hirst's and Crewe's critiques therefore do not undermine Hall's basic arguments regarding the hegemonic character of Thatcherism. Powellism and Thatcherism were hegemonic discourses in the sense that they proposed new visions of the social order and successfully stigmatized alternative visions so that their political projects appeared to be the only credible frameworks for the interpretation of the national crisis. Hegemony does not depend on the explicit and unequivocal expression of support for specific initiatives; hegemony involves the far more subtle deployment of naturalization strategies which ultimately reduce opposition discourse to unintelligibility. Specific Thatcherite policies were unpopular and individual Labour proposals were widely supported, but a majority of the electorate agreed with Thatcher that there was 'no alternative'. For hegemony theory, these results are neither accidental nor paradoxical; they demonstrate, instead, the complex effects of political (mis-)identifications and representational strategies.

Chapter 2

Derrida's 'infrastructure' of supplementarity

I have argued that new racism and Thatcherite homophobic discourses share a similar spatial structure: they both position the enemy figure, the black immigrant and the dangerous queer, outside the imaginary familial nation. The construction of these outsider figures is performative in the sense that the very frontiers of the 'threatened' familial nation are only defined in the context of 'foreign invasions'. What, then, is the nature of the frontier which divides the 'outsider' figures and the familial nation? How can these figures be, at one and the same time, the 'enemies within' and the 'foreign invaders'? How can the familial white Christian nation be simultaneously represented as a precarious space which urgently requires re-fortification and as an a-historical essence to which 'we' can always return? Derrida's writings on the 'infrastructure'[1] of supplementarity offer many valuable insights for the analysis of the strategic deployment of political frontiers.

The deconstruction of Powellian essentialism

For Powell, English whiteness and foreign blackness are radically different: not only do they belong on opposite sides of the proper national frontier, they also have fundamentally different metaphysical characteristics. English whiteness takes the form of the utterly immutable core of the nation, while foreign blackness operates as a floating corrosive element which threatens to destroy the white English way of life. Powell also distinguished between the British nation and the British Empire in both spatial and metaphysical terms. In the 1960s, Powell became convinced that decolonization had greatly contributed to the disintegration of British national pride. Too many Britons thought that their country had only obtained its 'greatness' through imperial conquest, so that decolonization appeared to doom Britain to a new era of mediocrity. He addressed this problem in several speeches on the Empire. I shall analyse these speeches in detail in chapter 4; for our purposes here, it should be noted that the Empire took on specific metaphysical characteristics in Powell's speeches. It was a dangerous myth, he argued, that Britain had become 'great' through imperialism. The Empire should not be regarded as an integral part of the nation; it had been created through a series of blunders and irrelevant decisions, and – according to Powell – had contributed little to the nation's wealth. In other words, Powell re-constructed the British nation-British Empire relation as an inside–outside or essence–accident relation. He argued that the Empire could have been added to or subtracted from the metropole with virtually no effect on its greatness. He metaphorically situated (white-)Englishness as the timeless core of Britain; the true English spirit, he claimed, had remained virtually unchanged through various international traumas, and could always be recovered in its pure form.

Powell's discourse on the Empire, then, could be described as essentialist. Not only is (white-)Englishness conceptualized as the unchanging 'inside', it is also privileged over the accidental 'outside': it is (white-)Englishness alone which shapes the British nation, not its external foreign 'adventures' and colonial appendages. Essentialist discourse claims that essence is prior to accident, separate from accident, and always recoverable in its pure form. It should be emphasized that we cannot predict the political effects of a discourse based on its essentialist or anti-essentialist form. Many aspects of new racism discourse and Thatcherite homophobia are actually quite anti-essentialist in their conceptualization of identities, while many effective resistance strategies are constructed around essentialist identity claims.

Instead of offering an a priori political evaluation of an essentialist text, we should pay close attention to the ways in which the relation between the 'inside' and the 'outside' is represented. The category of the accidental allows essentialist discourses to account for differentiation and variation while simultaneously claiming that essence always remains absolutely the same. Essentialist discourse claims that accidental differences are wholly non-constitutive; they are supposed to be purely external to essence. Repetition, the absolutely identical return of the same essence, is supposed to be guaranteed by the absolutely impermeable boundary between essence and accident.

Deconstruction constitutes an infiltration and subversion of essentialism, rather than a simple rejection of essentialism altogether.[2] Where an essentialist discourse claims that the essence–accident relation is structured so that essence is prior to accident, separate from accident and always recoverable in its pure form, deconstruction can show that the accidental is always 'inside' essence as its condition of possibility. Deconstruction works on the claims which are made concerning the nature of the frontier between the two terms in this relation. Because it is supposed to be external to essence, the accidental is supposed to be wholly unnecessary to essence. Aristotle compares the accidental to a non-rational variation which cannot be conceptualized, such as the unforseen disruption in the voyage of a ship when it is blown off course by a storm.[3] When something 'goes wrong' in the 'normal course of things', the accidental category allows an essentialist text to locate these disruptions as non-necessary externalities so that the integrity of essence is maintained. Deconstruction, however, shows that the boundary between essence and accident is always being violated. There is *always* a possibility in every 'normal course of things' that something will 'go wrong';[4] essence is *always* exposed to the possibility of accidents. The accidental is supposed to be a purely random chance variation, but deconstruction reveals that it is actually structured in terms of an alternative order. By showing the alternative structure of the supposedly un-structured, deconstruction begins to break down the strict separations between essence–accident and necessity–unintelligibility.

Necessity can therefore be located exactly where it is not supposed to be, namely in the accidental. Conversely, the accidental can also be located on the wrong side of the frontier: it can always be shown that that which is represented as an external accident actually functions as the 'outside' against which the supposedly prior, separate and independent essence, the 'inside', is constituted. Against Powell's essentialism, for example, it can be shown that the external accident, the Empire, was absolutely central to the organization of British nationalisms since the late nineteenth century. In the late nineteenth and early twentieth centuries, the discourse of imperial nationalism, which included elements of racial superiority, monarchism and Social Darwinism, made its mark throughout domestic British culture. References to imperial nationalism were common in popular cultural forms like advertising, theatre, cinema, radio, religious discourse, youth organizations, official rituals and ceremonies, educational curricula and juvenile literature. Overtly imperial organizations also became prominent at this time. While the 'average' British citizen may not have had an extensive knowledge of the Empire, the imperial nationalist discourse nevertheless constituted a 'world view' which united the various fragments of the British nation in terms of the sense of a shared superiority over and against the non-European world. The saturation of the popular culture with references to the colonized other served to locate the 'lowest' 'under-classes' in Britain as superior to the highest 'native' elite, and to remind them of their equal place in the great national colonization project, 'an enterprise conducted by the State and great commercial companies, protected by the army and navy ... sanctified by the Church [and] tinged with a sense of moral crusade'.[5] Imperial nationalist discourse therefore had a tremendous impact upon British society: '[it] contributed to the complacent habit of superiority which created what might be called "protected markets of the mind" in Britain, intellectual shells which were only really shattered, like their economic equivalents, in the 1960s'.[6] Powell was quite rightly concerned about the impact of decolonization on British nationalism. The accidental 'outside' had in fact contributed to the constitution of the essential 'inside' in the sense that the Empire played a key role in the construction of an imaginary national space which transcended class and regional differences. However, the Powellian representations of the colonized 'other' and blackness are ultimately self-contradictory. Powellism says that the racial 'other' is entirely external to Britishness, but it actually reorganizes the unification of the (white-)British nation through its 'call to the barricades' against black immigration. Powellism never achieves the recovery of a pure essence; it only unifies dispersed elements in opposition against the 'foreign invader'.

Deconstruction does not reject the possibility of identity, determinacy and repetition entirely. It shows that instead of being grounded on an absolutely prior 'inside' core, identity is only possible to the extent that the 'inside' is 'supplemented' by the 'outside'. Every essentialist text *says* that identity is possible because essence is prior to accident, separate from accident and wholly recoverable in its pure form. It can nevertheless be *shown* that in these same texts, identity is constructed as an 'inside' which always has the accidental 'outside' within itself as its condition of possibility. Essentialist identity claims always strive to conceal this fundamental dependence of the 'inside' space on 'outsider' figures. Deconstruction's approach to identity therefore amounts to the following paradox: identity is never purely possible, for identity is always dependent on that which is 'outside' identity, and it always differentiates itself in its shifting relations with its othernesses; but identity is never purely impossible, because there always remains something irreducibly other against which an 'inside' can be constructed. Another way of phrasing this paradox is to say that otherness is that which makes identity impossible and possible at the same time. To put this in strategic terms, resistance against authoritarian essentialist identity claims must take a dual form. It is not as if Powellian racism is successfully defeated as soon as it is shown that Britishness depends upon its enemy figures for its constitution, and that Britishness is historical, plural, contextual and so on. The unification of dispersed fragments against excluded figures of otherness by discourses such as Powellism must be taken seriously, for identity games do have actual material effects. Even if Powellism is self-contradictory, or, in some senses, because Powellism is self-contradictory, it works: it builds on already sedimented forms of common sense to propose a new hegemonic solution to the 'national crisis'. The deconstruction of racist discourses such as Powellism should be supplemented by alternative identity claims which intervene on the same popular field and propose radically different articulations of racial and national signifiers.

Supplementarity in Rousseau and in the representation of black immigration

Essentialism's concealment strategy is therefore organized in terms of its representation of otherness. To the extent that otherness is depicted as a non-essential addition, as something which is purely extra, then the façade of the essentialist text is maintained. To the extent that otherness escapes this metaphysical erasure, and is shown instead as the condition of possibility of the very integrity of the 'inside' essence, then otherness becomes transformed. Instead of playing the role of a purely harmless and cosmetic addition, it becomes instead the subversive supplement: it positions itself as the necessary completion to the 'inside', and in this manner shows that the 'inside' has always remained incomplete on its own.[7] To protect itself, then, the essentialist text must neutralize the threat of subversion by managing the representation of otherness. In the case of Powellism and Thatcherism, the importance of constructing borders through the externalization of blackness – by representing the Empire as irrelevant, radical blacks as inspired by American movements, black migrants as 'outsiders' rather than the descendants of the workforce which created much of Britain's wealth and so on – cannot be overestimated. The new racism flickers constantly between representations of blackness as a pure addition, as a wholly foreign population which can be simply 'repatriated' back to their 'home' countries, and representations of blackness as a dangerous supplement, as an insidious element which has thoroughly penetrated education curricula and local government policies. This apparently contradictory complex of representations nevertheless has extremely consistent effects: the supplementarity of blackness promotes white-British solidarity against the enemy within, while the accidental appearance of blackness allows white-Britishness to appear as absolutely invulnerable, as an unaffected a-historical essence which is not dependent upon racist solidarity for its constitution.

Supplementarity also has a temporal dimension which is equally useful for political analysis. Otherness can be represented as an unnecessary late arrival which imperfectly mimics that which is already in place, while a deconstruction of that representation can show that otherness and mimicry were already at work in the origin. Derrida emphasizes this temporal dimension of supplementarity in his intervention into Rousseau's arguments concerning the role of writing in education. Rousseau describes literature as an essential aid in education, and yet, at the same time, insists on its dangerous character and issues strict rules for its use. For Rousseau, education should be nothing but a process of reconstituting nature. Modern Europeans have to reconstitute nature because, in Rousseau's terms, they have become distanced from their true nature through civilization: the development of socio-economic inequality, status hierarchies, high culture, the arts and letters and the institution of private property. They can only 'return' to nature, then, through its reconstitution. Ironically, it is the civilizing process of education itself which makes up for the deficiencies of their corrupted nature. Rousseau warns, however, that this substitution of the written version for the real nature must be done as little and as late as possible. The written representation of nature may seductively lead the student away from nature towards the pursuit of unnatural goods. Writing possesses this seductive potential because it appears to be a purely natural and innocent means of assistance in this 'return' to nature.[8]

Although Derrida works with Rousseau's *Essay on the Origin of Languages*, I have chosen the *Discourse on the Origin of Inequality* for analysis. Rousseau's arguments are quite similar in both texts, but the latter text has been granted a more central place in the Western political theory canon. I should also point out that I am using the male pronoun in this discussion of Rousseau's conception of the state of nature because he excludes females from rationality. For men, the exercise of 'virtue' means the development of independence, autonomy and self-control; for women, it means the development of dependence, servility and self-inhibition. Male citizens in the social contract obtain their freedom through their participation in the formulation of equitable and just laws. Females become free only insofar as their husbands are free and the male community of citizens succeeds in realizing the general will; they play a crucial role in guiding males towards good behaviour, but they can only perform their supplementary function if they remain absolutely subservient to males.[9] In the *Origin of Inequality*, Rousseau even suggests that males become increasingly feminine to the extent that they are distanced from their natural state of freedom through the civilizing process: 'as [natural man] becomes sociable and a slave, he grows weak, timid and servile; his effeminate way of life totally enervates his strength and courage'.[10]

Rousseau attempts to characterize 'man's' original condition in terms of immediacy and completion. He asks us to imagine 'man' in the state of nature, a state of being prior to the development of the 'artificial' practices of civilized 'man'. Unlike Hobbes, Rousseau holds that 'natural man' lives in a harmonious relationship with nature which provides the means for the immediate gratification of his desires. Rousseau states, 'I see him satisfying his hunger at the first oak, and slaking his thirst at the first brook; finding his bed at the foot of the tree which afforded him a repast; and, with that, all his wants supplied.' The only goods which natural 'man' recognizes are 'food, a female and sleep', and he only fears 'pain and hunger'. Because 'natural man' must provide for his needs without the assistance of modern machinery, the body of the 'savage' remains robust, balanced and whole. '[The savage has] the advantage of having all [his] forces constantly at [his] disposal, of being always prepared for every event, and of carrying [him]self, as it were, perpetually whole and entire about [himself].' Instead of becoming caught up in the individualistic and competitive effects of *amour-propre*, a feeling which only arises in civilized society and which brings about endless conflicts, natural 'man' is moved by the 'love of self', a naturally compassionate attitude towards all other beings. The Rousseauian state of nature is therefore a solitary and yet, from the male point of view at least, a peaceful condition.[11]

As the supposedly natural object of 'natural man's' desire who is obtained and consumed with the force of immediate gratification, we could imagine that 'natural woman' experiences this original condition as a state of perpetual fear and violence. Within his misogynist and heterosexist framework of 'natural' gender differentiation, however, Rousseau argues that women have unlimited heterosexual desires, and as continually desiring beings women always consent to sex even when their natural shame forces them to feign non-consent.[12] By assuming that unlimited and male-centred heterosexual desire governs sexual behaviour in the pre-cultural condition of the state of nature, Rousseau implicitly argues that any contemporary cultural norm which 'represses' this desire is illegitimate. His theory is in this respect vulnerable to Foucault's critique of Freud's conception of the repression of desire. There is no pre-cultural 'original' desire – heterosexual or otherwise – which is later subjected to 'repression' in contemporary Western culture; rather, multiple institutions within our culture hegemonically produce that which appears to be an 'original' desire.[13] Rousseau in this sense violates his own rules regarding the construction of the state of nature. 'The only goods [natural man] recognizes in the universe are food, a female and sleep: the only evils he fears are pain and hunger.'[14] 'Natural woman's' body is reduced to the status of a 'natural good', like food, water or shelter; 'natural man's' immediate consumption of 'natural woman' is reduced to the absolutely instinctual act of gratifying a bodily urge – an act which is supposed to be absolutely prior to any cultural intervention. Rousseau's image of 'natural man' 'consuming' 'natural woman' in the state of nature actually reads male-centred heterosexuality, a fragile product of contemporary Western culture, back into a supposedly pre-cultural condition.

As a condition of pure immediacy, the state of nature has a distinct temporal form. Whereas civilized society is characterized by 'sudden and continual changes which arise from the passions and caprices of bodies of men living together', the state of nature takes the form of an absolutely timeless and harmonious flow: 'all things proceed in a uniform manner'. Immersed in the immediacy of 'natural' life, 'natural man' does not have to bridge the gaps between past 'now's, present 'now's and future 'now's. The undisturbed soul of 'natural man' is 'wholly wrapped up in the feeling of its present existence, without any idea of the future, however near at hand; while his projects, as limited as his views, hardly extend to the close of day'. In the following passage, Rousseau once again violates his own rules: his 'state of nature' is supposed to be a hypothetical construct which does not correspond to any contemporary cultural situation which has been marked by civilization. He does not hesitate, however, to reach for a racist metaphor in his discussion of temporality in the state of nature. Rousseau writes, 'Such, even at present, is the extent of the native Caribbean's foresight: he will improvidently sell you his cotton-bed in the morning, and come crying in the evening to buy it again, not having foreseen he would want it again the next night.'[15]

According to Rousseau's climatological schema in the *Social Contract*, 'the native Caribbean' is an inhabitant of a 'hot country'. Unlike 'cold countries' like England, 'hot countries', such as Africa and the Indies, are quite fertile. Because the peoples of 'hot countries' consume much less than their northern counterparts, and their lands produce a large surplus with relatively little labour, they are naturally suited to a despotic form of government. The southern peoples' surplus, Rousseau argued, ought to be consumed by a despotic government because of the corrupting effects of this potential wealth: 'it is better for this excess to be absorbed by the government than dissipated among the individuals'.[16] The lands in the northern countries with colder climates, by contrast, yield much smaller surpluses. Because the northern peoples are not endangered by corrupting surpluses, there is no need for the benevolent consumption of the excessive fruits of the people's labour by a despotic government. The inhabitants of the 'cold countries' are therefore best suited to a democratic form of government.

Because the land in 'hot countries' is supposedly more fertile, its cultivation requires less forethought and less disciplining of one's immediate passions for future gain. From Rousseau's viewpoint, the 'native Caribbean' is only behaving in the irrational manner which is typical of the climatologically conditioned cultures of the 'southern' peoples. His geo-psychological reasoning may strike the contemporary reader as bizarre. Rousseau's point is that the development of reason is contextual, and that climate plays an important role in that process. At the same time, however, he contradicts himself: the inferiority of women and non-Europeans obtains for every possible context. It is of course no small coincidence that he groups Caribbeans, Africans and Persians and 'Asiatics'[17] together in the general category of irrationality in an eighteenth-century European text, and that Rousseau's theory legitimates the colonization of these peoples in the name of universal justice.

The identity of the 'native Caribbean' in the *Origin of Inequality* remains somewhat mysterious: he could be one of the very few indigenous peoples who escaped the Europeans' genocidal occupation of the islands or an African slave on a European plantation. After the banning of slavery, indentured Asian workers were brought to the Caribbean by the British, but we can assume that the account in Rousseau's text pre-dates their arrival. In short, the very conception of a 'native Caribbean' from an eighteenth-century European perspective is a strategic fiction which conceals the brutality of European racist domination: the European explorers, colonizers, slave-traders and plantation-owners had almost totally eradicated the forms of life which had existed among the indigenous peoples of the Caribbean. A Eurocentric analysis of the native Caribbean's culture would indeed relegate it to the status of the 'un-civilized', but 'un-civilized' is not the same as 'pre-civilized'. Even on Rousseau's own terms, the eighteenth-century 'native Caribbean' is not a good example of 'natural man', for his condition is marked through and through by European civilization. Deviating from his own methodology, Rousseau constructs an analogy between 'natural man', who is supposedly absolutely prior to (European) civilization, and one of the products of European civilization – the slave or the colonized indigenous person. Rousseau nevertheless takes his enslaved and colonized condition as a 'natural' and 'original' condition of inferiority: although European 'man' has made the problematic transition to civilized society, the 'native Caribbean' remains 'even at present' locked within the original state which European 'man' has left far behind. Rousseau therefore performs a manoeuvre which is typical of many racist discourses: the legitimation and concealment of racial domination through the idealization of the racial 'other' as a primitive. Strictly speaking, then, Rousseau's 'natural man' is specifically the ancient ancestor of modern European man – the 'founding father' of European civilization. Rousseau could, within his Eurocentric framework, draw imperfect analogies between 'natural man' and the contemporary colonized, but – within his schema – the irrational colonized would never found a 'proper' civilization.

Because 'natural man' lives in the continual present, he has no anticipated fears or unfulfilled desires, he has no knowledge and he does not need to use signs: 'his imagination paints no pictures'. Against Condillac's assumption that humans have always had language, Rousseau claims that in the state of nature 'there was no communication among men and no need for any'. Consequently, there is no possibility of identity: 'the same persons hardly met twice in their lives, and perhaps then, without knowing one another or speaking together'. Children do not even recognize their mothers after being weaned.[18]

Language develops only when the immediacy of the state of nature is interrupted. The original language of 'natural man' is the 'cry of nature'. In the case of the original cry, however, there is supposed to be an absolute proximity between the signifier and the signified. The cry is 'excited only by a sort of instinct on urgent occasions, to implore assistance in case of danger, or relief in case of suffering'. In the 'ordinary' course of civilized life, in which immediacy breaks down and 'more moderate feelings prevail', the cry is 'of little use'. 'Men' invented 'more numerous signs and a more copious language' as their ideas began to 'expand and multiply'. 'They multiplied the inflexions of the voice, and added gestures, which are in their own nature more expressive, and depend less for their meaning on a prior determination.' Gestures, however, depend on full presence, the presence of both the indicated object and the gesturing subject for the audience: 'hardly anything can be indicated by gestures, except objects actually present or easily described, and visible actions'. As immediacy breaks down even further, 'men' had to replace gestures with spoken signs. Because 'men' wanted to express their past and future experiences, gestures became inadequate. Conventional spoken signs, unlike gestures, can represent something absent. Because they can have meaning without being linked to any immediately present object, they do not bear 'the same relation to any particular ideas [and] are better calculated to express them all'.[19]

For Rousseau, this compensation for the loss of original presence through signification introduces the risk of corruption. In the *Essay on the Origin of Languages*, Rousseau argues that the written sign ultimately replaces the spoken sign. The members of the original speaking community did not use the written sign, because in their state of immediate empathy with one another they did not need to make use of this additional replacement. Once that immediacy is interrupted, the written sign stands in for the spoken sign. Written devices, such as accent marks, are used to represent the oral intonations of the absent speech. Accent marks, however, never make up for the fullness of intonation; they are invented by people who remain strangers to the original speaking community. The transcription of the original spoken signs in writing entails not only the replacement of the absent speech, but also the addition of new meaning. The written sign does not merely re-present the spoken sign; the copy marks themselves begin to signify something slightly different. Writing threatens to degrade the original language by adding something new to its re-presentation of the original, so that differences are introduced between the original and the transcription. The *introduction* of this difference constitutes a moment of danger for Rousseau; not only has the presence of the original language not been faithfully reproduced, but the corrupted transcription now threatens to take the place of the complete original.[20]

Derrida's intervention into Rousseau's text shows that even on Rousseau's own terms, this utterly undifferentiated origin never took place. For all his claims concerning originary immediacy, Rousseau nonetheless recognizes that the 'cry of nature' which precedes language is wholly incoherent precisely because it is *inarticulate*, not-yet-marked-by-articulation. The addition of articulation is not an 'unhappy accident', but a necessary and 'natural progress'. Language is always already constituted by the endless additions and substitutions of new terms, consonants, tenses and quantity. Where Rousseau says that difference in language only develops with the use of writing, as writing introduces a gap between the original and the transcription, Rousseau's own text shows that the coherence of language depends upon difference. Language is in this sense 'born out of the process of its own degeneration'.[21] Rousseau's text is therefore caught up in, and riven by, two opposed movements. Rousseau 'declares what he wishes to say', that articulation and writing come later to language and corrupt its originary integrity, but he also 'describes that which he does not wish to say', that the spacing work of articulation, or arché-writing, operates at this origin of language itself.[22] Rousseau protects the wholeness and purity of his original language and the state of nature by relegating difference to a secondary and external position. The representation of writing as an accidental addition is therefore deployed to support Rousseau's primary aim, that of defending his conception of the origin as full presence and pure immediacy. Derrida shows, however, that writing, in the sense of a representation of something absent which is at the same time the construction of a space between the representation and the represented, is supplementary. It must be at work in the origin, such that its spacing effects have always corrupted even the first moment of presence. Because Rousseau's text explicitly forbids this conception of spacing and difference in the origin, this double self-contradictory movement in Rousseau's text can only be shown by working within and against the text, by showing the work of the infrastructures – in this case, supplementarity – which is already there in the very structure of the text.

In the *Origin of Inequality*, Rousseau's text also shows, in spite of itself, that difference is at work within and against originary presence. Although (European) 'natural man' is supposed to live in absolute harmony with nature, he is already different from animals: he is perfectible and he has the capacity to take decisions. Whereas an animal is driven purely by instinct, 'natural man' always exercises, to some extent, his free will in his decisions. The instinctual movements of animals are already determined by natural necessity, while the decisions which are taken by 'man' are contingent. Even in the state of nature, 'the brute cannot deviate from the rule prescribed to it', whereas ' }man frequently deviates from such rules to his own prejudice'.[23] To be human, then, is to be subjected not to the absolute necessity of nature, but to the necessity of taking decisions which are never already fully determined. Nature speaks to animals and they 'obey her voice', but natural 'man' always knows that he is free to resist nature's command. Rousseau equates the contingency of free will with immorality, excess, illness, depravity, a distancing from nature, speech and death. 'Hence it is that dissolute men run into excesses which bring on fevers and death; because the mind depraves the senses, and the will continues to speak when nature is silent.'[24]

Ultimately, the male citizens in the social contract are able to distinguish between 'good' and 'bad' decisions: 'good' decisions conform to the universal standards of virtue and justice which are themselves independent of human conventions.[25] The proper development of reason, however, depends on artificial supplements: 'man' only acquires the capacity for making 'good' decisions through a developmental process. Males only come to realize that the curbing of the passions, the formation of the social contract and the constitution of laws which embody the universal standards of virtue and justice are necessary conditions for the realization of their true freedom once they have experienced the disastrous state of war. Their male descendants re-learn the lessons of the founding fathers through education. The artificial institutions of the social contract, the formulation of man-made laws and education are therefore central to the cultivation of reason and the preservation of man's natural condition – freedom. Hirschmann writes:

> Reason, then, develops only in a nonnatural context; hence the justice that [reason] develops, though universal, is moral and artificial. As a moral value, justice must apply equally to all. It must be reciprocal, coming from all and applying to all. So these 'natural' standards of political morality come to have a real existence only in the artificiality of political society.[26]

Education, then, is necessary to the reconstitution of 'man's' natural freedom, and yet, because of its artificial character, it remains a dangerous supplement.

New Right discourse exhibits many tensions around the spatial, temporal, mimetic and vicarious aspects of supplementarity which are similar to the anxieties in Rousseau's texts. The New Right often represents blackness and queerness as wanting to take the place of the 'original' white-Christian-Britishness and heterosexual normalcy. Black immigrants were welcomed by many British companies and governmental agencies in the 1950s as a supplemental workforce which could compensate for the post-war labour shortages. Much of the subsequent official policy and popular discourse on race turned on the following question: could the otherness of the black workers be adequately contained and assimilated, so that their presence would remain purely accidental and functional; or would they radically transform Britain's inner city neighbourhoods, classrooms, and local and national government? The black immigrant was also regarded as a total 'stranger' to Britain – a 'new settler', an exemplary 'late arriver'. As I shall argue in more detail in chapter 4, the Asian and Afro-Caribbean immigrants were actually not 'strangers'; they were already quite familiar with British colonialism. They had in a sense been in Britain all along: their foremothers and forefathers had worked as slaves, indentured labourers and underpaid workers for the British for generations. In both legal and symbolic terms, the black immigrant was not really an immigrant; she was only moving within a system which already included her. Her inclusion was not the fruit of a paternally granted privilege because she had already won the right of inclusion within British society through her labour and that of her ancestors. However, the supplemental representations around black immigration conceal these truths about her history and erase her rights. They invent the fiction of a pre-existing British border, place her on the other side and keep her waiting for favours.

Like all new racisms, anti-black immigration discourse invokes the myth of a homogeneous and indigenous English race. It is taken for granted that the status of 'being here first' establishes a privileging of the white-British population *vis-à-vis* the black immigrant, while the 'being here first' status of the colonials and indigenous peoples counted for absolutely nothing in the imperial tradition. Homosexuality is also represented temporally in British New Right discourse in a contradictory manner. Because everyone is supposed to be vulnerable to homosexual seduction, homosexuality is not confined to a fixed proportion of the population, but is present at birth as a possibility for everyone. Homosexuality must nevertheless be made to come later; legal distinctions are made between the age of consent for homosexual acts as opposed to heterosexual acts, and popular movements attempt to cleanse the classroom of queerness. The assertion of lesbian and gay rights, especially in the context of the small but significant advances of leftist policies at the local government level, was re-interpreted by the Thatcherites as an illegitimate mimicry of democratic principles. Section 28 demonized homosexuality not only as a dangerous subversive force, but as a vicarious 'pretender' to the real thing: heterosexuality and the patriarchal nuclear family.

The management of supplementarity – the reduction of necessary compensatory elements and penetrating invaders to harmless and external additions – is also central to the New Right's representation of the 'enemies within'. The neutralization of these supplements' corrupting effects, however, never takes the form of a simple and blunt exclusion. Drawing from Nietzsche's conception of nihilism and Foucault's theory of bio-power relations in chapter 3, I shall attempt to show how the subversive potential of otherness as supplementarity is at least partially neutralized through the multiplication of difference, and the separation of difference from what it can do.

The politics of deconstruction: theorizing identity without the presumption of immediacy

Before turning to Nietzsche and Foucault, however, I would like to raise a particularly difficult and yet important question: what are the strategic effects of deconstruction? In strategic terms, there is nothing inherently 'progressive' about anti-essentialism: in Thatcherite Britain, it was often the right who would engage in subversive re-appropriations and who would lecture the left on its essentialist conception of natural political subjects. It is worth repeating, then, that the deconstruction of a hegemonic discourse, and the weakening of naturalized horizons of intelligibility, is in itself an insufficient form of resistance. It is not as if the legacies of Thatcherism are effectively countered as soon as Thatcherism's inconsistencies, metaphysical ruses and representational strategies are shown. Post-structuralist political theory should never lose sight of the fact that the disruption of a hegemonic space is inextricably linked with the re-construction of alternative spaces through identity claims. To return to Lacan's metaphor in his 'Mirror Stage' essay, the imaginary constitution of identity produces a kind of 'body-armour' which is both restrictive and yet necessary to one's self-defence. Identity claims give us the sense of being located within a partially bounded order whose incomplete frontiers operate simultaneously as the defences against disruption and the limits of our freedom. We cannot remain in the non-spatializable moment outside all identity claims: every subversion of a hegemonic space depends upon the resources of marginalized spaces, and the defence of the possibilities which are opened up through subversion depends in turn upon the construction and reinforcement of alternative spaces. The effects of deconstructive strategies vary according to the contexts of their deployment and their articulation to specific identity claims.

Deconstruction therefore cannot deliver any political promises; on its own terms, it cannot claim a vanguardist, truth-revealing role for itself. It may be useful in this respect to mark the distance between deconstruction and Barthes' mythology. In his essay 'Myth Today', Barthes attempts to show the constructed, historical and particular character of 'bourgeois' discourse which presents itself as natural, a-historical and universal. In this respect, Barthes' mythological studies are an important precursor to Foucauldian genealogy. Barthes radicalized semiology by applying it to analyses of popular

culture and by focusing on the centrality of politics to the constitution of meaning. Citing Marx, Barthes argues that even 'the most
natural object contains a political trace'.[27] The concealment of historicity in bourgeois discourse is therefore entirely strategic: bourgeois discourse represents itself as de-politicized speech by erasing
its political trace structure.

Barthes' early formulations in 'Myth Today' are nevertheless
problematic in many respects. Barthes usefully draws attention to
the play between different orders of signification; connotation 'para-
sitically' re-positions the signified which is established at the level of
denotation as a new signifier. With this fundamental parasitism, the
absolute fixing of the value of the sign is impossible. Meaning is only
constituted through this endless process in which every definition
can be re-defined, and every signified can become a signifier.
However, Barthes is himself caught up in the myth of a pure origin:
he argues that bourgeois discourse 'impoverishes', 'distances' and
'distorts' the pre-mythological order which is supposed to be absolutely prior to all parasitism and mimicry.[28] Barthes attempts to
restore the purity of the origin by showing how bourgeois discourse
distorts the original order of signification.

Barthes also claims that the form of a specific discourse, such as
'bourgeois myths', is determined by the subject position from which
it is supposed to have been deployed. This straightforward categorization of discourse is problematic in two respects. First, we cannot
predict the political effects of a discourse based on its form alone,
since there are for every 'form' an infinite number of possibilities for
articulations with different political 'contents', and, indeed, the pure
separation of 'form' and 'content' is itself impossible. Second, we
cannot define a discourse in terms of the subject position 'from
which' it appears to have been deployed, since the appearance of
that subject position as a prior 'author' of 'its' discourse is itself a
fiction which is created as an effect of discourse. Barthes nevertheless
proposes the following typology: only the language of the producers
and the colonized constitutes truly non-mythological political discourse, while only bourgeois discourse is capable of mythological
parasitic mimicry. The 'revolutionary' language of the producers
and the colonized cannot be mythical because it is essentially a
language of action in which there is an absolute proximity between
the signifier and the signified. Barthes writes, 'Wherever man speaks
in order to transform reality and no longer to preserve it as an image,
wherever he links his language to the making of things, meta-

language is referred to a language-object, and myth is impossible.' The 'oppressed' can only have a 'poor, monotonous [and] immediate' language, which is 'always the same, that of his actions'; whereas bourgeois discourse takes the form of a metalanguage, for the oppressed, 'metalanguage is a luxury, he cannot yet have access to it'.[29]

Barthes' argument may appear to be persuasive. In activist discourses, it is often assumed that the discourses of the oppressed have a privileged and immediate access to the truth. Statements in feminist discourses, for example, sometimes take the form, 'As a woman, I know that x, y, z, are true.' This kind of statement rests not only on the assumption of the natural immediacy of 'woman' to truth, but also on the assumption that the definition of 'woman' is an entirely straightforward matter. In this manner, the exclusions of others from this subject which claims to be universal, such as the exclusion of black feminist positions in the articulation of a 'universal' feminist argument, are concealed. It is often similarly argued in activist debates that theoretical questions around representation are ultimately irrelevant to actual struggles. In these moments, it is supposed to be already perfectly clear exactly who the enemy is, exactly how the enemy should be fought, and exactly who 'we', the 'oppressed', are. Activist discourses therefore often represent themselves as discourses of immediacy in the same way that Barthes represents 'revolutionary' discourse.

This assumption of immediacy is highly problematic. The claim that the 'oppressed' enjoy an immediate relation to the world is derogatory in that it assigns a 'primitive' status to the 'oppressed'. Whereas the rest of society is supposed to be capable of participating in rich, heterogeneous and differentiated language-games, the 'oppressed' remain confined within a condition of immediacy in which critical thought and self-reflection are impossible. Barthes' conception of the non-mythological character of colonized discourse has a racist primitivizing effect which is similar to that of Rousseau's comparison between (European) 'natural man' and the eighteenth-century 'Caribbean native'.

The idealization of the discourse of the oppressed as a naturally self-enclosed immediacy functions as an apparatus of containment which punishes any violation of its supposedly 'natural' boundaries. hooks addresses this form of social control in her comments on soliloquy. She states that as a black woman, she was taught to speak, but 'to talk a talk that was in itself a silence'. 'Our speech, the "right speech of [black] womanhood", was often the soliloquy, the talking into thin air, the talking to ears that do not hear you – the talk that is simply not listened to.'[30] With this disciplinary containment of their discourse, the problem for black women is not to overcome silence but to transform their disempowered speech. Where black women break the boundaries of that containment, as Anita Hill did in her testimony against Clarence Thomas, or Lani Guinier did in her academic articles, they are often pathologized. President Clinton originally nominated Guinier, an African-American, for the position of Assistant Attorney-General with responsibility for civil rights, but withdrew the nomination after strong right-wing opposition. Throughout the controversy, Guinier's academic writings were radically misinterpreted and no official effort was made to correct these misinterpretations. Black women like Hill and Guinier are represented in official discourse as a social problem, as an object of discourse rather than a subject who is capable of producing coherent versions of official discourse. With the distortion of her positions on the Voting Rights Act, Guinier was dismissed as a 'quota queen', a term which immediately invokes the derogatory name for poor black women, 'welfare queen'. In official discourse on race and gender, there is no significant difference between Guinier, a tenured professor of law, and a single mother on public assistance if both of these persons are black women.

hooks states that where black women exceed the boundaries of soliloquy, they are punished in terms of both physical abuse and madness. In Britain, 40 per cent of all blacks in National Health Service hospital beds in 1984 were classed as psychiatric patients. There are several 'black-specific' categories of mental illness currently in use: 'West Indian psychosis', 'paranoia', 'religious mania', and, for Asian women, 'marital psychosis'. Compared to whites, black psychiatric patients are far more likely to receive physical treatments (electro-convulsive therapy and drugs), and at higher intervals and dosages, while they are also far less likely to receive non-physical treatment (psychotherapy and counselling).[31] Resistance for those subjects whose subjectivity is erased by sexism and racism and policed by violent and pathologizing technologies of social control entails a political struggle against the strategic idealization of soliloquy. As hooks argues,

> Moving from silence into speech is for the oppressed, the colonized, the exploited and those who stand and struggle side by side, a gesture of defiance that heals, that makes new life and

new growth possible. It is that act of speech, of 'talking back', that is no mere gesture of empty words, that is the expression of our movement from object to subject – the liberated voice.[32]

The claim, then, that the oppressed remain permanently locked in a child-like and primitive state of immediacy in which their discourse can only constitute a naive soliloquy is far from innocent. Because they are supposed to be trapped within these natural boundaries, it seems natural in turn that the oppressed can only be represented by an external agency. Barthes' claim that the 'oppressed' cannot have access to metalanguage is therefore similar to Marx's claim that a class which has not yet developed a full consciousness of itself as a class cannot have access to the means of representation: 'they cannot represent themselves, they must be represented'.[33] The treatment of Hill and Guinier are two cases in point. While hostile Senators used psychological 'evidence' to pathologize Hill, the press represented Guinier's mainstream views on democratic rights as extremist absurdities. Williams writes:

> Guinier's own insistence on retaining *her* meaning of *her* words was thrown back at her as 'denial' or as evidence of opportunism, shiftiness, lying or insanity. . . . The he-said-or-she-said of the [Thomas–Hill] hearings gave way to a weirdly disempowering game of 'she-*says*-she-said'. Over and over I saw her picture on television, her lips moving, but the sound being given to a voiceover that described all the awful crackpot things she *meant* when her lips moved like that.[34]

The disciplinary containment of women of colour and other targets of social control always operate behind the apparently harmless fictions of their natural immediacy. It is because of their authoritarian potential, rather than their essentialist form, that radical democratic projects ought to be quite wary of immediacy claims. The post-structuralist critique of immediacy, then, can be a useful tool for resistance against authoritarian erasure. Deconstruction, as opposed to Barthes' mythology, does not claim to stand outside the philosophical text, and does not position itself as a privileged knower who unveils the truth which has been distorted for, or concealed from, the deluded masses. In 'doing' (as if it were not always already 'done') deconstruction, there is no choice;[35] instead, one finds oneself participating in the supplementation of the text in which one was always already immersed, and in which the supplement had always already 'taken place'. Spivak locates the Derridean text in terms of a double bind. On the one hand, the critic finds herself intoxicated with the lure of a way out of the closures of metaphysics (as if this were possible), a promise of an infinitely pleasurable fall into the abyss. On the other hand, the critic finds herself attempting to master the text, to show the text (arrogantly enough) what the text does not know and to speak as if (ignorantly enough) she knows what she is saying. The critic never overcomes this double bind; she can never choose to situate herself unequivocally either inside or outside metaphysics. In spite of our best intentions, 'we *must* do a thing *and* its opposite, and indeed we desire to do both, and so on indefinitely'. Unlike mythology, then, deconstruction admits, on its own terms, that it ultimately betrays itself. Deconstruction does not claim that it takes a special form which sets itself apart from other discourses; like every other text, the deconstructive text is a 'perpetually self-deconstructing movement that is inhabited by différance'.[36]

This self-betrayal which is essential to deconstruction can also be compared to the ultimately self-contradictory character of identity games. On the one hand, even the most essentialist strategy which aims to fix an identity always has the effect of differentiating and postponing identity. To present itself as universal, rather than particular, an identity must function across as many different contexts as possible. Since every articulation is performed in a specific context, however, the 'same' identity is always contextually redefined. The 'same' identity is always shifting across different contexts in a manner which is analogous to the necessary failure of the signifier to retain the 'same' meaning across different repetitions. Instead of being grounded in terms of an essence, the 'same' identity only retains an unidentifiable minimal remainder across its different contexts.[37] On the other hand, even the most deconstructive critique of the fixity of an identity always simultaneously re-constitutes identity. The deconstructive critique must be intelligible for someone else at some other time and place. It must therefore take place within some particular language game and it must make use of discursive elements which are borrowed from other contexts and re-deployed.

Even the most radical critique of identity, and even the most naive championing of absolute indeterminacy, reproduce some degree of sameness and identity. Martin and Mohanty rightly insist that where critiques posit only an 'indeterminacy' in the place of totalization, they are engaging in a strategic concealment of their positionality. These texts fail to recognize the 'critic's own situatedness in the social' and refuse 'to acknowledge the critic's own institutional home'.

> The claim to a lack of identity or positionality is itself based on privilege, on a refusal to accept responsibility for one's implication in actual historical or social relations, on a denial that positionalities exist or that they matter, the denial of one's own personal history and the claim to a total separation from it.[38]

Identity games therefore cannot be totally mastered or transcended. Even though 'we' can never fully occupy a position, the forces of 'position effects' – the ways in which 'our' failed positionings nevertheless place 'us' within power relations – should be recognized. In some cases, it is absolutely vital that resistance discourses speak the impossible, such as the claim to a lesbian identity in the face of the virtual erasure of lesbianism from official discourse. (I shall return to the structure of the erasure of lesbianism in chapter 5.) Foucault, who often expressed his suspicions around identity politics, explicitly defended identity claims in an interview on gay politics. On the one hand, he describes sexuality as 'something that we ourselves create', and argued that instead of regarding sexual liberation as a discovery of an already determined sexual truth, 'we have to create gay life [and] to become'.[39] He questioned the validity of categories such as 'gay painting' and a separate gay culture, and asserted, 'we have to create culture'. He emphasized that identity can become a self-administered technology of social control.

> If identity becomes the problem of sexual existence, and if people think that they have to 'uncover' their 'own identity', and that their own identity has to become the law, the principle, the code of their existence; if the perennial question they ask is, 'Does this thing conform to my identity?', then, I think, they will turn back to a kind of ethics [which is] very close to the old heterosexual virility ... The relationships which we have to have with ourselves are not ones of identity, rather they must be relationships of differentiation, of creation, of innovation ... we must not think of this identity as an ethical universal rule.[40]

On the other hand, Foucault also recognized that identity claims – even when they are made on the 'ground' of 'natural' differences – can in certain contexts promote resistance against authoritarianism. His interviewers state that one of the practical effects of the conception of sexuality as naturally fixed is that gay activism sometimes limits itself to demands for rights and tolerance. Foucault responded,

'Yes, but this aspect must be supported. It is important, first, to have the possibility – and the right – to choose your own sexuality.'[41] A mobile approach to political practices, such as Sandoval's 'oppositional consciousness',[42] depends precisely upon this complex juxtaposition of strategies around identity. Identity can be a source of pleasure, a basis for the creation of new forms of relations and cultural expressions, and the stronghold from which political gains against authoritarianism can be won. Strategies which posit identities and which have these effects should be defended, even if they are organized around a natural, rather than constructed, sense of identity. At the same time, the strategies which challenge identity claims are useful in terms of their interruption of the self-disciplining effects of rigidified identities.

In an article on Caribbean cinema and photography, Hall offers a similar distinction between two ways of thinking 'cultural identity'. The first involves the recovery of a 'true self' and the excavation of a 'hidden history' which, in its positing of a common past, constructs an imaginary reunification of the collective subject in resistance, against the dispersals and fragmentations of slavery, colonialism and contemporary racisms. The second viewpoint recognizes the significant differences which continually postpone the return to/arrival of a common origin. In this second moment, hybridization – the multiple borrowings from African, native-American, European and black American sources, the 'mixes of colour, pigmentation, physiognomic type; the "blends" of tastes that is Caribbean cuisine; the aesthetics of the "cross-overs" and "cut-and-mix", to borrow Dick Hebdige's telling phrase, which is the heart and soul of black music' – is understood as the 'essence' of the Caribbean identity.[43] Hall's reading of Derrida's (non-)conception of différance in this article is profoundly political: he is acutely aware of both the impossibility of, and the inevitable exclusionary effects of, identitarian imaginaries. He rejects, for example, the conceptualization of diaspora as 'those scattered tribes whose identity can only be secured in relation to some sacred homeland to which they must at all costs return, even if it means pushing other people into the sea'. For Hall, this exclusionary imaginary is 'the old, the imperializing, the hegemonizing, form of "ethnicity"'.[44]

Hall nevertheless exhibits a deeply felt empathy with the strategic attempts to recover the 'true self'. Referring to the imaginary reunification of the black peoples of Africa, the Caribbean, the United States and Britain in the photography of Armet Francis, Hall writes:

No one who looks at these textual images now, in the light of the history of transportation, slavery and migration, can fail to understand how the rift of separation, the 'loss of identity' which has been integral to the Caribbean experience, only begins to be healed when these forgotten connections are once more set in place. Such texts restore an imaginary fullness or plenitude, set against the broken rubric of our past. They are the resources of resistance and identity, with which to confront the fragmented and pathological ways in which that experience has been reconstructed within the dominant regimes of cinematic and visual representation of the West.[45]

Deconstruction can be used to show that these two moments – the identity claim and the differentiation/postponement of identity – are supplementary moments, rather than freely chosen alternatives or two discrete stages. They contradict one another, and yet they simultaneously constitute the condition of possibility for each other.

Deconstruction can also be used to show that even when 'we' speak from 'our own' positions, it is always possible that 'our' strategies will produce effects which actually contradict 'our' intentions, and 'our' representation of 'ourselves' as the 'oppressed' does not in any way protect 'our' strategies from this essential possibility. This is not to say that deconstruction de-legitimizes resistance strategies, that because deconstruction shows that every strategy always betrays itself, deconstruction promotes a total withdrawal from activism.[46] This is also not to say that all claims are equally valid from an anti-essentialist perspective. If power relations were no longer constitutive of the social, then all claims would be equally normal. The normality of each claim would be established as soon as it conformed in some minimal way with an already established language game. In actual history, this moment of pure relativism is infinitely postponed: even though a claim may be coherent within a particular language game, it is accepted as normal only to the extent that other competing claims are hegemonically excluded as incoherent. Its normalization therefore depends upon the hierarchical status of its context *vis-à-vis* other contexts, and that status is in turn an effect of contingent power relations.

The competition for legitimation and normalization through the fundamentally political strategy of representation brings competing claims into a mutually subversive battle. For example, the new racism's claims around the natural foreign-ness of blackness constituted a direct response to liberal anti-racist discourse. These claims only achieved a normalized status to the extent that movements such as Powellism re-defined official and popular discourse on race and excluded pro-racial-tolerance 'permissiveness' as unthinkable. As the anti-'permissiveness' backlash was re-deployed against the lesbian and gay community in the 1980s, the claim that homosexuality was being 'promoted' had an effect on resistance strategies in turn. Whereas radical lesbian and gay activists had long insisted on a social constructionist approach to sexual identities, the community leaders and politicians who claimed that sexuality was fixed at birth became hegemonic in defining the community's response to the Thatcherites. It would be absurd to describe these identity claims as 'equally normal' *vis-à-vis* their competitors; their normalization depended not on abstract rules of coherence but on the configurations of power relations.

The 'grounds' for choosing between opposed claims are strategic and contextual, rather than objective. Even if the choosing subject is but a strategic myth, and the structure around the decision is itself undecidable,[47] decisions are nevertheless always taken. As Rousseau argues, the necessity of taking decisions, which are themselves never fully determined by necessity, is the very principle of the 'human condition'. The only choice which we can never make is whether or not we will choose. The choices which 'we' always find 'ourselves' to have already 'taken', however, are only 'taken' within specific contexts. The effective re-positioning of an alternative claim as a thinkable position, against the operation of the hegemonic horizon which excludes it as unthinkable, depends upon the specificities of its articulation: it will only 'take hold' to the extent that the hegemonic rules of exclusion have already been weakened, and to the extent that the alternative claim is articulated with other already normalized positions.

Deconstruction's radical contextualization, then, can be counterposed to the dangerous arrogance of mythology: deconstruction shows that immediacy is impossible for every discourse, and that the effects of a strategy cannot be predicted in advance by asserting that it is determined by the subject position 'from which' that strategy is deployed. The tools of deconstruction can be used to remind 'ourselves' that even if an identity claim does have liberatory effects in one context, the re-deployment of this 'same' strategy in a different context may actually have authoritarian effects. Deconstruction, insofar as it is deployed in this manner, does not license a new list of privileged knowers, but, on the contrary, promotes the kind of 'self'-criticism which interrupts the reproduction of authoritarianism in the guise of resistance.

Chapter 3

Separating difference from what it can do: nihilism and bio-power relations

Contemporary racist discourses, such as the British new racism, usually promote the differentiation of racial otherness: they include some aspects of blackness as the pseudo-assimilable, and they use this inclusion to legitimate the demonization and exclusion of other blacknesses as the unassimilable. The new racism defines the blackness which it wants to exclude not as that which is not-white and therefore inferior, but as that which is inherently anti-British. This 'cultural' definition of race opens up the possibility for a disciplinary differentiation of blacknesses.

Again, the new racism's disciplining of blackness through differentiation is not really 'new'. Colonial discourses are also structured around multiple inclusions and exclusions: a small elite class is Europeanized and assimilated, while the 'native' masses are regarded as the enemies of culture itself. In Homi Bhabha's terms, the 'agonistic' mode of colonial authority does not simply silence or repress racial differences; it actually promotes new differentiations. With this (re-)production of differences, the stereotypical figures of racist colonial discourse, such as 'the simian Negro [and] the effeminate Asiatic male', become fundamentally split subjects. Bhabha concludes that colonial subjection would not be possible without this 'discrimination between the mother culture and its bastards, the self and its doubles, where the trace of what it disavowed is not re-pressed but repeated as something *different* – a mutation, a hybrid'. Insofar as the colonial presence is represented as an 'original', and yet is only constructed through repetition and defined in terms of discriminatory differentiation, the colonial presence itself remains fundamentally split. For Bhabha, this essential ambivalence at the core of colonial authority is basic to the possibility of resistance: that which operates as the 'conditions of dominance' can be subverted

and transformed into the 'grounds of intervention' through camou-
flage, mimicry and the representation of the 'insignia of authority' as
nothing but a mask.[1]

Immigration, policing and the multiplication of racial differences

The post-war official discourse on race in Britain has reproduced the
colonial differentiation of blacknesses in many forms. In the 1960s,
for example, the Labour Party explicitly combined its policies on
black immigration and race relations.[2] In 1965, the Labour government both renewed the 1962 Commonwealth Immigration Act and
passed a Race Relations Act. The 1962 Commonwealth Immigration
Act established the first *de jure* distinction between British passport-
holders: every British passport-holder who had not been born in the
United Kingdom or Ireland, or who had been issued her passport by
the government of a colony, was subjected to new immigration
controls. During imperial rule, the citizens of the British colonies and
the citizens of the United Kingdom had both held the same passport
and had both enjoyed the same right to enter the United Kingdom.
The 1962 legislation aimed to adjust the definition of Britishness to
the 'realities' of de-colonization through the re-inscription of a new
British frontier. It set the white-British colonial administrators and
their families who wanted to return from the Commonwealth countries, and the descendants of the white Britons who had migrated to
Commonwealth countries, apart from the non-white colonized,
even though both groups were British subjects. The technicalities
around place of birth and the origin of the passport allowed for the
regulation of immigration in terms of race. Because the movement of
non-white peoples to Britain largely took place in the post-war era,
differentiations between British subjects in terms of birthplace and
the origin of their passports in the 1960s operated as racial differentiations. Although black immigration was not altogether halted by the
1962 legislation, it was controlled through a new employment
voucher scheme.

When the Labour government renewed the 1962 legislation in
1965, it defended its policy on the grounds that these racially biased
controls would improve race relations.[3] Under its dual approach, the
'equal' treatment of black persons would be promoted, but only after
immigration legislation had already excluded the unassimilable.
Designed as public order legislation, the Labour government's 1965

Race Relations Act prohibited discrimination on racial grounds in places of public resort and penalized incitement to racial hatred. It did not address discrimination in housing and employment. Although it originally classified the racial breach of public order as a criminal offence, it was amended – in the context of a small Labour majority in the House – to secure bi-partisan support. After it was amended, the Act made racial public order offences civil misdemeanours and merely obliged offenders to submit to the Race Relations Board's conciliation procedures. Although Labour was returned to power in 1966 with a large majority, it did not introduce comprehensive legislation against racial discrimination in the areas of housing, employment and public and commercial services until 1968. Once again, its 1968 Race Relations Act was passed in tandem with specifically anti-black immigration legislation, the 1968 Commonwealth Immigrants Act. Home Secretary James Callaghan explicitly linked the two pieces of legislation together. He stated, 'This [immigration] Bill ... must be considered at the same time, and in accordance with, the ... Race Relations Bill... Both these Bills are ... essentially parts of a fair and balanced policy on this matter of race relations.'[4] Roy Hattersley summed up the Labour Party's juxtaposition of exclusions and inclusions around race: 'without integration, limitation is inexcusable: without limitation, integration is impossible'.[5]

Race relations legislation does not only promote the 'equal' treatment of the admissible blackness; it also treats virtually *all* explicitly radical statements on race – racist or anti-racist – as 'equal' threats to the public order. Section 6 of the 1965 Race Relations Act prohibited the incitement of racial hatred.[6] In 1967, five black activists were charged with this offence. Michael Abdul Malik, a leading member of the Racial Adjustment Society, was convicted under the Race Relations Act for 'anti-white' comments which he made in his address to a meeting in Reading. He was sentenced to twelve months' imprisonment, and his appeal was refused. Four members of the Universal Coloured People's Association were also prosecuted for inciting racial hatred against whites for their statements at Speakers' Corner in Hyde Park, London. They were fined a total of £270.[7] The very legislation which is meant to promote racial equality has been used in these and other cases to reproduce the disciplinary differentiation of colonial and immigration discourse – the differentiation between the assimilable and the unassimilable blacknesses.

Policing discourse reproduces these differentiations even further.

Blackness, especially young male blackness, was linked with criminality in an unprecedented manner in the 1970s. The policing of the
Afro-Caribbean community dramatically intensified as the popular
media conjured up images of black 'crime waves'.[8] As the policing of
the black community became more highly organized, however,
extensive efforts were made to represent the policing frontier not
simply as the line between whites and blacks, but as the line between
different blacknesses: the law-abiding blacks who conducted themselves in a sufficiently British manner versus the dangerous blacks
who, through their criminality, proved themselves to be recalci-
trantly anti-British. For example, the Asian community, although still
considered 'black', was policed differently than the Afro-Caribbean
community. In his influential text, *A Theory of Police/Immigrant Relations*, John Brown distinguishes between the 'quiet evasion of the
Asians [and] the thick skinned aggression of the West Indians'.
Brown claims that Asian crime takes place only within the Asian
community, and has a 'cerebral, sophisticated and organized' character. He depicts West Indian crime, by contrast, as publicly visible,
'unskilled or semi-skilled', 'casual and physical', 'impuls[ive]' and
'disorganized'.[9] Gilroy argues that the denial in police discourse of a
'specifically *racial* dimension to the rising volume of attacks on black
people' is supported in large part by the 'racist construction of Asian
passivity': 'this image ... has provided the counterpart to the wild
and lawless West Indian'. He points out that this caricature of Asian
passivity is fundamentally contradicted by Asian militant resistances, but that the investment by police discourse in the Asian/West
Indian differentiation is such that this caricature has remained
intact.[10]

Gilroy shows that the differentiation of blacknesses and the inclusion of assimilable blackness is central to British New Right discourse
on race. In their 1983 election campaign, the Conservative Party
placed an advertisement in the ethnic minority press which represented the Conservatives as the truly inclusionary party, as opposed
to the exclusionary Labour Party. The poster featured a photograph
of a young black man, and its main text stated, 'Labour says he's
black. Tories say he's British.' It also declared that the Conservatives
view the British people not as 'special' groups which are differentiated according to race, but as equal citizens: 'With the Conservatives, there are no "blacks", no "whites", just people.' Gilroy points
out, however, that it is not just any blackness which is promised
acceptance here, but only a solitary male. The figures of the black

woman and the black family, which are often linked with the threat of fertility in racist discourse, remain absent. This male figure is also wearing a business suit, signifying his already assimilated status as an entrepreneur.[11]

A similar juxtaposition of assimilatory inclusions and exclusions can be found in the speeches of the then Home Secretary Douglas Hurd. Speaking at a Conservative Party weekend conference in January 1989, Hurd argued that the Home Secretary aims first and foremost to protect the nation from crime, and to protect the freedoms of individuals. Hurd explicitly insisted that anti-discrimination measures had to be combined with the regulation of racial otherness. He stated, first, that 'racial discrimination is not only wrong, but hostile to any sense of common nationhood or hope of social peace', and, second, that 'strict immigration controls' remained necessary. 'The two go together. I am certain that the creation and maintenance of [immigration] restrictions were indispensable in helping to drain the poison from discussions about immigration and race relations.'[12]

In a speech delivered at the Central Mosque in Birmingham one month later, Hurd focused on the problem of 'absorbing large numbers of people from very different religious and cultural traditions'. Implicit throughout the speech is the assumption that most of the responsibility for this 'absorption' lies in the hands of the black and Asian communities themselves. Hurd expressed his 'admiration' for the religious faith of British Muslims and 'their continuing regard for the family', and stated that 'no one is asking you to abandon either your faith or your traditions'. He urged Asian Britons, however, not to 'isolate [themselves] from the mainstream of British life', to learn English and, with reference to death threats against Salman Rushdie, to obey British laws. Throughout the speech, Hurd portrayed British society as an essentially open and tolerant space in which racial discrimination is exceptional, rather than systemic. He stated that immigrants such as 'Dutch Protestants, Huguenots, Jews fleeing from Russia or from Germany' had always been welcomed to Britain, and that freedom of expression was protected by British law. (In fact, Jewish refugees in the early twentieth century actually faced anti-Semitic immigration legislation and popular movements,[13] and the Thatcher government actually exploited the weaknesses of Britain's unwritten constitution to the full by introducing notoriously draconian censorship measures.) Above all, Hurd distinguished between the 'vast majority of British Muslims [who] are hard-working, law-abiding men and women', and the violent minor-

99

ity. He pointed to the 'growing numbers' of blacks and Asians among 'police officers, magistrates, local councillors or Parliamentary candidates' as 'increasing signs of black and Asian Britons playing their full part in the mainstream of our national life'.[14]

Immigration discourse continues to differentiate blacknesses and to promote assimilation. In 1984, the appeal against a deportation order by the Asian-British family, the Pereiras, received the support of many right-wing newspapers, including the *Daily Mail, The Times* and the *Daily Telegraph*. In this campaign, however, the Pereiras were represented as an *extraordinary* Asian-British family: the reports stressed that they were English-speaking Catholics who had become well integrated into the mainstream culture of their village. The Pereiras ultimately won their appeal. Ronald Butt, whom Gilroy describes as a 'new right ideologue', claimed that the most important factor in their successful appeal had been the

> approach that Mr. and Mrs. Pereira had to living in Britain and the attitude towards them of their English neighbours ... they played an active part in village life ... they were popular ... in short, they showed a positive commitment to Britain and to the English way of life.[15]

The Pereiras case can be compared to the unsuccessful deportation appeal on behalf of a young woman and her child who had both been the victims of her ex-husband's violent attacks. The immigration adjudicator stated:

> her knowledge of English is limited and her association with this country is largely concerned with the better standard of living she enjoys here ... the overriding reason for all her actions since coming here has been a desire to obtain a residential qualification by marriage to almost anyone of acceptable age ... or in any other way open to her.[16]

British immigration legislation inscribes the national frontier at multiple and local sites, thereby perpetuating racial differentiations. Immigration regulations bisect marriages, non-marital partnerships and parent–child relationships within the black and Asian communities. (The same is true for gay male and lesbian relationships, regardless of race.) Women who are settled in Britain but who do not have British citizenship cannot bring their husbands into the country to join them, whereas non-British men have the right to bring in their wives and children. British women face more legal restrictions than British men in bringing in foreign spouses. James Callaghan, the Labour Home Secretary, explained that the government feared that unless male immigrants were allowed to bring in their wives and children, British society would be inevitably faced with 'social problems'. The Women, Immigration and Nationality Group concluded that Callaghan was indirectly expressing the widespread concern among white British men that '"their women" might become associated with these "wifeless" black men'.[17]

Since the 'primary immigration' of blacks had been already tightly controlled in the 1960s and early 1970s, the anti-black immigration lobbies of the 1970s and 1980s have campaigned for increased restrictions on the movement of dependants into the country. The 1968 Commonwealth Immigrants Act initiated the specific regulation of dependants: it introduced a voucher system in which a controlled number of vouchers were issued to the heads of households. Each voucher entitled the head of the household, who was usually male, and particular types of dependants, defined in relation to him, the legal right of entry. Immigration officials were highly unlikely to recognize the status of black and Asian women who were heads of households, even if they were widowed, divorced or deserted. The maintenance of the *de jure* distinction between the rights of immigrant men and women to bring in their spouses and children has been defended in terms of sexist and racist arguments – that women are the mere appendages of men, that a wife should follow her husband, that black and Asian women do not work,[18] that without the moderating presence of a wife, black male sexuality is dangerously excessive, and that black and Asian male dependants take away the jobs of white British workers. In practice, the applications for the entry of the women and children who are dependants of black and Asian immigrants often meet with delays, arbitrary procedures and refusal. Asian women who applied for entry as dependants have been subjected to particularly abusive investigations of their status. In 1978, for example, it was revealed that immigration officials were conducting vaginal examinations on Asian fiancées of men who were already settled in Britain. They believed that these examinations were necessary to establish the virginity of the incoming fiancées, on the assumption that non-virgin applicants were lying about their status.[19] This incident is but one example of the extent to which British racist discourse assumes that black and Asian women's bodies are public property, as opposed to the highly private character of the bodies of economically privileged white British men. The vaginal examinations were only halted after a sustained campaign by Asian women and their allies.

The racism in immigration legislation and policing practices does not, therefore, take the form of a total exclusion of racial otherness. This racism is in fact more effective and more insidious: it includes some aspects of blackness, but only at the cost of the assimilation of that blackness, and only to support the exclusion of the unassimilated blackness. This differentiation of otherness as a strategy for neutralizing the subversive threat of otherness can also be found in British New Right discourse on sexuality. In the parliamentary debates on Section 28, distinctions are consistently made between the homosexuality which is admitted as an assimilable element within the social order, and the homosexuality which is identified as unassimilable and is excluded. The British New Right does not promote a homogeneous vision of the social order, but actually multiplies difference to neutralize the threats of subversion. In this chapter, I shall attempt to provide a theoretical account for this strategy of managing difference through the separation of difference from what it can do.

Before turning to Nietzsche's and Foucault's texts, however, it should be emphasized that no one actually occupies the positions of the assimilated homosexual or the assimilated black. To identify the differentiating strategies of the right is not to accuse actual black conservatives of being 'inadequately' black. Stephen Carter offers several examples of the deployment of this racist argument from a white 'progressive' standpoint. In opposing a black Republican's bid for the Senate, a *New York Times* editorial argued that the candidate would have been a 'misfit in the Congressional Black Caucus'. A white Representative, Pete Stark, attacked the policies of Louis Sullivan, an African-American who served as George Bush's Secretary of Health and Human Services. He claimed that Sullivan was a 'disgrace to his race' because of the adverse effects of Bush's health policies on black African-Americans. Sullivan replied, 'I don't live on Pete Stark's plantation.'[20] Black conservative figures such as Supreme Court Justice Clarence Thomas clearly should be opposed because of their right-wing views and policies. However, the opposition against black conservatives should not position them as racially 'inauthentic', just as the opposition against Thatcher should never have indulged in sexist 'handbag-swinging' caricatures. The portrayal of Thatcher as a masculinized woman in satirical texts such as the television programme *Spitting Image* is a sexist and anti-lesbian example of the white male leftist tendency to dismiss as 'unnatural' those women and blacks who do not fit into the left's patronizing image of its 'natural' constituency.

The inscription of frontiers and the sexual/national body

The juxtaposition of assimilatory inclusions and disciplinary exclusions in British New Right discourse on race and sexuality can be usefully analysed in terms of Nietzsche's and Foucault's theoretical frameworks. Their genealogical approach facilitates the investigation of the conditions of possibility of identity claims, namely the clarification of the conditions in which a particular articulation becomes hegemonic. Hegemonic identity claims become stabilized spatial fantasies: they give us a sense of belonging to a bounded social order. Like phenomenology, genealogy takes the form of re-activation, the problematization of the spatial fantasies which we have come to take for granted. Genealogy shows that those identity claims which operate as if they were guaranteed by necessity itself have only been installed through habitual repetitions and the violent exclusion of alternatives. Genealogy is in this sense a politicized phenomenology: it is a return to 'origins', but only in the sense of a return to the contingency of identity, rather than the Husserlian return to essences. What, for example, were the conditions in which the Powellian and Thatcherite definition of the white British familial nation became normalized, so that the regulatory differentiation of blacknesses in immigration and policing discourse appeared to be natural and non-political expressions of an already-given national interest? The racially defined immigration legislation of the 1960s, 1970s and 1980s reconstituted the national body in the context of the post-colonial crisis in frontiers. The bounded, coherent and hegemonic character of the racially exclusionary post-colonial Britishness is, for genealogy, not an a-historical fact but a problem requiring critical investigation.

The genealogical approach has been taken up by Butler in her theory of the performative character of sex and gender categorization. She argues that Foucault re-works Nietzsche's conception of the internalization of the law by showing that this process takes the form of incorporation. Through incorporation, 'bodies are produced which signify the law on and through the body; there the law is manifest as the essence of their selves, the meaning of their soul, their conscience, the law of their desire'. The bounded body is not a neutral surface which is already constituted before discourse, and discourses do not merely struggle to dominate already defined bodies. Any apparently prediscursive being is a constructed fiction which legitimates the extension and intensification of disciplinary strategies. The body is marked out as a discrete entity, as a coherent sexed, classed, gendered, racialized and sexualized formation, through exclusions, prohibitions and the 'disciplinary production of the figures of fantasy'. Butler shows that deviations from the sex/gender/sexuality rule of the compulsory heterosexual order are not accidents which can be quarantined in the residual sphere of the unnatural to preserve the rule. By conceptualizing gender as the effect of performative practices, she undermines the distinction between 'natural' and 'unnatural' articulations. All gender practices are copies of copies; constructed through the recitation of past practices, they all have the same ontological status. If one sex/gender/sexuality articulation appears as a 'natural' position, it has only won that appearance through the violent suppression of alternatives as 'unnatural'. Insofar as habitual repetitions install the illusion of a prediscursive, desire-governing 'self', the 'political regulations and disciplinary practices which produce that ostensibly coherent gender are effectively displaced from view'.[21]

The exclusion of various blacknesses from Britishness through the regulation of immigration can be compared to the exclusion of subversive gender practices. Butler argues that reproductive heterosexuality has become a hegemonic order through the deployment of what she calls the 'gender border control'. This apparatus constitutes and continually mobilizes the frontier between the fictitious inner core of the 'self' and the supposedly external social field. The externality of the social is of course an illusion, but insofar as this illusion remains convincing, the inner 'self' appears to be an absolutely primary source of desire, and social relations appear to be secondary or even irrelevant to the truth of the 'already' sexed and gendered self. In other words, the social regulation of gender and sexuality is legitimated in terms of the logic of the supplement: the relegation of the social to an outside and latecomer status conceals the fact that the constitution of a 'normal' sexed, gendered and sexualized inner 'self' fundamentally depends upon extensive familial, educational, medical, moral and legal intervention. Insofar as compulsory heterosexuality operates as a hegemonic discourse, it is taken for granted that sexuality naturally 'follows from' gender and sex. Compulsory heterosexuality represents heterosexuality as the logical corollary to an immutable nature, when it is of course a fragile institution which persists only with the assistance of numerous socio-political props. Compulsory heterosexuality also rules out lesbian sexuality as unthinkable: the natural passivity of femaleness is supposed to make an autonomous women's sexuality impossible. I shall show in chapter 5, for example, that lesbianness is only represented in British New Right discourse as a 'pretender' figure, a failed copy of the real thing.

Where compulsory heterosexuality represents sexuality and gender as if they 'followed from' the 'fact' of biological sex, Powellism represents national allegiance as if it 'followed from' the 'fact' of race. Powell posited an a-historical white-Englishness as the inner core of Britishness, and relegated Britain's imperial tradition to the external sphere of the accidental. These representations allowed him to argue that the (white) British people had to recover their true Englishness by promoting the 'natural' exclusion of blackness from Britishness through immigration controls. In the 1980s, many Thatcherites reproduced this aspect of Powell's discourse. Norman Tebbit was responsible for Thatcherism's most blatant dismissal of British blackness as an oxymoronic impossibility. Tebbit, the former Chairman of the Conservative Party and MP for Chingford, organized a backbench revolt against the Conservative government's own British Nationality (Hong Kong) Act in 1990. This Act gave 50,000 members of Hong Kong's corporate, professional, public service and military elite the right to obtain British passports for themselves and their families before the transfer of the colony to the Republic of China in 1997. Cabinet ministers defended the bill in the House of Commons as a measure that would offer reassurance to the 'key personnel' in Hong Kong. They argued that this reassurance was especially important in the wake of the June 1989 Tiananmen Square massacre. Tebbit insisted in the debate that even the elite citizens who passed the rigorous point system[22] were irreducibly alien. Referring to the Conservative Party's 1987 election manifesto which opposed increased immigration, Tebbit stated:

> These pledges were made because these islands of ours are already overcrowded, and in the belief that great waves of immigration by people who do not share our culture, our language, our ways of social conduct, in many cases who owe no allegiance to our culture was, and is, a destabilizing factor in society.[23]

Tebbit also made two journalistic contributions to the debate. Writing in the *Field* on 'What It Means to be British', he stated that Britain's 'sense of insularity and nationality has been bruised by large waves of immigrants resistant to absorption'.[24] In an interview in the *Los Angeles Times*, he stated that too many Asian Britons failed the 'cricket test' by supporting Indian or Pakistani teams rather than the British: 'It's an interesting test. Are you still harking back to where you came from or where you are?'[25] When reporters and Asian leaders challenged him, he defended his 'cricket test' remarks and reiterated his claim that Asian Britons had not become truly integrated into British society.[26]

Tebbit and other prominent Tories do of course contradict their racially exclusionary positions around British nationality in various strategic contexts. One of the first controversies which confronted John Major after he succeeded Thatcher as Prime Minister in 1990 was a dispute within the Conservative Party concerning the nomination of a black man as the party's candidate in the almost all-white Cheltenham constituency. John Taylor, a barrister, a former Home Office adviser and speech-writer, and a Conservative councillor in Solihull, West Midlands, became the first Conservative candidate of Afro-Caribbean descent selected to fight a 'safe' seat for the party. Taylor's selection quickly became a testing-ground for the Conservatives' official discourse on race.

Taylor's selection was not entirely without precedent. The Conservative Party had already selected four other black and Asian candidates to fight the 1992 election: Lurline Champagne, Qayyum Chaudry, Mohammed Khamisa and Andrew Popat, but they were all contesting seats which were held by Labour and the Liberal Democrats. In 1892, an Asian-British lawyer, Mancherjee Bhownaggree, was selected to fight a winnable seat in the London borough of Bethnal Green. Bhownaggree went on to win against the Liberal incumbent and only lost the seat in 1906 in a Liberal landslide. However, when the Cheltenham Conservatives' constituency meeting proceeded with the formality of voting on Taylor's selection on 1 December 1990, the vote was split 111 in favour and 82 opposed. Only Taylor, out of the 254 applicants, had been shortlisted by the local Conservative Party executive association. Although the party officials had followed the usual shortlisting procedure, various local members charged that Taylor had been inappropriately imposed on the Cheltenham constituency by the Conservative Party Central Office. Some members explicitly referred to Taylor's race in their objections. Party member Bill Galbraith publicly admitted that he had stated in the selection meeting, 'We should not let bloody niggers in this town.' He later commented, 'I am not remotely racist but I don't think that he's the right man for this town.'[27]

Tebbit and other prominent Conservatives represented Taylor as the kind of black Briton who is so assimilable that his race virtually disappears. Tebbit declared, 'The black issue is irrelevant. [Taylor] thinks of himself as British, Conservative and public-spirited.'[28] Chris Patten, the Conservative Party Chairman and Kenneth Baker, the Home Secretary, immediately expressed their support for Taylor. William Waldegrave, the Health Secretary, called for Galbraith's expulsion from the Conservative Party. Monica Drinkwater, the Cheltenham constituency party chairman, also claimed that the dispute was centred on the selection process, and 'had nothing to do with Mr. Taylor being black'.[29] A petition to review Taylor's selection nevertheless received 139 signatures from local party members. Taylor was only confirmed at a local association meeting on 10 February 1991 and the vote remained split 406 in favour to 164 against, with 60 abstentions and 7 spoiled ballot papers.

Taylor himself resolutely refused to focus on the issue of race in his statements to the press. Referring to his father, a Warwickshire cricketer, Taylor said, '[He] always told me to keep my eye on the ball and that is what I am doing.'[30] Taylor described Galbraith not as a racist, but as one of a group of 'rebel members' who were 'not prominent local Conservatives'.[31] Taylor's statements reveal the close affinity between his own approach to race and that of the Conservative Party. An interviewer for *The Times Saturday Review* wrote, '[Taylor] has little time for blacks and Asians who complain about racism holding them back.' He quotes Taylor's own explanation of his position:

> That's why I joined the Conservative party. It's got a positive message, to go out there and make something of yourself. John Major's shown us that's possible, whereas the Labour party just whinges, tells us you're downtrodden, but doesn't suggest any solutions.[32]

Taylor also stated that while he supported increased hiring of blacks in police and public offices, he strongly opposed 'positive discrimination'.[33]

The Conservative leadership's defence of Taylor was entirely strategic: although it necessitated completely self-contradictory statements from Tebbit on the possibility of an authentically British blackness, it also allowed the Major government to distance itself from Thatcherism. In a speech on 4 December 1990, Major declared to the House of Commons that his government would work to create a classless and compassionate British society in which merit would be duly rewarded. Responding to the criticisms of Taylor's selection, he stated, 'There should be no artificial barrier of background, religion or race', and that Galbraith's racist opinions were 'not sentiments that have any place in our party'. A report on Major's speech in the *Daily Telegraph*, a conservative national daily newspaper, put the Thatcher/Major comparison in the following terms:

> The 1990s, [Major] said, should be a decade of opportunity. But in marked shift from the rhetoric of Thatcherism, he said that, amidst the competitive thrust of life, there should be genuine compassion for those who needed a helping hand.[34]

In his first months in office, Major faced the challenge of overcoming the legacy of Thatcher's increasing unpopularity through 1990, especially around the poll tax and her belligerent stance on Europe. In this context, the marginalization of Galbraith's explicit racism and the championing of Taylor's assimilable Tory statements were used by Major as an opportunity to represent his government as a 'caring and sharing' project, in direct contrast to the exclusionary Thatcher years, and without advancing a single new policy initiative.

The distinction between assimilable and unassimilable blackness is also deployed in new racism discourse in the organization of consent for racist policies. As I shall demonstrate in chapter 4, Powell proudly pointed to the support which he received from his Asian and Afro-Caribbean constituents on many different occasions. Winston S. Churchill, MP, has reproduced Powell's populist image of a multi-cultural anti-immigration bloc. In a 28 May 1993 speech, Churchill called for a 'halt to the relentless flow of immigrants to this country, especially from the Indian sub-continent'. He suggested that nothing less than the preservation of 'the British way of life' was at stake.

> Mr. Major seeks to reassure us with the old refrain, 'There'll always be an England ...' and promises us that, fifty years on, spinsters will still be cycling to Communion on Sunday mornings – more likely the *Muezzin* will be calling Allah's faithful in the High Street mosque![35]

The most remarkable aspect about Churchill's discourse is his strategy for responding to his critics – which included the Prime Minister and other members of the Cabinet, and the editorial staffs of virtually every 'quality' newspaper: *The Guardian, The Independent on Sunday, The Times, The Sunday Times, The Sunday Telegraph* and *The Daily Telegraph*. Churchill wrote two feature articles in the tabloid press in which he claimed that the real views of the British people on immigration were being censored by the 'political class' and the media. He positioned himself as the true spokesperson for 'the people', not only by pointing to the large amount of supportive mail which he had received, but also by emphasizing the fact that many of his supporters were not white.

> In the past week I have received thousands of letters, running at 100-to-1 in support of what I have said including, it is worth pointing out, for those like my Parliamentary colleague Mr. Keith Vaz MP who accuses me of 'racism', from those of Jamaican, Nigerian, Guyanese and Asian origins.[36]

In Churchill's feature article for the *Sun*, he presents excerpts from sixteen letters which he received after his Bolton speech. Only one of the letter-writers, an Asian man born in Nairobi, criticizes his position. Of the fifteen supportive letter-writers, four identify themselves as non-whites: a Nigerian, an anonymous person who describes her/himself as Asian, an Iraqi and a Bangladeshi.[37] In response to a letter from me about his remarks, Churchill sent me copies of his speech and press releases. In his cover letter, he wrote:

> I also attach for your information copies of articles which I have contributed to *The Daily Mail* and *The Sun* newspapers, outlining the background to my remarks, as well as the amazing degree of support I have received from the public at large, including several members of the ethnic minorities in this country.[38]

The production of a black or Asian supporter for a racist policy allows new racist discourse to turn the logic of the left's 'identity politics' discourse against itself. According to the most reductionist versions of 'identity politics', the validity of a truth claim depends upon the immediate relationship between the person who is making the claim and the matter at hand: only a woman can know women's interests, only a black person can know black people's interests, only a gay man can know gay male interests and so on. The new racism therefore borrows the legitimating structure of 'identity politics' discourse and finds itself a Clarence Thomas to dismantle affirmative action or a Dinesh D'Souza to denounce 'political correctness'[39] and an Asian Briton to support anti-Asian remarks about immigration.

White leftists should not dismiss conservative people of colour as misguided victims of false consciousness, but we also cannot leave the job of responding to minority conservatives to our minority colleagues in the anti-racism struggle. The only effective response to this situation is for white leftists to do our homework on our own racism, to come to the debates well armed with the knowledge of the actual histories of people of colour, and to be prepared to say to any conservative who is promoting a racist policy – regardless of their own race – that they are, quite simply, wrong.

The mastery of difference through interpretation

While Nietzsche's and Foucault's genealogical approach can be used to undermine the strategic naturalization of bodily fantasies, their texts can also be used to show that the inscription of the frontier which constitutes the body and/or nation never takes the form of a singular repression or a total exclusion. Nietzsche's conception of the subject as a divided and self-punishing self who is invented only within the confines of the other's value system, and Foucault's theory of the disciplined body as a self-partitioning micro-formation which is re-inserted into harmonized macro-formations, constitute powerful frameworks for the analysis of the endless circulation and productivity of differentiations. Authoritarian discourses such as Powellism and Thatcherism should be analysed in terms of Nietzsche's and Foucault's conception of the domestication of difference through the incitement of differentiation, rather than as models of total exclusion and repression.

Foucault draws extensively upon Nietzsche's conceptualization of history as a fundamentally nihilistic process in his theory of bio-power relations. Nietzsche's conception of nihilism is based on his unique understanding of the will. For Nietzsche, the will is irreducibly multiple and heterogeneous; the state of harmonious unity is utterly incompatible with the will. The will is not a thing but an endless confrontation with another will. This confrontation takes the form not of brute collision of discrete bodies, but of an infinite effort to exercise the other, by entering the other, commanding the other, making the other obey, operating the other, making the other other than itself. Wherever there is will, there is a relation between dominated and dominating, commanding and obeying. At the same time, however, 'domination' is never total. If a will does not operate on another will which remains distinct from itself, it ceases to be a will.

A will is a will only insofar as it wills the obedience of another, and it can only will another will. There is only will insofar as the multiplicity and heterogeneity of the wills are preserved, and insofar as the 'dominated' will remains a recalcitrant otherness which at least partially escapes total neutralization.[40]

The wills express themselves in the form of forces. Forces are capable of both engendering effects and being affected by other forces; indeed, the magnitude of a force can be measured in terms of its capacity for being affected by another force. A distance is nevertheless always preserved between the forces as they affect one another so that they can never be fully comprehended by one another. Forces relate to one another by appropriating things, but these objects themselves are nothing but sedimented force-effects.[41] It is the forces, and not subjects or subject positions, which deploy strategies; that which appear to us as subject positions are the effects and the contested objects of the forces. The juxtaposition of forces which overdetermines every positioning process infinitely postpones the full occupation of subject positions. In Yamato's model of oppression, for example, internal forces supplement external ones. She argues that each oppression depends upon its relation with other oppressions: 'racism is supported and reinforced by classism, which is given a foothold and a boost by adultism, which also feeds sexism, which is validated by heterosexism, and so on'. In addition, however, the effective operation of an oppression also depends upon the installation of its 'flip-side', namely the 'internalized version of the "ism"'. Because they operate as mutually dependent forces, an increase in the externalized aspect of an oppression is always twinned with an intensification of its internalized aspect.[42] Ultimately, the reproduction of an 'external' oppression as an 'internal' force, or, in other words, the mimetic incitement of the 'oppressor within', calls the external/internal boundary into question. If the formation of myself as a self were inextricably linked with the reproduction of the oppressor/oppressed dyad within me, then my vision of my true inner self which resists the 'oppressor within' may be itself a metaphysical illusion which has already been installed to promote self-disciplining in the guise of resistance.

For Nietzsche, there is no 'nature' which is outside the endless contest between forces, just as for Foucault there is no identity and knowledge outside power relations. The 'sense' of a thing, and its very being, depends upon the configuration of forces at a particular moment. The contest between forces, their attempts to master things through interpretation, is therefore endlessly creative. Interpretation does not come later to an already established body; racist immigration discourse does not arrive after the constitution of the British nation, and the heterosexist regulation of gender and sexuality does not simply interpret an already sexed body. The body is not merely a stage for the struggle between forces; the boundedness, coherence and concreteness which are fundamental to every body are wholly constituted by forces over time.[43] The genealogy of a body works against the interpretation effects of the forces by un-masking the constitutive bodily fantasies which present themselves as natural origins, and by revealing the violent struggles which are at work behind every normalized body.

Interpretation is central to *ressentiment*, the first phase of nihilism. In a highly problematic figuration, Nietzsche depicts *ressentiment* as the slave's revenge against the master. The slave works to transform the master through re-evaluation: she interprets the master as the 'evil one' so that she can represent herself to herself as good. Nietzsche's positing of the master as a being who is capable of affirming herself before her encounter with the slave[44] constitutes a recourse to an impossible prediscursive order. His emphasis on the creativity of the slave, and on her deployment of metaphysical fictions, is nevertheless extremely useful for the analysis of authoritarian discourse. The slave situates herself as morally superior to the master by interpreting both herself and the master as autonomous sovereign subjects. She thereby re-positions herself as the one who has chosen to be a better subject, as having chosen to suffer domination, while the master is represented as the one who has chosen to dominate the slave.[45] The subordinated slave becomes superior through the fiction of her self-mastery: she represents herself as a substance which is prior to the discursive field of the forces.

The fiction of the autonomous subject can become a powerful strategic weapon. Thatcherite discourse, for example, made extensive use of this device. Wherever leftist criticisms of Thatcherite policies were based on structural analyses, and were organized in terms of collective struggles, Thatcherism deployed the myth of the self-sufficient and freely choosing individual who was responsible for her own impoverishment, under-education, unemployment, malnourishment, lack of housing and so on. Thatcher's dramatic claim that 'society does not exist' only served to strengthen this individualistic negation of the socio-political conditions of oppression.

The racial character of Nietzsche's conception of the noble morality of the master limits the value of his formulations for political analysis. Nietzsche depicts noble morality as a pure-blooded blonde beast figure, refers to the advance of democracy as an attack by the non-Aryans on the Aryans, and argues that goodness was originally defined as the blonde-headed, 'in contradistinction to the dark, black-haired aboriginal inhabitants'.[46] Kaufmann, one of the English translators of the *Genealogy of Morals*, argues that Nietzsche's racial representations are ambiguous. He states that Nietzsche is referring to 'ancient Greeks and Romans, the Goths and the Vandals', rather than nineteenth-century Germans in this passage. Kaufmann also insists that 'the "blond beast" is not a racial concept and does not refer to the "Nordic race" of which the Nazis later made so much. Nietzsche specifically refers to Arabs and Japanese ... and the "blondness" presumably refers to the beast, the lion.' Nietzsche himself explicitly equates the 'blonde beast' with both European and non-European peoples: 'the Roman, Arabian, Germanic, Japanese nobility, the Homeric heroes, [and] the Scandinavian Vikings'.[47] In any event, a discourse may be ambiguous and self-contradictory and yet still have deeply racist and anti-Semitic effects. Balibar argues that although Nietzsche regarded anti-Semitism as the 'politics of the feeble-minded', 'this in no way prevented him from taking over a large part of racial mythology himself.'[48] In the terms of O'Brien's typology, Kaufmann could be described as one of the 'gentle Nietzscheans' who 'explain away the more ferocious aspects of the philosopher's writings'. O'Brien recognizes that Nietzsche's main target is Christianity, and that Nietzsche rejected 'vulgar' anti-Semitism. However, O'Brien also shows that from a Nietzschean perspective, there is nothing more Jewish than Christianity: Nietzsche held that it was the Jews who originally transformed 'noble' morality into Christian values. In this sense, Nietzsche rejected vulgar anti-Semitism because it was not anti-Semitic enough. He differed with his contemporary anti-Semites because they did not realize that their own Christianity was the product of a Jewish transvaluation of values.[49]

Even with these racist and anti-Semitic traces within his texts, Nietzsche's critique of German nationalism, and his distinction between high and low cultures, can be used as an effective framework for analyses of racism. Nietzsche links the development of German philosophy, science and culture to brutal torture: 'one has only to look at our former codes of punishments to understand what effort it costs on this earth to breed a "nation of thinkers"'. He lists the following practices: stoning, breaking on the wheel, quartering, boiling of the criminal in oil or wine, flaying alive, cutting flesh from the breast and the 'smearing of the wrongdoer with honey and leaving him in the blazing sun for the flies'. He states that it is only with these practices that the Germans have acquired a collective 'memory', a sense of national loyalty and a philosophical culture. Reason and patriotism, which are expressed in the citizen's apparently consensual acceptance of the national social contract, are neither natural nor original. They are not produced spontaneously and on their own, but are only created with the *assistance* of torture.[50] The torturing of the contract-breaker is therefore not an accidental externality to German culture; torture is its necessary supplement. For Nietzsche, as for Gramsci, consensus and coercion are inextricable. The apparently autonomous decision to consent to the contract, whether it is the racial-national contract or the patriarchal heterosexual contract, is a strategic fiction. The demonization of contract-breakers serves not only to demonstrate the costs of subversion, but also to conceal the fact that free choices are impossible.

Although some form of force is a necessary condition of the formation of any social contract, the degree of dependency on this supplement varies from context to context. In 'low' civilizations, the offence of a contract-breaker is viewed as the most serious offence against the entire social order. The contract-breaker is thrust outside the social order and infinitely punished in a process which is designed to invent a sense of guilt. In 'high' civilizations, by contrast, the contract-breaker is seen as a much less dangerous figure. The highest civilization would be one in which those who do harm to it would not be disciplined at all. The contract-breaker would be represented as accountable, but not as guilty.[51] Higher civilizations do not aim to confine and to quarantine difference; they tolerate and even promote infinite differentiations. For Nietzsche, his contemporary German culture was a 'low' civilization precisely because it could not tolerate the presence of the criminal. Nietzsche's argument remains profoundly ambiguous. The Nietzschean approach to the social contract romanticizes the criminal, just as Rousseau's misogynist theories of 'man''s 'natural' desire for the immediate consumption of a female body, and of woman's infinite heterosexual desire, romanticizes the rapist. However, the 'criminal' is also a metaphorical 'out-law', a symbolization of an otherness which escapes the containment of social boundaries, a subversive variation of the social rule. 'Higher' social orders, then, tend to have more negotiable limits; they tend to offer a much greater space for alternative articulations. A 'higher' social order would be less threatened by the introduction of social differences, through developments such as black immigration or the establishment of lesbian and gay communities, for it would accommodate the supplemental subversion of social relations without resorting to a disciplinary response. At the same time, it would promote the formation of a vibrant civil society and the democratic tolerance of non-authoritarian differences so that it became increasingly less vulnerable to authoritarian discourses such as racism and homophobia.

The 'cultural racism' of the British New Right can be analysed from this perspective. The new racism presents difficulties for anti-racist discourse because it takes the form of a 'cultural racism'. New racists such as Tebbit argue that insofar as blacks and Asians escape the neutralizing process of assimilation, they remain inherently anti-British. For the new racism, recalcitrant un-assimilable blackness should be separated from assimilated blackness and excluded. The new racism anticipates and attempts to neutralize the anti-racist critique of its exclusion of blackness in two ways: it does not claim that whiteness is superior, and it does include some blackness as a quasi-legitimate element within British society. Because the new racism is organized in terms of cultural differences, rather than biologically fixed differences, it can present itself as a legitimate political project. The discourse of Ray Honeyford is a case in point. Honeyford was a headmaster in a Bradford school in which over 90 per cent of the students were Asian-British. He was dismissed from his position after he published strong criticisms of the council's multicultural education programme in *The Times Educational Supplement* and the *Salisbury Review*. He became a leading figure in the right-wing anti-multiculturalism campaign; he even attended a Downing Street symposium on educational policy that was chaired by Thatcher herself. In his articles, he argued that multiculturalism was promoting 'anti-British prejudice' to the extent that it was causing a white backlash against blacks and Asians. He further equated multiculturalism with feminism, radical politics and 'hard core left-wing political extremists'.[52] Seidel notes that because Honeyford made no reference to the presence of institutional racism in the education system, multiculturalism was represented as a cultural invader that subverts a tolerant and ordered society. The dominant white British culture was thereby positioned as a beleaguered victim, while a small initiative on behalf of an oppressed minority was transformed into an overwhelming threat.[53] Through these inversions of power relations, racial otherness was constructed as a corrosive external force bent on the total destruction of the 'peaceful' (white) British way of life; arguments around natural superiority and inferiority were entirely absent. Gilroy comments that 'the anti-racists, who were quick to brand [Honeyford] as a racist, were less able to demonstrate why and how this was the case'. The 'cultural qualities' of his racism 'prevented it from being recognized as racism at all'.[54]

By shifting the analysis from claims of natural superiority and inferiority to the representation of racial otherness, it becomes possible to trace the racist aspects of Honeyford's discourse. By representing Afro-Caribbean and Asian children as the offspring of a 'settler' population, he reinforces the racist myth of an authentic 'British' people – the white Christian English – and situates the racial minorities as a naturally alien group which has no right to a place within British spaces and institutions. His fictitious construction of an 'authentic' British education strengthens the strategic concealment of political interventions in the curricula, so that its particular class, racial, religious and political content is taken for granted. With these illusory constructions of the 'authentic', his discourse promotes an uncritical defence of the 'true' Britishness against the 'outsiders'' subversion. The British New Right's vision of an ideal British society is highly intolerant towards otherness; it only includes elements of othernesses, such as certain blacknesses and certain homosexualities, insofar as their alterity has been domesticated. Its imaginary British society is in this sense constructed around racist and anti-queer exclusions. The disciplining of difference is not accidental to the new racism and the New Right; it is the supplement which is necessary to its interpretation of Britishness. From a Nietzschean perspective, the type of Britishness which is promoted by the British New Right is a 'low' civilization, for it responds to the multiplication of racial and sexual differences with authoritarian strategies.

Self-punishment, self-surveillance and self-differentiation

In Nietzsche's account, the strategies of evaluation, interpretation and containment through the deployment of metaphysical fictions are central to the slave's revenge. The slave's attempt to domesticate the master, or, in other terms, the authoritarian strategy of neutralizing difference, never achieves a final resolution. Haunted by the traces of past differences, slave morality, in the form of the 'man of *ressentiment*', turns away from the enjoyment of difference in 'new things' and engages in increasingly rigid, obsessive and repetitious attempts to cancel out difference. The slave's revenge through interpretation is neither an accident nor a singular event; the pure affirmation of difference which Nietzsche ascribes to noble morality is impossible. In Deleuze's terms, the active forces of noble morality make difference an object of pleasure, affirmation and difference. The reactive forces which animate the slave's revenge separate difference from what it can do; they tend to adapt, neutralize and domesticate difference. Active forces are always intertwined with reactive forces in history; for Nietzsche, 'man is domesticated man'. Nihilism, the devaluation and depreciation of the play of difference, is not an event within history; nihilism is the very principle of history.[55] Although Nietzsche problematically constructs an 'original scene', the relation between the slave and the master, and although he indulges in the fantasy of a 'post-historical' 'overman', he consistently argues that there is no escape from nihilism within history.

Through her interpretation of herself and the other as autonomous subjects who have freely chosen their positions, the slave takes her revenge by gaining the right to make the other accountable for her otherness. The second and third forms of nihilism, bad conscience and the ascetic ideal, are organized around the internalization of interpretation and accountability. Again, the very term, 'internalization', is inadequate; because the prediscursive autonomous subject is a strategic fiction, there is no sense of a bounded internal space which is prior to the effects of the reactive forces. It is through the imposition of a 'form' or, in other words, the creation of a 'soul', that noble morality becomes a self-conscious subject.[56] Self-consciousness is therefore inextricably linked with the acceptance of the evaluation structure of the other. The judgement of the other becomes the very structure for the apparently autonomous 'self'-formation of the self. Nietzsche's subject is in this sense a subject of a lack: in her very formation, the self conceives of herself as lacking in comparison to the ideal of goodness which is constituted by the other. Finding herself guilty, she sets about the endless process of rehabilitation through the increasingly repetitious and compulsive practice of self-punishment.

The construction of a self-punishing self is of course impossible without some form of legitimation. In his discussion of the ascetic ideal, Nietzsche argues that the apparently disinterested claims of philosophical discourse conceal the extent to which these claims allow for the advance of authority. In Gramscian terms, the philosopher 'organizes consent' for the normalization of her claims by borrowing the already-normalized discursive form of the ascetic priest. Nietzsche states, 'The ascetic priest provided the repulsive and gloomy caterpillar form in which alone the philosopher could live and creep about.'[57] Against philosophy's claims of disinterestedness, Nietzsche insists that discourse is impossible except through masks.

The in-formation of the self in terms of the ascetic ideal is a wholly creative process. Nietzsche depicts the ascetic priest-philosopher as a fraudulent and malicious 'healer' figure, and the self-condemning force-complexes as her patient. The ascetic priest-philosopher wounds the healthy, infects these wounds, exploits the dependence of the wounded to tame them and then guides the wounded towards a pseudo-recovery. She 'trains' the sick by encouraging them to engage in mechanical activity, with a daily regimen, regular schedules and work assignments. The ascetic priest-philosopher incites the self-construction of a simulacrum, a pseudo-life. The pleasurable and creative character of the pseudo-life in turn promotes the further containment of the forces. At the highest moment of this training, the pale facsimile of the pseudo-life presents itself as the only possible formation. The ascetic priest-philosopher's 'healing' depends upon the normalization of metaphysical fictions; it begins when the sick recognize themselves as selves. Through their 'recovery', the sick accept that their sickness has a cause, and that that cause can be found within themselves. They accept that they are to blame for their own sickness.[58] If nihilism begins with the containment of otherness through interpretation, it becomes an effective disciplinary mode insofar as otherness is separated from its potential subversiveness: the accused becomes in-formed by the metaphysical enclosures which she constructs for herself. The nihilistic reactive forces do not eliminate otherness; they attempt to manage otherness by separating difference from what it can do.

The continuities between Nietzsche's and Foucault's conceptions of the domestication of difference are striking. In *Madness and Civilization*, for example, Foucault argues that the modern asylum is organized around the incitement of guilt. The keeper of the asylum encourages, rather than represses, the discourse of the madman. The madman is subjected to the keeper's regularized observation to the extent that he begins to incorporate the keeper's gaze. The madman gradually accepts the moral code of the keeper, takes responsibility for his madness and promises to restrain himself. He lives in 'perpetual anxiety, ceaselessly threatened by Law and Transgression'. The madman only becomes a subject, an autonomous choosing self, insofar as he acknowledges that he could have done otherwise, and therefore justly deserves punishment. It is only through the process of becoming the guilty object for the other that he becomes a subject.[59] Ultimately, the newly created judging and punishing element within himself takes the place of the external other, such that this process of objectification/subjectification takes the form of localized and self-perpetuating repetitions.

From a Foucauldian perspective, authoritarian discourse does not merely strike the surface of its targeted othernesses; it penetrates their spaces, seizes hold of their logic, separates otherness from its subversive potential, and attempts to achieve total domestication by turning otherness against itself. Foucault shows, for example, that the intervention into madness by some physicians of the classical age was organized in terms of parody. They held that madness was a 'movement of reason reasoning with itself', rather than an absence of reason. Madness is represented by these physicians as a simulacrum-text, an otherness which adopts a corrupted form of the normal, so that it transforms the normal into the ridiculous. The subversive dimension of the simulacrum-text lies in its capacity to expose the normal text to mimicry, parody and mockery. The simulacrum-text's adoption of the form of the normal, however, also makes it vulnerable to a counter-strategy. Physicians in the classical age sometimes took the grammar and meanings which were already established in the text of madness seriously. They attempted to use the pseudo-structure of madness to turn the madness-text's illusions against themselves. For example, a man who believed that he had been damned was presented with a man dressed as an angel who absolved him of his sins. A man who refused to eat because he thought that he was already dead was presented with a group of men dressed as the dead who were eating. These interventions work with the structure of the illusion, but they also introduce a degree of difference, 'a ruse, or at least an element which surreptitiously alters the autonomous operation of the delirium'. The counter-illusion simultaneously confirms the illusion and 'turn[s] [it] back upon itself'. An invalid who believed that an animal was living inside his body was fed a purge and, as he vomited, an animal was thrown into the sink with his discharge.[60]

The counter-illusion paradoxically borrows the strategy of the illusion: as the illusion mimics the normal, the counter-illusion mimics the illusion. The success of the intervention depends upon the physician-actor's ability to borrow the discursive mask of the madman. The counter-illusion takes the form of a theatrical acting out of the illusion, an externalization of an internal text. This theatrical representation places the illusion on a plane outside the mind of the madman where the discourse of the normal already has an advantage in determining the grammar of the text: the *mise-en-scène* all occurs within the institution of confinement. That advantage, however, is won through force and deception. There are two assumptions which are implicit in the physicians' initiatives: first, that the mere acting out of the illusion is in itself insufficient (the logical structure of the illusion is such that the illusion will not self-destruct), and second, that there is no necessary reason for the madman to prefer the normal to the illusion. Because the return to the normal is not strictly necessary, it can only be guaranteed through violence and artifice, the representation of the illusion-with-a-difference that the madman is forced to watch. This type of neutralization of a simulacrum-text therefore undermines any claim to necessity for the discourse of the normal: the normal shows itself to be grounded on contingency and structured by parody to the same extent as its impersonator, and guaranteed not by the inevitable unfolding of necessity, but by force. As such, the counter-illusion cannot rule out the possibility of other subversive re-interpretations of the normal.

The parodic intervention into the discourse of otherness is not, of course, peculiar to this medical discourse; authoritarian discourse organizes consent precisely by taking up already popularized discursive forms and re-orienting them towards authoritarian ends. Hall's critique of the abstract character of leftist alternatives to Thatcherism focused on their failure to work with the logic of popular concerns around race, racism, the family, sexuality and so on. Far from calling for the capitulation by the left to Thatcherite strategies, Hall insisted that Thatcherism had effectively erased leftist alternatives from the political agenda by turning leftist logic against itself, by re-defining local government socialism as tyranny, anti-racism as an attack on democratic freedoms, pro-lesbian and gay policies as the promotion of AIDS, environmental controls as a surrender of national sovereignty to European bureaucrats and so on. In other words, Hall grasped the creative and parodic character of Thatcherism's re-definition of the political agenda. He argued that the left had to examine the weaknesses of its positions – which had allowed for this thorough transformation of political values in the first place – and that leftist alternatives had to transform the Thatcherite logic against itself in turn.

Hall does not address one other aspect of Thatcherism which is relevant to the incitement of self-judgement, namely Thatcherism's ability to mobilize, or even to invent, self-surveillance. Hall points to the support for Thatcherism among 'traditional Labour supporters' such as workers, women, blacks, lesbians and gays and so on. From a Nietzschean and Foucauldian perspective, however, a study of Thatcherism should also analyse its incitement or exacerbation of the differentiations among these othernesses. In chapter 5, I shall make only a small gesture in this direction by looking at some of the letters to the editors of queer publications in the late 1980s which express sympathy for the Thatcherite attack on queer activism. The Thatcherite invocation of the 'good homosexual' did not fall on deaf ears. Even in this limit case, in which there was tremendous popular support for the attack on the lesbian and gay community, Thatcherism worked organically, encouraging the 'good homosexual' stance against dangerous queerness, and promoting the separation of queer difference from what it can do.

Foucault develops his theory of the creative and interventionary character of authoritarianism further in his conceptualization of bio-power relations in *Discipline and Punish* and *The History of Sexuality*.[61] For Foucault, bio-power relations emerge with the founding of modern institutions, such as the prison, the factory, planned workers' neighbourhoods, the modern school, the modern army and so on. In these institutions, law-breakers are not merely superficially marked by the sign of the sovereign authority's power, they are brought within the machine-like structure of the modern disciplinary institution and inserted into its system of spatial distributions and temporal controls. If Bentham's panopticon model for the modern prison serves as the symbolic prototype for all modern institutions, it is the torture and execution of criminals which exemplifies the structure of power relations in the classical period. The earlier form of intervention had proved unreliable. The markings of torture and execution were only administered in the context of irregular spectacles; the sovereign's intervention tended to remain almost totally external to the constitution of the subject's identity. The sovereign's text, the broken body of the accused, was also vulnerable to subversive interpretations by the crowd. The public execution was often turned into a popular carnival in which rules were inverted and authority was mocked.[62] Foucault does not offer this model of repressive and totally exclusionary power merely to account for the differences between the classical and modern periods. Foucault's point is that even though power has taken radically different forms in contemporary societies, it is still regarded as an external and repressive force which emanates from a single centre. He also points to the tremendously seductive aspect of the myths around power. Political practices are widely organized around the assumptions that power distances us from our true selves and that it ultimately leaves our inner truths intact. No one can escape these all-pervasive illusions: we always find ourselves attempting to recover and to liberate our true selves. For Foucault, liberation strategies are not just theoretically problematic; they may also conceal, or even promote, the multifarious ways in which disciplinary regimes extend their grip throughout the social.

Foucault reiterates Nietzsche's argument that the advance of the domestication of difference depends upon the creation and normalization of metaphysical fictions, such as the fiction of the prediscursive and substantive subject. *The Genealogy of Morals, Discipline and Punish* and *The History of Sexuality* also share an emphasis on the role of the domestication of difference through the multiplication of difference. Bio-power's incitement of differentiation stems from its fundamentally contradictory logic: it simultaneously partitions the body and reassembles the individualized parts to form a disciplined whole. The intricate dressage of disciplinary technologies individuates at the micro-level through, for example, marching drills, table manners, handwriting instruction, safer sex practices, body-building exercises and so on. At the same time, the trained individual parts are inserted back into a totality at the macro-level which is harmonized through large-scale state policies, such as the management of the birth rate and immigration flows, employment and education policies, large-scale urban planning, national health care programmes and so on. Instead of repressing difference and life itself, bio-power 'endeavours to administer, optimize and multiply [life], subjecting it to precise controls and comprehensive regulations'.[63]

Foucault depicts the targets of the disciplinary technologies as recalcitrant othernesses. The delinquent's delinquency is never finally eliminated by incarceration discourse, just as the deviance of the hysterical woman, the masturbating child, the Malthusian couple and the perverse (male) adult is never finally corrected through the regulation of sexuality. Bio-power comprehends the remainder, however, in the sense that the uncorrected deviance is put to use. The masturbating child, for example, became the object of new forms of surveillance by 'parents, families, educators, doctors and eventually psychologists'. Masturbation was not eliminated, of course, but its significance was enlarged so that it gradually became understood as a threat to the 'future of the entire society and species'.[64] With the invention of a sexualized child's body, parents had to question their parenting techniques, teachers had to submit their pedagogical practices to increased regulation and scrutiny, doctors had to develop new methods of examination and intervention, architects had to re-design school dormitories and so on. The impossibility of the total domestication of otherness becomes the support for the circulation of disciplinary technologies, the incitement of self-surveillance and, indeed, the invention of new selves.

Gilroy's analysis of the policing of blackness in the 1970s and 1980s can be usefully read in terms of Foucault's analysis. The emergence of the modern disciplinary institutions marked a shift from exclusions, such as the banishment of the madman or the execution of the criminal, to assimilatory inclusions, such as the treatment of the insane in psychiatric hospitals or the incarceration of the offender within the modern prison. Gilroy similarly insists that the criminalization of the young black male in the 1970s marked a distinct shift in popular and official racist discourses. Racist representations of blackness had tended to focus on the 'threat' of miscegenation and black immigration until the 1970s. In other words, the popular and official racist responses to anxieties around blackness had been expressed largely in the form of demands for the separation of blackness from the white social order. In the 1970s, by contrast, the demands in racist discourses shifted toward the disciplining of blackness within the social order. In the context of new popular panics around black criminality, inner-city unrest, and the numbers of non-white and non-Christian students in the schools, demands were made for the intensification of the policing and the bureaucratic management of blackness. Spatial differentiation technologies were central to this new regime. Gilroy notes that the London Metropolitan Police responded to the inner-city riots and concerns about (black) 'street crime' by re-organizing the policing of London in terms of an 'area-based approach'. By differentiating blacknesses in terms of the geographical distribution of black criminality, the new approach allowed the Metropolitan Police to single out 'high-crime neighbourhoods' for 'particularly intense forms of police surveillance and control'. Insofar as the putative threat of anti-British blackness was not contained, this 'failure' was highly productive: concerns around black male criminality were used to bring otherwise private matters onto the official agenda. Lord Scarman's Home Office Inquiry Report on the 1981 Brixton riots, for example, includes discussions of the generational differences in black families (the difference between the 'strictness' of 'first-generation' black immigrant parents and the 'permissiveness' of their British-born children), the insufficient presence of male authority in black families and the political-spiritual views of the Rastafari.[65]

Foucault's theory of bio-power relations remains limited by functionalist and totalizing tendencies. In his discussion of the strategic deployment of the delinquent figure within incarceration discourse, for example, it appears that we can only engage in resistances which allow the disciplinary technologies to extend endlessly throughout the social. Against the repressive model, Foucault insists that prohibitions incite multiple resistances which always to some extent subvert the prohibitory order. He often seems to suggest, however, that every subversion merely becomes a new target for discipline and surveillance, such that bio-power ultimately obtains a totally comprehensive grip on virtually every possible resistance. Foucault states in *Discipline and Punish*, for example, that the reversals of power relations can only be temporary, and that the triumph of bio-power is a 'perpetual victory' which is 'always decided in advance'.[66] A similar tension can be found in Foucault's conception of the rules of a discursive formation. In the *Archaeology of Knowledge*, for example, Foucault states that an analysis of a discursive formation should uncover the rules which govern that formation. He argues that rules are predetermining: their operation supposedly guarantees that only one specific set of relations, strategies and statements is possible for every particular context.[67] In this schema, parodic subversions through alternative re-articulations would be ruled out in advance as impossible. The horizons which established the limits of coherence would not be open to contestation and counter-hegemonic strategies; ultimately, they would remain impervious against any political intervention. Virtually every possible resistance would be already mapped out and anticipated. The predetermined conformity of every resistance with the rules of the formation would ensure that it merely provided a new occasion for the further advance of disciplinary technologies.

In these passages, then, Foucault's theory of bio-power is quite similar to the theories of hegemony as total domination which I outlined in chapter 1. Once again, hegemony can also be conceptualized as a formation which normalizes itself through the marginalization of alternatives as incoherent. In this second approach, a hegemonic formation never obtains the all-encompassing closed status which Foucault envisions in his bio-power theory. Foucault's Nietzschean re-conceptualization of discursive rules is nevertheless quite compatible with the hegemony as normalization approach. In 'Nietzsche, Genealogy and History' Foucault rejects his previous argument in *The Archaeology of Knowledge* that rules are pre-determining. He fully recognizes that parodic resistances can indeed turn a formation's rules against themselves. It is the queer forces – the bent, the inverts and the perverts – who triumph in history through the re-appropriation of the rules.

> Rules are empty in themselves, violent and unfinalized; they are impersonal and can be bent to any purpose. The successes of history belong to those who are capable of seizing these rules, to replace those who had used them, to disguise themselves so as to pervert them, invert their meaning, and redirect them against those who had initially imposed them; controlling this complex mechanism, they will make it function so as to overcome the rulers through their own rules.[68]

From this second perspective, Foucault suggests that the possibilities of subversive resistance are, in logical terms, infinite; the only limits to social change are contingent, historical and contextual. The tension in Foucault's thought between these two perspectives is never fully resolved.

Genealogy and race

Foucault's texts are almost totally silent on racism, colonialism and nationalism. His brief references to the eugenics movement, and to the racial character of nineteenth-century European discourses on population management,[69] are inadequate exceptions to this erasure. However, Foucault does offer a rich analysis of the relation between genealogy, race and European identity in 'Nietzsche,

Genealogy and History'. He states that genealogy concerns itself with 'descent', but in a peculiar sense: instead of positing a unified self whose essential core places her unambiguously within a specifiable lineage, genealogy depicts the individual as an irreducibly differentiated complex. Foucault explicitly links 'descent' with 'race', and argues that claims around the purity of 'descent' operate as strategic concealments. Citing Nietzsche, he states that when the nineteenth-century Germans attempted to account for their complexity by claiming that they possessed a double soul, 'they were simply trying to master the racial disorder from which they formed themselves'. The genealogical excavation of the differences beneath the racial purity claim therefore works against the 'soul [which] pretends unification' and the 'self [which] fabricates a coherent identity'. Genealogy undermines all evolutionary theories: 'it disturbs what was previously considered immobile; it fragments what was thought unified; it shows the heterogeneity of what was imagined consistent with itself'.[70]

The fictions which constitute the body are central to 'descent' claims. Unlike traditional history, genealogy has no constants; for genealogy, the body is 'moulded' and 'imprinted' within historically specific regimes. The body simultaneously serves as the 'surface of events', the bearer and record of historical markings, the site in which the 'dissociated self' organizes its 'illusion of a substantial unity', and a 'volume' whose 'perpetual disintegration' allows for the genealogical critique of uninterrupted evolutions and substantial unities. At some moments, Foucault represents genealogy as a witness to the endless failure of identity. He states, for example, that genealogy attempts 'to reveal the heterogeneous systems which, masked by the self, inhibit the formation of any identity'. At other moments, genealogy becomes an interventionary force itself. It aims 'to introduce discontinuity into our very being'; its purpose is 'not to discover the roots of our identity but to commit itself to its dissipation'. In any event, Foucault consistently argues that the racial character of the body is not simply given as an a-historical fact; like every other aspect of the formation of the body – individual or national – racializations are strategic fictions which only appear as prediscursive givens within specific historical contexts.[71]

Genealogy can also be deployed against the constitutive nostalgia of white-Christian-Europeanness. Traditional histories offer the possibility of an essential affiliation with previous moments of 'high civilization'. For the 'confused and anonymous [white-Christian-]

European' of the nineteenth and twentieth centuries, these strategic connections with past monuments open up the 'possibility of alternate identities, more individualized and substantial than his own'.[72] Martin Bernal's *Black Athena* is an excellent example of the genealogical approach at work.[73] Bernal investigates the strategic character of the radical shift in the historiography on ancient Greece in the eighteenth and nineteenth centuries. In his terms, the 'ancient model' was displaced by the 'aryan model' at that time. According to the 'ancient model', which roughly corresponds to the conventional view among Greeks in the classical and Hellenistic periods, Egyptian and Phoenician colonization and Near Eastern cultural influences constituted the foundations of ancient Greek culture. Modern European historians developed an alternative 'aryan model' through which Greek culture is understood as the result of an invasion by the 'racially pure' Hellenes from the north. The 'aryan model' conceptualizes ancient Greece as the product of Indo-European influences, rather than African and Semitic ones. It replaces the racial mixture in the Greek origin with an uncontaminated Europeanness by devaluing the Egyptian and Phoenician cultures, and by keeping them at a distance. Bernal does not limit his study to the advance of competing truth claims around the origins of Greece. He also explicitly calls attention to the effect of racism, anti-Semitism and 'continental chauvinism' on apparently neutral scholarly research. For Bernal, this fundamental historiographical shift should be explained in terms of the Eurocentrism of the Romantics, eighteenth- and nineteenth-century racism and Christian anxieties around the ancient Greeks' recognition of the importance of Egypt. Because ancient Greece is supposed to constitute 'the epitome of Europe' and 'its pure childhood',[74] the definition of the origins of Greek civilization is the definition of Europeanness itself. Bernal's Foucauldian point is that the 'scholarly' re-definition of the origins of ancient Greek civilization was influenced by, and contributed to the legitimation of, hegemonic racist and anti-Semitic discourses in eighteenth- and nineteenth-century Europe.

Foucault argues that genealogy attempts to interrupt these dangerous racial readings of European history through parodic subversions. Genealogy re-reads 'monumental history''s 'excessive deference' and 'veneration' for past epochs as 'masquerade'.[75] It does not, of course, replace masquerade with the 'real thing' or a true narrative. Genealogy aims instead to show the contingency of all historical narratives, and the multiple possibilities of identification. It displaces 'the identification of our faint [white-Christian-European] individuality with the solid identities of the past' in favour of 'our "unrealization" through the excessive choice of identities'.[76] Foucault's argument should not be mis-read as promoting an individualistic 'anything goes' voluntarism. For genealogy, identities are wholly constituted through the inevitable and endlessly shifting practice of adopting discursive masks. In ontological terms, all identifications are equally 'unreal', all identities are equally precarious and all masquerades are equally contingent. The insistence that – logically speaking – the possibilities of identity claims are infinite can be used to heighten our awareness of the contingent and historical character of even the most normalized identities and rules of exclusion.

Chapter 4

Powellism: the black immigrant as the post-colonial symptom and the phantasmatic re-closure of the British nation

Essentialist identity claims always betray themselves and ultimately remain impossible, but they nevertheless can have tremendous material effects in specific historical contexts. The Powellian construction of an essentially racist conception of Britishness in the post-colonial 1960s is a case in point. A traditional 'history of the referent'[1] approach to Powellism would place Powell's anti-black immigration campaign within a more or less unified tradition of similar campaigns, and would take the meaning of terms such as the 'black immigrant' for granted. In my analysis, I shall attempt instead to draw out Powellism's genealogical precedents, its historical specificity and the ways in which it laid part of the foundation for Thatcherism. I shall focus on questions pertaining to the representational structure of Powellism. If de-colonization amounted to the traumatic loss of a necessary supplement, like the loss of a vital body part, then Powell's representation of the Empire as an accidental irrelevance amounts to a strategic suppression of the trauma.

The term, 'immigrant', is defined in the *Oxford English Dictionary* simply as 'one who or that which immigrates; a person who migrates into a country as a settler'. The *Webster's Dictionary* entry reiterates this basic definition, but then adds that the immigrant is 'not previously known' in the new habitat. It defines 'immigrant' as 'one who immigrates; a person who comes to a country to take up permanent residence; a plant or animal that becomes established in an area where it was not previously known'. In some situations, however, this distinction – the boundary between those who are 'previously known' and those who are 'not previously known' within a certain space – is the product of re-written histories. It cannot be overemphasized that the status of entire black populations was abruptly changed precisely at the time of de-colonization. Although they had been British passport-holders with full legal rights to settle in the United Kingdom, they became foreign immigrants who were subjected to extensive immigration controls. It was through the invention of the black immigrant that the work of forgetting the dependency of the metropole upon the periphery was carried out.[2] The colonized had in fact been 'known' very well: the fruits of their labour had been consumed for centuries, references to the 'native' were pervasive in popular culture at the height of Empire, and the entire imperial project had contributed significantly to the unification of the British nation. By re-naming the colonized as 'immigrants', these supplemental populations were suddenly re-defined as the late additions to an already complete body. The 'known' colonized became 'unknown' 'strangers' in the land of their own making. Above all, the movements of these peoples provided the occasion for the re-closure of the broken body. The specifically anti-black immigration laws offered a solution to the post-colonial crisis of national identity. Powell succeeded in transforming the popular resistance against black immigration into a broadly based social movement. The anti-black immigration discourse, unlike the other single issue 'backlash' movements of the 1960s, functioned as the stage upon which previously unrepresented elements of dis-illusionment with the political system, frustrations around the shortcomings of Labour and the Conservatives' consensus approach and anxieties about the 'permissive society' found their official voice.

Powellism unfolded in three phases. In the first, from the 1950s to the mid-1960s, Enoch Powell became the MP for Wolverhampton South-West, developed his unique position on de-colonization and expounded his monetarist views. In the second, he emerged as a populist parliamentary maverick in the late 1960s by speaking directly to 'the people' on black immigration. In the third, Powellism began to operate in the early 1970s as an actual political force. Powell's support rivalled that of his party leader and many of his positions were taken up by mainstream Conservatives. However, his uncompromising rejection of the Conservative government's poli-cies *vis-à-vis* Europe subsequently destroyed his own leadership bid and left his support bloc in a temporary state of disarray.

Forgetting the trauma of de-colonization: Powell on the Empire, 1950–65

Powell took up the position that the Empire had been absolutely irrelevant to Britain only after it had become clear to him that nothing could be done to stop de-colonization. During a 1947 election campaign, for example, Powell stated that the Labour Party was promoting the 'eclipse of the whole Empire, which is the structure on which we are dependent for our very existence'.[3] Powell's first important statement in the House of Commons on de-colonization took the form of an intervention against the Royal Titles Act. This law changed the British monarch's title from 'Head of the British Empire' to 'Head of Commonwealth'. For Powell, the changed title signified the displacement of the British imperial system with a hollow pretence. From his perspective, the Commonwealth merely covered over the loss of the Empire, and allowed the British people to ignore the fact that the colonies had unilaterally rejected the 'mother country'.[4] With the Suez crisis of 1956 and the Mau Mau campaign in Kenya from 1952 to 1959, Powell became even more convinced that the relations between Britain and the former colonies had to be completely re-evaluated. In an article written under a pseudonym in *The Times* (2 April 1964) entitled 'Patriotism Based on Reality, Not on Dreams', Powell described the Commonwealth as a 'gigantic farce', and a 'disastrous encumbrance from which Britain must break free'.

By 1964, Powell had altogether dropped the argument that Britain had been dependent on the colonies for its very existence. He argued that the British had to reject two powerful and harmful myths, that 'Britain was once a great imperial power' and that 'Britain was once the workshop of the world'. If they continued to believe that the strength of their nation had depended on its ability to dominate its colonies, then de-colonization would only signify the end to British greatness. In other words, these two 'bad myths' were structured according to a supplementary logic, and, as such, revealed the fundamental weaknesses within the metropole. Powell proposed an entirely different myth. He argued that British imperial rule was extended through a series of blunders, misfortunes and entanglements, and that the Conservatives invented the Empire at the turn of the century because 'about that one could make stirring speeches without needing actually to alter anything'.[5]

By representing the Empire as accidental and external, Powell was able to claim that Britishness had remained essentially the same through the imperialist period and would not be significantly altered by de-colonization. Powell argued that just as the Athenians had discovered that their sacred olive tree had somehow survived the sacking of their city, so too were the British, 'at the heart of a vanished Empire and the fragments of demolished glory, [able] to find, like one of her own oak trees, standing and growing, the sap still rising from her ancient roots to meet the spring, England herself'. Because the nation was essentially uninvolved in the Empire, 'so the continuity of her existence was unbroken when the looser connections which had linked her with distant continents and strange races fell away'.[6] Powell's championing of the 'pure' and 'true' Englishness which could be so easily recovered is deeply ironic. Historians generally agree that Britain is one of the most ethnically differentiated nations within Europe.[7] As early as the Norman Conquest of 1066, 'the English people' included Celts, Gauls, Romans, Angles, Saxons, Jutes, Danes and Norsemen, and the separation between the Welsh, Scottish and English sovereignties had already been fully established.

This forgetting of the metropole's dependency on its periphery and the profound differentiation in its origin is central to contemporary British racist discourse. As Hall argues,

> The development of an indigenous British racism in the post-war period *begins* with the profound historical forgetfulness – what I want to call the loss of historical memory, a kind of historical amnesia, a decisive mental repression – which has overtaken the British people about race and Empire since the 1950s. Paradoxically, it seems to me, the native, home-grown variety of racism begins with this attempt to wipe out and efface every trace of the colonial and imperial past.[8]

It is in this respect that the racist response to de-colonization can be analysed in terms of the psychoanalytical category of the trauma. An event is traumatic insofar as the subject is unable to respond adequately to a failure in her defensive boundaries. In medical discourse, trauma means any injury where the skin is broken as a consequence of external violence. Freud compared the traumatized subject to a 'living vesicle' whose protective shield had been breached by an excessive amount of external stimuli. Psychoanalysis insists on the relative character of the traumatic event. A subject's response to a given event is shaped by her predisposition; the same event might provoke entirely different responses from different subjects with higher levels of tolerance.[9] For example, the differences between the responses of the British and the other Europeans to de-colonization and post-colonial black immigration could be explained in terms of their different political contexts. It was the political articulations around British de-colonization which gave this radical reconstruction of the national frontiers a traumatic value. These articulations – such as Powellism – certainly were shaped in part by Britain's imperial past, but de-colonization in itself did not have to become a political trauma.

Forgetting is one of the signs of trauma. Caruth states that the traumatized person 'carries an impossible history within [herself]'; she is gripped by thoughts or dreams about events which she failed to perceive fully when they originally occurred. She passed through the traumatic event apparently unharmed, only to have symptoms emerge after a period of latency. She does not totally forget or distort the traumatic event; after the delay, her thoughts or dreams about the event may be almost perfectly literal representations. The traumatic event itself can only be borne by the subject if she forgets it in the actual moment of its occurrence. The force of the event for her – given her specific predisposition, her low level of tolerance for the event, the context of its occurrence, and so on – is such that she is unable to understand it in that moment.[10]

Powell's denial of the historical presence of blackness within Britishness as the latter's necessary supplement can therefore be described as an immediate forgetting, which is typical of a traumatic experience. While it is true that the 1950s and 1960s saw an unprecedented movement of Asian, African and Afro-Caribbean peoples to the United Kingdom, blackness had always been integral to imperial Britain. In economic terms, for example, black slaves, indentured workers and free labourers made an enormous contribution to British wealth. The triangular structure of the slave trade ensured that in a material sense, the black slaves on distant plantations were present in the very heart of industrializing Britain. In the mid-eighteenth century, British ships transported tens of thousands of Africans to the West Indies each year. Slaves were purchased on the West African coast for guns, spirits and finished cotton goods. One in seven of the slaves survived the brutal conditions of the middle passage across the Atlantic to labour on the Caribbean and American plantations. The raw materials from the plantations, such as sugar, cotton and tobacco, were then shipped to Europe's manufacturing and refining centres. The triangular slave trade contributed as much as one-third of the capital which was invested in industrializing Britain's economic development. Slave-traders claimed that the labour of one slave in the West Indies provided the capital which was necessary for the employment of six workers in Britain.[11] As Beverly Bryan, Stella Dadzie and Suzanne Scafe put it, 'It was the blood, sweat and tears of Black women and men which financed and serviced Europe's Industrial Revolution, a revolution which laid the basis for Europe's subsequent domination and mono-poly of the world's resources.'[12] An entire popular pro-slavery litera-ture emerged, including numerous tracts, pamphlets, handbills and books. In addition to the economic arguments, this discourse drew upon anthropological and biblical sources to assert the inferiority of the African, and the moral, spiritual and physical benefits of slavery.[13]

Returning slave-traders sometimes brought Africans back to Britain as their servants. Other Africans won their freedom by fighting on the British side in the American War of Independence, but many were forced by economic circumstances to join the black beggars in London as soon as they were freed. Free black labourers and escaped slaves worked in the English ports, but they were often kidnapped and sold back to slave-traders bound for the West Indies. In 1772, the Mansfield judgement virtually outlawed the removal of slaves from England back to the colonies. The black population in London numbered between 15,000 and 20,000 in the late eighteenth century – almost 3 per cent of the total population of the city. Given the impoverished state of the freed slaves, the absence of black women, various 'repatriations' of the freed slaves to Africa, and the shipments of black 'free labourers' to the West Indies, the black population steadily declined through the nineteenth century.

After the abolition of slavery, British plantation-owners and mining companies turned to India as a source of labour. Indentured workers from India were imported by the British to Mauritius, British Guiana, Trinidad, Jamaica, Ceylon, Malaya, Burma, South Africa and East Africa. Asian workers, like the African slaves, obtained a material presence in the British 'motherland' through their labour. Hall states:

> In each of these phases [the slave trade and plantation system of the seventeenth century, the imperial conquest of India in the eighteenth century, and the expansion of British trade to Latin America and the Far East in the nineteenth century], an

economic and cultural chain – in short, to be brutal, the imperialist chain – has bound the fate of millions of workers and peasants in the colonial hinterlands to the destiny of rich and poor in the heartland of English society ... If the blood of the colonial workers has not mingled extensively with the English, then their labour-power has long entered the economic blood-stream of British society.[14]

In the 1950s and 1960s, the repression of this knowledge – that blackness had already established a substantial material presence within Britain – supported the dismissal of alternative representations of the Afro-Caribbean and Asian migration to Britain. As the descendants of enslaved and colonized workers, these peoples already had a legitimate share in British wealth. In other words, as supplemental, rather than accidental, elements, they were not immigrating across an inside-outside frontier, they were moving within a system which already included them. Lauretta Ngcobo quotes Margaret Prescod-Roberts and Norma Steel's insistence on this alternative representation.

We had every right to move, for although we had worked hard in our former communities, generating wealth in the Caribbean over hundreds of years, we had been left poor. All the wealth we made was stripped away and taken to these 'mother' countries. We came to share the wealth that we ourselves had created, claiming what was legitimately ours.[15]

Powell's representation of the English nation as the self-sustaining, invulnerable, eternal and essential source to which Britain can always return operates as a phantasmatic construction. Like all fantasies, his image of England is a purely non-contradictory space which is absolutely purified of all subversions and interruptions. In a 1968 speech, for example, Powell argues that race relations legislation is absolutely unnecessary. He states that unlike the 'American negro' who was brought to that country as a slave, the 'Commonwealth immigrant' came to Britain as a 'full citizen'. Ignoring the experience of entire generations of workers, women and ethnic minorities, he claims that Britain is a 'country which knew no discrimination between one citizen or another'.[16] This is not to say that we only need to pull away Powell's phantasmatic 'myth' about the non-dependency and non-discriminatory character of Britishness to reveal the underlying truth. In psychoanalytic terms, there is no experience of reality outside some kind of phantasmatic structure.[17] The fantasy analogy should be used instead to draw attention to the constitutive character of Powell's representation. Zizek argues that fantasies operate as the 'support for our "reality" itself' by structuring our actual social relations. Instead of offering an escape from reality, they 'offer us the social reality itself as an escape from some traumatic, real kernel'. The fantasy is not produced after the organization of the subject and her desires has been completed; it does not merely stage the fulfilment of the already constituted subject's wishes. On the contrary, the fantasy 'constructs the frame enabling us to desire something'. It is through the fantasy that the objects of desire are given: 'through fantasy, we learn how to desire'. The fantasy's frame is structured so that we experience our world as a wholly consistent and transparently meaningful order.[18] By its very structure, the Powellian phantasmatic construction of the post-colonial British nation displaces the cause of all disorder onto external sources: since Britain is an essentially complete, independent and unified nation-space, any interruptions within that space must be caused by foreign elements.

Zizek's conception of fantasy is not simply one more version of the scapegoat model. Racist Britons did of course blame the black immigrant for socio-economic antagonisms, but this is only half the story. The scapegoat model takes the 'outsider' status of the black immigrant for granted, and assumes that 'the British people' functioned like an already fully-formed subject with completely organized desires. The displacement of disorder onto the foreign element plays a part in the very construction of these 'inside' and 'outside' spaces. Powell's phantasmatic representation of Britain drew upon various organic racist traditions to promote a racially exclusionary conception of Britain which masked the traumatic experience of de-colonization.

Although Powell's interventions around de-colonization form an important part of his overall approach to race, his speeches received little attention at this time. Powell's monetarist views on the economy and political principles hardly won him any favour with his party leadership. The formation of Powell's right-wing political agenda took place against the backdrop of the post-war consensus. In the years immediately after the war, both Labour and the Conservatives committed themselves to the welfare state and 'mixed-economy' policies. This new social contract called upon trade union leaders to forgo 'excessive' militancy in return for a stable economy and full employment. The disciplinary dimension of the post-war consensus, in which all legitimate political forces were supposed to find adequate representation within the 'neutral' and 'post-ideological' state, was heightened by the unequivocal commitment by the Labour government to the American 'free world' side of the Cold War. Hall *et al.* associate the 1945–51 Labour government with the political retreat of the left: 'throughout Western Europe, the Cold War had the effect of driving every major political tendency into the middle ground, where political life was stabilized around the key institutions of parliamentary democracy and the "mixed economy"'.[19]

The post-war consensus discourse became increasingly hegemonic through the 1950s, as working-class living standards improved, social mobility increased and trade union leaders vigorously supported the 'mixed-economy' approach. The introduction of new technologies and the expansion of the state sector gave rise to the formation of new middle-class strata. Labour and Conservative leaders proclaimed that Britain had entered the endless era of pragmatic, class-less and antagonism-free politics in which the primary distinction between the two parties consisted in management expertise. On the question of race, however, the 'middle ground' consensus was actually right-wing, rather than centrist. The post-war recovery of the 1950s coincided with the super-exploitation of black workers and the total failure of the welfare state to assume any responsibility for the immigrant populations. In the 1960s, both the Conservatives and Labour leaderships shifted their positions even further to the right: they explicitly linked 'race relations' tensions with excessive black immigration, and supported blatantly racist immigration legislation.

Powell established his own independent political agenda outside the post-war social democratic consensus. During the negotiations around de-colonization and the founding of the Commonwealth, Powell called for a spirited defence of Britain's sovereignty. Against the bi-partisan support for welfare state policies and state intervention in the economy, Powell championed monetarist policies and free market capitalism. For Powell, 'socialist' interventionary policies only distorted the egalitarian and democratic effects of the free market. He argued that 'excessive' government expenditures on social services were inflationary, and that the welfare state bureaucracy and national economic plans only displaced the democracy of the free market with authoritarianism. He defined Tory philosophy in terms of pro-free market ideals, individual responsibility and 'family values' in an article which he wrote in 1950 – almost thirty years before the rise of Thatcherism. He stated:

> The Tory believes that inequality is not only natural and inevitable, but within a sound society is of infinite value. He sets definite limits to the sphere of government and the responsibilities of the state, and would preserve and strengthen those of the individual and the family.[20]

As a 'professional' politician coming from a lower-middle-class background, Powell was himself the very embodiment of the Conservatives' shift away from their party's former aristocratic tendencies. However, Powell's policies were largely dismissed as bizarre in the 1950s and early 1960s. By the time that the party leadership took a decisive turn towards the Powellian themes of the free market, monetarism, individualism and family values in the 1970s, Powell's outspokenness on black immigration, the European Common Market and Northern Ireland had earned him permanent ostracism.

It should also be noted that Powell's views on black immigration and the assimilation of the black populations were somewhat ambivalent in the 1940s and 1950s. Mercer argues that the shift in Powell's position on race in the mid-1960s was so great that it took the form of a 'radical volte-face'.[21] It is true that Powell joined other Tories in criticizing the Labour government's 1948 British Nationality Act. This law established an official distinction between British subjects on the basis of nationality for the first time in the history of the Empire. It established two separate categories for 'Commonwealth citizens' and 'citizens of the United Kingdom and its colonies'. These distinctions were designed to allow for autonomous legislation on citizenship by independent Commonwealth countries such as Canada, Australia and India. Some Tory leaders opposed the Act because they believed that it prepared the way for selective immigration controls. Powell's opposition to the Act, however, had nothing to do with its potential effect on immigration. His concern was that the Act legally recognized the constitutional autonomy of the former Dominions and the former colonies, thereby giving an official status to the process of de-colonization. During a 1953 debate in the House of Commons, Powell stated

> The British Nationality Act, 1948, removed the status of 'subject' of the King as the basis of British Nationality, and substituted for allegiance to the Crown the concept of a number of separate

citizenships combined together by statute. The British Nationality Act thus brought about an immense constitutional revolution, an entire alteration of the basis of our subjecthood and nationality, and since the fact of allegiance to the Crown was the uniting element of the whole Empire and Commonwealth, it brought about a corresponding revolution in the nature of the unity of Her Majesty's Dominions.[22]

It is also true that Powell accepted, in his own way, the argument that black immigrants could be integrated into British society. As late as 1964, Powell wrote that the Conservative Party wanted

to see the coloured immigrants no less integrated into the life and society of what is now their homeland than any other group, such as the Jewish community or the thousands of Poles living in Britain today. No other prospect is tolerable.

He also pledged to oppose anyone who claimed that there is 'any difference between one citizen of this country and another on the grounds of his origin'. These comments were included in Powell's contribution to a feature on 'The Immigrant Problem' in the *Wolverhampton Express and Star*. Powell's own article was entitled, 'Integration is the Only Way – Over Many Years'.

However, Powell always attempted to escape the charge of racism by insisting that he did not believe that the black race was inherently inferior to the white race. As is the case for new racism discourse in general, his rejection of this type of racial difference is perfectly compatible with his racist insistence on the essentially alien character of blackness. For all the appearance of a 'tolerant' attitude towards blacks that these statements might create, Powell's racism emerges clearly in the article. He makes a direct link between 'excessive' numbers of black immigrants and 'undesirable social problems'. He also insists that the 'idea of immigrants as an unassimilated element in our society, living apart in certain districts and following only certain occupations, is insupportable'. For Powell, the failure of assimilation was not a problem because black Britons would be denied full equality, but because it left this naturally alien population concentrated in undisciplined centres of otherness: 'Any substantial addition to the immigrant population would defer assimilation indefinitely and entail upon Britain the evils of a deeply divided nation and society.'[23] By 1964, Powell did not have to qualify the term 'immigrant' with 'black'; this equivalence had become a common-sense association.

Mercer also rightly points out that Powell explicitly speaks as the representative of his black constituents in his *Wolverhampton Express and Star* article. Powell states that black immigration controls would contribute to 'the interests of everyone, and most of all the immigrants themselves'. Referring to his regular meetings with his constituents, he points out that many Afro-Caribbean and Asian Britons had sought his aid as their MP, and that he was 'glad to serve them'. However, Powell continued to speak in the name of the sensible black citizen throughout his most explicitly racist period in the late 1960s and early 1970s. In a 1968 speech at Eastbourne, in which he spoke out against 'reverse discrimination' and called for an official 'repatriation' programme for blacks in Britain, he claimed that demands for increased black immigration controls had 'come as much from my [black] immigrant constituents as from the rest, if not, more so; in this matter I was convinced of speaking for and in the interest of all my constituents'. Here, as elsewhere, Powell strategically 'de-racializes' his racist attack on black immigrants by constructing a racially inclusive image of his supporters, and by stating that his real enemy was the 'tiny minority' in control of the 'channels of communication'. Their crime was the promotion of censorship and disinformation; he charged that they would 'resort to any device or extremity to blind both themselves and others' on the question of black immigration.[24] Powell therefore uses the image of his black supporters to represent his discourse as a moderate and objective exercise in counter-disinformation.

There was, in short, no effective discontinuity or 'radical volte-face' in Powell's discourse. He opposed the 1948 legal distinctions between British subjects only because they gave de-colonization a *de jure* status. He accepted the inclusion of the 'good assimilable black', but consistently argued that the main purpose of assimilation was the disciplining of the otherwise dangerously alien black population, and that this inclusion had to be supported by the exclusion of the 'dangerous black invader'. Although he spoke in the name of his black constituents, he invoked the image of his black supporters only to de-racialize his consistently racist discourse.

The black immigrant as a supplementary symptom: Powell's populist anti-black immigration campaign, 1965–70

The emergence of Powell as a populist leader can only be understood in the context of rising concerns in both popular and official discourse regarding black immigration. In the 1940s and 1950s, the black migrants from the Caribbean and Asia were often regarded as an important source of surplus labour, but were nevertheless treated as inferior. In the context of the acute post-war labour shortages in the 1950s, several private British companies placed job advertisements in Caribbean newspapers. London Transport, British Railways and various hospitals established special recruitment schemes with the West Indian governments. The promise of employment for the inhabitants of the impoverished West Indies, even in low-paid and unskilled positions, brought unprecedented numbers of migrants to Britain. Some of these migrants were already familiar with the country, having served in the armed forces during the Second World War. Most of them would have chosen to migrate to the United States, but the 1952 McCarren–Walter Immigration Act had almost completely banned West Indian immigration. A somewhat smaller migration of peoples from India and Pakistan to Britain began in the later 1950s. The manager of the Smethwick Labour Exchange reported in 1955 that the 'coloured labour from the Commonwealth is greatly easing the labour shortage. The labour turnover among these immigrants is lower than average, and firms formerly hesitant about employing them are now doing so to a considerable degree.'[25]

In spite of the importance of their work, black immigrants had to deal with extensive discrimination. They were placed in low-skilled occupations and refused promotions, regardless of their qualifications. They had to contend with quotas and even bans on 'coloured labour' by the management of several private firms. In exceptional circumstances, a small number of black workers were placed in skilled and supervisory positions, but their white co-workers often staged walk-outs to protest these promotions. Black immigrant workers were also turned away by the majority of white landlords, estate agents and building societies. They were forced to live in overcrowded hostels, to rent the worst types of local government housing or to finance their own mortgages with groups of friends, often for the purchase of condemned housing.

Intensified forms of racism emerged in the late 1950s. An argument between a black man and a white man at a public house in Nottingham in 1958 led to a full-scale white riot against blacks. The young white male Teddy Boys conducted 'nigger-baiting' sprees in various inner-city areas. Crowds of other whites would sometimes gather at the scene of a 'nigger-hunt' and encourage the white attackers.

White violence became especially intense in the Notting Hill area of West London, where the fascist White Defence League's graffiti, leafleting and newspaper-selling had become commonplace. In September 1958, white mobs rioted for several days and nights in Notting Hill, assaulting blacks on the streets and attacking the homes of blacks with petrol bombs. The British chapter of the Ku Klux Klan stepped up its campaign in 1961, with several death threats against black leaders, poster campaigns and cross-burnings. The *Smethwick Telephone*, a local newspaper in the Birmingham area, featured a series of articles and letters in the early 1960s which reflected the rise in popular racist concerns. White journalists and letter-writers charged that the hygiene practices of the black immigrants were uncivilized, that whites were threatened by the spread of infectious diseases from black neighbourhoods, that the mixing of races in the classrooms was causing a decline in educational standards and that white women were endangered by black male 'pimps', seducers and rapists.[26]

By the early 1960s, a fully-fledged anti-black immigration movement had been established. Groups such as the Birmingham Immigration Control Association campaigned for a ban on 'Commonwealth' – meaning black – immigration, compulsory tuberculosis testing for immigrants and the deportation of immigrant criminals. The Union Movement, which consisted of reorganized elements of Oswald Mosley's pre-war British Union of Fascists, the League of Empire Loyalists and the White Defence League also campaigned against black immigration. Inside Parliament, several Tory backbenchers actively lobbied for specifically black immigration controls, including Cyril Osborne, Norman Pannel, Harold Gurden and Martin Lindsey. Peter Griffiths won the Smethwick seat for the Conservative Party in 1964 with an explicitly anti-black immigration campaign. In his election leaflet, he declared,

> I shall press for the strictest possible control of immigration. We British must decide who shall or shall not enter our country. So vital a matter cannot be left to other Governments. Overcrowding and dirty conditions must be ended. There must be no entry permits for criminals, the unhealthy or those unwilling to work. Our streets must once again be safe at night.[27]

When asked to comment on the unofficial slogan, 'If you want a nigger neighbour, vote Labour', Griffiths stated – in populist tones similar to those of Powell and Thatcher –

> I should think that is a manifestation of the popular feeling. I
> would not condemn anyone who said that. I would say that is
> how people see the situation in Smethwick. I fully understand
> the feelings of the people who say it.[28]

Griffiths' explicit statements were exceptional: few other Conservative and Labour candidates discussed race and immigration in their campaigns.

The Conservative Party nevertheless shifted its position on black immigration at this time. The Conservative governments of the 1950s had totally ignored the discrimination which the black immigrant population faced in employment and housing. Conservative politicians had merely promoted the work of local voluntary organizations in 'assimilating' the new communities, and left these organizations' Victorian paternalistic structures intact. Blacks were under-represented in the leadership of the voluntary bodies which were working in the black communities, and black associations were rarely consulted. J.B. Williams, the chairman of the Inter-Departmental Committee on Colonial People in the United Kingdom, commented in 1951 that the 'integration' of the new black communities into Britain was a matter for the voluntary sector and remained 'entirely outside the scope of official action'.[29]

By the mid-1960s, several influential Conservatives had accepted the importance of government intervention, but only in the form of anti-black immigration laws. Many explicit calls for black immigration controls were made from within the Conservative Party. Sir Alec Douglas-Home, the Conservative Prime Minister, vigorously defended his government's 1962 Commonwealth Immigrants Act in a 1964 election campaign speech.

> What had been a trickle of immigrants from the Common-
> wealth was developing into a flood. We saw that if it was not
> brought under control it would create very serious social and
> economic problems, so we brought in legislation. The Socialists,
> aided by the Liberals, opposed it all along the line. But for the
> Act, an additional 300,000 immigrants with their families,
> perhaps nearer a million people, would have come in – an
> influx with which it would have been impossible to cope.[30]

In 1965, the Conservative Party front bench gave considerable support to Osborne's ten-minute rule bill which would have prohibited all immigration from the Commonwealth, except for those applicants whose parents or grandparents had been born in the United Kingdom.

Labour also shifted towards an anti-black immigration position: although it had opposed the Commonwealth Immigrants Bill in 1962, it pledged to renew this law in its 1964 manifesto. Labour's position was deeply influenced by Patrick Gordon-Walker's electoral defeats and popular opinion data. Gordon-Walker, a member of the Labour shadow cabinet who was labelled a 'nigger lover' because he had opposed black immigration controls, lost both his Smethwick seat to Griffiths, and a safe seat in a 1965 by-election. A private poll which was published at the time of Gordon-Walker's second defeat indicated that 95 per cent of the respondents supported 'stringent control of coloured immigration'.[31] As Labour changed its policies, the difference between the two major parties on race and racism largely became a difference in rhetoric rather than substantial leadership. In 1965, the Labour government published a White Paper on immigration which strengthened the 1962 black immigration controls and reaffirmed its basic argument that race relations management depended primarily upon the control of black immigration.

Labour also continued to pursue a liberal pro-multicultural, pro-tolerance-for-diversity approach to racial antagonisms. Mercer argues that the discourse of Roy Jenkins, the Labour government's Home Secretary, is indicative of Labour's overall approach to racism. He notes that Jenkins basically equated racism with 'prejudice'. In a 1966 speech, Jenkins stated that Labour aimed to promote racial 'integration', which he defined as 'equal opportunity, accompanied by cultural diversity, in an atmosphere of mutual tolerance'. He maintained that integration was blocked first and foremost by prejudice: irrational resentment, fearful and ignorant responses to blacks, scapegoating for inadequate social services and so on.[32] Jenkins' argument therefore reduced systemic, institutionalized and historically symptomatic racism to a problem of individual psychology. In this sense, there is a strong similarity between the Labour and Conservative positions. When Douglas-Home rejected Labour's proposals for anti-race discrimination legislation in a 1964 election speech, he stated that 'the avoidance of friction between immigrants and the rest of the population must largely be a question of personal attitudes'.[33] This individual psychology approach failed to recognize the extent to which racist representations and logics had become thoroughly intertwined with organic philosophies. When the first 'race relations' legislation was passed by the Labour government in 1965, the official anti-prejudice project remained a largely bureaucratic initiative. Mercer comments that Labour's multiculturalism was limited because it was 'articulated "from above" as part of the bureaucratic apparatus of social democracy's interventionary state'.[34]

In other words, Labour's multicultural anti-prejudice discourse represented racism as an external accident which could be added or taken away from post-colonial British society without any fundamental transformation of its most basic structures. Instead of explicitly taking on the task of working through the British imperial legacy, with the aim of breaking the dependent link between Britishness and racism as its national supplement, Labour de-politicized racism: it became purely a matter of individual behaviour. The pro-tolerance, anti-prejudice discourse could be summed up in terms of a simple maxim: 'Be kind to "our friends from overseas", then racism will disappear.'[35] When black power organizations called for a far more radical approach to racism, they were dismissed as 'extremists'. Hall *et al.* comment:

> For several months [during the rise of Black Power in the United States in 1967 and 1968], the media and race-relations officials refused to believe that anything so 'violent' and un-British as Black Power could take root amongst 'our West Indian friends'. Typically, they dubbed anyone who tried to describe or influence young blacks in the cities as 'racialist' and 'extremist'.[36]

As the laissez-faire approach of the Conservatives allowed the government to ignore its responsibilities *vis-à-vis* the settlement of the immigrant communities in the 1950s, Labour's anti-prejudice approach legitimated the suppression of public discourse on race and racism in the 1960s. The 'be kind to our friends from overseas' principle was translated into a policy of censorship. Hiro comments that although there was no 'conspiracy of silence' on racism, many BBC television producers, newspaper editors and trade union leaders downplayed the intensity of popular racist opinion by 'balancing' news features, refusing to publish representative samples of letters from the public, and quietly frustrating grass-roots initiatives.[37] This is not to say that officials should have freely given racists and fascists official platforms for their views. By merely suppressing racist discourse, however, rather than confronting it head on and working through its logic, these intellectual leaders contributed to a growing sense that the 'common "man"' was simply not being heard by the governing elite. To return to the trauma metaphor, working-through involves both the interpretation of the traumatic event and an overcoming of the resistances to that interpretation through discourse. Freud states that it is only by ' "becoming more conversant with this resistance" that the patient is enabled to carry out the working-through'.[38] The censorship of explicit racial discourse cut both ways: it blocked alternative anti-racist interpretations – the speeches by radical black activists, for example – and it suppressed racist statements. Instead of exposing racist resistances to vigorous public debate, with substantial anti-racist leadership by official spokespersons, racists were actually protected from anti-racist interpretations. It could also be argued that this censorship created favourable conditions for Powellism: like all successful populists, Powell ultimately emerged as the 'liberator' of 'the people's' repressed truths.

Without a thorough working-through of the de-colonization trauma, the black immigrant became the post-colonial symptom. As Lawrence argues, 'the "alien" cultures of the blacks are seen as either the cause or else the most visible symptom of the destruction of the "British way of life"'.[39] Fantasies are always accompanied by symptom-figures: since fantasies construct a perfect order, imperfection must be displaced onto the supplementary symptom. Once the symptom figure is constructed as the cause of disorder, a coherent account can be given for the inconsistencies between the supposedly complete and unified order, and the endless series of failures, incompletions and contradictions which continually disrupt the order. Not only is the symptom external to the fantasy order, it demarcates its very frontiers. Because it symbolizes that which cannot be integrated into the fantasy order, it marks out that order's limits of tolerance.[40]

Racist exclusions ensured the constant reinforcement of the symptomatic construction of the black immigrant. New pressures on the British economy accelerated the disruption of white workers' positions in the manufacturing sector and the disintegration of white working-class neighbourhoods. At the same time, the majority of black workers were locked into the lowest-paid occupational positions, such as unskilled manufacturing and service sector positions. The low incomes of the black workers and the racist exclusionary practices of white landlords, local government housing agencies and building societies led to the concentration of the black communities in the most run-down and overcrowded inner-city areas. Although they had to bear the brunt of socio-economic hardships themselves, the black communities were defined in racist discourse as the most potent signifier of the post-colonial national decline.

Other economic and political developments also created favourable conditions for Powell's populist movement. Persistent economic problems led to a weakening in the hegemonic status of the bi-partisan consensus approach. After a period of relative economic stability, the British political agenda in the 1960s was dominated by concerns around balance of payments deficits, unemployment and a decline in manufacturing investment. At the same time, the de-centralization and internationalization of British manufacturing decreased the effectiveness of government interventions. Industrial disputes also escalated in number and intensity throughout the 1960s. Industrial management had secured agreements from union shop stewards for sustained productivity rates in exchange for greater union control over work practices. In response to lay-offs and downward pressures on wages, the rank and file ignored the management–union leadership consensus and staged numerous short-term work stoppages. The work-stoppage statistics provide dramatic evidence of the extent to which British workers no longer felt included in the consensus: as much as 95 per cent of all strikes during the 1960s were not officially endorsed by union leaders.[41]

Confidence in the existing two-party electoral system also declined. In 1950, Labour and the Conservatives won the support of 93.2 per cent of all actual voters, and 73.2 per cent of the total electorate. These figures decreased continually through the 1960s. By the October 1974 election, the two parties won only 75 per cent of all the votes cast, representing merely 54.9 per cent of the total elector-ate. In 1964, Labour and the Conservatives won all but nine seats, and the latter all went to the Liberal Party. Even under the British 'first past the post' electoral system, a total of thirty-nine seats were won by the smaller parties in October 1974: thirteen by the Liberals, eleven by the Scottish Nationalists, three by the Welsh Plaid Cymru and twelve by the Northern Ireland parties. With the failures of both parties' economic policies, and increasing disenchantment with the social-democratic consensus, voters were increasingly attracted to solutions which were offered outside the two parties' official pro-grammes. Although the party leaderships gradually became more polarized – the Conservative Party shifted towards authoritarian and free-market doctrines in the 1970s, and party activists within Labour increasingly rejected the leadership's 'narrowly parliamentary approach' – alternatives from the party 'grassroots' and from outside parliament won increasing support in the interim. Political views on both the right and the left which had previously been considered too extreme gained much more support at this time.[42]

The Labour government failed to provide an adequate response to this growing sense of disenchantment with the political system. Labour owed its narrow 1964 election victory in part to its articulation of anti-elitist positions. Harold Wilson's championing of technological advance and modernization was coupled with an attack on the Conservative Party: he claimed that it was dominated by aristocratic amateurs who knew nothing about modern industrial technology. He also charged that the Tories promoted an outmoded sector of industrial management which had achieved its decision-making positions on the basis on class privilege, rather than merit. The Wilson government did introduce significant reforms in the civil service, the education system and public housing, which to some extent contributed to a dissolution of rigid class barriers. However, Wilson's anti-elitist reforms were juxtaposed with disciplinary corporatist policies. In 1968, having already failed to defend profits through voluntary wage agreements and legislated wage ceilings, the Wilson government proposed a bill which would have outlawed unofficial industrial action. Wage-control councils, commissions and boards only provoked a greater sense of resentment among workers. The number of working days lost in strikes remained constant at about 2.6 million days per year between 1964 and 1967. For 1968, 1969 and 1970, the figures jumped to 4.7, 6.8 and 11.0 respectively. By the June 1970 election, wage controls had ended, legislation against unofficial strikes had failed and wage rates had recovered, but Labour's credibility continued to decline. Although the Wilson government had presented itself as the party which rewarded merit, and which could increase the wealth of both capital and the working class, its policies contributed to the popular sense of alienation.[43]

Some elements of political disaffection were re-organized in the form of extra-parliamentary movements. The 1960s saw the development of the nuclear disarmament campaign, and the emergence of radical leftist student groups, anti-Vietnam war protests, feminist organizations and black power militancy. Although the British version of 1968 did not feature the almost revolutionary mobilizations of the French workers and students, and the British 'counterculture' was much smaller than the American 'tune in and drop out'

148

hippie phenomenon, 1968 nevertheless became a turning-point towards the social and political polarizations of the 1970s and 1980s. Marxist groups such as the International Socialists and the International Marxist Group flourished on the left. Neo-fascist groups, such as the British National Party (the result of a merger between the White Defence League and the National Labour Party) and the newly formed National Front also became increasingly visible in British inner cities. Catholics in Northern Ireland demanded equal rights, after more than four decades of institutionalized discrimination. The authoritarian response to this demand gradually set the stage for the militarization of Northern Ireland and the resistance struggle.

Right-wing political elements also took aim against the moral 'permissiveness' of the 1960s. New legislation was introduced on a wide range of 'morality' issues: gambling, suicide, obscenity and censorship, Sunday entertainment, capital punishment, divorce, contraception, abortion and homosexuality. While these reforms generally reinforced the distinction between the public interest and private conduct, established the sovereignty of adult individual consent in the private sphere and restricted state intervention to the public sphere, they were not unequivocally 'liberal'. Contraception and family planning services, for example, were made more widely available partly in response to right-wing concerns about the higher birthrates among the 'lower orders' and black communities. The 1967 Sexual Offences Act simultaneously decriminalized homosexual activities between adult men in 'private' and sharpened the definitions of various 'public' homosexual offences. This so-called 'permissive' moment actually ushered in a new era of the sexual policing: between 1967 and 1976, 'indecency' charges for consensual acts involving adult males in 'public' places doubled, prosecutions trebled and convictions quadrupled. The reforms of the 1960s had both liberalizing and authoritarian effects, and, according to numerous studies, the sexual behaviour of British youth remained fairly conservative.[44]

The notion that an excessively tolerant political elite was inflicting its 'permissiveness' campaign on a threatened nation nevertheless gained widespread credence. 'Moral entrepreneurs', such as Mary Whitehouse of the National Viewers and Listeners' Association, became highly popular single-issue campaigners. It was in the context of full-scale moral panics around 'hooligan' youths (the 'mods' versus 'rockers' riots, and, in the later 1960s, student protests), crime, pornography, drugs and excessive 'permissiveness' in general, that the image of the beleaguered 'silent majority' which was not adequately represented within the official electoral system was first constructed. The 'signification spiral', which according to Hall *et al.* accompanied the typical moral panic, is remarkably similar to the overall logic of Powellism. Whereas the 'moral entrepreneurs' linked a specific moral issue to other social problems – such as the equation of student activism with a-political hooliganism – Powellism constructed an entire chain of associations around the black immigrant – so that the black immigrant appeared to be inextricably linked with unemployment, inadequate social services, the decline of the British inner cities and so on. The moral panics of the 1960s were organized around imaginary thresholds of tolerance; invariably, these limits were threatened with violation or had already been violated. Sexual 'permissiveness', for example, was supposed to lead to nothing less than the complete destruction of British society. With Powellism, the limits were of course no less imaginary and no less historical; they were the national borders themselves which were endlessly re-created through official immigration policies. The moral entrepreneurs and Powell equally viewed the 'permissive' and 'tolerant' intellectual as the unknowing mouthpiece, or even the treasonous promoter, of the subversive forces. Hall *et al.*'s description of the moral backlash against the 'permissive' intellectuals could also be applied to Powellism: 'the soft, misguided "liberals" leading an innocent public into decadence, the "hard core" mopping up in their wake, as moral life sank into a den of iniquity ... the hunt for "subversive minorities" and "liberal dupes" had begun'.[45] In both the moral panic discourse and Powellism, a counter-imaginary was constructed in which the dire consequences of the failure to deal with the threat to the social order were graphically symbolized. In both cases, sensationalistic accounts of the total breakdown of social order in the United States provided the stage for this counter-imaginary. Finally, both the moral panics and Powellism produced specific demands for 'firm steps': the enhanced empowerment of the state and the deployment of an authoritarian response.

Racist interpretations of two specific events in 1967 and 1968 renewed popular concerns around black immigration and prepared the way for a specifically Powellian 'signification spiral'. The demonstrations and riots which followed the assassination of Martin Luther King on 4 April 1968 were apprehensively received in the British press. *The Times* reported that the riots were a 'black rampage that subjected the U.S. to the most widespread spasm of racial disorder in its violent history'.[46] Powell reiterated the popular representation of black militancy as a foreign invader from the United States. On 20 April, he argued that 'that tragic and intractable phenomenon which we watch with horror on the other side of the Atlantic ... is coming upon us here by our own volition and our own neglect'.[47]

A small influx of Asians from Kenya was also defined as a danger-ous foreign invasion. Imperial patterns of migration and the his-torical legacy of indentured labour had led to the settlement of Asians in East Africa. During the process of de-colonization, the British government had agreed with the first independent Kenyan government in 1963 that those in Kenya who held British passports would be given the chance to retain their British citizenship. In 1967, the Kenyan government announced that any person who had not taken up Kenyan citizenship could only remain in Kenya on a temporary basis. About 7,000 Kenyan Asians emigrated to Britain each year between 1964 and 1966, and 8,443 entered Britain between January and September of 1967. Net figures for 1967, however, show that there was a net emigration from Britain of 84,000. The immi-gration of the Kenyan Asians – who remained British passport-holders – was nevertheless portrayed by Powell and others as nothing less than a national emergency.

It was in the context of these developments – the official legiti-mation of racism through immigration legislation, coupled with a weak 'multiculturalism' discourse and the censorship of explicit racial discourse; increasing socio-economic tensions; a growing sense of alienation from the political system, political polarization and the rise of extra-parliamentary activism; the organization of single-issue anti-permissiveness movements on the right; and the demonization of American black activism and Kenyan Asian immi-gration as foreign invasions – that Powell emerged as a tremendous-ly popular spokesperson for the anti-black immigration lobby. The bi-partisan consensus approach on socio-economic issues, including black immigration, operated hegemonically: alternatives were ruled out as unthinkably divisive. While the official leaders focused on economic problems, tensions increasingly gathered around issues which were not included on the official agenda. Powell's anti-black immigration campaign ultimately challenged the entire hegemonic consensus discourse.

Although he spoke about race on many occasions in the late 1960s, it was his speech at the Birmingham Conservative Political Centre on

20 April 1968 which won him enormous support and extensive media coverage. This address has been informally named as Powell's 'rivers of blood' speech because of the analogy which Powell drew between himself and the ancient Roman who saw the Tiber foaming with blood. Powell's 'rivers of blood' speech was timed to coincide with a debate on new race relations legislation. The Labour government's Race Relations Bill (1968) was once again linked with specifically black immigration controls. In response to Powell's campaign around the Kenyan Asians, and to the demands for new controls by the Tory shadow cabinet, the government passed the Commonwealth Immigrants Act in February 1968. This law restricted the entry of British passport-holders only to those who had been born in the United Kingdom or who had a father or grandfather who had been born in the United Kingdom. These patriarchal blood ties with Britain were called 'patriality' rights. Because of the timing of de-colonization and the post-colonial migrations, the birthplace distinctions operated as explicitly racial distinctions, separating the white English offspring of the colonizers from the colonized. Individual 'non-patrial' British passport-holders had to apply for one of the 1,500 work vouchers. The dependants of already settled Commonwealth immigrants were also subjected to new restrictions.

The Race Relations Bill, which was introduced in April, was supposed to assure equal opportunity for black Britons in employment and housing. Powell believed that the bill would legitimate reverse discrimination and would punish white Britons for their 'natural' expression of hostility towards the black invaders. Although the shadow cabinet agreed with Powell to vote against the bill, his disregard of his party leadership was such that he virtually ignored the official Conservative strategy; he delivered his 'rivers of blood' speech on the Saturday before the Race Relations Bill debate. Powell deliberately timed the speech, and designed it around explosive metaphorical constructions, to achieve maximum coverage in the Sunday newspapers.

Powell's speech is centred on two main devices. First, Powell graphically portrays the Labour government's discourse on race as censorial, absurd, illogical, divisive and dangerous. In his introductory remarks, for example, he states that the most unpopular and yet 'most necessary' task for the politician is the 'discussion of future grave but, with effort now, avoidable evils'. He then situates himself as the spokesperson for one of his white constituents, a 'quite ordinary working man'. He reports that his constituent had pledged to settle his children overseas and had then stated, 'In this country in fifteen or twenty years time the black man will have the whip hand over the white man.' The 'whip hand' metaphor dramatically invokes the conception of authority reversal: with post-colonial immigration and the dangerous pro-tolerance measures of the government, the whip had passed from the white hand – the hand of the plantation slave-owner and his white English descendants – to the black hand. Powell interrupts his account of his discussion with his constituent to consider the effects of his own speech. He situates himself as the courageous truth-teller who, in the name of 'the people', will openly express that which has been hegemonically suppressed as the unspeakable:

> I can already hear the chorus of execration. How dare I say such a thing? How dare I stir up trouble and inflame feelings by repeating such a conversation? The answer is that I do not have the right not to do so. ... What he is saying, thousands and hundreds of thousands are saying and thinking.[48]

Through this structure, Powell takes on the role of the organic intellectual: he promises to resist the censorship of the truth by the mainstream political leaders to liberate the repressed confessions of 'the people'.

Powell reiterated his populist claim to speak for 'the people', in defiance of official censorship, in his 16 November 1968 speech on black immigration. Once again, Powell insists that he speaks for both his white and black constituents. He states that the negative reaction to his anti-black immigration campaign revealed a 'deep and dangerous gulf in the nation': not between the 'indigenous popu-lation' and 'the [black] immigrants', but between 'the people' and the nation's political and intellectual leaders.

> I mean the gulf between the overwhelming majority of people throughout the country on the one side, and on the other side a tiny minority, with almost a monopoly hold upon the channels of communication, who seem determined not to know the facts and not to face the realities and who will resort to any device or extremity to blind both themselves and others.[49]

Powell often underlined his populist claims by reading directly from his constituents' letters. In the 'rivers of blood' speech, he recites excerpts from a letter which was supposedly sent to him by a woman constituent. The true origin of this text is of course irrelevant in terms of its effects. By switching into the voice of the letter-writer,

Powell distances himself from the letter's actual content. This device allows Powell to deploy the 'neutral representative' strategy which is central to New Right discourse. Griffiths, Powell and Thatcher often claimed to be merely quoting 'the people' when they made their most racist remarks, just as Dame Jill Knight and other anti-queer extremists claimed to be only reflecting 'normal' opinion. Having constructed extremist bigotry as the voice of the majority, they sometimes even agreed that the racists and anti-queer bigots were 'going too far'. They nevertheless insisted on the 'natural'-ness and validity of extremist bigotry, and argued that it was the very targets of racist and anti-queer discourse who were to blame for the escalation of these antagonisms in the first place. In other words, by speaking as the representative of 'the people', the New Right intellectuals could disown their own extremism and position themselves as moderate officials who could resolve the potential disruption of national unity. They could even argue: We know very well that 'the people' are exaggerating some of their claims about blacks and queers, but they are on the whole sensible people; we must remove the cause of their natural concerns.

In his 16 November 1968 speech, for example, Powell presents a long list of grievances from his white constituents about the behaviour of their black neighbours. He explicitly admits that 'there is no reason to suppose that [blacks] are more malevolent or more prone to wrong-doing'. He nevertheless argues that this is 'not the point'. 'With the malefactors among our own people we have got to cope; they are our own responsibility and part of our own society. It is something totally different when the same or similar activities are perpetrated by strangers.'[50] It was the supplementary 'stranger' status of the black immigrant, and not the behaviour of the black populations themselves, which supposedly provoked the concerns of the white constituents. No amount of counter-truths about the personal standards and law-abiding behaviour in the black communities could disrupt Powell's claim to represent the 'natural' views of the 'silent majority'. All he needed to do was to find the same proportion of criminals among blacks that could be found among whites to support his argument.

In his 'rivers of blood' speech, Powell juxtaposes his populist truth-telling with a second device: the representation of black immigration to post-colonial Britain as a dangerous inversion of frontiers. In this respect, Powell's selection of this particular letter, from the hundreds of letters which he received on black immigration, is highly significant. In the passage which he quotes in his speech, the letter-writer tells a supposedly true story about a 'white woman old-age pensioner'. She lives on a 'respectable' street in Wolverhampton. She 'lost' her husband and both her sons in the war and now must support herself. After turning her family home, her 'only asset', into a boarding-house, she managed to establish a relatively secure income.[51] The fate of the elderly white woman and her house are central to the narrative in the letter, but these figures also play an important metaphorical role. The house in the story metaphorically represents the nation itself, with the woman as the spirit of the white British people; we re-live the experience of post-war recovery through her story. With the loss of the male soldiers in the family, Britishness is separated from the violence of its war-time and imperialist past; all that remains is an ageing feminine innocence. In his study of racist whites' complaints about blacks, Foot found that the alleged victims of black wrongs were often 'old ladies'.[52] A community liaison officer of the Oxford Committee for Racial Integration commented that the entire story in Powell's speech was repeated to her by a white complainant.[53] The fact that the story is taken from racist folklore which plays on myths around masculine chivalry and feminine victimization does not of course diminish its role as a political parable.

The letter-writer continues her story: 'the [black] immigrants moved in', the woman's white tenants 'regretfully' moved out, one house after another was 'taken over', the tranquillity of the street is replaced by 'noise and confusion' and the pensioner becomes the last white person in her street. The description of the street's decline is organized around an extremely rich set of supplementary metaphors. The 'outsiders', the black immigrants, are represented as vicarious invaders: the newcomers attempt to invade the house and to take the place of the pensioner. The black neighbours ask to use her phone and become abusive when she refuses. The enquiries of black tenants and home-buyers are depicted as sinister threats. The pensioner becomes afraid to go to the shops, and when she does, she is surrounded by 'wide-grinning piccaninnies' who call her a 'racialist'. The pensioner retreats to her home, and her telephone becomes her 'lifeline'.[54] Her retreat dramatically symbolizes white Britons as a besieged minority. Whereas she is cut off from her white community by the insidious black presence which has 'taken over' her street, the vital socio-economic links which bind the white British culture together were – in Powell's view – being destroyed by the black invader. The black invader figure – in its aggressive behaviour and in the absence of virtually any reference to black femininity – takes on a masculine predatory character, and the pensioner's helplessness and white femininity are heightened even further. Powell's account subtly invokes the entire imperial mythology of the black rapist who preys upon white women. The urge to protect the pensioner from the invading blackness consequently takes on the racist and misogynist force of a lynch mob.

The boundaries of the pensioner's home are ultimately violated. 'Windows are broken. She finds excreta pushed through her letter-box.'[55] The failure of the protective boundaries around the pensioner represents the failure of the British national borders in the face of post-colonial black immigration. For Powell, the reference to excrement is not unusual. He also links excrement with black immigrants in another speech. He reads a letter from a doctor which tells the story of a young white English couple who are 'intimidated out of their flat by their [black] landlord by verbal abuse and filth smeared on and around their toilet'.[56] In Foot's study of racist complaints, racist whites often associated blacks with excrement, refuse, blocked drains, public urination, prostitution, obscene language, uncontrolled sex, strong and unpleasant food odours, noisy parties and the use of black children by black parents to express their hatred of whites.[57] This chain of equivalences in a sense reproduces the colonial representation of blacks as childlike savages who refuse to become 'civilized' through the regulation of their bodies. Black bodies in the new racism, and queer bodies in Thatcherite anti-queer discourse, always exceed their 'proper' limits.

In the context of Powell's 'rivers of blood' speech, however, the excrement signifier also represents the post-colonial inversion of national orifices. Powell's speech is a response to the new wave of racist anxieties around the Kenyan Asian immigration. The Kenyan Asians were the unwanted 'residue' who were being expelled by an African government. Under imperial rule, it was nourishment – goods purchased under the favourable imperial agreements – which was extracted from the colonies and admitted into Britain. Unwanted populations flowed only in the opposite direction: convicts were sent, for example, to Australia, and religious outcasts fled to the Americas. The failure of the house's orifices –the letter-box, the front door and the telephone – to regulate the flow of nourishment and waste and to protect the pensioner from the black invasion metaphorically represents the failure of Britain's national boundaries after de-colonization.

It should also be noted that in terms of actual housing standards, the equivalence of black immigrants with excrement is deeply ironic. For many of the blacks who moved into previously all-white neighbourhoods, it was the white Britons who were uncivilized. The houses which the black immigrants bought often had inadequate plumbing facilities. A comprehensive housing study revealed that the newcomers usually improved the value of their houses: they often added the first indoor lavatory, modern sink or bath to the structure.[58]

Trapped within her failing home in the midst of a racial invasion, the pensioner then turns to her local government and asks for a reduction in her rates (local taxes). An official, a 'young girl', deals with her request. The 'young girl' advises her to let some rooms in her house. When the pensioner explains that the 'only people she could get were negroes', the 'young girl' replies, 'Racial prejudice won't get you anywhere in this country.' As a young person, she represents the naive and even dangerous pro-tolerance approach of official discourse. Through her gendered voice, Powell feminizes the pro-tolerance Labour Party, just as the Thatcherites homosexualize the left through the promotion of homosexuality crisis. Powell's misogynist and heterosexist abjection of the feminine and his denigration of socialism are combined in this passage to reinforce his racist representations. With the placement of the state's affairs in a naive young girl's hands, rather than those of chivalrous adult men, the nation's most valued capital – the white women who are exchanged between white men – is exposed to the risk of black violation.

Anti-racism is also expressed in the voice of a bureaucrat who cannot understand the realities of the pensioner's situation. The abstract terms of the young girl's warning contrast sharply with the rich detail of the pensioner's story. Powell associated the anti-discrimination policies of the Labour government with the worst forms of communist authoritarianism; for him, only the right-wing political intellectuals actually practised democratic principles and listened to 'the people'. The story ends as the letter-writer abruptly shifts from her narrative to the political moral: 'When the new Race Relations Bill is passed, this woman is convinced she will go to prison. And is she so wrong? I begin to wonder.'[59] Ultimately, the real enemy is the Labour government which is supposedly allowing

unlimited black immigration and passing laws which criminalize the
expression of natural racist sentiments.

Powell reiterated his supplemental representation of blackness as
a vicarious invader in his 16 November 1968 speech. In his statements regarding the actual numbers of black peoples in the United
Kingdom, Powell argues that a qualitative change in the impact of
black immigration occurs whenever the quantities of incoming
blacks become 'excessive'. He states, for example, that even though
blacks are not 'more prone to wrong-doing', it is perfectly reasonable for white Britons to become intolerant towards their black
neighbours 'above all when [the black wrongs] occur in the course
of an increase in the numbers of those strangers and an extension of
the areas which they occupy.' He offers an analogy between black
immigration and the settlement of large numbers of archbishops.

> If it were known in my home village that the Archbishop of
> Canterbury were coming to live here, we should undoubtedly
> ring a peal on the church bells. If it were known that five arch-
> bishops were coming, I should still expect to see my neigh-
> bours exchanging excited congratulations at the street corners.
> But if it were known that 50 archbishops were coming, there
> would be a riot.[60]

The race-neutral analogy, and the highly revered status of the
analogous object – the archbishops – masks Powell's overall
strategy. Because the black populations are supposed to become
more dangerous to the British people insofar as they enter the
country in greater numbers and remain concentrated in specific
areas, Powell effectively represents black immigration like a viral
infection. He discusses the allegedly higher birthrate among the
black population in great detail. He agrees that insofar as an 'immigrant element [is] thoroughly absorbed into a host population, [it
will] tend to have the same birth rate'. He nevertheless insists that
the black population in Britain has not been sufficiently integrated,
and that they have consequently not changed their less civilized
sexual 'habits'.

> To suppose that the habits of the great mass of [black] immi-
> grants, living in their own communities, speaking their own
> languages and maintaining their native customs, will change
> appreciably in the next two or three decades is a supposition so
> grotesque that only those could make it who are determined
> not to admit what they know to be true or not to see what they
> fear.[61]

The viral cycle of the enemy population is therefore self-perpetuating: as blacks arrive in larger numbers, they are less likely to become assimilated, more likely to reproduce at a higher rate and more likely to resist integration in the future. Powell's numerous references to immigration statistics and birthrates reveal his profound anxiety regarding black male virility and black female fecundity. It was only with the neutralization of this sexual potency through assimilation, like the absorption of a virus through an immune system response, that the black body's sexual threat to the British nation could be overcome. This image of the enemy's body as a self-perpetuating virus lodged within the body of the normal, threatening to burst the fragile boundaries between the two bodies, thereby endangering the very life of the normal through lethal contamination, would of course become central to the hegemonic representations of gay male bodies in the context of the 1980s AIDS panic.

Powell underlines his argument that the black populations continued to resist assimilation in the conclusion of his speech: 'The West Indian or Asian does not, by being born in England, become an Englishman. In law he becomes a United Kingdom citizen by birth; in fact he is a West Indian or an Asian still.' He argues that the black immigrants were not individuals who had 'uprooted' themselves from their homelands. Because of their social ties with their relatives who remained abroad, Powell argues that 'it is much nearer the truth to think in terms of detachments from communities in the West Indies or India or Pakistan encamped in certain areas of England'.[62] In this passage, Powell's representation of the black immigrant as a supplemental 'outsider' figure takes yet another form. He points to the financial remittances sent by the black workers to their relatives abroad, and argues that the scale of this outflow of capital 'would astonish anyone not closely acquainted with the actual phenomenon of Commonwealth immigration in this country'. Through these statements, the black immigrant becomes not only a dangerous invader, a black rapist who violates white mothers, an aggressive masculine shit which forces its way into the feminine mouth and a lethal viral infection, but a leech-like parasite as well.

The representation of the black immigrant as a nutrition-draining parasite is particularly significant in the post-colonial context. The perverse reversal of the imperial boundaries is completed as the unwanted foreign populations install themselves in the heartland of the 'mother country's' body and establish the flow of nutrients back to the foreign bodies. This representation totally obscures the exploitation of the peripheral economies by the metropole, which occurs wherever adult workers who have been raised and educated abroad are employed. By bringing in adult immigrant workers, British capital does not have to bear the costs of reproducing their labour.[63] The original cost of rearing and educating these workers was borne by the already under-developed peripheral economies. Although it is true that the immigrant workers' remittances to their friends and relatives who remained in their countries of origin became an important source of capital for the peripheral economies, these payments were made out of the wages earned by the immigrant workers, and not out of the profits of their employers. The exportation of these savings did of course constitute a loss in terms of the British balance of payments, but it was far outshadowed by other outflows, such as foreign investment and the importation of consumer luxury goods.

The real 'leech' in Powell's account was therefore British capital: through racist discrimination, the immigrant workers were even more exploited than their white counterparts, and the peripheral economies were never compensated for the enormous cost of producing the adult labourer in the first place. With the introduction of the 1962 immigration controls which specifically admitted professionals and skilled workers, and barred unskilled workers from entry, the costs to the peripheral economies escalated further. The workers whose reproduction costs were the highest – the doctors, dentists, nurses, teachers, technicians and so on who had the most education and training – and whose skills were vital to the peripheral economies were lost forever to the metropole, while the unemployed unskilled workers were not allowed to emigrate with them. Immigration controls in this sense actually restored the imperial organic system: 'nutrients' – the adult skilled workers and professionals – were withdrawn from the periphery, all other elements – the deported and repatriated immigrants, and the unsuccessful applicants – were rejected as unwanted 'waste', and the periphery was locked within this organic system – through the 'first world's' underdevelopment of the 'third world' – so that it could not escape.

The effectiveness of Powell's populist representations became evident immediately after his 'rivers of blood' speech on 20 April 1968. Headlines in the *Sun* and the *London Evening Standard* read: 'Immigration: the Powell Explosion' and 'Race: Powell's Bombshell'. Powell's legitimization of the 'natural' racist resentment against the black peoples in Britain struck a chord throughout the electorate. Schoen emphasizes the novelty and importance of Powell's populist strategy: 'One of the country's leading political figures, a man of Cabinet rank and experience with a powerful aura of cerebral severity, had made all his own the cause of the pubs and clubs, the bingo-halls and the football terraces.'[64] Edward Heath, the Leader of the Conservative Party, and his Shadow Cabinet did not disagree substantially with Powell. Heath himself called for voluntary 're-patriation' of black immigrants and further racially structured immigration controls in a *News of the World* article on 21 April. It was the populist style of Powell's campaign, and Powell's implicit challenge to the party leadership, which irritated Heath. Heath dismissed Powell from the Tory Shadow Cabinet for making a speech which he considered as 'racialist in content and liable to exacerbate racial tension'. Powell responded with a letter which received headline coverage across the country. Powell charged that Heath often gave the impression that he play[ed] down and even [unsaid] policies and views which [Heath] held to be right for fear of clamour from some sections of the press or public. The entire Shadow Cabinet agreed with Heath's decision to dismiss Powell. Schoen estimates that no more than forty-five of the Conservative MPs continued to support Powell. The majority of the Tory parliamentary party believed that he had damaged the Conservatives' reputation. Several members of the free market lobby abandoned Powell because of his racist extremism.[65]

The leading Conservatives' disapproval of Powell's speech stood in marked contrast to his tremendous popular support. London dockers and meat porters – traditional Labour voters – marched on Parliament in protest against Powell's dismissal.[66] Between 60 per cent and 75 per cent of the electorate agreed with what they regarded as Powell's view on black immigration, and disagreed with Heath's decision. Analysts found that these views did not vary significantly across class, party, age or regional differences. Opinion polls also found that opposition against the Race Relations Bill increased after Powell's speech: while 53 per cent approved of the bill earlier in the month (April 18–21), only 30 per cent did so after Powell's speech (April 26–29). Powell received 105,000 letters of support in only the first week after the speech. In a May 1968 poll, 74 per cent stated that they agreed with the speech, 69 per cent stated that Heath was wrong to dismiss Powell from the Shadow Cabinet, and 24 per cent stated that they preferred Powell to succeed Heath as Leader of the Conservative Party.[67] Violent attacks on blacks increased dramatically directly after Powell's speech, just as 'queer-bashing' would suddenly increase during the AIDS hysteria and Clause 28 debates almost twenty years later.

The black immigrant as the prototypical enemy within: Powell and the Conservative Party, 1970–4

Although the Labour government pursued various initiatives in the name of racial tolerance, such as the second Race Relations Act and an inner-city development scheme, it also closely followed the Conservatives in a further shift to the Powellian right on immigration. After Powell proposed a government programme for the voluntary 'repatriation' of black immigrants to their countries of origin, the Home Secretary James Callaghan stated, 'The Social Security Minister will now repatriate *any* immigrant family that is unable to pay for itself and wants to return home.'[68] When Powell demanded a total ban on black immigration, including the dependants of already settled immigrants, Heath responded with a call for further anti-black immigration controls, and the Labour government introduced a new entry certificate scheme for Commonwealth dependants.

The 1970 election campaign began without any significant statement on race or immigration by either party leadership. Labour and the Conservatives had developed a 'tacit understanding between [themselves] to smother a controversial debate on race'.[69] When Powell published his Election Address on 30 May, calling for a total ban on immigration and rejecting Heath's pro-Common Market stance, Heath merely stated, 'Mr. Powell isn't saying anything that he hasn't said before.'[70] Once again, the parties formed an almost complete consensus on race and attempted to suppress open debate, thereby allowing Powell to strengthen his populist stance.

The bi-partisan silence on race was broken by Tony Benn, a Labour MP. On 3 June, Benn accused Powell of mounting a fascist campaign against black immigrants, and attacked Heath for remaining silent on racism and immigration. However, because Labour had already joined with the Conservatives in shifting the centrist, 'moderate' and official position towards the Powellian right, Benn's argument was left exposed as unthinkably radical. When asked to comment on Benn's speech, the Prime Minister Harold Wilson 'made it clear that the speech, electorally, was very damaging to Labour, that he had not known of it in advance, and that, had he known of it he would have had the offending passages removed'. On 11 June, Powell spoke about black immigration in Wolverhampton. He alleged that the British people were being misled about immigration statistics, and that 'there are at this moment parts of this town which have ceased to be part of England'. The next morning, Heath changed his tactics and devoted a press conference to 'a matter of the utmost importance, which is that of immigration and race relations in Britain'. He implicitly attacked Powell by stating that he had a far less pessimistic view of race relations, but nevertheless outlined the Conservatives' proposals for the 'strictest possible control of immigration'.[71] On 12 June, the Conservatives remained 12.4 per cent behind Labour in the polls.

On 13 June, Powell delivered his 'enemies within' speech in Northfield, Birmingham. Powell's antagonistic distinction between the white British 'victims' of black immigration and the treasonous intellectual supporters of the black 'invasion' and 'reverse discrimination' is central to this speech. He expands the chain of enemy figures to include the radical student movement, the Northern Irish civil rights movement, black activists, the pro-third world lobby and the anti-apartheid movement. He argues that this bloc of enemies is more dangerous than Imperial Germany and the Nazis had been because it is 'invisible or disguised'. He claims that these extra-parliamentary forces on the left aim at nothing less than 'revolution' and the 'actual destruction of nation and society as we know or can imagine them'.[72]

Powell underlines the primarily intellectual character of the 'enemies within': he states that they deploy 'psychological weaponry' and engage in 'anarchist brainwashing'. Using their hegemonic grip on the 'organs of communication', the 'enemies within' repeat strategic 'absurdities' until the 'will' of the 'victims' is broken. The British are thereby made to think and to say untruths, and are made to forget and to leave unsaid the truth. Again, it is the 'permissive' intellectual, and not the 'enemy' group itself, which poses the greatest threat. The leading newspapers, for example, are singled out for their criticism of Powellian racism. 'Newspapers like the *Sunday Times* denounce it as "spouting the fantasies of racial purity" to say that a child born of English parents in Peking is not Chinese but English, or that a child born of Indian parents in Birmingham is not English but Indian.' The leaders of both parties are criticized for ignoring the issue of black immigration and for becoming 'mesmerized into accepting from the enemy the slogans of "racialist" and "unChristian" and applying them to lifelong political colleagues'. Academics and church leaders are also attacked for their support for educational reforms and aid to the third world.[73]

With this attack on the intellectual elite, Powell's speech can be located in a right-wing British tradition which extends back to Burke.[74] Like Burke, Powell inverts the democratic/anti-democratic distinction. The leftist intellectuals who speak in the name of democracy actually threaten to impose an unjust and artificial programme onto 'the people'. The advance of the left would therefore entail the suppression of 'the people's' truths, which they had slowly formulated through the experience of uninterrupted generations. The triumph of the left would actually mean the defeat of 'the people', for it would bring about the destruction of their natural hierarchy – the very principle of their entire way of life. In Powell's own terms, the leftist intellectual is like a 'social engineer' who treats the British like 'pawns or counters'.[75] Powell invokes the Burkean tradition by championing the 'truths' of 'the people's' experience, and by representing leftist movements as sinister authoritarian forces.

If revolutionary subversion essentially originates in France for Burke, it is the United States which constitutes the source of subversive otherness for Powell. In describing the evils of student activism, for example, Powell first asserts that American universities have become the 'permanent scene of violence and disorder'. He claims that they have fallen from the 'control of authority' and that they 'only exist and are administered upon terms dictated by the enemy'. He then argues that the 'same enemy in his student manifestation' has 'terrorized' various European cities and has 'brought down one of the strongest European governments'. He finally states, 'In this country we have seen the institutes of learning systematically threatened, browbeaten and held up to ridicule by the organizers of disorder.' By the very order of his statements, which move from the United States to Europe to Britain, Powell emphasizes his basic argument that firm measures must be taken to stop the British revolutionary forces from imitating their European and American counterparts. Powell also refers to civil disturbances in American cities and to the ways in which 'crowd behaviour' has had an undue influence on the American government.

> We have seen one city after another in the United States engulfed in fire and fighting, as the material for strife provided by the influx of Negroes into the Northern States, and their increase there, was flung into the furnace of anarchy.[76]

This construction of a counter-fantasy – the image of the United States as nothing but anarchical chaos thanks to the effects of student and black activism – plays a dual role. It serves, first, as an apocalyptic warning about the consequences of allowing the revolutionaries' advance. Second, its representation of subversion as an essentially foreign element operates as a support for Powell's phantasmatic erasure of the antagonisms which are organic to Britain. The British fascination with the breakdown in American society continues to this day; the supplements to the weekend newspapers often include sensationalistic stories about inner-city crime, racial antagonisms and 'political correctness' in the United States.

The seditious imitators of the American and European revolutionaries are, for Powell, essentially opportunistic. Where the real enemy in the 'rivers of blood' speech was the Labour government, which cynically exploits black immigration to promote its 'permissive' agenda, Powell's real enemy in this speech is the leftist intellectual who seizes upon 'natural' racial antagonisms to promote her cause. In the final analysis, Powell has to reconcile his image of blacks as essentially backward and uncivilized figures with his representation of the tremendous advance of the 'enemies within': the black immigrant may, in her simple presence, pose a lethal threat to the nation, but she herself lacks the intellectual cunning to transform that threat into an actual campaign. Powell states:

> 'Race' is billed to play a major, perhaps a decisive, part in the battle of Britain, whose enemies must have been unable to believe their good fortune as they watched the numbers of West Indians, Africans and Asians concentrated in her major cities mount towards the two million mark, and no diminution of the increase yet in sight.[77]

Powell's placement of the term, 'race', between quotation marks in his written manuscript should not be confused with the use of similar punctuation by post-structuralists such as Gates. Where Gates marks his challenge to racial essentialism through this notation,[78] Powell's strategy is entirely different. He states:

> The most perfect, and the most dangerous, example of this process [of anarchist brainwashing] is the subject miscalled and deliberately miscalled, 'race'. The people of this country are told that they must feel neither alarm nor objection to a West Indian, African or Asian population which will rise to several millions being introduced into this country. If they do, they are 'prejudiced', 'racialist', 'unChristian' and 'failing to show an

example to the rest of the world'. .... It is even heresy to assert the plain fact that the English are a white nation.[79]

Powell wants to shift the terrain of his argument on black immigration from race – where the liberal pro-tolerance discourse had made considerable advances in defining the limits of the sayable – to nation – where Powell faced very little opposition. Powell's fusion of the terms 'white British nation' was actually supported, rather than contradicted, by the Labour government's official discourse, namely in the form of its racially defined immigration legislation. His attempt to weaken the racial character of his argument, so that he appears to be saying, 'We British would resist any invader; they just happen to be black', further legitimizes his discourse in the face of anti-racist criticism. It also supports his construction of an entire chain of enemy figures: if the enemy is only accidentally black, then other elements, regardless of their race, might join forces with the black enemy. Powell's point here is that apparently white Britons (their whiteness of course becomes suspect to the extent that they engage in subversion) can be just as dangerous as the black American revolutionary or the black immigrant in Britain. The subversive white Briton can be even more dangerous: because her otherness is invisible, she can penetrate Britain's key institutions much more effectively than her black comrades.

For Powell, it is the entire discourse around race which serves as the transnational mode of transmission of the American 1960s 'revolution' to Britain. He states, 'the exploitation of what is called "race" is a common factor which links the operations of the enemy on several different fronts'. He then describes, in the sensationalistic terms quoted above, the development of racial antagonisms in the United States. Finally, he suggests that the enemies within Britain are watching the increasing numbers of black immigrants settle in the country's major cities with keen anticipation. For Powell, it is the racialized distortion of the 'plain facts' around immigration which constitutes the 'most perfect' and 'most dangerous' 'example' of 'anarchist brainwashing'. Because Powell holds that radical black activism originates in the United States, he implicitly argues that it is through the imitation of these American blacks that the British intellectuals have learned their new subversive strategies. Once again, Powell forgets the importance of colonial ties. While the black civil liberties and black power movements in Britain were influenced by their American counterparts, British blacks also looked to the contemporary struggles and historical traditions of resistance in Asia, Africa and the Caribbean for their political inspiration.

For the majority of Powell's audience, however, the references to racial antagonisms in the United States and the emergence of the new activist movements in Britain struck a strong and deep chord. In the late 1960s, numerous anti-'permissiveness' campaigners, newspaper editors and television producers created the sense that anarchy reigned in the United States and that Britain itself faced a new, bewildering and deeply threatening series of attacks. In Powell's discourse, American radical black activism and black immigration operate as the sources, the prototypes and the exemplars of this entire attack. In other words, Powell constructs black activism and black immigration as the *point de capiton*, the signifier which retroactively gives an apparently chaotic field of elements a meaningful structure.[80] Powell not only paid attention to the emerging social antagonisms which had been more or less excluded from the official agenda of the election campaign, he offered an entire explanatory structure for their emergence, and constructed that explanation around the racial terms which had already been legitimized by both of the major party leaderships.

Again, the timing of Powell's speech was crucial. It drew headlines in all the Sunday papers, and it was featured as the leading story in the *Sunday Mirror*, the *Sunday People* and the *News of the World*. A Conservative Party private poll showed that 48 per cent of the electorate had heard about the speech, and 67 per cent agreed that Powell had 'made sense'.[81] *The Times* declared that Powell's speeches on 11 and 13 June had 'dealt the Tory leader's new-style election campaign a serious body blow. For Labour, it is an unsolicited gift.'[82] The Conservatives had shifted substantially towards strong law-and-order policies at their Selsdon Park conference before the election. Heath nevertheless used Powell's speeches to represent the Conservatives as both anti-black immigration and pro-multicultural tolerance. Having already declared his substantial support for Powell's demand for a virtual ban on primary immigration and an official 'repatriation' scheme on 12 June, Heath nevertheless distanced himself from Powell in a statement issued on 14 June. He claimed that the Conservatives were advocating 'rational' and 'humane' policies, and stated, 'My colleagues in the Shadow Cabinet and I will never use words to support actions which exploit or intensify divisions in our society and so damage the interests of the nation as a whole.'[83]

The election was won later that week by the Conservatives with a majority of 31 seats and an overall swing to the Conservatives of 4.7 per cent. Harris Poll analysts suggest that in spite of Powell's attack on Heath's leadership, it is 'highly probable that on balance Powell helped the Conservative cause rather than damaged it'. They estimated that Benn committed 'one of the main blunders of the campaign' by 'bringing out the Powell issue', and that Heath would have lost more than he gained by dismissing Powell from the Conservative Party.[84] They also found that immigration was virtually the only policy area in which the voters had decisively preferred the Conservatives instead of Labour. Butler and Stokes concluded from their study that 'even if Mr. Powell was far from being the spokesman of the party, it is hard to doubt that he had succeeded in associating the Conservatives with opposition to immigration in the public mind'.[85] Powell himself received between 5,000 and 6,000 letters during and immediately after the election, and only 60 of them were critical of his views.[86] Throughout the election campaign, he received as much or even more national press attention than Wilson or Heath; one-fifth of the total election coverage in *The Times* was devoted to Powell alone.[87] Studlar found that the Tories had gained 6.7 per cent of the vote specifically because of their stronger stance on immigration, and commented that 'this is the first indication that a social issue could have the same impact on the British electorate that economic and class issues do.'[88] National Opinion Polls estimated that the last-minute swing to the Conservatives and the poor turn-out among Labour supporters was due largely to Powell's influence. One in five of the voters who had intended to support Labour stated that they had become more likely to vote Tory because of Powell's campaign. Of the non-voters, 65 per cent stated that they had been influenced by Powell, and seven out of eight of these abstainers reported that they had moved towards the Tories in response to Powell's speeches.[89]

In line with Heath's pre-election promise, Powell was firmly excluded from the new Tory cabinet. His popularity was not immediately affected by this ostracism: at the height of the 1972–3 panic over the Ugandan Asian immigrants, the Conservative leadership once again shifted its immigration policies towards Powell's position and Powell actually overtook Heath and narrowly trailed Wilson in the polls as a popular choice for prime minister.[90] However, Powell's support rapidly declined after he implied that he would support Labour because of its opposition to Britain's entry into the EEC, and subsequently refused to stand in the February 1974 election. Although Powell returned to parliament as an Ulster Unionist, and remained an outspoken critic on government policies, especially on the EEC and Northern Ireland, he became an increasingly marginal political figure.

Margaret Thatcher may have won the Conservative leadership in February 1975 on a technicality. Many Conservative backbench MPs would have preferred Powell if he had not betrayed the party by praising Labour's stance on Europe. If Heath had resigned immediately after the October 1974 defeat, William Whitelaw probably would have won.[91] Keith Joseph was the prominent leadership candidate from the party's right wing, but his bid was ruined when he made a disastrous speech on social class and eugenics.[92] In any event, it was Thatcher who championed the anti-black immigration, anti-nationalization, anti-collectivist, monetarist and pro-free enterprise policies which Powell had promoted for years. Powell had shown that a radical right-wing programme would be profoundly popular with large numbers of British voters, but he ultimately lacked the tactical skills to capitalize on his leadership potential.

The Powellian imaginary and Thatcherism

There were many important precedents for Powell's anti-black immigration campaign. The single-issue anti-'permissiveness' backlash had already brought several social and moral issues into the arena of public debate, and had already given shape to the popular sense that the existing political structure was not adequately responding to popular concerns. Powellism also drew upon the entire anti-immigration tradition which preceded the post-war migration of black peoples to Britain. Writing on the 'alien menace' in the early 1930s, A.H. Lane makes several Powellian-sounding charges against the immigrant population. He argues that immigrants take away housing and employment from settled Britons, draw on social services and benefits without contributing to the national economy, carry diseases and engage in unhygienic practices, foment social unrest and revolutionary plots, exploit British women through prostitution, run gambling dens and, most importantly, infiltrate and seize control of key industries, the financial system, the BBC, the film industry, the educational system – from elementary schools to the London School of Economics – and the 1929–31 Labour government. For Lane, however, the 'alien' enemy within of the 1930s consisted primarily of southern and East Euro-peans, Russian communists, Irish Catholics and German Jews. Lane makes virtually no mention of Africans and Afro-Caribbeans, and attacks only the leftist and Ghandhian Asians as anti-British enemies. He states:

> The policy of our Government is being dictated or inspired by foreigners bent on wrecking the British Empire and working in conjunction with Aliens and traitors living in it. Among those enemies are not only our avowed enemies the International bandits who, having enslaved the Russians, are working to expel the British from Asia and to stir up revolutions in every part of our Empire, but, also, Communists at all points of the globe; Germans thirsting to revenge the defeats inflicted by us and our allies on the Vaterland; certain International financiers; and the Brahmans.[93]

Powell's focus on specifically black immigrants does of course have some historical precedents: anti-black immigration legislation dates from Queen Elizabeth I's 1601 expulsion of the African 'Negroes and blackamoors' from England, and white seamen and stevedores rioted against the employment of Afro-Caribbeans in several ports in 1919. Asians and Africans were not, however, the main targets of immigration policies until the 1960s. Only the 1925 Special Restriction (Coloured Alien Seamen) Order had singled out black immigrants before this time, and it had had only a minor effect on migration flows.

Although scientific arguments in favour of the natural superiority of the 'advanced' white Christian Anglo-Saxon race over the 'back-ward' Asians, Africans and Caribbeans were widely accepted in Victorian society,[94] immigration discourse was organized around other figures. In the nineteenth century, it was the Irish immigrant who was demonized as lazy, diseased, criminal and immoral. The Russian and East European Jews who came to Britain in the late nineteenth and early twentieth centuries to escape persecution were the chief focus of immigration concerns before the Second World War. Lane's discourse in fact reflects the popular debate on Jewish immigration at the turn of the century. The Jewish worker was represented by the anti-alien lobby as peculiarly suited to survival on extremely low wages. Anxieties around the Jews' effects on the employment of low-skilled Britons escalated into full-scale demands for immigration controls. Although legislation sharply curtailed Jewish immigration at the outbreak of the First World War, the Jewish community was subjected to vicious attacks in the 1930s when anti-Semitic organizations such as Oswald Mosley's British Union of Fascists marched openly in the streets. Jewish refugees were refused entry into Britain throughout the 1930s, and 'enemy aliens' from within the settled British population were restricted in their movements, interned and deported to Canada and Australia. In some cases, the deportees were subjected to horrific abuse during their voyages.[95]

The immigration legislation of the 1960s therefore had an important precedent in the legal discourse on 'aliens' in the early twentieth century. Immigration was virtually unrestricted through the nineteenth century. The late-eighteenth-century controls were lifted after the Napoleonic Wars. The only significant piece of nineteenth-century immigration legislation was the 1870 Extradition Act, which merely provided for the deportation of criminals who were wanted in foreign countries. The 1905 Aliens Act marked a sharp departure from this laissez-faire tradition. Its ban on the entry of 'undesirable aliens' who came to Britain on 'immigrant ships' bearing more than twenty third-class passengers was specifically aimed at destitute Jewish refugees. Absolute powers were granted to the Home Office to prohibit any alien from landing, without appeal, in the war-time Aliens Restriction Act of 1914. In 1919, this Act was renewed without any substantial changes, and its provisions substantially remained in effect until the 1960s. The 1919 Aliens Restriction Act gave immigration officers and the Home Secretary complete authority to refuse entry or to deport any alien in the interests of the 'public good'. From Foot's accounts of the parliamentary debates on this law, it is clear that it was directed against the East European and German Jews first and foremost.[96] The 1960s anti-black immigration discourse is therefore not the first case in which popular bigotry against an internal enemy figure was legitimized in official immigration discourse. The 1960s controls were only unique in that they reconstructed the figure of the alien in the post-colonial context, so that the 'undesirable' Jew was displaced by the Commonwealth black. Many of the arguments in favour of controlling the non-white Commonwealth immigrants are directly analogous to those of the anti-Semitic, anti-alien lobby of the early twentieth century. In both cases, the response to the perceived threat to the national order by the incoming subversive element was the re-definition of the national body itself through the deployment of new frontiers.

Of all the anti-'permissive' movements of the 1960s, Powell's anti-black immigration campaign was unique in that it moved from a

single-issue movement to become one of the most important challenges to the hegemonic bi-partisan consensus discourse. The cross-
class dimension of the Powellian bloc was central to the force of this
challenge. At the height of his popularity in the late 1960s and early
1970s, Powell's support 'mirrored the electorate':[97] it spanned
virtually every class and geographical divide. Commenting on the
dockers' and meat porters' pro-Powell march to Parliament, *The
Economist* declared, 'Not in living memory have groups of workers
across the country gone on strike in favour of a Tory politician, as
they did for Enoch Powell.'[98] Other demonstrations in support of
Powell took place in Birmingham, Coventry, West Bromwich, South-
ampton, Southall, Nottingham, Gateshead, Norwich, Preston and
Tilbury. Virtually all of the trade union opposition against Powell
came from the shop-steward leadership rather than the rank and file.
In London, it was students, rather than workers, who faced the
dockers in counter-demonstrations.

We can assume that some of Powell's working-class supporters
already voted for the Conservatives before he launched his anti-
black immigration campaign. Political analysts generally estimate
that as much as one-third of the working class (defined in terms of
the Registrar-General's classifications) voted for the Conservatives in
the 1970s. There is, however, strong evidence that Powell's appeal
extended beyond this traditional Conservative voting bloc. Of the
voters who changed their vote from Labour to another party at the
1970 election, 53 per cent agreed with the survey statement: 'Powell
is the only politician I really admire in Britain.' Trade union and
non-trade union members were just as likely to agree with that
statement.[99] Thatcher owed much of her electoral success to the
support of skilled workers who had traditionally voted for Labour.
Powellism prepared some of the ground for this reorganization of
class allegiances by constructing a broad-based movement in the
1960s and 1970s.

Powell's cross-class appeal cannot be analysed in terms of the
scapegoat model. According to this model, racism emerges among
the economically insecure insofar as a non-white figure is successfully blamed for economic problems. The scapegoat explanation
takes the boundaries between inside spaces – the British nation – and
outsider figures – the black immigrant – for granted. It also cannot
explain the diversity of Powell's supporters. Powell's supporters did
not just include the unemployed and the middle-class voters who
believed that they faced declining incomes. Schoen's research shows

that the Powellians came from all economic backgrounds and that on the whole they were not particularly concerned about unemployment or their standard of living. The only factor which is common to almost all of Powell's supporters – besides their opposition to black immigration – is their sense that they were not adequately represented in the existing political system. Schoen argues that Powell's support should be analysed in two phases. In the first phase, 1968–70, Powellians did not express sentiments of alienation and disillusionment to any remarkable degree; they overwhelmingly backed Powell simply because of his anti-black immigration stance. In the second phase, 1970–5, Powell's support bloc became a diverse coalition of voters who were greatly dissatisfied with the political system as a whole. At a time when confidence in Heath and Wilson was at an all-time low across the electorate, Powellians demonstrated an even greater than average sense of alienation. Powellians were far more likely to say that it was difficult to see any difference between the Conservatives and Labour, that neither of the two leading parties represent the views of 'people like me', and that both the Conservatives and Labour had failed to solve the most important problems facing Britain. Schoen concludes that while 'racial conservatism' remained the strongest characteristic which united the Powellians, general disillusionment became the second most important variable in structuring attitudes towards Powell in the period leading up to the February 1974 election.[100]

The scapegoat model also cannot account for the political effect of racist movements. Powellism did not just blame the black immigrant for economic problems; it re-defined the entire political terrain by organizing a right-wing populist resistance against the hegemonic centre. Powellism was one of the key factors which led to the shift towards the right in both the Labour and Conservative parties in the 1970s. As Mercer argues, 'Powell did not "make racism respectable": he transformed the moral threshold of legitimacy itself.'[101] Powellism was not, of course, the only political force which promoted the dissolution of the hegemonic consensus discourse; underlying structural economic weaknesses and numerous social tensions would have remained intractable problems for the consensus leadership with or without him. The importance of Powellism lies both in its timing – its operation in the midst of a tremendous economic, social and national identity crisis – and in its construction of a radically new vision of British society which answered some of the most pressing questions around political representation.

In this sense, Powellism took the form not of an isolated demand, or an individual myth, but of an imaginary. Powell's phantasmatic reconstruction of Britain as a naturally white, antagonism-free and racially exclusionary space which was unaffected by de-colonization responded to the very concerns about national identity which had become unrepresentable in consensus discourse. Labour and Conservative governments did pass anti-black immigration legislation, but the two major parties did not grant race a prominent position on their official agendas. Where Labour did deploy the pro-tolerance strategy to counteract popular racism, this initiative was not sufficiently radical in its approach, and was undermined by Labour's own racist immigration laws. The key to the transformation of the Powellian demands into an imaginary which destabilized the consensus discourse lies in its populist form. A new vision of the social becomes an imaginary to the extent that it effectively represents itself as the only possible social order, rather than just one possible order among many alternatives.[102] Because Powell's supporters felt that the existing political structure was so unresponsive to their concerns, and that Powell was the only political leader who spoke for them, they regarded Powell not only as their leader on race and immigration, but as the only true symbol of democratic representation. Without this transformation, Powell would have remained a single-issue campaigner who could never have emerged as a challenger for the leadership of the Conservative Party.

The black immigrant was deployed in Powellian discourse as a prototypical symptom: it provided the discursive 'glue' which held Powell's vision together. It should be noted that after popular racist discourse had begun to coalesce around the black immigrant figure, the actual movements of black peoples became increasingly irrelevant to the effectiveness of racist representations. Many of Powell's initiatives, such as his opposition to the entry of the Kenyan Asians, dealt with the immigration of almost insignificant numbers of people. Like the disciplinary discourse's representation of the delinquent in Foucault's *Discipline and Punish*, Powell deployed the black immigrant figure in a manner which allowed his movement to profit from the 'failure' of immigration controls. Even the arrivals of small groups of black immigrants in the context of net migration outflows were used by Powell to promote the sense that the nation was being invaded, and that the mainstream politicians were not listening to 'the people'. Powellism's aim to close the nation against the influx of blackness was in this sense infinitely unobtainable. If Powell had succeeded in bringing in new legislation which barred every single non-white worker, dependant, student and tourist from entering the United Kingdom, and forcibly deported ('repatriated') every black Briton, the appeal of Powellism would not necessarily have diminished. In Eastern Europe, for example, anti-Semitism is now increasing in areas in which pogroms and the Holocaust have almost entirely wiped out the Jewish community. Anti-Semitic and racist discourses are quite capable of mobilizing resistance against Jewish and black cultural elements and 'ways of thinking' which are supposed to circulate like a cultural virus throughout vulnerable social groups. The threat of the enemy's return can also be used to represent a dominant social group as an endangered and beleaguered 'minority' even after the so-called enemy group has been brutally excluded. The argument that the political influence of racist movements such as Powellism can be effectively eliminated through the introduction of greater racist immigration controls should therefore be entirely rejected.

Because Powell was so much more than a single-issue campaigner, many regarded him as one of the most influential spokespersons for the New Right movement within the Conservative Party. The New Right strongly advocated a full-scale attack on the welfare state, a rejection of the 'socialist' consensus approach to economic problems and the elimination of 'permissiveness' in educational and state policies. New Right figures believed that the welfare state had removed the disciplinary mechanisms of unemployment and poverty, and had diluted the individual's sense of obligation to society. From this perspective, the increased affluence of working-class youth and the expansion of the welfare state only promoted moral corruption. Heath focused almost exclusively on economic strategies while the Conservatives were in opposition from 1964 to 1970. It was therefore the right wing of the party which actively engaged in the re-definition of Conservative positions on social issues. The New Right did not, of course, win control over the leadership of the party at this time, but it did exercise a great deal of influence over party policies. At the Selsdon Park conference in 1970, for example, the Conservatives adopted strong law-and-order policies and a much tougher stance towards the trade unions. They pledged to allow market forces to rule in industrial relations, housing, welfare and the distribution of income. Although they did not respond to Powell's call for the dismantling of all nationalized industries, the free operation of the exchange rates and a purely monetarist approach to the economy, the Conservatives took up many of the Powellian and New Right demands.[103]

The official racism of the 1970s differed from its 1960s precedent only in the site of its application: the black immigrant was displaced by the black criminal as the prototypical national enemy, while national frontiers and their immigration official guardians were increasingly supplemented by criminal laws and the policing, judicial and prison systems. Hall argues that race remained the 'framework through which the crisis [was] experienced [and] the means by which the crisis [was] to be resolved' in the 1970s.[104] Race became the primary means through which British politics shifted from the 'construction of consensus' of the 1950s and 1960s to the popular authoritarianism of the 1970s. The 'law and order' campaigns aimed primarily against the black criminal became a stage upon which the governing authorities could represent themselves as 'tak[ing] tough measures for tough circumstances' without addressing underlying social and economic problems. Most importantly, the 1970s authoritarian campaigns – which linked a whole range of striking workers, feminists, lesbian and gay activists, Irish nationalists, leftist teachers and progressive intellectuals together with the black criminal as national enemies – were legitimated in the populist forms of discourse which had been central to Powell's success. Hall states:

> It is, above all, the language of racism which has the effect of connecting the 'crisis of the state' *above* with the state of the streets, and little old ladies hustled off pavements in the depths down *below*. That is to say, it makes the 'crisis' real for ordinary people.[105]

Racially defined law-and-order discourse continued to play an important role through the 1980s. The intensification of policing in inner-city areas was invariably depicted as an a-political exercise in social control. In 1981, civil disturbances took place in Brixton, Toxteth, Moss Side and Manchester. Brixton, a London neighbourhood, has a high unemployment rate, especially among young black men and women, and a long history of tensions between the community and the police. When Thatcher was asked in the Commons whether social deprivation, high unemployment and inadequate housing had contributed to the community's frustrations, she flatly disagreed. She argued that 'nothing that has happened with regard to unemployment would justify those riots'.[106] The Thatcherites' demands for the expansion of the police force led to substantial expenditures on crowd-control technologies and equipment, including vehicles, weaponry, communications devices and protective body-armour. These armaments later played a key role in the defeat of the miners' strike in 1984–5. Lord Whitelaw, the former Home Secretary, stated, 'If we hadn't had the Toxteth riots, I doubt if we could have dealt with Arthur Scargill [leader of the National Union of Mineworkers].'[107]

As a libertarian, Powell might have privately opposed some aspects of the Conservative Party's shift to the right. Powell in fact differed from his New Right colleagues on several issues. He rejected right-wing Conservative proposals for education vouchers, post-graduate student loans and legislation against unofficial strikes. He made no important statements on policing, criminality and law and order – with the exception, of course, of his attack on demonstrations. He voted for the abolition of capital punishment and co-sponsored the private member's bill which would have decriminalized homosexuality in 1965. There were significant differences, then, between Powell's monetarist and right-wing libertarian programme and Thatcher's juxtaposition of anti-intervention policies in economic matters with an authoritarian moralistic approach to social issues. On the question of 'family values' and the status of women, by contrast, Powell and Thatcher held the same fundamentally anti-feminist position. In a debate on the 1981 Nationality Act, Powell argued that nationality should only be transmitted through the male line. He stated that nationality 'is tested by fighting', that it was men alone who should fight to defend their nation and that women should remain in the home. Powell dismissed alternative views on gender and the family as unnatural: 'Societies can be destroyed by teaching themselves myths which are inconsistent with the nature of man.'[108] Powell later intervened in the debate on embryo research in 1983 on the anti-abortion side with a private member's bill, the Unborn Children (Protection) Bill.[109]

In any event, surveys show that Powell's supporters consistently agreed with his anti-black immigration policies alone; they either did not know about the rest of his political programme or simply ignored the contradictions between their own views and Powell's positions in other policy areas. His supporters were far more likely to call for the retention of the death penalty, punishment for student activists and restrictions on trade union activities than the population as a whole.[110] Powellism greatly contributed to the escalation of racial antagonisms; Powell's own right-wing libertarianism did nothing to block the popular transformation of his anti-black immigration racism into the law-and-order racism of the 1970s and 1980s.

If the inconsistencies between Powell, the New Right and his anti-'permissive' bloc of supporters had little effect on the influence of Powellism, the ambiguities in Powell's own populist approach were more important. Powell's ostracism from the Conservative Cabinet heightened the popular sense that the party was extremely out of touch with 'the people'. However, Schoen estimates that Powell could have gained even more support if he had concentrated on building an 'anti-system movement using racial antagonism and general disillusionment as the central elements'. Powell remained caught between his populist strategy of speaking directly to the electorate and his profound lack of trust in the undisciplined forces of popular mobilizations. Schoen concludes that '[Powell's] commitment to the parliamentary system has been so strong that he has been unable to bring himself to emphasize the weaknesses in something he is resolutely committed to'.[111] Powell also failed to organize his supporters: he all but ignored the Powellian backbench MPs, constituency activists and the group of businessmen who encouraged him to stand for the Conservative leadership.

Thatcherism emerged out of four political developments: the popular backlash against the 'permissive' 1960s; the turn towards law-and-order government under Heath and Callaghan; the shift from corporatism, Keynesian fiscal policies and welfare state interventions to anti-collectivism, monetarism and anti-statism; and the re-definition of British nationalism through Powell's populism.[112] Again, Powell was personally opposed to some of the authoritarian policies of the radical right, but his libertarian positions on issues such as capital punishment and homosexuality did not receive much attention. Powell cannot, of course, be directly credited for the shift in economic strategies. His supporters remained largely unaware of his monetarist and free market platform. When Thatcher turned against Heath's corporatist programme, it was Keith Joseph and John Hoskyns who developed the Conservatives' new monetarist approach to inflation, employment, the money supply, labour unions and government intervention.[113] The work of popularizing monetarism was accomplished by other political figures as well: Callaghan's Labour government, for example, launched the first significant attack on the welfare state. Powell nevertheless made an indirect contribution to the shift towards monetarism and anti-statism. By linking the demonized black immigrant to the excesses of

the state bureaucracy, and by equating – through racist articulations
– the consensus discourse with the authoritarian censorship of the
'people's truths', he prepared the way for the right-wing attack on
the welfare state. The Thatcherites successfully deployed a similar
strategy when they promoted their attack on local government
autonomy through racist and anti-queer demonizations in the 1980s.
The popular transition from Keynesianism to monetarism could not
have taken place on the level of abstract economic theories alone; it
depended on the formation of a new organic common sense around
monetarist principles, and the construction of a whole range of
demonized symptom figures played a key role in that process.
Powell's construction of the black immigrant community as an 'alien
encampment' was in this sense an important precedent for
Thatcher's 'welfare scrounger': both figures supposedly exploited
the openness of the 'permissive' state and contributed to the already
'unfair' taxes and rates burden of the average (white) British citizen.

Thatcher differed from Powell on race in one important respect:
she was far more effective in representing her racist views as the
moderate position which stood between extremist demands from
both the right and the left. She benefited in this regard from the rise
of the National Front in the 1970s, and from the shift in her own
party, even among the pragmatic 'wets', to the right. Powell always
had to contend with Heath's criticisms which marginalized him as a
right-wing extremist; Thatcher was much more free to situate her
own extremism as a sensible and mainstream position.

Thatcher devoted an entire speech to immigration in January 1978.
Her tough stance on black immigration reassured her right-wing
backbenchers at a time when she was tactically obliged to make
several concessions to the Tory 'wets' and to present only a moderate right-wing critique of the Labour government. Her text reproduced much of Powell's discourse.

> If we went on as we are, then by the end of the century there
> would be 4 million people of the New Commonwealth or
> Pakistan here. Now that is an awful lot and I think it means that
> people are really rather afraid that this country might be
> swamped by people with a different culture. And, you know,
> the British character has done so much for democracy, for law
> and done so much throughout the world, that if there is a fear
> that it might be swamped, people are going to react and be
> rather hostile to those coming in.[114]

In a BBC Radio phone-in programme, five days before the 1979
general election, Thatcher reasserted her position, stating, 'Some

people do feel swamped if streets they have lived in for the whole of their lives are really now quite, quite different.'[115]

Like Griffiths and Powell, Thatcher claimed to be acting as a responsible representative who merely reflects existing anxieties. She characterized the views of her racist constituents as natural and justifiable sentiments, and located the source of racial antagonisms in the black population. Where Powell 'forgot' the dependency of Britain on its Empire, Thatcher 'forgot' the political debts that the white British owed to the incoming black populations precisely because the British had 'done so much throughout the world'. The *Sun*'s report demonstrates the extent to which Thatcher was successful in representing her position as a mediation between the extremists on the left and right. In a front-page story and an editorial, the *Sun* described the National Front as a group of 'twisted little men' who promoted a programme of 'crackpot economics, jingoism and odious racialism'. It concluded that it 'no longer matters what these revolting people say' because the Tories had 'grasped the immigration nettle', and that 'no reasonable person – black or white – could quarrel' with Thatcher's demands for new anti-black immigration legislation.[116]

In the Conservative Party's 1979 election manifesto, the Tories pledged to introduce further immigration controls against dependants and fiancé(e)s, and more restrictive citizenship legislation. Thatcher's government subsequently passed the 1981 British Nationality Act which eliminated the discrepancies between Britain's nationality and immigration laws by abolishing the citizenship rights of various categories of colonials and ex-colonials. For example, the British citizenship of the East African Asians – the very people who had already lost the right to immigrate into Britain in 1968 – was completely taken away from them.

The groundwork for the 1981 Nationality Act had already been laid in the 1971 Immigration Act. The 1971 law restricted the 'right of abode' in the United Kingdom to 'patrials': persons who were born in the United Kingdom; or persons who obtained British citizenship through adoption, registration or naturalization; United Kingdom citizens who had immigrated from another country and settled in the United Kingdom for a continuous period of five years; and Commonwealth citizens who had a parent or grandparent born in the United Kingdom. It established a voluntary 'repatriation' payment scheme, whereby the government would pay for the travelling expenses of any 'non-patrials' who wished to settle permanently in another country. Police officers and immigration officials were granted the right to arrest any person suspected of violating the immigration regulations without a warrant. After this law was passed, the Home Office and Scotland Yard established the National Immigration Intelligence Unit, which dramatically symbolized the shift from differentiating blacknesses at the 'outer' boundaries of the nation in the 1960s to the more localized surveillance and disciplining of blacknesses at the 'internal' borderline of criminality in the 1970s and 1980s. As for the holders of work vouchers, the 1971 Act reduced the Commonwealth immigrant worker to the status of a *Gastarbeiter* or guest worker.[117] Each work permit was restricted to a specific job at a specific location. It could be renewed only after an initial twelve months at the discretion of government authorities, and the worker could not change his or her job without government approval. Hiro estimates that because the 1971 law created a new 'loophole' for the white descendants of Britons in Australia, New Zealand and Canada – if their parents or grandparents had been born in the United Kingdom, they did not have to qualify for the work voucher scheme – it actually would have allowed for an increase in total immigration.[118] With the entry of the United Kingdom into the European Economic Community in 1975, European workers, by contrast, were given free access to the British labour market. When the 1971 Act went into effect in 1973, it virtually brought an end to primary black immigration.

The concept of 'patriality' in this law was taken directly from the 1968 Commonwealth Immigrants Act which the Labour government had passed to exclude the Kenyan Asians. With the 1971 Act, the boundaries of the nation became officially conceptualized in terms of familial blood ties. The then Home Secretary, Reginald Maudling, declared:

> It is said that most of the people with patrial status will be white. Most of us are white, and it is completely turning racial discrimination on its head to say that it is wrong for any country to accord those with a family relationship to it a special position in the law of that country.[119]

The centrality of the familial metaphor in distinguishing between the 'true' British and the pretenders would be proven once again in the 1987–8 parliamentary debates on the prohibition of homosexuality. Just as the very peoples whose labour had given Britain its prominence in the developed world were disowned as unwanted foreigners, so too would an entire British gay male and lesbian population be characterized as an un-British invasion from the immoral outside. Where the racist privileging of white familial ties resulted in legislation which tore black families apart, right-wing concerns about protecting children from sexual corruption led to the forced separation of hundreds, perhaps even thousands, of lesbian mothers from their children. The familial definition of the British frontiers which was deployed in the 1980s attack on the lesbian and gay community therefore had an important precedent in the racist closure of the nation in the post-colonial 1960s. Although white British gay men and lesbians do of course enjoy the socio-economic benefits of their white Britishness, their democratic rights – the right to free speech, democratic representation, privacy, the right to be free from arbitrary policing and so on – were nevertheless dramatically reduced in the anti-queer climate of the 1980s. It is not surprising, then, that Thatcherite anti-queer discourse reserved a 'special position' for the black lesbian; according to the New Right calculus, she was placed at the furthest possible distance from the white familial nation.

Chapter 5

Thatcherism's promotion of homosexuality

Section 28 of the Local Government Act 1987–88
Prohibition on promoting homosexuality by teaching or publishing
material

28.– (1) The following subsection shall be inserted after
section 2 of the Local Government Act 1986 (prohibition of
political publicity) –

2A – (1) A local authority shall not –
(a) intentionally promote homosexuality or publish material
     with the intention of promoting homosexuality;
(b) promote the teaching in any maintained school of the
     acceptability of homosexuality as a pretended family
     relationship.

(2) Nothing in subsection (1) above shall be taken to prohibit
the doing of anything for the purpose of treating or
preventing the spread of disease.

(3) In any proceedings in connection with the application of
this section a court shall draw such inferences as to the
intention of the local authority as may reasonably be drawn
from the evidence before it.

(4) In subsection (1)(b) above 'maintained school' means –
(a) in England and Wales, a county school, voluntary school,
     nursery school or special school, within the meaning of
     the Education Act 1944; and
(b) in Scotland, a public school, nursery school or special
     school, within the meaning of the Education (Scotland)
     Act 1980.

(2) This section shall come into force at the end of the period
of two months beginning with the day on which this Act is
passed.

Section 28 of the Local Government Act 1987–8, which passed into
British law on 9 March 1988, first appeared in the context of a private

member's bill introduced in the House of Lords by Lord Halsbury on 12 December 1986. According to the original wording of this first bill, local authorities were to be prohibited from giving 'financial or other assistance to any person for the purpose of publishing or promoting homosexuality'. During its third reading in the House of Lords the bill was amended, so that the teaching of the acceptability of homosexuality as a 'pretended family relationship' would also be prohibited. In the House of Commons, it passed through second reading and received unanimous support at the Committee stage. Like most private member's bills, however, this first bill failed to progress beyond the Committee stage; its significance was more symbolic than juridical.

The bill was nonetheless effective in preparing the way for the homophobic elements in the subsequent 1987 Conservative Party election campaign. One official party poster featured four books with the titles, *Young, Gay and Proud, Police Out of School, Black Lesbian in White America* and *Playbook For Children About Sex*. The main text of the poster stated, 'Labour's idea of a good education for your children'.[1] The play of racial and sexual images in this poster was by no means incidental; the construction of the equivalence, Labour = 'excessive' local government = high rates = 'loony left' = permissiveness = radical blackness, queerness, feminism = erosion of the entire social order, was central to the 1987 campaign.[2]

In the new parliamentary session, a local government bill was introduced which aimed to force local authorities to award works contracts only through competitive tendering and to dismantle all their contract compliance schemes relating to the employment of minorities. The 'free market' was to replace the interventions by local bodies. As the forty-fourth piece of legislation on local government introduced since 1979, the Local Government Bill 1987–8 on one level simply constituted yet another attack on the autonomy of the local authorities, one more attempt to reduce them to de-politicized service delivery points. At the Committee Stage, however, a version of Lord Halsbury's bill to prohibit local authorities from promoting homosexuality was added as a new clause. The motion to make the clause stand as part of the bill passed at that sitting without a vote, although the Opposition could have insisted on a division. Clause 28 received disproportionate consideration throughout the subsequent debates in both Houses. In the House of Lords, amendments to the clause were passed, most notably the amendment which prohibited the 'intentional' promotion of homosexuality. These amendments were accepted by the House of Commons, and the bill received Royal Assent on 9 March 1988. Section 28 came into effect two months later. From its introduction to the final division, discussion of this particular clause accounted for approximately 26 per cent of the debates on the entire bill.[3]

The homosexualization of local government autonomy

Section 28 was therefore a late addition to an anti-local government, anti-union, anti-black and anti-feminist bill. The unique location of this legislation on homosexuality in a local government act is not accidental. Local authorities had to a limited extent become a counterweight to central government in the late 1970s and early 1980s. In some cases, such as that of the Greater London Council (GLC), local governments became the sites of new leftist coalitions, in which the demands of feminists, black activists and lesbians and gays were granted an unprecedented degree of legitimacy. However, instead of recognizing the democratic character of these modest advances in the representation of popular demands at the local level, the Thatcher government responded with the abolition of the GLC, the re-definition of progressive policy changes as the will of un-British pressure groups, and the demonization of elected local councillors as the tyrannical 'loony left'.

The abolition of the GLC was fully in line with the centralist project of Thatcherite 'parliamentarism',[4] which aimed to reduce the political terrain to two spheres, the enterprising individual and her family on the one hand, and the central government on the other. No interruption in the simple relation between these two spheres was tolerated. What must be underlined, however, is that the organization of consent for centralization, through the equation of local government autonomy with the illegitimate subversion of the social order, was not a natural phenomenon. It was achieved through complex discursive strategies; the strategic invention of a crisis around the promotion of homosexuality operated as one of these legitimating strategies.

I have already referred in chapter 1 to the Labour defeat in the February 1987 by-election in Greenwich. According to Hewitt, the 'gays and lesbians issue' cost the Labour Party many votes. Aides to Kinnock called this problem of political imagery the 'London effect'. It should be recognized that the 'London effect' and the 'loony left' smears were substantially linked with local governments rather than some aspect of central government. The only notable exception to this linkage is the 'loony left' smear campaign against Labour candidate Peter Tatchell during the 1983 Bermondsey by-election. Tatchell, a gay man and a grass-roots socialist activist, was branded by the press as a 'Militant poofter' for his critique of British parliamentary democracy and for his support for lesbian and gay rights. The Liberal/SDP Alliance candidate, Simon Hughes, ultimately won the Bermondsey seat – a traditional Labour stronghold – following an explicitly homophobic Liberal/SDP campaign. Although he was branded a 'Militant' extremist, Tatchell actually faced opposition from both the right wing and leftist Militant tendencies within the Labour Party. Many of his Labour opponents made homophobic remarks about his candidacy. When Labour Party Leader Michael Foot took false information about Tatchell's views on extra-parliamentary activism at face value and denounced him, Neil Kinnock, who was then Shadow Cabinet spokesperson on education, declared, 'I'm not in favour of witchhunts but I do not mistake bloody witches for fairies.'[5] During the Darlington by-election, which occurred a few weeks after Tatchell's defeat in Bermondsey, Roy Hattersley remarked, 'Thank God there are no poofs in this by-election.'[6] Tony Benn was the only prominent Labour Party figure who consistently supported Tatchell.

The Tatchell controversy was structured around the equation of homosexuality with a treasonous assault on parliamentary democracy; Tatchell's opponents misrepresented his support for grassroots activism as a call for a communist revolution and fused his homosexuality together with his alleged political extremism. One anonymous election leaflet featured two sketches, one of the Queen and one of Tatchell wearing lipstick and with pencilled eyebrows. Under the headline, which asked, 'Which Queen Will You Vote For?', the text read,

> Peter Tatchell is an outspoken critic of the Queen and Royal Family – he believes that the monarchy should be abolished. The people of Bermondsey have always been loyal to the Crown. Many Bermondsey families lost loved ones during two world wars. They fought and died to save their country – on the other hand Tatchell ran away from his home in Australia to avoid fighting for his. Soldiers from this area also fought in the Falklands – needless to say Tatchell stabbed our boys in the back by opposing the war. Tatchell is a traitor to Queen and country.[7]

The leaflet invited people to ring Tatchell's private telephone number and to visit him at his council flat, and supplied his telephone number and address. Instead of focusing exclusively on Tatchell's homosexuality as an isolated issue, the leaflet articulated several symbolic elements to Tatchell's sexuality. It reflected the entrenched status of extremely conservative views about democracy and Britain's unwritten constitution, the intense debates within the Labour Party around defence policies and the post-colonial revival of jingoistic militarism in the wake of the Falklands/Malvinas War. For right-wing bigots, Tatchell's homosexuality summed up virtually every negative aspect of the Labour Party.

The subsequent homophobic campaigns against local government socialists reproduced the homosexuality = anti-democracy equation, but shifted the site of this homophobic discourse away from parliamentary politics to local government issues. Although moral conservative lobbying campaigns transformed the promotion of homosexuality into a national issue, they consistently aimed at progressive Labour-led local authorities as the seat of the problem. During the May 1986 local election in the London borough of Haringey, Bernie Grant, the then Labour council leader, was attacked because he supported modest proposals for the introduction of 'positive images' of lesbians and gays in local schools' sex education curricula. The Tottenham Conservative chairman Peter Murphy sharply criticized Grant's policies in a front-page story in a local newspaper. He stated that 'no person who believes in God can vote Labour now. [The Labour proposals are] an attack on ordinary family life as a prelude to revolution.' When, following the election, the newly established Lesbian and Gay Unit of Haringey Council wrote to school head teachers and merely requested that 'positive images' of lesbians and gays be promoted in the schools, local Conservatives responded with even greater hyperbole. In a press release entitled, 'Family Life Under Grave Threat', the Tottenham Conservative Association declared that the proposals constituted 'a bigger threat to the normal family than even the bombers and the guns of Adolf Hitler'. Murphy himself added that the council's pro-lesbian and gay rights policy was 'part of a Marxist plot to destabilize society as we know it'.[8]

Various parent groups emerged to campaign aggressively against the council's policies – or, more accurately, against the popular perception of the council's policies. I shall discuss the fact that some of these parent groups were not genuine 'local' groups below. In any event, they were quite successful in transforming their local conflict into a national issue. They circulated petitions, leafleted private homes, threatened to withdraw children from the council schools, proposed a referendum for ratepayers and attempted to close schools down with one-day pickets. The Haringey protests brought statements of concern from Kenneth Baker, the then Education Secretary, and Lord Swinton, the education spokesman, on local government decisions around homosexuality in school curricula. Two right-wing national groups, the Conservative Family Campaign and Christian Action, Research and Education (CARE) launched new lobby campaigns against the promotion of homosexuality by local governments.[9] It was in the context of these protests and campaigns that Lord Halsbury's bill was introduced in the House of Lords in December 1986. Again, it should be noted that the Halsbury bill's ban against the promotion of homosexuality was aimed specifically against local governments. Government spokesmen expressed their general support for the Halsbury bill, but argued that the 1986 Education Act and a forthcoming code of practice against local government publicity would provide adequate protection against 'improper' local government initiatives. The 1986 Education Act did in fact transfer jurisdiction over sex education in school curricula from local government officials to school governors.

The 1987 general election advertisements which linked Labour to the promotion of homosexuality also referred specifically to local government initiatives. Prior to the election, Haringey Council distributed a leaflet to ratepayers' homes which defended its pro-lesbian and pro-gay policies. The leaflet listed various resources on the topic; it included the text, *Young, Gay and Proud*, and stated that the text was suitable for thirteen-year-old readers.[10] The Conservative Party subsequently released the advertisement which listed four book titles, including *Young, Gay and Proud* during the general election. In addition to this official campaign, the Committee for a Free Britain launched a series of unofficial advertisements against Labour. One of the Committee's advertisements featured Betty Sheridan, a member of Haringey's Parents Rights Group. Sheridan stated, 'I live in Haringey. I'm married with two children. *And I'm scared*. If you vote LABOUR they'll go on teaching my kids about GAYS & LESBIANS instead of giving them proper lessons.'[11]

Section 28 should therefore be regarded as the product of a concerted effort on the part of extra-parliamentary right-wing groups and Conservative Party members to homosexualize leftist local governments. The prohibition of the promotion of homosexuality was not, in this sense, an irrational product of prejudice; it was, instead, a coherent deployment of highly charged statements and images. Homophobic discourse is nevertheless widely treated in lesbian and gay publications and community projects as if it were the effect of an irrational prejudice. On an interpersonal level, homophobic exclusions can be quite irrational: someone might claim to respect lesbian and gay rights in abstraction and yet insist on their own 'right' to treat actual lesbians and gays with disrespect; parents of adult lesbians and gays often refuse to acknowledge their children's coming out and continue to plan for their heterosexual future; and, in extreme cases, bigoted families pretend that their living lesbian or gay relative is dead. On a structural level, however, even the most irrational homophobic discourse can take the form of a coherent and effective authoritarian strategy.

The argument that all homophobic discourse is irrational is supported by two implicit assumptions: first, that people who engage in homophobic discourse are motivated by an irrational fear of the unknown, and second that if the myths about lesbians and gays were countered by effective positive images and 'truths', this homophobia would dissolve to make way for a tolerance of difference. However, homophobic discourse is organized not around a fear of otherness but around an obsession with otherness. This obsession is structured symptomatically: insofar as homophobic representations effectively displaced and condensed a whole range of anxieties onto the queerness signifier, queerness began to function as a supplement to Thatcherite discourse. Queerness became one of the enemy elements which supported the phantasmatic construction of the family as the antagonism-free centre of the British nation. Positive image campaigns and truth-telling about sexual minorities are also not straightforward matters; these strategies can dangerously escalate into what I shall call the 'evidence game', and can reinforce a differentiation which is basic to homophobic discourse: the good homosexual/dangerous queerness distinction. These strategies may win 'tolerance' for homosexuality, but there are many different types of 'tolerance'. Some types of 'tolerance' are won only at the expense of further excluding the less assimilable elements of the lesbian and gay community. Some positive image campaigns, for example, may promote the acceptance of white, middle-class professional gay men in monogamous relationships who demonstrate impeccable bourgeois taste, so that working-class and non-white male queers, lesbians, bisexuals and sex-trade workers are placed even further outside the social norm. The homophobia-as-irrational-prejudice analysis and the 'positive images' strategy can fail to address the ways in which class, race, gender and sexuality are articulated together, and therefore may risk the reinforcement of oppression in the name of '[white] gay [male] rights'. Given the extremely hostile environment in Haringey, we can only imagine the courage of the officials who stood behind the council's proposals for a positive images campaign. We can nevertheless speculate as to the possible shortcomings of similar campaigns if they were actually implemented.

Resistance against homophobic discourse has to deal with the deep investments which have been made in the demonization of queerness. As Zizek states with reference to anti-Semitism:

> It is not enough that we must liberate ourselves of so-called 'anti-semitic' prejudices and learn to see Jews as they really are – in this way we will certainly remain victims of these so-called prejudices. We must confront ourselves with how the ideological figure of the 'Jew' is invested with our unconscious desire, with how we have constructed this figure to escape a certain deadlock of our desire.[12]

Zizek argues that instead of presenting what could be called positive images of Jews, anti-Semitism can only be defeated insofar as it is recognized that the 'Jew' is a symptom figure which facilitates the 'stitch[ing] up [of] the inconsistency of our own ideological system'. Merely demonstrating that Jews really do not run the international banking system, engage in international conspiracies, prey upon children and so on is insufficient. The anti-Semite could respond: Well, they've fooled you too, or: They're even more clever than we thought, and so on. It should be argued instead that 'the anti-semitic idea of Jew has nothing to do with Jews'.[13]

The anti-Semite, like the racist and the anti-queer bigot, derives tremendous satisfaction from her symptom; the symptom operates as the principle of organization for the subject's enjoyment. Even after the symptom is interpreted – after the subject realizes that her slip of the tongue reveals some unconscious desire, or after it is shown that the black immigrant operates as the symptom of post-colonial nationalism – the subject may still cling to her symptom. Zizek insists that interpretation of the symptom may not disrupt the subject's attachment to it. Following Lacan, he argues that the end of the psychoanalytic process is 'identification with the symptom'.

> The analysis achieves its end when the patient is able to recog-
> nize, in the Real of his symptom, the only support of his being
> ... You, the subject, must identify yourself with the place where
> your symptom really was; in its 'pathological' particularity you
> must recognize the element which gives consistency to your
> being.[14]

It should be noted, once again, that Zizek is not simply stating that
anti-Semitic discourse 'scapegoats' the Jew as the figure who is to
blame for the system's failures. Zizek's point is that there would be
no system whatsoever without the symptom. As the element which
'stitches up the inconsistency of an ideological system' and 'gives
consistency to being', the symptom is prior to the system.

Zizek's analysis of anti-Semitism can be re-applied to homophobic
discourse. 'Positive images' which attempt to locate homosexuals as
equal members of the 'normal' would fail to address the Thatcherite
identification with the queerness symptom. The Thatcherites were
covering up some of the tremendous ruptures and contradictions in
their discourse through their campaign against the promotion of
homosexuality. 'Positive images' offer an interpretation of homophobic discourse, and construct a counter-discourse, but they do not
interrupt the entire process whereby the coherence of a political
project is established through the construction of demon figures. The
investment in that process remains unchallenged. In response to a
'positive images' campaign, a Thatcherite could have replied: Well,
maybe these particular homosexuals are normal, but our children are
still at risk from the loony left's promotion of homosexuality. Even if
the positive images did block the demonization of a particular type
of homosexuality, they would not necessarily block the circulation of
the demonization process to new figures: other queers, leftist intellectuals, multiculturalism, radical blacks, feminists and so on.

The evidence game

What were the discursive initiatives which created the appearance of
a crisis around the promotion of homosexuality? In what follows, I
shall examine the discourse of the supporters[15] of Section 28, with
specific emphasis on the parliamentary debates. I shall attempt to
show that this discourse can be usefully considered as a complex
ensemble of strategies. The most salient strategy in this discourse is
organized around truth claims and the provision of 'evidence' to
substantiate these claims. The supporters were able to set into

motion a self-reinforcing circulation of their truth claims, such that each claim became situated in what could be called an 'evidence game'. The evidence game is extremely seductive; when truth-claiming is located on a site in which uncertainties and anxieties have become concentrated, we can become seduced by the game's play of truths and counter-truths. Although we may think that we are resisting the original truth claiming by providing counter-evidence, we may actually be reinforcing the game itself.

For example, the arguments of the supporters of Section 28 were based first and foremost on the proposition that a campaign to 'promote homosexuality' by local authorities *did* exist and that its subversive effects were devastating. Several speakers, such as Dame Jill Knight, specialized in the provision of 'evidence' in a complex circulation of mythical figures. A wide variety of texts were cited, ranging from GLC policy statements to children's sex-education materials produced wholly independently of local authorities, to a political manifesto written by a non-governmental gay and lesbian group. These disparate texts were listed as if they were equivalent and as if they were representative of many other similar texts. They were invariably discussed out of context, misattributed and mis-quoted. At one point, Knight quotes a passage from a sex-education text which she incorrectly claims to have been 'promulgated by a local council'; she then directly proceeds to situate her 'evidence' by quoting passages from a radical critique of the family by the Gay Liberation Front written in 1971.[16] The argument is presented as if it were self-explanatory: any effort to place homosexuality on an equal plane with heterosexuality is seen to constitute a subversive 'pro-motion', because behind even the most apparently harmless toler-ance of homosexuality lies a deep conspiracy to undermine the entire social order. 'Promotion' can be 'proven' in this context merely by referring to discourses in which homosexuality is included as a legitimate element; the citation of exact cases of the actual and explicit promotion of homosexual acts to minors is unnecessary.

Early speakers in the debates make several fallacious charges. It is claimed that lesbian and gay books were displayed in two Lambeth play centres, that the book *Young, Gay and Proud* was recommended for children by the Inner London Education Authority and stocked by a Haringey library, that the text *Jenny Lives With Eric and Martin* was stocked at an ILEA teacher centre and that the publisher of the latter text was grant-aided by the GLC. These fallacies then become self-perpetuating: later speakers cite the same 'evidence' as if its legitimacy and significance were already well-known. In the final debates, the simple act of speaking the names of five local authorities, Camden, Haringey, Lambeth, Brent and Ealing, is deemed sufficient to evoke the figure of the 'promoter' of homosexuality. Local council support for lesbian and gay youth groups is presented as if the local councils invented these organizations to brainwash teenagers, when such organizing actually originated in the lesbian and gay community. Furthermore, although the speakers claim to be concerned with the welfare of children, they also cite publications and policies aimed at adults.

The myth that a campaign to promote homosexuality existed is therefore constructed through the repetition of truth claims. The productivity of these repetitions is remarkable: even though the truth claims are so vulnerable to counter-truth claims, they are, in another sense, absolutely invulnerable to them at the same time. The supporters' discourse is in this sense structured in terms of what has been called the 'magic of reiteration'. The illusion of reality can often be created through repetition, even if the repeated element would lack any degree of validity in other contexts. The propaganda techniques of totalitarian regimes are often organized in terms of this production of truth through repetition.[17]

The most forceful truth claiming in support of Section 28 is organized around interpretations of popular opinion. Opinion polls in which 83 per cent of the respondents stated that they 'do not approve of schools teaching that homosexuality is on par with heterosexuality', 43 per cent stated that they 'do not approve of homosexual relationships between consenting adults' and 85.9 per cent agreed that the promotion of homosexuality should be prohibited,[18] are offered as conclusive evidence of the necessity of the Section. The relatively few public protests in support of the Section are presented as the true expression of the 'average ratepayer'. With these claims, the evidence game becomes even more complex. Supporters can agree that the 'promotion of homosexuality' is a mythical construction, but they can nevertheless argue that the signs of popular concern irrefutably indicate the necessity of prohibitive legislation. Patrick, a Conservative MP, states:

> I accept that [the Section] is needed ... I know that parents often object to the fact that such teaching *appears* to be available in the schools. Whether it is in fact available is not the argument.[19]

The supporters never recognize, however, the context of these 'popular' concerns, the fact that widespread anxiety and misinformation about AIDS, and the supporters' own fallacious claims about local government activities, preceded these poll findings and protests. The supporters also do not admit that most of the leaders of these protests were not 'average ratepayers' but members of right-wing activist groups. In Haringey, leaflets which opposed the local council's policies on homosexuality were published by 'Concerned Parents and Citizens of Haringey' in association with 'The New Patriotic Movement'. The latter group has links with the extreme right-wing Moonie World Unification Church.[20] The local Parents' Rights Group published national advertisements during the 1987 election which claimed that a Labour victory would mean that children in the schools would be taught about 'Gays and Lesbians instead of proper lessons'. The ads were financed by The Committee for Free Britain which shares an address with the Moonie Church. The Parents' Rights Group itself denounced the Moonie support for the 'New Patriotic Movement', but it formed unusual political alliances of its own. At one point, it announced plans to pursue court action against Haringey Council with the support of the Union of Democratic Miners, the union which had represented the miners who opposed Scargill's National Union of Mineworkers strike.[21] Through the evidence game, the strategies which operate behind the apparently organic 'local parents' group' are concealed. A mythical narrative is instead constructed: first, there were the excesses of the 'promoters', then the expressions of popular concern and, last, the legitimate response of the supporters in the form of the Section. The truth claiming conceals the extent to which the supporters' discourse is constitutive of that which appears to be its enemy, the 'promotion campaign', and of that which it appears to be representing, 'popular opinion'. Using an extremely reductionist conception of democratic representation, the supporters position themselves as the true spokespersons for 'the people', against the authoritarian leftist local government councillors. Their so-called democratic discourse completely fails to recognize that the protection of the rights of minorities over and against the tyranny of majorities is basic to any democratic system.

Furthermore, the truth-claiming of the supporters constitutes a framework which organizes both the supporters' discourse, and, for the most part, the opposers' discourse. For example, when the Section is introduced in Committee, Cunningham, the Labour spokesman on local government affairs, emphasizes that it has never been the policy of the Labour Party to promote homosexuality. What Cunningham does not do is to question the manner in which the supporters express their concerns about homosexuality, or to defend the existing policies of Labour-led local governments; he only attempts to distance the Labour Party from the alleged phenomenon. In his intervention in the same Committee debate, Bernie Grant, a newly elected backbench Labour MP, takes an entirely different approach. Instead of arguing about whether or not a campaign to promote homosexuality actually exists, he presents a detailed defence of Haringey's modest proposals for changes in school curricula. Reading from a council report, Grant states that the aim of responsible teaching is to 'reflect the reality of actual experiences of children' and to give the children 'the confidence to manage their relationships with integrity' and to encourage them to establish non-exploitative friendships and relationships based on 'equality and respect'.[22] From this and other similar contributions to the debates, it can be seen that while it is true that a very small number of local authorities established lesbian and gay units, offered support to gay organizations and explored the possibilities of promoting the 'positive images' of lesbians and gays through their programmes, these initiatives were very few in number, were often mere proposals for change, and were shaped by measured, principled and cautious thinking.

However, within the opposers' discourse, interventions such as Grant's were exceptional. The opposers generally pursued Cunningham's line of argument, an attempt to show that a campaign to promote homosexuality simply did not exist. Whereas Grant directly confronts the 'loony left' and 'promotion of homosexuality' figures deployed in the supporters discourse, most of the opposers focus on demonstrating that the supporters' claims are untruthful.[23]

In strategic terms, the problem with the opposers' counter-truth strategy is that the charges of the supporters, for all their fictitious character, were tremendously effective. Not only were they widely believed, but they moved many people to positive action: to repeat the charges to others or to write to their MP. The signifying function of discourse on the promotion of homosexuality was to represent and to give permission to otherwise disorganized or unspoken anxieties, and that function could not be nullified through counter-truths. The senselessness of the supporters' charges did not in any way diminish the authority of their claims. Anyone who felt that the supporters' claims 'spoke' to her was perfectly capable of saying: Well, I know very well that some of these stories are untrue, but we still have to do something about this crisis. This was, after all, the very response of Patrick which I have quoted above. This had also been one of Powell's tactics. In his 16 November 1968 speech, he listed the alleged wrongs of black landlords in great detail and then anticipated his critics by admitting that blacks were not more 'malevolent or more prone to wrong-doing' than whites. Like Patrick, however, he insisted that the actual facts were irrelevant; any degree of wrongdoing by blacks was totally unacceptable. Powell and the supporters of Section 28 therefore play both sides of the evidence game: they make extensive truth claims, but when they are challenged at the truth game level, they insist that the truth game itself is entirely beside the point.

The 'promotion of homosexuality' is not a hypothesis which can be rationally proven or disproven; it is a symptom of underlying ruptures in the social. Even if one symptom could be treated with the remedy of counter-truth, the ruptures it conceals will produce other symptoms, forming a chain of elements. The symptom-work, condensation and displacement, representation and iteration, can never be completed. The symptom is situated on the terrain of excess,[24] a permanent, futile and yet highly productive struggle of representation. The counter-truth discourse, insofar as it also 'believes in' truth, can even escalate the symptom-evidence game by taking the truth claims seriously.

Homosexuality as the subversive supplement: invader, seducer, monster, pretender

Rather than playing the evidence game by offering counter-truths, resistance discourses ought to analyse the conditions of effectiveness of truth claims. In the place of counter-truth claiming, we should engage in 'symptomology', an investigation of the structure, and the strengths and weaknesses, of the supporters' truth-claiming discourse. Why was this expression of anxiety around homosexuality, in this particular form, at this particular juncture, so persuasive? Why did the conception of the erosion of the social order through the promotion of homosexuality seem to 'sum up' otherwise disparate concerns, concerns about disease, morality, children and the family, and the relations between central government and local government? Why did the devotion of extensive official discourse to this conception of homosexuality, at this particular time, appear to be a legitimate exercise?

In the late 1980s, discourse on homosexuality was thoroughly intertwined with discourse on AIDS. In terms of the Section 28 supporters' discourse, discourse on AIDS plays a key role in two different ways. First, the AIDS phenomenon is strategically interpreted so that homosexuality no longer appears to be one social element among many, but is represented as a threat to the very existence of other social elements. For example, Baroness Cox stated in the House of Lords, 'I cannot imagine how on earth in this age of AIDS we can be contemplating gay issues in the curriculum.' Knight similarly states in the House of Commons, 'Some of that which is being taught to children in our schools would undoubtedly lead to a great spread of AIDS.'[25] She also argues that Section 28 is necessary because 'AIDS starts with and comes mainly from homosexuals' and only 'spreads to others' later.[26] This interpretation of AIDS, so that 'homosexuality' appears to be equivalent to 'threat to others', is of course only one possible interpretation. The AIDS syndrome does not live in an empirical group of people; indeed, the groundless equation, male gayness = AIDS, is an extremely dangerous strategy of denial by heterosexuals and lesbians of their own risks and responsibilities.[27] The HIV virus associated with AIDS is transmitted by practices which cut across all social groupings, and an individual's imaginary location in a so-called 'low risk group' provides absolutely no protection from the virus. Safer sex and drug use practices stop the virus; moral hierarchies have no place in AIDS discourse. The search for the origin of AIDS is in turn nothing more than an attempt to ground this denial of the risks to heterosexuals; claims about the African and homosexual origins of AIDS are shaped more by racist and anti-gay fantasies than by reputable medical research.[28]

Although the supporters of Section 28 engage in several strategic misinterpretations of the AIDS phenomenon, their statements on AIDS build up a legitimating structure which is fundamental to their homophobic discourse in general. The construction of the myth of the promotion of homosexuality is effective in part because it is preceded by the articulation, homosexuality = threat to all other elements in the social. Statements on AIDS, both by officials like Knight and by the popular press, prepared the way for Section 28. However, discourse on AIDS is also re-represented in the discourse on Section 28. AIDS 'hysteria' has generated a great deal of hostility towards lesbians and gays, from everyday discrimination to 'queerbashing'. Section 28 gives this expression of hostility an officially sanctioned and apparently disinterested form. Many individuals would not consider violent or hostile acts towards homosexuals as socially acceptable acts. By contrast, the act of agreeing with an elected official that 'our' children are being threatened by a campaign to promote homosexuality is more readily understood as a socially acceptable act. As was the case in Powellism, Section 28 creates the structure in which an otherwise unspeakable 'private' concern can be brought into the public sphere and given a proper place in 'public' official discourse.

The statements about AIDS by the Section 28 supporters are also organized according to a precise structure which is reproduced throughout their discourse. In her claim about AIDS, Knight appears to be expressing her fears about the threat of *illness* here. It should be noted that this expression is organized in terms of supplementary inside-outside metaphors. In Knight's discourse on AIDS and homosexuality, 'homosexuality' is represented as an element which is inherently opposed to the 'norm'. This opposition, however, is given a precise spatial and temporal structure. Homosexuality is equated with a disease which begins outside the 'norm' and later spreads into the 'norm' and contaminates the 'norm'. Her discourse therefore locates homosexuality both as a lethal medical threat and as a foreign invader. By representing homosexuality as an element which wants to cross the boundaries which protect the social order, however, the discourse of the supporters paradoxically creates a sense of a threatened space, the 'natural social order', the 'inside'. Already in the most exclusionary aspect of Knight's homophobic discourse, there is no simple opposition, the 'norm' versus homosexuality. There is instead a complex of spaces, and fundamental attributes are ascribed to each spatially located element as if they were inherent characteristics. The 'norm' appears to have been there first, as the natural space, and homosexuality appears to have come later, as that which essentially wants to contaminate the natural space from the outside. It is of course only with the invader figure that the 'norm' takes on this appearance. The threat of the supplementary outside is reworked to produce that which it could otherwise interrupt, the sense that the 'norm' is an absolutely primary, complete and self-contained space.

Knight's discourse therefore only appears to be about nothing more than illness. The anxieties she voices are actually about the disruption of the social order in general. In other words, these are anxieties about subversion in the broadest sense. The hegemonic interpretation of the AIDS phenomenon, which equates AIDS with male homosexuality with promiscuity with death, is actually a strategic response to perceived threats of subversion of the heterosexual patriarchal order through the advances of the radical sexual liberation and feminist movement. This interpretation should be located genealogically, within the long tradition of similar representations of subversive social elements and popular anxieties about prostitution, pornography, abortion rights, the provision of contraception to persons under the age of consent, sex education, various diseases, communist infiltration, immigrant populations, crime 'waves', drug 'crazes', 'hooligan' youths and so on.

Sontag demonstrates through historical research that the 'foreign invader' figure has been central to the medical response to disease for centuries. The bubonic plague and cholera were also depicted as foreign invasions. Xenophobic discourse in the late nineteenth century depicted the immigrant as the bearer of cholera, yellow fever, typhoid fever and tuberculosis. For Sontag, the representation of disease as a foreign threat is a basic element in European identity.

> Part of the centuries-old conception of Europe as a privileged cultural entity is that it is a place which is colonized by lethal diseases coming from elsewhere. Europe is assumed to be by rights free of disease.[29]

When Tory MPs demanded HIV screening for immigrants travelling from the Third World in the mid-1980s, they were speaking within a well-established tradition. Health checks played an integral role in the controls against Jewish immigrants at the turn of the century. Jews were widely regarded as tuberculosis carriers who threatened the European populations with 'degeneration'. Popular anxieties around foreigners as carriers of disease were expressed in the early 1960s, when anti-black immigration movements demanded compulsory health examinations for all immigrants. The British Medical Association legitimized these demands by calling for health checks for all black immigrants after a minor outbreak of smallpox in Bradford in 1966.[30] The privileging of Europe as a disease-free space, and the depiction of Europe as 'colonized' by foreign disease, is especially ironic in light of the fact that it was the European 'explorer', conqueror and settler who introduced deadly epidemic diseases which wiped out entire indigenous populations. The foreigner = disease articulation nevertheless reinforces the representation of the British nation as a healthy body, whose immigration controls must operate like the skin, the immune system and the bodily orifices in the assimilation of nutrients and the repulsion of dangerous elements. The British obsession with border controls against continental rabies is in this sense an important precursor to the hegemonic discourse on AIDS. The representation of disease as originating in foreign elements also mobilizes the militarization of discourse on immigration. If foreigners are regarded as a diseased 'invading force', then their arrival appears to necessitate an all-out military defence of the national borders, with the usual war-time suspension of respect for human rights.

Each of the foreign invader figures, such as the disease-ridden Jew, the black American revolutionary, the leech-like Asian immigrant, the criminal Rastafarian, the fanatical Muslim fundamentalist and the promiscuous gay man, is depicted as invading the social order from the outside and, at the same time, threatening it from within. Fundamental anxieties are organized around this interruption, and a simulated consensus is forged against the figure of the 'invader' or the 'enemy within'. 'We' only have a sense of a Thatcherite Britishness, for example, by virtue of a series of staged confrontations, resistances to the belligerent Argentinian invader, the swamping by black immigrants, the revolutionary plot of the communist miners, the treasonous advance of the 'loony left' and so on. Knight's presupposed sexual 'norm' only appears as such through its representation in opposition to diseased and uncontained homosexuality. The hegemonic discourse on AIDS is therefore about subversion in that it is an expression of anxieties about subversion, it is a representation of the threat of subversion in the figure of the diseased gay male invader, and it offers compensation for anxieties about subversion by creating a sense of a consensus.

The supporters' discourse on Section 28 is structured in part in a similar manner as the hegemonic AIDS discourse. It is taken for granted that a space of sexual normalcy exists as the primordial and natural space, and that, although that space is threatened by the homosexual invader, it remains for the time being uncontaminated. At the same time, however, the supporters' discourse is contradictory, for it contains a vision of the space of the sexual 'norm' as already thoroughly contaminated by queer otherness. In this second representation of the threat of subversive difference, homosexuality is not simply a threatening invader from the outside, but has taken on the properties of a seducer, a floating element whose corrosive effects are already experienced throughout the space of the 'norm'.

This second representation becomes particularly striking in the context of the supporters' expressions of their views on the development of sexuality. The supporters unanimously agree that sexuality is not fixed biologically at birth and that virtually every child and teenager is vulnerable to sexual corruption through 'improper' teaching. Quoting from the Wolfenden Report, Lord Halsbury argues that because 'people's sexual orientation [is] not fixed at any particular stage, but is stabilized around the middle twenties', school-leavers are still 'open to seduction', and must be protected until that age.[31] In contrast to Knight's taking-for-granted of the resilience of sexual normalcy as a primordial space, here there is no such certainty: anyone is open to seduction.

This representation of homosexuality in the form of the predatory seducer is not just an isolated distortion of the 'truth' of homosexuality. Homosexuality was in fact originally conceptualized in official discourse in terms of the seducer/victim relation. The early sexologists, who worked with a behaviourist framework, divided male homosexuality into two types: the invert and the passive homosexual. The invert, who actively pursued the passive homosexual, was supposed to be homosexual by nature. The passive homosexual, by contrast, was supposed to be basically heterosexual; he only became homosexual through the invert's seduction.[32] Official representations of homosexuality are often structured in terms of this theoretical framework. The image of the vulnerable young man who is threatened with perversion by the older male homosexual seducer has been normalized in official discourse. When the Wolfenden Committee, a 1957 Home Office inquiry into the legislation on homosexuality and prostitution, recommended the de-criminalization of male homosexual practices, it distinguished between the sexual practices involving persons over the age of 21, and those involving younger persons. Their report stated:

> We should not wish to see legalized any forms of behaviour which would swing towards a permanent habit of homosexual behaviour a young man who without such encouragement would still be capable of developing a normal habit of heterosexual adult life.[33]

The Committee concluded, with the unanimous support of their medical witnesses, that sexuality is fully established at the age of 16. Focusing on the figure of the young male 'victim' of male homosexual seduction, they nevertheless stated: 'A boy is incapable, at the age of sixteen, of forming a mature judgement about actions of a kind which might have the effect of setting him apart from the rest of society.'[34] The 1967 Sexual Offences Act, which finally put the

Wolfenden recommendations into law, decriminalized consensual sexual practices in private places between male adults. However, the Act also constructed an age of consent distinction. British law recognizes the ability of young adults to consent to heterosexual sex once they reach the age of 16. Under the 1967 Sexual Offences Act, by contrast, the age of consent for male homosexual acts is 21. Legislation currently before Parliament would only partially reduce this distinction by setting the age of consent for male homosexual acts at 18.

The obsessive surveillance of young people's sexuality is a logical corollary to the assumption that homosexuality is essentially predatory and that virtually every young person is open to corruption. Homosexuality must be displaced from the childhood space in which the 'true' sexuality is carefully nurtured; if homosexuality is to emerge, it must do so later. In other words, this discourse on homosexuality is organized in terms of the logic of the supplement in a manner which is strikingly similar to the logic of Rousseau's discourse on signification and Nature. The paradoxes are of course obvious: homosexuality is represented as potentially present in the originary moment of childhood, and yet must be made to come later; heterosexuality, the 'natural' sexuality, does not 'naturally' develop but must be produced through intervention; if every 'normal' child can be seduced by the 'not-normal', then there is something in the essence of normalcy that turns the 'normal' against itself; the 'normal' would not be 'normal' without its relation to the 'not-normal'; thus the very idea of normalcy depends on an ever-present threat from the 'not-normal'; with the play of contamination and dependency between the two terms, the distinction between the 'normal' and 'not-normal' ultimately fails and so on. This self-contradictory thinking does not collapse into incoherence, however, but fuels an obsessive concern for the production of normalcy in a world in which nothing can be taken for granted, especially the sexual development of the apparently most 'normal' child. 'Natural' sexual development, then, cannot be left to 'nature' but must be actively created through an intensely interventionist project of social transformation.

Having examined these discursive operations of the supporters' discourse, we can now grasp the logic behind the precise wording of Section 28. The supporters say that they do not want to eliminate services for lesbians and gays, and that they do recognize the importance of discussing homosexuality in the classroom. Many emphasize that they are not against homosexuals *per se*. A government spokesman defends the inclusion of the vague term homo-sexuality in the Section, instead of the more precise 'homosexual acts', because he is concerned that local authorities are attempting to 'sell' the 'whole gamut of homosexuality, homosexual acts, homo-sexual relationships, even the abstract concept'.[35] Homosexuality becomes a threat to the extent that it takes the form of subversive difference, to the extent that it invades the space of the 'norm' from the outside, or circulates throughout this space as a seductive float-ing element. Whereas both the *Oxford English Dictionary* and *Web-ster's Dictionary* define the *homosexual* as someone who is inclined towards erotic acts with someone of the same gender, *Webster's* further defines homosexuality as the *manifestation* of sexual desire toward someone of the same gender. The crisis which the support-ers' discourse aims to forestall relates to uncontained homosexuality – the visible violation of the norm through an excessive exhibition of queerness. The Section treats homosexuality like a monster, like an evil element which must be shown as a warning to the good, but only in strictly supervised conditions.[36] Just as Powell used the American radical black activist as a monster figure, as a warning to the British about the subversive potential of the 'enemies within', the supporters of Section 28 invoke the image of the male homosexual seducer to warn 'the people' about the over-'permissive' local government programmes. From the point of view of the supporters' discourse, the problem is not the existence of an invisible sexual minority, or the acts of consenting adults in private; it is the dis-ruption of the social order by subversive difference. The dangerous potential of subversive difference is realized insofar as its circulation is encouraged and made public, that is, insofar as it is 'promoted'. Consequently, the main section of Section 28 does not refer to persons (homosexuals) or acts (sodomy), but prohibits the 'pro-motion of homosexuality'.

The second part of the Section, the prohibition of the 'teaching of the acceptability of homosexuality as a pretended family relation-ship', is also constructed in terms of an attack on subversive queer-ness. The supporters say that they want to make illegal any discourse organized by a local authority which 'portrays' homosexuality as 'the norm',[37] grants homosexuality a 'more favourable treatment, a more favourable status, or wider acceptance [than heterosexual-ity]',[38] or suggests that the '[homosexual] lifestyle is desirable over another'.[39] Homosexuality not only wants to invade the space of the 'norm' from the outside, and to circulate seductively throughout the space of the 'norm', it also wants to take the place of the 'norm' by presenting itself as the pseudo-'norm'. The crisis here is the possibility of deception: the possibility that homosexuality may be accepted as legitimate, as a 'norm'. The supporters' discourse instead names homosexuality as a false 'norm', its family relations as simulacra and attempts to make a distinction in law between the pretender and the real thing. Here again their discourse is grounded in paradox: they believe that the distinction between the pretender and the real thing is necessary, and that drawing this distinction is a task appropriate for official discourse; yet the very necessity of such a distinction is indicative of its impossibility. Necessary and yet impossible, but always productive; these are the hallmarks of the supporters' discursive project.

The 'good homosexual'/dangerous queer differentiation

The supporters' discourse is opposed to homosexuality insofar as it takes the 'form' of the subversive supplement, the invader, monster, seducer and pretender. There is a distinction, then, between homosexuality as subversive difference, which disrupts the social order, and homosexuality as accidental difference which can be added to the social order without any fundamental transformation. This distinction is made in explicit terms throughout the supporters' discourse. The law-abiding and not-diseased *subject* who keeps her expression of difference strictly behind closed doors in a monogamous relationship with another adult, the 'good homosexual', is distinguished from the publicly flaunting *element* which strives to reproduce itself by seducing the innocent young. This element could be called the 'dangerous queer'.[40] Lord Halsbury, for example, argues that it is important to distinguish between 'responsible' homosexuals and their 'exhibition[ist]', 'promiscuous' and 'proselytizing' counterparts.[41] Lord Monson says that he recognizes the 'genuine' rights and freedoms of homosexuals, but emphasizes that these rights pertain only to the 'bedrooms of consenting adults' and not to 'propaga[tion]'.[42] Other Section 28 supporters recognize that the lesbian and gay community is currently facing a violent backlash, but they attribute that backlash to the work of the dangerous queer, rather than to their own discourse. Conservative MP Wilshire says that it is the 'arrogan[ce], self-assertive[ness], aggressive boastfulness and self-glorification' of some homosexuals which has offended the 'majority of people'.[43] Dickens, another Tory MP, argues that lesbians and gays who want support against the 'queer-bashers' should accept the decriminalization of homosexuality 'gently and steadily and not expect too much'. In an unintentionally revealing *double entendre*, he concludes, '[homosexuals] are only likely to get that support [against violent attacks] if they stop continuing to flaunt their homosexuality and thrusting it down other people's throats'.[44]

The distinction between the good homosexual and the dangerous queer is made on both qualitative and ontological grounds. The good subject is *closeted* in every sense of the term, hidden and contained within closed frontiers, while the subversive element *comes out of the closet*, shows itself in its own self-staged spectacle and refuses to be contained. The goodness of the 'good homosexual' consists precisely in her self-disciplining, self-limiting, fixed subject status, an otherness which knows her proper place. The dangerousness of subversive queerness lies in its unfixity and 'excessiveness', its insatiable drive towards expansion and self-reproduction, its contamination of the space of normalcy through its entry of the wrong orifices, and, above all, its pursuit of unlimited pleasure.

The 'good homosexual'/dangerous queer differentiation also takes place in many other official discourses on homosexuality. In the debates on Lord Halsbury's original bill, Lord Campbell, the Earl of Longford and even Dame Jill Knight express both their acceptance of law-abiding homosexuals and their alarm concerning the promotion of homosexuality.[45] The 1967 Sexual Offences Act and Clause 31 of the 1990–1 Criminal Justice Act also deploy a similar differentiation. The 1967 Act juxtaposed its de-criminalization of private practices between adult men with the strengthening of legislation for other practices. Like many other pieces of 'permissive' legislation in the 1960s, the effects of the Sexual Offences Act were contradictory. While it did shift 'the state' away from the regulation of the 'private' sphere, it intensified the regulation of the 'public' sphere. It introduced reinforced restrictions concerning offences involving 'minors', persons of less than 21 years of age, male soliciting and sexual practices in 'public' places. It defines the conception of 'public' place quite broadly as any place in which a third person is likely to be present. Section 31 of the 1990–1 Bill increases the severity of existing offences relating to 'public' sexual acts, including gross indecency (*any* display of affection and/or sexual contact other than buggery between two men in a 'public' place), procuring an act of indecency and soliciting ('cruising' between two men or between a formerly male post-operative transsexual and a man; no sex act need actually occur, and no exchange of monies need be involved). In 1989, 2,311 men were convicted for these soliciting, procuring and indecency offences in Britain.[46]

Both of these criminal laws target specific homosexual acts which are supposed to threaten the social order, rather than homosexuality *per se*. Section 31 of the 1991 Act defines the term, 'sexual offence', which is used in Section 2. Section 2 states that the length of a custodial sentence is to be commensurate with the seriousness of the offence, except in the case of a violent or sexual offence, where the court may impose a longer sentence. The latter terms are defined as follows:

> In this section ... any reference, in relation to an offender convicted of a violent or sexual offence, to protecting the public from serious harm from him shall be construed as a reference to protecting members of the public from death or serious personal injury, whether physical or psychological, occasioned by further such offences committed by him.

The government retained the term, 'psychological harm', which may be used to legitimate harsh sentencing for consensual adult gay male sex acts, in spite of extensive lobbying by lesbian and gay activists.

In one of the debates on Section 31, John Patten, then Home Office Secretary of State, declared, 'I fully understand the strong feelings evinced by Stonewall [a lesbian and gay legislative lobby group] and other organizations.' He nevertheless defended Section 31 in that it reflected only the 'existing structure of sexual offences as they affect homosexual activity and heterosexual activity'.[47] Patten also referred indirectly to the criticisms of the bill by lesbians and gays in a letter to Robin Squire, a Labour Party MP. He stated that he is 'of course concerned that the bill should be perceived as having an effect that was never intended', and that he planned to amend the bill so that the increased sentences would only be used 'in cases where there is a need to protect potential victims from serious harm from the offender concerned'. He added,

> I hope that, as a result, those who have been anxious about the possible effects of the Bill as it stands will be reassured that the only people who have anything to fear from the Bill are that small number of dangerous offenders from whose activities their intended victims need to be protected.[48]

In any event, because the Criminal Justice Act 1990–1 was added to an existing body of legislation which criminalizes consensual sex practices between men, the perpetrator of a victimless crime may now be classified as a 'dangerous offender'.

Like Section 28, the Sexual Offences Act of 1967 and Section 31 of the 1990–1 Criminal Justice Act differentiate between 'private' and 'public' homosexual discourse, identify 'private' homosexual discourse as a self-regulating, harmless, assimilable and accidental difference, and 'public' homosexual discourse as a flaunting, dangerous, unassimilable and supplementary difference. The dangerous homosexual element must be taught to regulate himself[49] by internalizing the surveillance strategies which transform him into a good homosexual subject. These laws do not exclude or repress or wage a total war against homosexuality, although they are often represented in this manner in the lesbian and gay press. They do not work to eliminate homosexual difference and do not promote a purely homogeneous heterosexual vision of British society. They actually differentiate *homosexualities*, and *promote* a homosexuality of a very specific type – that of the 'good homosexual' subject.

The 'good homosexual'/dangerous queer distinction is not peculiar to British homophobic discourse. When President Clinton originally declared that he intended to issue an Executive Order which would have directed the military to stop discriminating against lesbians and gays, the Joint Chiefs of Staff expressed their strong disapproval. After several months of negotiations, the Whitehouse and the Pentagon agreed a 'don't ask, don't tell, don't pursue' policy. According to its terms, military recruiters will no longer question applicants about their sexuality in order to screen out lesbians and gays, and commanding officers will no longer be allowed to conduct investigations about a soldier's or sailor's alleged homosexuality if the allegation is based on rumour alone. However, the new policy states that 'homosexual conduct' is incompatible with military service; any military personnel who engage in 'homosexual conduct', on-duty or off-duty, on-base or off-base, will risk dishonourable discharge. It defines 'homosexual conduct' quite broadly as a 'homosexual act, a statement that the [soldier or sailor] is homosexual or bisexual, or a marriage or attempted marriage to someone of the same gender'. The policy claims that evidence which merely shows that a soldier or sailor has frequented a lesbian and gay bar, read a homosexual publication or marched in a lesbian and gay rights march in plain clothes would not in and of itself constitute 'credible information' of 'homosexual conduct'. The extremely vague and broad terms of the policy nevertheless leave even the most discreet lesbian or gay man in the military vulnerable to prosecution. Although questions have been raised about the constitutionality of the military's censorship of discourse on homosexuality, American courts have traditionally found that the military is not bound by civil liberties provisions and legislation.

The new policy makes a critical distinction between merely being homosexual and displaying homosexuality: it states, 'sexual orientation will not be a bar to [military] service unless manifested by homosexual conduct'. In this sense, it reproduces the 'good homosexual'/dangerous queer distinction which is central to Section 28 discourse. The new policy therefore places impossible burdens of secrecy and discipline upon lesbian and gay soldiers and sailors. The policy fails to prioritize the elimination of the pervasive, violent and sometimes lethal climate of homophobia in the military; it demands conformity, first and foremost, from lesbians and gays rather than homophobic bigots. Its promise to include lesbians and gays is therefore a mythical promise, like that of the supporters of Section 28. It pretends to 'tolerate' lesbians and gays in the military – as long as they perform impossible acts of self-containment and self-erasure, and as long as they quietly endure institutionalized discrimination against them – and it promises to discipline only those who disrupt the military's secret homoerotic culture by flaunting her or his sexual difference. In actuality, it provides no protection whatsoever for lesbian and gay soldiers and sailors from homophobic persecution. The policy also has a disturbingly chilling effect on American society in general in that it legitimizes the argument that lesbians and gays do not deserve the same democratic rights, such as the right to free speech, which heterosexuals take for granted.

It should also be recognized that the 'good homosexual'/dangerous queer distinction is a consistently gendered difference. Lesbianness, as opposed to male gayness, is usually located within the 'good homosexual' category. Lord Halsbury, for example, argues that in contrast to the excesses of some male homosexual practices, lesbians are 'not a problem'. 'They do not molest little girls. They do not indulge in disgusting and unnatural acts like buggery. They are not wildly promiscuous and do not spread venereal disease.'[50] He claims that gay men attempt to conceal their dangerous practices by placing the term 'lesbian' before the term 'gay' in the names of community groups, so that the 'relatively harmless lesbian leads on to the vicious gay'.[51] This gendered distinction is consistent with legislation on sexual offences. Lesbian practices were not referred to in the 1533 Act of Henry VIII on sodomy, the 1861 and 1885 laws on sodomy and gross indecency, the 1898 Vagrancy Act, the 1967 Sexual Offences Act, or Section 31 of the 1990–1 Criminal Justice Act. When attempts were made in 1921 to include lesbian practices in the category of gross indecency, Lord Desart argued that this inclusion would be inappropriate in that it would only bring lesbian sex 'to the notice of women who [had] never heard of it, never thought of it, never dreamed of it'.[52]

The absence of the lesbian in criminal discourse is not due to a special benevolence towards lesbians on the part of juridical and parliamentary discourses. This lack, on the contrary, constitutes a deeply misogynist strategy, namely the erasure of the very possibility of any autonomous female sexuality. It is structured in terms of a sexist conception of women's subjectivity: that women are, by nature, passive, moderate, non-assertive, incapable of re-occupying sexual discourses on their own terms and so on. Roger Scruton, a British right-wing philosopher, claims female sexuality has, by definition, a 'moderating' presence. Because the 'moderating effect' of female presence is lacking in male homosexuality, the latter takes the form of an 'imperative force' which promiscuously seeks immediate gratification in a socially destructive manner. Lesbian sexuality, by contrast, lacks the male drive. As the mere addition of two moderating forces, lesbian sexuality is supposed to be centred on lasting partnership, and not on sexual excitement. Scruton concludes that a lesbian cannot possess the same sexual drive as a gay man, because if she did 'act like a man' in this way, she would no longer attract other women.[53] A similar erasure of lesbian sexuality has taken place in the United States in the context of AIDS research. When asked why the Center for Disease Control has not carried out any research on woman-to-woman transmission of the virus, an official replied, 'Lesbians don't have much sex.' Official discourse on AIDS has 'over-sexualized' the activities of gay men and 'desexualized' lesbian sexuality.[54]

In other words, Lord Desart, Scruton and the officials in medical institutions who fail to recognize that lesbians do indeed have an autonomous sexuality are all performing the same conflation of gender and sexuality. Many theorists, such as Gayle Rubin, contend that no one's gender – no one's masculinity or femininity – naturally determines their sexuality.[55] Read from a feminist perspective, their arguments are problematic on three counts. It is simply not true that all women are feminine and all men are masculine; indeed, the very terms, 'feminine' and 'masculine' are constantly being re-defined through subversive 'gender-bending' practices. Second, only sexist discourse equates femininity with absolutely passive behaviour; as many feminine men and women have shown, there is no contradiction between femininity and assertiveness. Indeed, this colonization of women within the so-called natural category of passive helplessness legitimates the de-authorization of women's discourse, such that our self-representation is displaced by paternal control. Finally, the articulation between an individual's gender identity – their femininity, masculinity or some other gendering – and their sexuality – their active or passive role-playing; their heterosexuality, bisexuality or homosexuality; their 'straightness' or 'kinkiness'; and so on – is entirely contingent. As the lesbian saying goes, one can be 'butch in the streets and femme in the sheets'; we simply cannot predict the ways in which gender and sexuality will coincide in any particular identity.

The erasure of lesbian sexuality supports the representation of lesbian political autonomy as an impossibility. When Lord Halsbury distinguishes between the morally bankrupt, disease-ridden and criminal gay man and the relatively harmless lesbian, he does nevertheless note that lesbians have become an active political force. Remaining consistent with his extremely misogynist conception of the gay male/lesbian difference, he maintains that the politicization of lesbians must have its origins outside the lesbian community. He claims that the 'loony left is hardening up the lesbian camp and they [the lesbians] are becoming increasingly aggressive'.[56] For him, the opportunistic male heterosexual leftists are the real instigators; it is only through their intervention that the naturally passive and quiescent lesbian is transformed into an activist. The idealization of the lesbian in the pro-Section 28 discourse therefore plays a similar function as Powell's distinction between the basically docile black immigrant and the radical African American revolutionary. Both of these representations perform deeply oppressive erasures of political autonomy and agency.

In Britain, the lesbian is nevertheless identified in official discourse as a dangerous element in two ways. First, the figure of the lesbian, or more precisely, the black lesbian, is used to invalidate the Labour Party's support for a whole range of feminist, black, disabled and lesbian and gay projects. This tactic was used, for example, in leaflets distributed by a Conservative Party local constituency association in Surbiton before the May 1991 elections. The leaflets claimed that the London Boroughs Grant Scheme should be eliminated so that 'public money' would no longer be spent on '"loony left" projects such as black lesbian groups'. References to the illegitimacy of funding for black lesbian projects were also made by both left- and right-wing politicians throughout the debates on the abolition of the GLC.[57]

Second, the lesbian is represented as a dangerous element in official discourse when she attempts to occupy the place of the parent. In the Section 28 debates, *both* gay male parents and lesbian parents were named as the pseudo-parents of 'pretend families'. Lesbian and gay male parenting has also been attacked through recent fostering regulations. Paragraph 16 of the guidelines to the 1989 Children Act instructed social services departments that

> It would be wrong arbitrarily to exclude any groups of people from consideration. But the chosen way of life of some adults may mean that they would not be able to provide a suitable environment for the care and nurture of a child. No one has the 'right' to be a foster parent. 'Equal rights' and 'gay rights' policies have no place in fostering services.

Paragraph 16 was only amended by the government after intensive lobbying by lesbian and gay activists. The final version replaces the last sentence with a more neutral statement, 'Fostering decisions must centre exclusively on the interests of the child.' It also states that 'the needs and concerns of gay young men and women [as foster children] must also be recognized and approached sympa-thetically ... Gay young men and women may require very sym-pathetic carers to enable them to accept their sexuality and to develop their own self-esteem.'

Lesbian parenting was nevertheless targeted again in the Human Fertilization and Embryology Act 1990. Conservative MP Ann Winterton tabled an Early Day Motion on 26 October 1989 which expressed 'profound concern' that lesbians had received artificial insemination by donors at a London pregnancy advisory service clinic. Winterton lobbied for the introduction of an amendment to prohibit the provision of this service to unmarried women, and to order the compulsory registration of all sperm donors, in the legisla-tion on embryo research. The government successfully added section 13(5) to the 1990 bill, which states:

> A woman shall not be provided with [artificial insemination] treatment services unless account has been taken of the welfare of any child who may be born as a result of the treatment (including the need of that child for a father).

Speaking to the amendment which introduced this section, the Lord Chancellor stated:

> Among the factors which clinicians should take into account will be the material circumstances in which the child is likely to be brought up and also the stability and love which he or she is likely to enjoy. Such stability is clearly linked to the marital position of the woman and in particular whether a husband or long-term partner can play a full part in providing the child with a permanent family setting in the fullest sense of that term, including financial provision.[58]

Wilshire, the Conservative MP who had played a key role in the Section 28 debates, attempted to move a further amendment. If passed, Wilshire's amendment would have restricted the provision of government-licensed artificial insemination services only to women who were in couples with men. Wilshire argued that the man in each of these couples should be 'treated as the father of any child carried by the woman as a result of the provision of those treatment services'. He declared:

> Our society is based on long-term commitments between adults in a family setting. It is based on a child having a mother and a father, and on the importance of family life ... Our social standards are deliberately being undermined, and it is high time for those of us who think that that is wrong to stand up and say, in words of one syllable, that we shall fight that decline and prevent it going any further.[59]

In a complete confusion of biological and social categories, he insisted that 'whatever goes on in the laboratory, a mother and a father are still required to produce'.[60]

Although Wilshire's amendment failed – other Tory MPs supported Wilshire in principle but expressed their reservations about the amendment's legality – it revealed much about the right-wing Conservatives' approach to the family. Lesbians were not particularly singled out in the debate; Wilshire's target was the self-created single-parent family of any type. He argued that his amendment 'will make it crystal clear that the deliberate creation of a legally fatherless child will not be permissible in this country'.[61] The only mention of lesbian parenting came in an intervention by a Labour member which was virtually ignored. The MPs in the Committee exchanged imaginary scenarios in which women sought impregnation through casual sex with men or saved the sperm of their dying husbands for future use. It should therefore be recognized that the restriction of lesbians' access to official insemination services is but one aspect of a broader assault on women's rights to control our bodies, and that the 'pro-family' lobby targets both unmarried heterosexual women and lesbians alike through these measures.

Artificial insemination clinics remain under pro-family surveillance, for they must follow government guidelines to retain their licenses. The April 1991 draft of these guidelines states that the doctors and counsellors of each clinic have to decide whether or not the prospective mothers who do not have male partners would be able to meet the child's needs fully. In the spring of 1991, claims were made in both the popular and 'quality' press that women who had not had sex with men should not be allowed to bear children. The rights of both lesbians and single heterosexual women were attacked on an equal basis in this so-called 'virgin birth' scandal. The specificity of the *lesbian* mother as a demonized figure was rather weak throughout the sensationalistic news coverage.

Lesbian parents, like single heterosexual mothers, are dangerous because, for the supporters of Section 28, they are pretenders to the real thing. When asked to clarify the meaning of 'pretended' in the second part of Section 28 which prohibits the teaching of homosexuality as a 'pretended relationship', Lord Halsbury says that 'pretended' means 'someone who is claiming to something', like a 'pretender to the throne'.[62] The lesbian parent is dangerous because she displaces the male head of the household. Lesbian parenting does not, however, constitute an autonomously defined *sexuality*. The demonization of the lesbian parent in this sense remains consistent with the sexist erasure of any autonomous female sexuality.

The lesbian figure is transformed, then, into a dangerous figure in official discourse, but only where racist and sexist discourse coincide with homophobic discourse to produce the black lesbian and the lesbian parent as specific demons. The very use of the term, 'lesbian', in the debates on Section 28 marks, in a peculiar way, an important milestone for lesbian politics, namely recognition of our presence in official discourse. Nevertheless, it should be underlined that for the most part, the lesbian figure is represented as the good homosexual as opposed to the dangerous queer.

Even in its most extreme moment, then, homophobic discourse did not take the form of a simple total war on homosexuals. The dangerous queer provided an infinitely threatening enemy who could be used as a symptom figure to 'stitch up' the inconsistencies in Thatcherite discourse. Because even the most modest pro-lesbian and gay rights statements had been equated with a moral and medical plague, virtually any group or initiative which dealt with the issue of homosexuality without condemning lesbians and gays could be used as further evidence of the sinister campaign. Furthermore, as the Nietzschean and Foucauldian approach to power relations suggest, differences were actually multiplied through the supporters' discourse: a mythical position of the wholly accepted homosexual was created, 'borderline' deviants were encouraged to distance themselves from the subversives, the subversives' resistances were depicted as the intolerable extremism which had to be met with an authoritarian response, and the mythical inclusion of the assimilable homosexuals cast the homophobic supporters of Section 28 as tolerant defenders of the social order. It is important to insist on the differentiating effects of Section 28 and other homophobic initiatives precisely because the right's anti-queer campaign is often represented in monolithic terms. These representations in turn support the strategic myth that the lesbian and gay community is an essentially homogeneous bloc and that gender, class and racial differences are virtually irrelevant to queer politics.

Some forms of anti-AIDS discourse reproduce this monolithic structure: gay men are represented as an utterly undifferentiated group with no significant political links with lesbians or the feminist movement. Bersani, for example, represents American gay men as an essentially disempowered bloc. He develops this argument through a comparison with African Americans.

> While it would of course be obscene to claim that the comfortable life of a successful gay white businessman or doctor is as oppressed as that of a poverty-stricken black mother in one of our ghettoes, it is also true that the power of *blacks as a group* in the United States is much greater than that of homosexuals.[63]

Bersani recognizes that the political gestures towards the African American community – the nomination of a few blacks to decision-making positions, civil rights initiatives, the direct appeals to the 'black vote' and so on – are perfectly compatible with the intensification of racist oppression. He nevertheless insists that 'a few blacks will always be saved from the appalling fate of most blacks in America, whereas there is no political need to save or to protect any homosexuals at all'.[64] For Bersani, even the most affluent white gay man is totally unrepresented.

Frequently on the side of power, but powerless; frequently affluent, but politically destitute; frequently articulate, but with *nothing but a moral argument* – not even recognized as a moral argument – to keep themselves in the protected white enclaves and out of the quarantine camps.[65]

It is of course true that sexuality does not operate exactly the same as race in political discourse, and that gay men have been singled out for vicious attacks by the American and British right since the popularization of the gay male excess = AIDS = death equation in the mid-1980s. This does not mean, however, that affluent white gay men are politically powerless. They are extensively represented in terms of their maleness, whiteness and middle-class positions, often to the exclusion of women, people of colour and the working class. Although the official response to AIDS has been extremely inadequate to say the least, it should be recognized that where the pitifully few resources have been devoted to AIDS education and research, the needs of white gay men have sometimes taken a priority over those of women and racial/ethnic minorities. ACT-UP has pointed out that all women and men of colour have been excluded from drug trials for AIDS-related illnesses, that women on average die much faster than men after an AIDS diagnosis, and that a Person-with-AIDS' life expectancy after diagnosis in New York can be predicted with reference to their location in one of the city's ethnic- and class-defined neighbourhoods.

Bersani's comparison is therefore inaccurate, and his narrow definition of political power, framed in terms of interest group politics rather than a structural analysis, is misleading. While it is true that a few African Americans have finally been admitted to powerful governmental, military and judicial posts, it is also clear that when other people of colour attempt to bring an anti-racist agenda into institutional hierarchies, they face tremendous resistance. If a handful of conservative African Americans are 'saved', but only to mask the intensification of racism throughout American society, then their entry into the national elite does not substantially alter the exclusion of the majority of African Americans.

To represent affluent white gay men as 'politically destitute' is to ignore the fact that their homosexuality is simply not the only aspect of their identities which determines their socio-economic and political privileges. If they were indeed totally excluded from the political system, if hegemonic official discourses made no effort to represent them as middle-class white men, or as 'good homosexuals', and if those representations were totally irrelevant to the construction of gay male identities, then they could be excused from all political responsibility. This claim to an utterly 'outside' status for affluent white gay men is a phantasmatic construction which only promotes the more reactionary elements within gay male discourse.

The continuities across racist and homophobic discourses

Having demonstrated the differentiation between the good homosexual and the dangerous queer in the supporters' representations of homosexuality, the strategic necessity for the supporters simultaneously to include the former and to exclude the latter from their vision of the social order remains to be shown. First, however, it is important to note that the supporters' demonizing strategies are not 'new', but have already been developed in discourses on other social elements. The construction of a crisis is a mythical but effective evidence game; the use of otherness as a common enemy against which the concealment of social ruptures becomes possible; the representation of that otherness as an invader, a monster, a floating interruption and a pretender; the division of otherness into legitimate and illegitimate camps; the pseudo-acceptance of the former as harmless difference and the exclusion of the latter as dangerous difference; all these strategies are also at work in the New Right discourse on race and nation. The 'panic' about the numbers of 'New Commonwealth' immigrants in the later 1960s was the product of an evidence game organized by Powellian discourse. The crises of the Kenyan Asian immigrants and the promotion of homosexuality campaign were constructed through representational strategies. In both Powellian discourse and the debates on Section 28, blackness and homosexuality are not just represented as something other, and they are not simply excluded. They are represented instead as threats to the social order insofar as these othernesses take the 'form' of a subversive supplement, and these threats are managed through strategies of differentiation and representation. In both cases, a demon figure is not just simply imposed onto 'the people'; the New Right works instead to organize already available anxieties – anxieties about de-colonization and the disintegration of the nation in the 1960s, and anxieties about AIDS, the collapse of the family, the advance of feminism and sexual liberation movements and affirmative action for racial minorities in the 1980s. Where Powell used the figure of the black immigrant to address the rise of an anti-demo-cratic bureaucracy and the collapse of consensus discourse, the supporters of Section 28 use the figure of the self-promoting homo-sexual to depict local governments as authoritarian and to promote central government control over local government. Powellism created an open-ended list of 'enemies within', the extra-parliamen-tary movements which worked partially 'outside' official discourse on the level of intellectual reform. Discourse on Section 28 reiterates the Powellian-Thatcherite racial logic. The Powellian version of the new racism helped to prepare the place for the self-promoting homosexual in the long list of 'enemies within', black immigrants, radical students, Irish activists, socialist school teachers, critical journalists, progressive intellectuals and so on.

The juxtaposition of criminal, sexual, racial and national themes in the four book titles featured in the Conservative Party's campaign poster cited above makes sense because it works within this Powellian–Thatcherite tradition. 'Invader-ness' is not fixed in terms of a single 'concrete' enemy, but circulates to new figures. The reader of the poster is prompted to think, as we fought against the blacks to exclude them (through the immigration laws) and to regulate their criminality (through new policing discourses), so too must we join together to defeat the perverts in the classroom. The white line of the immigration queue and the thin blue line of inner city policing is reproduced in homophobic discourse in the form of an obscure division between the 'proper' and 'improper' teaching on homo-sexuality.

In New Right discourse, whiteness, Britishness and heterosexual-ity are represented as if they ought to correspond to a given set of people; at the same time, supplementary difference is seen as con-taminating these essential attributes. The very whiteness and British-ness of school children is represented as natural and yet fragile. The controversies in the 1980s about 'multiculturalism' and putatively illegitimate approaches to the Empire demonstrated the extent to which white Britishness was regarded as vulnerable to corruption through radical black influences. The teaching of 'multiculturalism', the content and form of the British history curriculum, and the appropriate quantitative mix of children from different ethnic back-grounds in places such as Dewsbury were extensively debated throughout the 1980s.[66] From a radical perspective, some of the 'multiculturalism' initiatives are just as suspect as the 1960s race relations laws which were used against black activists. Beverly

Bryan, Stella Dadzie and Suzanne Scafe argue that Black Studies and multiculturalism were often used in secondary schools as a form of social control: the new curricula were supposed to placate black parents and educators who were concerned about the miseducation of black students. They make the important distinction between multicultural curricula, which emphasize cultural differences, and anti-racist curricula, which emphasize the analysis of power relations.[67] From the New Right's perspective, however, even the most timid step in the direction of multiculturalism constitutes an illegitimate politicization of the classroom. Regardless of actual skin pigmentation, parenting and apparent 'normalcy', the white child is seen by the Thatcherites as someone who needs protection from these subversive elements; her true identity must be actively produced through proper teaching.

In the Thatcherite discourse on multiculturalism and the promotion of homosexuality, the classroom is situated as the supplement to the family. The classroom must perform an impossible task, that of completing the natural development of the child. The 'proper' space for the development of racial and sexual identities is nevertheless supposed to be the space of the family. In the context of the Section 28 debates, the supporters argue that teachers and other local government officials are 'strangers' from 'outside the home', and that the teaching of sexuality ought to 'start in the family unit'.[68] The teacher, then, should only complete the work of the parents and should not interfere. The supporters' arguments imply that it is only in the absolutely normal space of the family, a space of known blood relatives, and organized, strictly hierarchical, relations, that subversive difference can be adequately resisted. Their representation of the family as a perfect antagonism-free space is, of course, deeply ironic in light of the prevalence of violence against women and child sexual abuse within familial settings.

Thatcher's own statements demonstrate the extent to which the promotion of homosexuality crisis was manufactured with direct reference to the multiculturalism debate. At a Conservative Party conference in October 1987, Thatcher explicitly attacked schoolteachers for politicizing the school curriculum. She ridiculed the inclusion of multiculturalism in the schools by suggesting that the notion of 'anti-racist maths' was absurd. She then declared, 'Children who need to be taught to respect traditional moral values are being taught that they have the inalienable right to be gay.'[69] The problematization of the space and frontiers of the classroom in the late 1980s with regard to the otherness of blackness follows from the thinking of identities as always susceptible to illegitimate influences, and this is precisely the thinking that runs through the supporters' discourse on Section 28. The worst villains in the 'promotion of homosexuality' story – teachers, cultural workers, progressive politicians and intellectuals in general – are also the villains of Powellian and Thatcherite discourse on race. In Powell's speeches, the most treasonous enemy is not the black immigrant, but the apparently harmless journalists, academics, politicians and even church officials who spread the corrosive message of tolerance.

The Powellian–Thatcherite argument – which is reproduced in the discourse of the supporters of Section 28 – is that the most sinister advances of the left, including socialism and tolerance for blacks and queers, have been made on the terrain of moral and intellectual reform – or, in the right's terms, 'social engineering'. From this perspective, the role of the intellectual is seen as critical in that it is through intellectual activity that identities are constructed and otherness is managed; the 'permissive' intellectual commits a crime against society in that her interventions weaken the frontiers which would otherwise facilitate the exclusion and neutralization of supplementary difference. It is not accidental, then, that Section 28 prohibits the *intentional* promotion of homosexuality; what this encourages is an intellectual self-examination, a policing of one's own intentions. The Earl of Caithness says that Section 28 is supposed to make any local authority involved in an initiative concerning homosexuality 'ask itself' about its legal position, and 'decide what its purpose is' in that activity.[70] Wilshire, who introduced Section 28, says it stands as a 'warning to the liberal and the trendy that you can go too far for society to tolerate'. A spokesperson for the National Council of Civil Liberties further comments, 'It's the self-censorship, the decisions taken by councils behind closed doors that make Section 28 so dangerous.'[71] Section 28 is therefore also located within a particularly effective tradition of anti-intellectualism – the tradition of insidious incitement to self-censorship.

There are several statements in the Section 28 debate which explicitly link race and the 'promotion of homosexuality'. Lord Halsbury states:

> We have for several decades past been emancipating minorities who claimed that they were disadvantaged. Are they grateful? Not a bit. We emancipated races and got inverted racism. We emancipate homosexuals and they condemn heterosexism as

chauvinist sexism, male oppression and so on. They will push us off the pavement if we give them a chance.[72]

National self-determination and civil liberties are here defined as privileges bestowed by a generous and 'permissive' society. The problem with 'permissiveness' for Halsbury is that that which appears to be a legitimate recognition of the basic rights of minorities is actually a fatal step on the slippery slope towards total anarchy. Furthermore, the products of 'permissiveness' are represented as an endless chain of disruptive social movements which build on each other's subversion in the advancement of increasingly absurd demands.

References to the link between discourse on race and discourse on homosexuality are also explicitly made by the opposers of Section 28. The GLC's proposals on 'heterosexism', which were published in the document *Changing the World*, were especially attacked by the supporters. This document was a report on homophobic discrimination which was written by a working group of lesbians and gay men in 1985. It included 142 recommendations for legislative and administrative reforms, and only one of these recommendations addressed 'heterosexism'. In his parliamentary speech on Section 28, Labour MP Ken Livingston addressed the supporters' criticisms of the GLC's pro-lesbian and gay rights stance. Livingston defines anti-heterosexism as the fight against homophobic discrimination and insists that anti-heterosexism is not the rejection of heterosexuality. He then constructs a parallel between different forms of discrimination: 'Heterosexism is exactly the same kind of term as racism or sexism. They all describe discrimination against a particular group or class or gender.'[73] With this analogy, Livingston borrows the logic of Halsbury's discourse and merely inverts it. Where Halsbury legitimates his homophobic discourse by reactivating racist anxieties, Livingston legitimates his opposition to homophobic discourse by reactivating anti-racist discourse. In a sense, both speakers are right and wrong: there are many continuities between discourse on race and discourse on sexuality, but there are also important specificities which are erased by these reductionist analogies.

One of the specificities of discourse on homosexuality – as opposed to discourse on race – is the articulation between anxieties around the dangerous queer and anxieties around the disintegration of the patriarchal nuclear family. British New Right discourse on blackness is ambiguous on this point: while the supposedly natural matriarchal tradition in black cultures, the fertility of black women and the promiscuity of black men, are often represented by the New Right as threats to the white familial nation, the Asian communities are also represented as exemplary preserves of pro-family standards. In the debates on Section 28, Tory MP Greenway stated that in response to the policies of the Ealing Council in support of lesbian and gay rights, he organized a 'conference on the family' in February 1987. He emphasizes that representatives from the Anglican, Catholic, Sikh, Moslem and Hindu communities attended this conference. He also insists that the Anglican, Catholic, Jewish, Sikh, Moslem and Hindu religions 'teach that homosexuality is wrong'.[74] Greenway is of course engaging in a strategic (mis-)interpretation of these religions here, but it is important to note the complexity of his manoeuvre. In this particular moment, the racist and anti-Semitic aspects of New Right discourse are suppressed, and a homophobic consensus is constructed around a campaign to preserve the patriarchal family. This consensus is cross-racial, cross-religious and cross-'Western'/'Oriental'. Where the Moslem faith is represented as backward and anti-European in the contexts of the Salman Rushdie crisis and Middle East foreign policy, it is held up as an exemplary model in the context of pro-family discourse.

There is, by contrast, very little ambiguity in terms of the representation of the relation between the dangerous queer and the institution of the family in New Right discourse: the self-promoting queer is regarded as an anti-family enemy. Stacey argues that there are important continuities between homophobic pro-Section 28 discourse and anti-feminist discourse.[75] Although Section 28 is widely regarded as a 'backlash' against the achievements of feminism, she argues that it actually represents a re-working of feminist discourse. Where feminists insist that sexuality and gender are socially constructed, the British New Right accepts this premise, but attempts to respond to the unfixed character of identities through intellectual interventions of their own. Stacey also compares the emphasis on the patriarchal family in pro-Section 28 discourse to feminist critiques. Feminists have recognized that with the rise in divorce rates and the numbers of 'non-traditional' families, the patriarchal family is in crisis. They hold that this crisis is related to women's resistance to the family's structural inequalities, and to the rejection by lesbians and gays of the institutionalization of heterosexuality as a compulsory, rather than chosen, practice. With Section 28, the New Right has shown that it has also recognized the fragile and ruptured character of the family. For the New Right, however, the failures of the family have nothing to do with its oppressive structure. They argue instead that the otherwise perfect family has been disrupted by figures which are, supposedly, external to the family, such as pornographers, prostitutes, pro-choice feminists and the dangerous queer. Stacey concludes that Section 28 does not mark a return to Victorian values, but constitutes a contemporary response to the feminist contestation of the organization of sexuality, gender roles and family relations.

For the Thatcherites, the family is the 'fundamental unit of society', and it is because the family has been 'stripped of so many of its rights and duties' that moral standards have declined.[76] In an interview in *Women's Own* magazine in November 1987, Thatcher urged the Church of England to take a 'more forthright' stance on AIDS and morality. She stated, 'A nation of free people will only continue to be great if family life continues and the structure of that nation is a family one.'[77] Again, the Thatcherite phantasmatic construction of the family as the basis of national morality is sharply at odds with feminist research on child abuse involving parental and sibling offenders, violence against women in the family and marital rape. Through their construction of the homosexual as the invader, monster, seducer and pretender, the Thatcherites displace the cause for the breakdown of the family onto an external figure. The dangerous queer therefore operates as one of the symptomatic supports for the phantasmatic representation of the family as an antagonism-free space, just as the black immigrant functions as one of the symptomatic supports for the re-constitution of the white British nation.

Even with this Thatcherite representation of lesbians and gays as an undifferentiated enemy of the family, the racial differences within the lesbian and gay community *vis-à-vis* the family should not be ignored. When black lesbians and gay men risk rejection by their families through 'coming out', their risk is even more intense than that of white lesbians and gay men because the black family often offers support against racist exclusions. In its promotion of the principle that every lesbian and gay man should come out in as many different situations as possible, sexual liberation discourse may have been insensitive to the actual experiences of black lesbians and gays. It should also be noted that the notion that black families are inherently more anti-queer than white families is a racist myth; this argument only constitutes the lesbian and gay version of the racist pathologization of the black family.[78]

222

The management of otherness in homophobic discourse

When the supporters of Section 28 speak of a distinction between the good homosexual and the dangerous queer, then, they are speaking inside the 'enemies within' tradition. Different moments in this tradition are not essentially the same, but a sufficient degree of continuity, a non-essential minimal remainder, is retained across them. In both the new racism and the Thatcherite homophobic discourses, otherness is divided into subversive difference and accidental difference: anti-British radical blackness versus the figures of the entrepreneurial assimilated black and the morally conservative black, and flaunting subversive queerness versus the closeted homosexual. In Nietzschean and Deleuzian terms, radical blackness and subversive queerness could be conceptualized as the products of the purely active forces, and the assimilated black and the closeted homosexual as the products of the purely reactive forces. These figures are in this sense ideal; no one can actually occupy these identities fully. Actual identification practices can only produce identity effects which approximate these ideals.

This theoretical conceptualization is nevertheless useful in that it emphasizes the complexity of identity strategies. Where social disruption is dealt with through the construction of a symptom figure, such as radical blacks or dangerous queers, various responses are possible. A democratic response would, first and foremost, insist on the full recognition of the inalienable rights of the target populations. Furthermore, a democratic response would demonstrate that the demonizations only concealed social ruptures – unemployment, political alienation, class and regional differences, the dislocation of traditional family structures, crises in national cohesion and so on – and that these ruptures would persist even if the campaign against the symptom figure were totally successful. Instead of taking the symptom logic for granted as natural and merely working within its terms, a democratic response would concentrate on the reactionary forces and volatile conditions from which the demonization originates. An authoritarian response would attempt to transform a vague sense of anxiety in popular discourse into a total war against a clearly defined symptom figure. An authoritarian response would call for a war-time suspension of the rights of the target populations.

Deploying the symptom as a constitutive supplement, an authoritarian response would utilize the campaign against the enemy figure as an opportunity to promote national unity; ultimately, the anti-democratic effects of the campaign against the symptom figure would be felt far beyond the specific site of this struggle.

British New Right discourse on race and sexuality in this sense tends towards the authoritarian type of response. Its effectiveness is actually enhanced by self-contradiction. At one moment, the Powellians and Thatcherites virtually exclude all blackness and homosexuality from the white British familial nation and the social is depicted as a simple two-camp system: the British versus the anti-British. At another moment, the Powellian and Thatcherite discourse invokes the tolerance tradition: mythical figures such as the good homosexual are constructed and explicitly included within the imaginary British community. In this second moment, the social is represented as a synchronic array of antagonism-free differences: the sense of a total civil war between the British and the anti-British is suppressed, and the British community is represented as an infinitely tolerant space which can accommodate virtually every difference.[79]

At closer inspection, however, these two moments are not just contradictory but are also complementary. The racist and homophobic antagonisms of the first moment can only be successfully dealt with through surveillance and discipline technologies: it is because blacks and homosexuals constitute subversive threats to the social order that they must be brought within the social order to some degree and turned against ourselves/themselves. The differentiation of otherness and the inclusion of trained otherness also facilitates the concealment of the exclusionary dimension of the discourse; it makes it possible to argue coherently, and effectively, that the British New Right is not racist or homophobic. To paraphrase Patten, the British New Right is quite fond of saying, 'the majority of blacks and homosexuals can be reassured that it's only those people who are dangerous to society that we're after, and some of those people only "happen" to be black and/or lesbian and gay'. That which is included, however, is a neutralized, simple difference; the 'cost' of inclusion is never explicitly recognized. This double manoeuvre also opens up the tremendously productive possibility of self-division and self-surveillance *within* an element of otherness, practised at a local level, in local discourses. I shall return to this theme below.

224

In the second moment, the moment in which the social is represented as an array of antagonism-free differences, the inclusion of the trained otherness allows Britishness to appear as truly all-encompassing. Because the assimilated blackness and homosexuality are included, and the excluded elements are represented as only accidentally black and homosexual, Britishness can be depicted as a truly universal space: the Noah's ark of differences. The British New Right's Britishness can therefore be represented as essentially 'tolerant', even though this 'tolerance' is actually constructed through extremely racist and homophobic representations. As Thatcher stated:

> People with other faiths and cultures have always been welcomed in our land, assured of equality under the law, of proper respect and of open friends. There is absolutely nothing incompatible between this and our desire to maintain the essence of our own identity.[80]

In a peculiar sense, Thatcher is right: othernesses have always been included, but only through the neutralizing process of assimilation, and only as the support for authoritarian exclusions. Through the mythical inclusion of the (impossible) figures of the perfectly assimilable black and the perfectly good homosexual, the British New Right's imaginary British community and its moral 'norm' can be represented as invulnerable; it permits the racist and homophobic Britons to say, 'look at how strong our nation is, "we" can actually live together with so many different peoples and still maintain our Britishness', and so on. 'We' are doubly reassured here: 'we' congratulate 'ourselves' on 'our' ability to 'tolerate', indeed to enjoy included difference; yet 'we' enjoy it in a safe, neutralized space – a walk in a zoo rather than a walk on the wild side.

The representation of Britishness in terms of the total war antagonism – the British versus the anti-British – must therefore be supplemented by an antagonism-free and infinitely tolerant representation of the British nation. The reverse is equally true. The imaginary British community cannot be simply represented as a virtually peaceful and all-inclusive system of differential elements. The exclusion of the demon symptom figures produces the order, the consensus, the sense of common purpose which is supposed to have been there all along. The exclusion of dangerous difference is necessary for the creation of a sense of unity ('our' nation, 'our' shared norm), yet the inclusion of difference is a necessary support for that exclusion. Differentiation is therefore promoted, rather than suppressed, through this exclusion/inclusion matrix, but, paradoxically, in the re-working of difference through this matrix, an appearance of consensus and closure is created and preserved.

It is of course true that some of the supporters of Section 28 do not participate in these complex manoeuvres *vis-à-vis* otherness. When Smith, a Labour MP, cites the escalation of physical attacks on lesbians and gays in general, and the arson attack on the offices of the community newspaper, *Capital Gay*, in particular, Kellett-Bowman, a Conservative MP, responds, 'Quite right ... there ought to be intolerance for evil.'[81] Fairbairn, a Conservative MP, claims incorrectly that homosexuality is classed as a 'psychopathological perversion' and lists unlimited aggression, sadism, masochism and criminality as equivalents to homosexuality.[82] Others further equate homosexuality with the total destruction of the social order, the institution of the family and even civilization itself.[83] The 'promotion of homosexuality' is represented as the 'thin edge of the wedge'. Lord Monson argues that lesbian and gay pride weeks cannot be publicly funded because there would be no grounds to refuse support to 'bondage pride weeks'; in his view, 'the possible permutations are endless'.[84] Wilshire says that if the promotion of homosexuality were made legal simply because homosexual acts had been decriminalized, this would 'lead to an "everything goes" in this country'. In an almost impossible twist of logic, he concludes that if the promotion of homosexuality were allowed, then other promotions of illegitimate elements, such as the promotion of racial hatred, would also have to be permitted.[85]

This discourse of bigotry, though not typical of the supporters' discourse, is put to use within it. Contrasting themselves to the bigots on the one side, and the 'loony left' on the other, the supporters are able to locate themselves as the centrist representatives of the moderate majority,[86] in a situation in which they would otherwise be themselves recognized as extremist reactionaries. Where Thatcher used the National Front to represent her stance as that of an official and moderate position which mediated between two extremes, the white fascists versus the black anarchists, the pro-Section 28 discourse also 'centres' itself between two extremes. The supporters actually express concern regarding the current backlash against lesbians and gays, and argue that the Section is the best remedy in that it will 'remove the source of the disquiet',[87] namely the 'unacceptable activities of a few extremist councils'.[88] The 'good homosexual' is therefore represented as the innocent victim of a backlash against homosexuals which ought properly to be directed against local authorities; indeed, it is implied that it is in the true interest of the lesbian and gay community itself to support the Section. The arguments of both the bigots and the opposers of Section 28 are represented in this context as equivalents, as equally disruptive extremisms – and the supporters' response to the crisis is represented as the only possible strategy for the restoration of order. Where Powell and Thatcher attempt to de-racialize their racism, the Section 28 supporters attempt to de-homosexualize their homo-phobic discourse. In both cases, these representations 'centre' poli-tical figures who would otherwise be recognized as extremists.

The management of otherness and the identities of lesbians and gays

I have referred to the strategy of inciting self-division and self-surveillance within a demonized population both in my discussion of Foucault's theory of power relations and in the above analysis of the multiplication of differences through Thatcherite homophobic discourse. The Thatcherite differentiations between the good homo-sexual and the dangerous queer have a significant effect not only on those homophobic extremists who want to depict themselves as tolerant, but also on lesbians and gays ourselves. The New Right discourse speaks persuasively to the element within the lesbian and gay community which 'wants to be good'; it seems to offer to the mythical good homosexual full inclusion in its imaginary British community. The homophobic representations in Thatcherite dis-course do not remain external to lesbian and gay identities. The New Right does not say 'no' to all homosexuality, but actually manages sexual difference by encouraging the development of a self-limiting homosexual subject. It does not invent a self-disciplining element and impose it onto lesbians and gays, and it is certainly not the author of the gendered and racial differences within the community. The New Right nevertheless mobilizes these differences, incites their development and puts them to work.

In the parliamentary debates on Section 28, Lord Halsbury reads a letter which he says is from a 'male homosexual'.

> I want to say how fed up I am with my fellow homosexuals. They have brought it upon themselves, their unpopularity. They are too promiscuous, too aggressive and exhibitionist. I cannot stand the sight of them. I wish they would keep them-selves to themselves.[89]

Again, the question of the document's authenticity is irrelevant. Regardless of whether or not he fabricated the letter, Lord Halsbury is explicitly positioning himself as the spokesperson for the good homosexual, just as Powell and Churchill spoke in the name of the black immigrant who supports racist immigration legislation.

Lord Halsbury's invocation of a self-limiting homosexual has a well-established organic basis. The distinction in the letter between the good homosexual and the dangerous queer is repeated in many other texts which are written by lesbians and gays ourselves. It is beyond the scope of this study to present a thorough analysis of the extremely complex responses to Thatcherite discourse on the part of lesbians and gays. I have focused almost exclusively on the official discourse of the New Right, and I have only mentioned black and lesbian and gay resistances in passing. Because the entire Gramscian-Foucauldian 'authoritarian populist' approach to political discourse holds that right-wing hegemonies are established through the organization of consent – rather than coercion or deception – this approach ultimately depends on studies which show the discursive effects of right-wing representations on marginal identity games. Did the hegemonic strategies of the Thatcherites actually succeed in inciting self-differentiation and self-surveillance among its demonized target groups, such as leftist intellectuals, militant trade unionists, blacks, Asians and other ethnic minorities, socialist politicians and lesbians and gays? The following selection of letters to the editors of British lesbian and gay publications is but an initial contribution to this type of research.

The opinions which are expressed in these letters also cannot be viewed as indicators of the 'average' lesbian and gay position. Of all the various peoples who engage in same-sex practices, only a minority identify as members of the lesbian and gay community. Only a small section of the community reads the lesbian and gay periodicals regularly, and only particularly motivated individuals bother to write letters to the editor. Editors select what they regard as 'representative' samples of 'acceptable' letters. Finally, I have selected, for the most part, those letters which demonstrate that their writers are attempting to occupy the impossible position of the good homosexual. It should be noted at the outset that letters of this type constitute a minority of the total number of letters which are published in British lesbian and gay publications. Many others express fierce pride in our movements, and still others deal with ordinary everyday events in our communities. It is nevertheless useful to draw attention to this non-representative sample because of the striking continuity – in terms of structure and metaphor – between many of the following letters and New Right discourse.

It is also significant that these letters were written against the background of a tremendous mobilization within the lesbian and gay community. Between 15,000 and 20,000 lesbians, gays and heterosexual supporters attended an anti-Section 28 march in Manchester in February 1988, and 40,000 marched in London in April. Although, by American standards, these are rather small numbers, the marches broke all previous British records for lesbian and gay protests. Numerous groups sprang up across the country, politicizing younger lesbians and gays, re-energizing older activists and bringing lesbians and gay men together in an unprecedented manner.

The anti-activist lesbian and gay letters which were written at the time of these mobilizations therefore constituted both a positive response to the New Right's invocation of the good homosexual, and 'our own' version of a right-wing backlash. In his February 1988 letter to *Capital Gay*, M. W. writes,

> As for 'closets', they are surely no worse than the 'ghettoes' built for us by the socialists, who, in spite of their rhetoric, promote intolerance, class hatred and division and create 'aware' minority groups for their own political ends. It is the socialists who have isolated us from mainstream society and identified us as outcasts. Their meddling in local government with theory and ideals has got us where we are now. The gay community is losing any credibility and respect it had through their antics. They caused the backlash.[90]

M. W. deploys many of the representational devices which are the hallmarks of New Right discourse: the equation of radical black activism, union militancy and queer resistance; the location of socialism as an anti-democratic extremism; and the depiction of lesbians and gays as passive pawns who are exploited by the opportunistic heterosexual left. Like Powell and Thatcher, M. W. depicts socialist politics as an authoritarian imposition of abstract social engineering. Performing yet another erasure of lesbian subjectivity, he focuses exclusively on socialist gay men and argues that through their activism they have become the architects of their own oppression.

Many letter-writers do discuss the role of lesbian activists with reference to two particularly effective publicity stunts. On 2 February 1988, three lesbians abseiled down from the Visitors' Gallery in the House of Lords onto the floor during a Section 28 debate. They shouted slogans such as 'Lesbians are angry!' and 'It's our lives you're dealing with!' J. J. writes to *Capital Gay*, 'One should remember that such actions may reinforce the idea that we are an extremist people requiring strict control. Isn't that helpful to our oppressors?'[91] W. B. (who signed his letter with a man's name) denounces the lesbian abseilers.

> They ... are harming the cause for toleration and understanding of gay problems... Maybe Clause 28 is right after all. And why gay men should be linked up with lesbians I cannot understand. Most lesbians dislike gays and vice versa.[92]

W. B.'s misogyny is reproduced by lesbian letter-writers. In May 1988, four lesbians protesting against the final passage of Section 28 disrupted a live broadcast of the BBC's *Six O'Clock News*. Their slogans were muffled by the crew, but presenter Sue Lawley abandoned her news text and stated, 'We have been rather invaded.' M. W. (who signs her letter with a woman's name), responds with a strong letter against lesbian activism. She states that she is 'sick' of the anti-Section 28 coverage in *Capital Gay*, claims that AIDS is a gay male disease and argues that the local councils and schools should not have become 'involved with gay politics'. Referring to the lesbians' protest, she states:

> We could also do with less of these dykes bursting into these news studios. Do they really believe that the sight of four masculine women screaming slogans at a pretty female newsreader is going to enhance the soiled image some gays have given themselves in this country?[93]

It is highly probable that most of these critics were already committed Conservative Party voters before the promotion of homosexuality crisis. An informal survey conducted by *Capital Gay* in the summer of 1987, found that 47 per cent of the lesbians and gays polled identified themselves as Tory voters.[94] In any event, it is remarkable that these lesbians and gays do not just support Thatcher's economic policies; they also took up many of the Thatcherite arguments around race and sexuality. Many of the letter-writers and contributors in the lesbian and gay press in the late 1980s strongly objected to the linkage between the Labour Party and lesbian and gay politics. In a February 1988 commentary, Peter Davies writes in *Capital Gay* that the left had 'damaged' the 'gay movement'. He explicitly agrees with Polly Toynbee's article in *The*

Guardian in which she argued that the lesbian and gay movement has 'nurtured within it the seeds of its own destruction'. Not hesitating to employ a racial metaphor, he states, 'Lesbians and gay issues have been colonized by the left-wing of the Labour Party. Now, in the mind of the public, gay equals "loony left"'. He concludes that lesbians and gays should build a 'non-sectarian movement', and that we should reject the GLC model – the construction of a cross-class and cross-racial coalition of oppressed minority groups.[95] Peter Campbell, the Vice-President of the Conservative Group for Homosexual Equality, distances himself from Toynbee's position, but reiterates the charge that the homophobic backlash has been caused by leftist opportunism.

> Section 28 is not the fault of gays protesting too much but of left-wing politicians crudely exploiting the gay cause and trying to buy the gay vote . . . To identify the gay cause with the left gives the homophobes the support and encouragement they most desire.[96]

Several letter-writers join these right-wing community leaders in attacking the left. On 2 May 1987, in the lead-up to the general election, *Capital Gay* ran a front-page editorial which promoted the March Against the Backlash in Haringey. This action, which was held in response to right-wing criticisms of the borough's pro-lesbian and pro-gay rights policies, was jointly organized by Haringey Black Action and Positive Images. The Broadwater Farm Youth Association, which serves a local public housing project with a large black population, led the march. More than 2,000 people took part in the action. A. B. comments in *Capital Gay*:

> Please do not lump the gay community with the failed politics of the left. As an issue we do not wish and cannot afford to be consigned to the political fringes. . . . Most gays are as angry at the continual exploitation by the left as by the ranting of the odd anti-gay maverick. Despite your feeble attempts, the Conservatives will rightly be elected for a justified third term.[97]

Given the specific character of the Haringey march, A. B.'s rejection of the political 'fringe' identity amounts to a racist stance against cross-racial coalitions. His argument in this sense reiterates the racially coded criticisms of the GLC which were widely circulated in the mid-1980s. A. B. also reproduces the Thatcherite de-politicization of homophobic discourse. He claims that the attacks on the community are accidental deviations committed by 'maverick' figures rather than the symptoms of fundamental political structures and invest-ments. Finally, his dismissal of *Capital Gay*'s political endorsements as 'feeble attempts' mirrors the Thatcherites' homosexualization and effeminization of the left.

Several letters in the lesbian and gay publications which were published in the late 1980s also express a tremendous sense of betrayal. Right-wingers state that they feel betrayed by the leftist community leaders. Lesbians and gays who report that they have been subjected to extreme forms of discrimination often express their intense disappointment with the lack of support from other community members. Many letters of the latter type were written by HIV+ gay men and people with AIDS. One writer explained that he had lost most of his gay friends, as well as his family, when he told them that he was HIV+.

> I am unable to work any more due to chronic HIV infections, my family, mother, father, brothers and other relations have broken off all contact with me, and I have been told that as far as they are concerned, I died. However, one would have thought that one's friends would have remained close, but no.[98]

The sense of betrayal among the community's right wing, and their criticisms of leftist lesbian and gay activists, peaked with the organization of increasingly militant resistances in the late 1980s and early 1990s. Right-wing criticism became particularly focused upon the direct action group, OutRage!, after it was founded in 1990. OutRage!'s out-reach actions in lesbian and gay clubs and gay male cruising-grounds were generally met with quiet support or apathy. The group staged several theatrical protests against police abuse, church bigotry, AIDS underfunding, censorship and sexism in the gay male community. Their flamboyant, high-visibility actions in crowded shopping areas and around tourist attractions were widely applauded by other lesbians and gays. A minority of community leaders nevertheless voiced their strong disapproval of OutRage!. Reproducing the Thatcherite hyperbole around the subversive activ-ities of the 'enemies within', they denounced the group's tactics. John Marshall, the editor of *Gay Times*, declared in an interview with a national daily newspaper, 'The biggest enemies of our movement are those gay people who have decided that we should be called queer.'[99] The Gay and Lesbian Humanists Association passed a motion at its 1991 annual general meeting to reject the use of the term 'queer'. In their press statement, they declared, '["Queer"] is a repulsive and wholly negative word. Its use is irrational and self-oppressive and risks dividing the lesbian and gay community when it is at its most vulnerable.'

Community attacks on militant activists peaked around the controversy about 'outing' in the summer of 1991. A group of gay men, Faggots Rooting Out Closeted Sexuality (FROCS), initially promised to the press that it would reveal a list of 200 closeted lesbian and gay politicians, church leaders and celebrities. The tabloid press, which had 'outed' a dozen politicians and celebrities in vicious smear campaigns, condemned the FROCS campaign as a 'fascist' plot which would ruin the lives of the people involved. FROCS thereby successfully revealed the deeply entrenched double standards around privacy in Britain – that leftist and marginal figures could be 'outed' without regard to their privacy, but that the sexual identities of 'establishment' figures are supposed to be protected by 'gentlemen's agreements'. After tremendous media coverage, FROCS ultimately revealed that the list did not exist, that its campaign was a hoax and that it had only wanted to 'expose the double standards, hypocrisy and homophobia of the media'.[100] R. H.'s letter is one of the many critical responses to the FROCS campaign.

> First we had OutRage! who have been attempting to make people use the word, 'queer', a word I bitterly resent. Now this FROCS group have decided to launch a poster campaign to 'out' gay MPs and celebrities. Who exactly are this group? No doubt made up of the usual, probably out of work lefties within the gay community. And who are they speaking for – certainly not me.[101]

If the Thatcherites were remarkably successful at harnessing internalized homophobia within the lesbian and gay community, and at inciting the reproduction of their discourse within lesbian and gay texts, their strategy also failed in one important sense. The incitement of self-surveillance has an extremely complex effect on the demonized group, for its excessive representations may actually bring that group to the attention of the wider population. As soon as it was attacked as an 'enemy within', the lesbian and gay community became officially recognized as a force that the right had to reckon with. The official deployment of explicitly homophobic strategies and representations also encouraged otherwise apathetic individuals to take a strong stand. Many closeted individuals came out, thousands participated in their first lesbian and gay protest march and hundreds emerged as committed activists and spokespersons.

Most of the individuals who were politicized around the Section 28 resistances will always remain suspicious of right-wing pro-tolerance statements. Just as Powell's speeches were followed by an upsurge in militant black resistances in the 1960s, Thatcher's final term in office coincided with a tremendous renewal of lesbian and gay militancy. Because of the numerous hesitations and contra-dictions within the Labour leadership on sexual politics, and because many of the newly politicized lesbians and gays retain conservative views on other issues, this renewed political constituency did not automatically become a bloc of Labour voters. Except for specific mobilizations at the local level, the new phase of lesbian and gay activism will probably remain a purely extra-parliamentary phenom-enon. The Thatcherite promotion of homosexuality will nevertheless be marked by British lesbian and gay historians as one of the greatest incitements to political activism that the community has ever seen.

H. B., who identifies herself as a lesbian, writes in April 1988 – after Section 28 was passed into law – 'I am gay – I have to thank Dame Jill Knight and David Wilshire. They gave me the courage to write it down ... to say it to my mother ... [and] to admit it to myself.'[102] R. F., a member of the Lesbian and Gay Youth Federation (LGYF) wrote an open letter to Thatcher.

> On behalf of the LGYF, I would like to thank you and all those behind Section 28 for pulling the lesbian and gay community together in a way never before imagined; for making our community stronger than it has ever been in the past; for bringing more people to admit to their homosexuality than ever before; for bringing more people onto our side than we could have ever done and most of all for promoting homo-sexuality more widely and more efficiently than we could have ever done ourselves.[103]

The prohibition of the promotion of homosexuality therefore had deeply ambiguous effects on the identities of lesbians and gays. It mobilized already existing differences within the community and incited the deployment of self-surveillance and self-demonizing tactics, but it also created the conditions for a profound politicization of the community against the Thatcherite attacks. However, this politicization was not met with adequate leadership on the left, and many of the vehicles of resistance at the local government level were destroyed through Thatcherism's centralist policies. The renewal of lesbian and gay activism consequently had little effect on parlia-mentary politics.

The emergence of an anti-queer activism backlash within the lesbian and gay communities during the Section 28 debates was not an isolated event. Gay liberation activists faced a great deal of criticism from closeted community members in the 1970s and 1980s. In the United States, lesbian and gay rights campaigns have often taken an assimilationist – 'we're just like you' – stance. Organizers in the lesbian and gay Campaign for Military Service, which is fighting the military ban on homosexuality, have deployed an explicitly patriotic lesbian and gay rights discourse. They have selected 'exceptional' lesbians and gays – white middle-class overachievers in the military – as spokespersons for their cause.[104] Retired United States Army Staff Sergeant Perry Watkins, who served fifteen years as an openly gay soldier, was not chosen by the Campaign as a spokesperson; Watkins is a black man who, when off duty, often took on the persona of Simone Monet, a singer, dancer and drag queen.[105]

A homophobic interpretation of the backlash within the lesbian and gay communities and of the assimilationist tendencies of some lesbian and gay rights groups would treat these phenomena as the specific effects of homosexual pathology on an individual level, namely a self-hatred which is supposed to be peculiar to lesbians and gays. A more accurate and more useful interpretation would begin with the homophobic forces themselves. Like any target of oppression, the lesbian and gay communities experience themselves as the objects of tremendously intensive and extensive surveillance. Anyone who deviates from gender and sexual norms in the slightest becomes immediately hyper-visible as a suspect queer; placed within the panopticon[106] of compulsory heterosexuality, lesbians and gays have to deal with a degree of scrutiny which our heterosexual counterparts will never know. Paradoxically, even as we become hyper-visible as targets of surveillance, either we are asked to remain invisible, or, in the case of lesbians and queers of colour, our very existence is often denied. One response to the panopticon condition is assimilationist: the structuring of lesbian and gay resistance around already normalized elements of the oppressor's discourse. A second response is subversion: the seizure of the panopticon condition as a strategic opportunity for the promotion of an unassimilated queerness which creatively resists and parodies the oppressor's discourse. In actual practice, most resistances combine some aspect of both of these responses in complex negotiations of contextual limitations and possibilities. A third response to the panopticon condition is other-blaming: the blaming of one particularly 'deviant' segment of the community for drawing the homophobic gaze towards the 'almost-normal' members of the community. The rage of the 'almost-normals' stems from the fact that they are caught up in the myth of authoritarian 'tolerance'. They actually believe that without the community's deviants – such as working-class bar dykes, black drag queens, leather fetishists, transsexuals, transvestites and socialist and anti-racist activists – they could peacefully 'pass' unnoticed in straight society. In other words, they make the crucial mistake of believing in the false promises of inclusion which authoritarian discourse offers them. In some cases, such as the anti-activist letters quoted above, or, in the United States, the *After the Ball* manifesto by Kirk and Madsen,[107] there is very little difference between the assimilationist position and 'other-blaming'. Where 'other-blaming' is quite common – as it was in Britain in the late 1980s and early 1990s – lesbian and gay activists find ourselves fighting against two different opponents who sound increasingly the same: the homophobic forces outside and within the lesbian and gay community.

Leftist essentialism, right-wing anti-essentialism

It is precisely on this 'ground' – the 'ground' of the constantly shifting identity games – that the discourse of the opposers of Section 28 becomes ineffective. The opposers' discourse fails in three ways. First, as noted above, it fails to confront directly the 'loony left' charge, and tends to conceal its own pro-lesbian and pro-gay elements, especially those within the Labour Party. Second, its position on the Section itself is often equivocal. Several prominent speakers, including Cunningham, the Labour spokesman on local government affairs, speak in favour of the Section in the first instance and only reverse their position after much lobbying from the grassroots of the party. Cunningham first says that he is opposed to the promotion of homosexuality, urges all Committee members to vote for its inclusion in the bill, and forgoes any amendment of, or division about, the Clause.[108] In the third reading, he says that the Clause must be amended to preserve the rights of lesbians and gays to 'equal treatment' but that he still supports it in principle.[109] In the final debates, he nevertheless declares that he has always been 'fundamentally opposed to the Clause'.[110]

Most important, however, is the failure of the opposers to recognize the impossibility of identities. Their discourse is largely structured around the argument that the Section is nonsensical because everyone's sexuality is fixed at birth, such that no promotion of any sexuality is possible.[111] Well-intentioned as they may be, the opposers, in arguing that homosexuality simply 'is', undermine the importance of the construction of alternative sexual identities and communities. If heterosexual and homosexual identities were established at birth, and if the very boundaries of sexual categories were inevitably fixed, then sexuality would no longer be a terrain of struggle. From this perspective, it would appear that homosexuals ought to organize merely to guide each individual to their 'true calling', and to constitute ourselves as simply one more bloc in a pluralist society. That the actual lesbian and gay movements are engaged in so much more than this – in the interruption of *everyone's* experience of sexuality and gender as fixed positions, and in the disruption of the structure of sexual categorization itself – would appear nonsensical and even illegitimate from this perspective. Yet homosexuality was often portrayed as a naturally fixed bloc in a system of separate and competing social blocs in the discourse of opposition against the Section.[112] The popularity of this approach indicates the extremely underdeveloped status of the thinking about identities in general, and sexuality and gender in particular, in many leftist discourses in Britain.

What the left often fails to recognize is that homosexual, gay and lesbian identities cannot be taken for granted, for, as historical constructs, they developed only in certain contexts, and will disappear in other contexts. It is true that many lesbian and gay activists and intellectuals remain suspicious about any attempts to enforce the normalization of lesbian and gay cultures; they, like Foucault, are proponents of endlessly creative sexual movements which would celebrate the multiplication of non-authoritarian differences. However, there is quite a difference between, on the one hand, the weakening of lesbian and gay identities and their displacement with new identities through our own creative practices, and, on the other hand, the marginalization of our political movements and the destruction of our entire culture by homophobic forces. Although we need to be on our guard against the rigidity of identity games, this does not mean that we ought to abandon our efforts to consolidate our fragile gains in the face of tremendous authoritarian bigotry. Again, we can only engage in the exploration of creative identity games once we have constructed fortified enclosures against homophobic forces through defensive identity games.

The opposers' discourse is excellent on one particular point, namely its insistence on the fact that the prohibition of the promotion of homosexuality is a thoroughly homophobic measure. The opposers were able to demonstrate that opposition to subversive queerness is essentially opposition to all queerness, since the occupation of the 'good homosexual' position is impossible. Section 28 thus gives symbolic license to homophobic bigotry even as it portrays itself as a tolerant mediation between extremes.

Yet there remains a tremendous absence in the discourse of the opposers: the argument that homosexuality *can* and *ought to be* promoted. This absence can at least partially be accounted for in terms of short-term strategies; clearly, it would have been a counterproductive argument in some contexts during Section 28 debate. It is important, however, to recognize the limitation in suppressing this argument, and the importance of taking up this proposition wherever possible. It is a myth that homosexuals constitute, and will always constitute, 10 per cent of the population, and that homosexuality pertains only to this fixed group; homosexuality survives only to the extent that it is promoted. In other words, the left tended to represent homosexuality as an accident which could be added or taken away without any effect on 'normal' society, and as an element which would remain intact throughout the homophobic political attacks from the right. For the supporters of Section 28, homosexuality operated like a supplement: they rightly claimed that lesbian and gay identities – like all identities – profoundly depend upon political intervention, and that if homosexuality were politicized, it could indeed have a tremendous subversive effect on the 'normal'.

It should be emphasized that sexual identities do not have a unique ontological structure. Sexual identities are not necessarily 'more' chosen, and are not more vulnerable to subversion than other identities, such as race. I would reject, for example, Sedgwick's conception that sexuality is less fixed than gender and race for every individual and context, and Gates' argument that biological sex is less of a 'trope' than race.[113] No identity is fixed in biological matter; all identities are socially constructed on a discursive terrain. As Butler rightly insists, even our notion of biological sex – our conception of what officially counts as properly 'male' and 'female' – has been constructed within specific contexts and is open to re-definition in new contexts.[114] Some identities may appear to be more fixed than others, but this appearance is only the effect of contextually specific strategies. We cannot tell in advance which identity game will operate as the nodal point for other identity games; we cannot predict which form of identity will hegemonically define other identities in any particular context. The strategic field in which we find ourselves negotiating identity games is never a configuration of 'our' choosing, and 'we' always experience it as a field into which 'we' have been 'thrown', but the field itself is vulnerable to subversive re-definition through new resistance strategies. Even with the most normalized identity games, there is always the possibility of interruption and subversion. The effects of the radical black movements in Britain can be compared with the effects of the lesbian and gay movements, in terms of their interruption of categories which present themselves as 'natural'. Black resistances have not only made the very identity 'black' a coherent and viable position; they have called the normalized meanings of whiteness and Britishness into question. The radical lesbian and gay critiques of compulsory heterosexuality and the necessity of the patriarchal nuclear family have had a similar anti-authoritarian effect. Together, these resistances have constituted the most radical challenges to the phantasmatic construction of the white familial British nation.

Conclusion

In *The Intimate Enemy*, Nandy[1] offers a provocative theoretical model of the relations between the colonizers and the colonized. He suggests that colonial forces operate in two complementary and yet distinct forms. The first form is basically organized around the violent conquest of the colonies by 'bandit-kings'. The 'bandit-kings' have no civilizing mission; they are influenced not by Eurocentric conceptions of progress or religious duty but by crude racist theories which reduce the racial 'other' to a sub-human status. The second form of colonialism, by contrast, is organized around the Westernization of the colonized. The 'bandit-kings' are displaced by the colonizers, the 'well-meaning, hard-working, middle-class missionaries, liberals, modernists, and believers in science, equality and progress'.[2] The colonizers do not violently eliminate the colonized; although they view the colonized as child-like, backward and dependent upon Europe for their progress, they do recognize the colonized as fellow human beings. The violence of the colonizers is a cultural and psychological violence: they take hold of the cultural difference of the colonized, they enter the culture of the colonized at local levels and they train the colonized to internalize Western values. Their colonizing intervention hegemonically installs the Western imaginary as the only possible social imaginary. '[Colonialism] helps generalize the concept of the modern West from a geographical and temporal entity to a psychological category. The West is now everywhere, within the West and outside; in structures and in minds.'[3] Through these dual processes, colonialism becomes so pervasive and so effective that even the anti-colonial forces reproduce the discourse of the colonizers. Colonialism maps out in advance the limits of legitimate resistance; it actually produces forms of 'official dissent' which, for all their oppositional appearance, conform quite closely to Western ideals. 'It is possible today to be anti-colonial in a way which is specified and promoted by the modern world view as "proper", "sane" and "rational". Even when in opposition, that dissent remains predictable and controlled.'[4] This containment of resistance is the 'ultimate violence which colonialism does to its victims'; colonialism 'creates a culture in which the ruled are constantly tempted to fight their rulers within the psychological limits set by the latter'.[5]

Many of these insights will already be familiar to readers of Foucault and Fanon. Nandy's two forms of colonialism resemble Foucault's distinction between juridico-discursive power and bio-power relations,[6] while the argument that colonialism produces its own domesticated forms of dissent echoes both Foucault on resistance and Fanon on assimilation.[7] The novelty of Nandy's theory lies in his discussion of sexuality: unlike Foucault, he does not neglect the racial aspect of sexual discourse, and, unlike Fanon, he does not explore the articulation of race and sexuality within a misogynist and heterosexist framework.[8] For Nandy, the institutionalization of Western values among the colonized entails, among other things, a transformation of their traditional sexual discourse. Where a traditional social order may have valued femininity as well as masculinity, and may have tolerated or even promoted androgyny and the constant confusion of gender and sexual positions, colonialism imposes the Western value system in which masculinity is valued over femininity, femininity in turn is valued over androgyny and male effeminacy, and gender and sexual deviants find themselves caught up in disciplinary strategies of sexual normalization. Nandy traces the remarkable impact of the British cult of the 'hyper-masculine' upon Indian culture. He argues, for example, that various sacred texts traditionally portrayed un-mediated masculinity and gender fixity in a negative manner, but that with the influence of Western ideals, many nineteenth-century Indian writers celebrated these same qualities in their reinterpretations of sacred texts.[9]

Nandy also suggests that, like all colonizing strategies, this particular disciplining of the colonized reproduces itself within the 'mother country'. The institutionalization of new gender and sexual norms in the British colonies has, as its mirror image, an escalation in the policing of gender and sexuality within Britain. Again, as Mackenzie[10] insists, colonialism is never an accidental appendage to the domestic culture of the 'mother country'; it has, for every class fraction and regional group, profound effects on social institutions and popular cultures. With reference to colonialism's promotion of 'hyper-masculinity', Nandy argues that the colonizing experience contributed to the masculinization of British culture. The de-valuation of 'feminine' pursuits and the exclusion of women from the public sphere were legitimated as new forms of masculine values, 'competition, achievement, control and productivity – new forms of institutionalized violence and ruthless social Darwinism' were promoted.[11]

Within this perspective, the presence of violent patriarchal and homophobic forces in post-colonial Western countries is no accident. For every brutal deployment of colonizing strategies, there was a persecution of an Oscar Wilde or some other gender/sexual deviant in the 'mother country'; for every Falklands or Gulf War, there will be many more rapes and queer-bashings 'back home'. The flourishing of both racism and homophobia in contemporary Western countries should be understood not only in terms of the specific histories of these forces, but also in terms of their common colonial past. This is not to say that these two forms of authoritarian-ism operate in exactly the same way; I have noted some of the differences between racism and homophobia in contemporary Britain, and there are, certainly, many others. Nevertheless, there are many important continuities between racism and homophobia. As racist colonialism constructs the mythical figure of the assimilated and Europeanized colonized, and sets her against her former sisters and brothers, the unassimilable 'natives', contemporary new racism invents the mythical figure of the assimilated black and speaks its anti-affirmative action policies in her/his name, and contemporary homophobia constructs the mythical figure of the 'good homosexual' and promises to include her within the normal in return for her denunciation of her fellow queers.

In this study, I have attempted not just to bring racism and homophobia onto the agenda of British political analysis as separate 'issues', but to show how these forces were central to two key moments in Powellian and Thatcherite discourse: the de-legiti-mation of consensus discourse in the late 1960s and early 1970s and the centralist attack on local government autonomy in the 1980s. Using the hegemony-as-normalization approach, rather than the hegemony-as-domination approach, and borrowing from Derrida, Nietzsche and Foucault, I have emphasized the complexity of, and interconnectedness between, racism and homophobia in contemporary right-wing official discourse in Britain. I have focused almost exclusively upon authoritarian discourse, and I recognize that any study which does not give equal treatment to resistance discourses risks the 'celebration' of authoritarianism as omnipotent. I would insist, however, that resistance discourses can only be effectively analysed once the complexity and contextual specificity of their authoritarian counterparts have been fully grasped.

Notes

Introduction

1 See, for example, Colin Leys, *Politics in Britain* (London, Verso, 1983); Tom Nairn, 'The Crisis of the British State', *New Left Review*, vol. 130, Nov.–Dec. 1981, 37–44; Peter Riddell, *The Thatcher Era and Its Legacy* (Oxford, Basil Blackwell, 1991).

2 Dennis Kavanagh, *Thatcherism and British Politics: The End of Consensus?* (Oxford University Press, 1987, 246–80); Beatrix Campbell, *The Iron Ladies: Why Do Women Vote Tory?* (London, Virago Press, 1987); Wendy Webster, *Not a Man to Match Her* (London, The Women's Press, 1990); Anthony King, 'Margaret Thatcher as a Political Leader', in Robert Skidelsky, ed., *Thatcherism* (London, Chatto and Windus, 1988), 51–64.

3 Peregrine Worsthorne, quoted in Ivor Crewe, 'Has the Electorate Become more Thatcherite?', in Skidelsky, ed., *Thatcherism*, 32.

4 Patrick Minford, quoted in Skidelsky, 'Introduction' in Skidelsky, ed., *Thatcherism*, 1.

5 *ibid.*, 1–2.

6 I have many reservations about the term 'homophobia', which I shall present in chapter 5. For all its shortcomings, this word has become widely accepted as a general term for anti-lesbian and gay discourse. I shall assume that it works well enough for now, although I do think that lesbian and gay activists need to come up with a better word.

7 Margaret Thatcher, speech at Cambridge University, 6 July 1979, in Thatcher, *The Revival of Britain: Speeches on Home and European Affairs, 1975–1988* (London, Aurum Press, 1989), 89.

8 *ibid.*, 95.

9 David Willetts, 'The Family', in Dennis Kavanagh and Anthony Seldon, eds., *The Thatcher Effect* (Oxford, Clarendon Press, 1989), 267.

10 The term 'black' has acquired two different meanings in British discourse. At times it connotes, in both racist and anti-racist discourse, a collectivity which includes 'Asians' – which, in the British sense, means peoples from India and Pakistan – and peoples of the

African diaspora from the Caribbean and Africa. At other times, it connotes the peoples of the African diaspora alone or in contrast to Asians. This ambiguity in usage is, of course, a part of the legacy of both British imperialism and the struggles against racism which are specific to the British post-colonial condition. See Beverly Bryan, Stella Dadzie and Suzanne Scafe, *The Heart of the Race: Black Women's Lives in Britain* (London, Virago, 1985), 170, for an explanation of the strategic usage of the term 'black', in the Organization of Women of Asian and African Descent.

11 Andrew Gamble, *The Free Economy and the Strong State: The Politics of Thatcherism* (Durham, Duke University Press, 1988), 250.
12 Antonio Gramsci, *Selections from the Prison Notebooks of Antonio Gramsci*, Quintin Hoare and Geoffrey Nowell Smith, eds. and trans. (London, Lawrence and Wishart, 1971); Ernesto Laclau and Chantal Mouffe, *Hegemony and Socialist Strategy* (London, Verso, 1985); Ernesto Laclau, *New Reflections on the Revolution of Our Time* (London, Verso, 1990).
13 Kavanagh, *Thatcherism and British Politics*, 57; emphasis added.
14 *ibid.*, 57.
15 Gamble, *The Free Economy and the Strong State*, 71.
16 *ibid.*, 200.
17 Zig Layton-Henry and Paul Rich, 'Introduction', in Layton-Henry and Rich, eds., *Race, Government and Politics in Britain* (London, Macmillan, 1986), 1–16.
18 Kavanagh, *Thatcherism and British Politics*, 73.
19 Ivor Crewe, 'The Labour Party and the Electorate', in Dennis Kavanagh, ed., *The Politics of the Labour Party* (London, George Allen and Unwin, 1982), 28, 34.
20 Ivor Crewe, 'How to Win a Landslide Without Really Trying: Why the Conservatives Won in 1983', in Austin Ranney, ed., *Britain at the Polls: A Study of the General Election* (Durham, Duke University Press, 1985), 176, 184.
21 Riddell, *The Thatcher Era and Its Legacy*, 185.
22 Hugo Young, *One of Us: A Biography of Margaret Thatcher*, (London, Macmillan, 1989), 262.
23 Quoted in Riddell, *The Thatcher Era and Its Legacy*, 215.
24 Young, *One of Us*, 259.
25 *ibid.*, 273.
26 Quoted in *ibid.*, 272.
27 Quoted in Anthony Barnett, 'Iron Britannia', *New Left Review*, no. 134, July–August 1982, 14, 17.
28 *ibid.*, 19.
29 *ibid.*, 24.
30 *The Times*, editorial, 14 May 1982, quoted in *ibid.*, 71.
31 Barnett, 'Iron Britannia', 87; Young, *One of Us*, 276–7.
32 Young, *One of Us*, 280.
33 Quoted in *ibid.*, 281.
34 Quoted in *ibid.*, 282.

35 Layton-Henry and Rich, 'Introduction', 10.
36 Other studies which focus on the role of race in British politics in the
   1970s and 1980s include: Layton-Henry and Rich, eds., *Race, Govern-
   ment and Politics in Britain*; Zig Layton-Henry, *The Politics of Race in
   Britain* (London, George Allen and Unwin, 1984); Stuart Hall *et al.*,
   Policing the Crisis: Mugging, the State, and Law and Order (London,
   Macmillan, 1978); Centre for Contemporary Cultural Studies, eds.,
   The Empire Strikes Back: Race and Racism in 70s Britain (London,
   Hutchinson, 1982); Paul Gilroy, *'There Ain't No Black in the Union Jack':
   The Cultural Politics of Race and Nation* (London, Hutchinson, 1987);
   David Edgar, 'The Free or the Good', in Ruth Levitas, ed., *The Ideology
   of the New Right* (Cambridge, Polity Press, 1986), 55–79; Gill Seidel,
   'The Concept of Culture, Nation and "Race" in the British and
   French New Right', in *ibid.*, 80–106; Jacqueline Bhabha *et al.*, eds.,
   Worlds Apart: Women Under Immigration and Nationality Law (London,
   Pluto, 1985); Brian Jacobs, *Racism in Britain* (London, Croom Helm,
   1988); Harry Gouldbourne, ed., *Black Politics in Britain* (Aldershot,
   Avebury, 1990). Again, it is regrettable that political scientists have for
   the most part ignored these important studies.
37 This figure is based on my own measurement of the columns in the
   Hansard Official Reports of the debates.
38 Etienne Balibar, 'Is there a Neo-Racism?', in Balibar and Immanuel
   Wallerstein, *Race, Nation, Class* (London, Verso, 1991), 19.
39 Gayle Rubin, 'Thinking Sex: Notes for a Radical Theory of the Politics
   of Sexuality', in Carole Vance, ed., *Pleasure and Danger: Exploring
   Female Sexuality* (London, Routledge and Kegan Paul, 1984), 267–319;
   Jeffrey Weeks, *Sex, Politics and Society: The Regulation of Sexuality Since
   1800* (London, Longman, 1981).
40 Gilroy, *'There Ain't No Black in the Union Jack'*, 57–9.
41 There are two exceptions to this generalization: Queen Elizabeth I's
   expulsion of African 'Negroes and blackamoors' from England in
   1601, and the 1925 Special Restriction (Coloured Alien Seamen)
   Order.
42 The symbolic spatial location of the HIV virus within excluded
   communities – such that the 'general population' appears to be
   invaded from an immoral outside – of course reaches its most explicit
   moment in immigration laws which bar HIV positive individuals
   from entering nation-states. Legislation of this kind is currently in
   effect in the United States.
43 My purpose in using the term 'identity games' is not to conceal their
   seriousness, but to draw a loose analogy between the discursive fields
   in which identity claims are made and the Wittgensteinian conception of language games. See Ludwig Wittgenstein, *Philosophical
   Investigations* (Oxford, Basil Blackwell, 1958).
44 I have not included the debates between Jessop *et al.* and Hall
   because their arguments and replies have already been well documented elsewhere. See Bob Jessop, *et al.*, *Thatcherism* (Cambridge,
   Polity Press, 1988) and Stuart Hall, *The Hard Road to Renewal* (London,
   Verso, 1988).

1 Thatcherism, the new racism and the British New Right: hegemonic imaginary or accidental mirage?

1 Stuart Hall, 'The Great Moving Right Show', in Hall and Martin Jacques, eds., *The Politics of Thatcherism* (London, Lawrence and Wishart, 1983), 19–39; originally published in *Marxism Today*, Jan. 1979.

2 *ibid.*, 29–30.

3 *ibid.*, 29.

4 Martin Durham, *Sex and Politics: The Family and Morality in the Thatcher Years* (London, Macmillan, 1991).

5 Cited in *ibid.*, 142.

6 Maureen McNeil, 'Making and Not Making the Difference: The Gender Politics of Thatcherism', in Sarah Franklin, Celia Lury and Jackie Stacey, eds., *Off-Centre: Feminism and Cultural Studies*, London, Harper Collins, 1991, 235.

7 *ibid.*

8 Donna Minkowitz, 'Outlawing Gays', *The Nation*, 19 October 1992, 420–1.

9 *The Manchester Guardian Weekly*, 6 September 1992, 11.

10 Quoted in *ibid.*

11 Geraint Parry, George Moyser and Neil Day, *Political Participation and Democracy in Britain* (Cambridge University Press, 1992), 247–50.

12 Roger Jowell, Sharon Witherspoon and Lindsay Brook, eds., *British Social Attitudes: The Fifth Report* (Aldershot, Gower, 1988), 112.

13 Selected data from *ibid.*, 118.

14 Hugo Young, *One of Us* (London, Macmillan, 1989), 153, 204–5.

15 On the conception of hegemony, see the remarkable continuities across the following works: Roland Barthes, *Mythologies* (London, Paladin, 1973), 143, 154–5; Donna Haraway, *Primate Visions: Gender, Race and Nature in the World of Modern Science* (New York, Routledge, 1989), 6; Ernesto Laclau, *New Reflections on the Revolution of Our Time* (London, Verso, 1990), 64; Judith Butler, *Gender Trouble* (New York, Routledge, 1990), 33, 56, 149; and Butler, 'Contingent Foundations: Feminism and the Question of "Postmodernism"', in Butler and Joan Scott, eds., *Feminists Theorize the Political* (New York, Routledge, 1992), 13.

16 Quoted in *The Manchester Guardian*, 6 June 1993, 15.

17 Antonio Gramsci, 'The Study of Philosophy', *Selections From the Prison Notebooks*, Quintin Hoare and Geoffrey Nowell Smith, trans. and eds. (London, Lawrence and Wishart, 1971), 325, 330, 335.

18 Slavoj Zizek, *The Sublime Object of Ideology* (London, Verso, 1989), 29.

19 *ibid.*, 82.

20 *ibid.*, 75.

21 Jacques Lacan, 'The Mirror Stage as Formative of the Function of the I', *Ecrits* (London, Tavistock, 1977), 1–7; and John Muller and William Richardson, *Lacan and Language* (New York, International Universities Press, 1982), 5–34.

22 James Scott, *Domination and the Arts of Resistance: Hidden Transcripts* (New Haven, Yale University Press, 1990), 79.

23 Stuart Hall, 'Blue Election, Election Blues', *The Hard Road to Renewal* (London, Verso, 1988), 259–67.
24 *ibid.*, 262.
25 *ibid.*
26 *ibid.*
27 *ibid.*, 264.
28 *ibid.*, 263.
29 Paul Hirst, *After Thatcher* (London, Collins, 1989), 11–35.
30 *ibid.*, 11.
31 *ibid.*, 12; emphasis added.
32 *ibid.*, 12, 15, 24–7, 27, 13.
33 *ibid.*, 16–17, 21, 22.
34 *ibid.*, 32.
35 See I. Crewe, 'The Electorate: Partisan Dealignment Ten Years On', in H. Berrington, ed., *Change in British Politics* (London, Frank Cass, 1984); P. Dunleavy and C.T. Husbands, *British Democracy at the Cross-roads: Voting and Party Competition in the 1980s* (London, Allen and Unwin, 1985); D. Robertson, *Class and the British Electorate* (Oxford, Basil Blackwell, 1984); M. Franklin, *The Decline of Class Voting in Britain* (Oxford, Clarendon Press, 1985); and R. Rose and I. McAllister, *Voters Begin to Choose: From Closed-Class to Open Elections in Britain* (London, Sage, 1986).
36 Hirst, *After Thatcher*, 33–4.
37 Ivor Crewe, 'Has the Electorate Become Thatcherite?', in Robert Skidelsky, ed., *Thatcherism* (London, Chatto and Windus 1988), 28–9.
38 Hall, 'Blue Election, Election Blues', 260.
39 *ibid.*, 32.
40 *ibid.*, 35–44.
41 Peter Riddell, *The Thatcher Era and Its Legacy* (Oxford, Basil Blackwell, 1991), 214.
42 Mary Douglas, quoted in Judith Butler, *Gender Trouble* (London, Routledge, 1990), 131.
43 Riddell, *The Thatcher Era*, 215. The complete passage in Riddell's text reads: 'My own view is that a central factor sustaining the Conservatives' political dominance has been Mrs. Thatcher's leadership style – as demonstrated during the Falklands War and at other crises like the miners' strike and the Brighton bombing – coupled with the prosperity of the majority of the population (at least those in employment). Of course, the divided opposition has made her task easier, but that division has been partly because the Tories have split the working class.'
44 Paul Gilroy, *'There Ain't No Black in the Union Jack'* (London, Hutchinson, 1987).
45 Ivor Crewe, personal correspondence, 15 June 1991.
46 Anthony Heath *et al.*, *Understanding Political Change* (Oxford, Pergamon Press, 1991), 47–8, 177, 279.
47 Crewe, 'Has the Electorate Become Thatcherite?', 33.
48 R. Jowell, S. Witherspoon and L. Brook, eds., *British Social Attitudes: The Fifth Report*, 36; and Roger Jowell, Lindsay Brook and Bridget

Taylor, with Gillian Prior, eds., *British Social Attitudes: The Eighth Report* (Aldershot, Gower, 1991), 7.

49 R. Jowell, S. Witherspoon and L. Brook, eds., *British Social Attitudes: the Fifth Report*, 35, 36, 137.

50 R. Jowell, L. Brook, and B. Taylor, with G. Prior, *British Social Attitudes: the Eighth Report*, 11, 7–8, 19.

51 *ibid.*, 19.

52 R. Jowell, S. Witherspoon and L. Brook, eds., *British Social Attitudes: the Fifth Report*, 36, 74.

53 *ibid.*, 74.

54 *ibid.*, 44.

55 *ibid.*, 78, 81, 82.

56 *ibid.*, 75, 76, 77.

57 *ibid.*, 40–2, 45.

58 Etienne Balibar, 'Is There A Neo-Racism?', in Balibar and Immanuel Wallerstein, *Race, Nation, Class* (London, Verso, 1991), 21–3.

59 Martin Barker, *The New Racism: Conservatives and the Ideology of the Tribe* (London, Junction Books, 1981).

60 Frantz Fanon, *The Wretched of the Earth* (New York, Grove Press, 1963), 41.

61 Frantz Fanon, *Black Skin, White Masks* (London, Pluto, 1986).

62 Enoch Powell, *The David Frost Show*, BBC, 3 June 1969, quoted in Barker, *The New Racism*, 40.

63 Quoted in Barker, *The New Racism*, 18.

64 Quoted in *The Guardian*, 13 July 1988, 20.

65 R. Jowell, L. Brook, and B. Taylor, with G. Prior, eds., *British Social Attitudes: The Eighth Report*, 191.

66 *ibid.*, 191.

67 *ibid.*

68 Nicholas Deakin, *Colour and the British Electorate, 1964* (London, Pall Mall Press, 1965), 1.

69 Dilip Hiro, *Black British, White British* (London, Eyre and Spottiswoode, 1971), 63–4, 69–70, 259, 263, 255.

70 Riddell, *The Thatcher Era*, 156.

71 Brian Jacobs, *Racism in Britain* (London, Croom Helm, 1988), 104.

72 *Manchester Weekly Guardian*, 28 February 1993, 3.

73 Quoted in Jacobs, *Racism in Britain*, 116–17.

74 Young, *One of Us*, 377.

75 Selected data from: *British Election Study, 1987, Codebook*, A. Heath, R. Jowell, Social and Community Planning Research, J.K. Curtice, Principal Investigators; ESRC Data Archive Reference 33066.

76 Selected data from: *British Election Study, 1987, Codebook*.

77 Gillian Peele, 'Parties, Pressure Groups and Parliament', in Patrick Dunleavy, Andrew Gamble and Gillian Peele, eds., *Developments in British Politics 3* (New York, St. Martin's Press, 1990), 81.

78 *ibid.*

79 Jacobs, *Racism in Britain*, 81–5.

80 Quoted in Michael Leapman, *Kinnock* (London, Unwin Hyman, 1987), 187.

81 Selected data from: *British Election Study, 1987, Codebook.*

2 Derrida's 'infrastructure' of supplementarity

1 The term, 'infrastructure' is taken from Rodolphe Gasché, *The Tain of the Mirror* (Harvard University Press, 1986), 185–224.
2 Vincent Descombes, *Modern French Philosophy* (Cambridge University Press, 1980), 136–52.
3 Henry Staten, *Wittgenstein and Derrida* (London, University of Nebraska Press, 1984), 16; Ernesto Laclau, *New Reflections on the Revolution of Our Time* (London, Verso, 1990), 18–19.
4 Staten, referring to Jacques Derrida, 'Signature, Event, Context', *Limited Inc* (Evanston, Northwestern University Press, 1988), 1–24; *Wittgenstein and Derrida*, 16.
5 John Mackenzie, *Propaganda and Empire* (Manchester University Press, 1984), 258.
6 *ibid.*, 255.
7 Jacques Derrida, *Speech and Phenomena* (Evanston, Northwestern University Press, 1973), 88–104 and *Of Grammatology* (Baltimore, Johns Hopkins University Press, 1976), 141–64; Gasché, *The Tain of the Mirror*, 205–12, and Staten, *Wittgenstein and Derrida*, 111–60.
8 Derrida, *Of Grammatology*, 146–51.
9 Nancy Hirschmann, *Rethinking Obligation: A Feminist Method for Political Theory* (Ithaca, Cornell University Press, 1992), 70.
10 Jean-Jacques Rousseau, 'A Discourse on the Origin of Inequality', *The Social Contract and Discourses*, G.D.H. Cole, trans. (London, J.M. Dent and Sons, 1973), 52.
11 *ibid.*, 47, 55, 48, 65–7.
12 Hirschmann, *Rethinking Obligation*, 71–2.
13 For a more detailed discussion of Foucault's critique of Freud, see Jonathan Dollimore, *Sexual Dissidence: Augustine to Wilde, Freud to Foucault* (Oxford, Clarendon, 1991), 106.
14 Rousseau, 'A Discourse on the Origin of Inequality', 55.
15 *ibid.*, 56.
16 Jean-Jacques Rousseau, 'The Social Contract', *The Social Contract and Discourses*, 228.
17 *ibid.*, 229.
18 Rousseau, 'A Discourse on the Origin of Inequality', 48, 56, 58, 59.
19 *ibid.*, 60.
20 Derrida, *Of Grammatology*, 227.
21 *ibid.*, 242.
22 *ibid.*, 229.
23 Rousseau, 'A Discourse on the Origin of Inequality', 53.
24 *ibid.*, 54.
25 Rousseau, 'The Social Contract', 191.
26 Hirschmann, *Rethinking Obligation*, 66. On the gendered differentiation of education and virtue, and the operation of the feminine private sphere as the necessary supplement to the male political sphere in Rousseau's *Emile*, see *ibid.*, 55, 63, 70–6.

27 Roland Barthes, 'Myth Today', *Mythologies* (London, Paladin, 1973), 111.

28 *ibid.*, 118, 121.

29 *ibid.*, 146, 148.

30 bell hooks, 'Talking Back', in Gloria Anzaldúa, ed., *Making Face, Making Soul = Haciendo Caras: Creative and Critical Perspectives By Women of Color* (San Francisco, Aunt Lute, 1990), 208.

31 Amina Mama, 'Black Women, the Economic Crisis and the British State', *Feminist Review*, no. 17, autumn 1984, 31. One of the omissions in Foucault's *Madness and Civilization: A History of Insanity in the Age of Reason* (New York, Vintage Books, 1973) is precisely this use of psychiatry as a gendered and racial technology of social control. On the pathologization of black women in prison, see Beverly Bryan, Stella Dadzie and Suzanne Scafe, *The Heart of the Race: Black Women's Lives in Britain* (London, Virago, 1985), 116–23.

32 bell hooks, 'Talking Back', 211. On black British women's writing, see Lauretta Ngcobo, ed., *Let It Be Told: Essays by Black Women Writers in Britain* (London, Virago, 1988).

33 Karl Marx, 'The Eighteenth Brumaire of Louis Bonaparte', *The Selected Works of Karl Marx and Frederick Engels* (Moscow, Progress Publishers, 1966), vol. I, 479.

34 Patricia J. Williams, 'Lani, We Hardly Knew Ye', *The Village Voice*, 15 June 1993, 27, 28.

35 Derrida, *Of Grammatology*, 125.

36 Gayatri Spivak, 'Translator's Preface', in Derrida, *Of Grammatology*, lxxvii, lxxviii.

37 On Derrida's conception of repetition as 'iteration', and the non-specifiable 'minimal remainder' which is retained across the corrupting chain of iterated repetitions, see Derrida, *Speech and Phenomena*, 50; 'Signature, Event, Context', 12 and 'Limited Inc a b c . . .', in *Limited Inc*, 53.

38 Biddy Martin and Chandra Talpade Mohanty, 'Feminist Politics: What's Home Got to Do With It?', in Teresa de Lauretis, ed., *Feminist Studies/Critical Studies* (Bloomington, Indiana University Press, 1986), 193–4, 208.

39 Foucault, 'Sex, Power and the Politics of Identity', interview by B. Gallagher and A. Wilson, *The Advocate*, 7 August 1984, 27. Although Foucault failed here, as elsewhere, to refer to women's sexualities, he did make passing references in the interview to lesbian history.

40 *ibid.*, 28.

41 *ibid.*, 27.

42 Chela Sandoval, 'Feminism and Racism: A Report on the 1981 National Women's Studies Association Conference', in Anzaldúa, ed., *Making Face, Making Soul*, 67.

43 Stuart Hall, 'Cultural Identity and Diaspora', in J. Rutherford, ed., *Identity: Community, Culture, Difference* (London, Lawrence and Wishart, 1990), 235–6.

44 *ibid.*, 235.

45 *ibid.*, 224–5.

46 This is, however, one possible reading of the following passage by Derrida, which is taken from his contribution to the Art Against Apartheid exhibition catalogue. 'Beyond a continent whose limits they point to, the limits surrounding it or crossing through it, the paintings gaze and call out in silence. And their silence is just. A discourse would once again compel us to reckon with the present state of force and law. It would draw up contracts, dialecticize itself, let itself be reappropriated again. This silence calls out unconditionally; it keeps watch on that which is not, on that which is not yet, and on the chance of still remembering some faithful day.' 'Racism's Last Word', in Henry Louis Gates, Jr., *'Race', Writing, and Difference* (University of Chicago Press, 1986), 338. Derrida's article on apartheid can be usefully compared to his critiques of Husserl's and Levi-Strauss' ethnocentrism in *Edmund Husserl's Origin of Geometry: An Introduction* (Stony Brook, Nicolas Hays, 1978), 80–1, 115; and *Of Grammatology*, 101–40.

47 Laclau, *New Reflections on the Revolution of Our Time*, 44, 60.

3 Separating difference from what it can do: nihilism and bio-power relations

1 Homi Bhabha, 'Signs Taken for Wonders: Questions of Ambivalence and Authority under a Tree Outside Delhi, May 1817', in Henry Louis Gates, Jr., ed., *'Race', Writing and Difference* (University of Chicago Press, 1986), 169, 172, 173, 181.

2 For a critical discussion of the Labour Party's positions on race, see Caroline Knowles, *Race, Discourse and Labourism* (London, Routledge, 1992).

3 A. Sivanandan, *A Different Hunger: Writings on Black Resistance* (London, Pluto, 1982), 17.

4 Dilip Hiro, *Black British, White British* (London, Eyre and Spottiswoode, 1971), 229.

5 Quoted by Errol Lawrence, 'Just Plain Common Sense: The "Roots" of Racism', in Centre for Contemporary Cultural Studies, ed., *The Empire Strikes Back* (London, Hutchinson, 1982), 94.

6 Section 6 states, 'A person shall be guilty of an offence under this Section, if, with intent to stir up hatred against any section of the public in Great Britain distinguished by colour, race or ethnic or national origins, (a) he publishes or distributes written matter which is threatening, abusive or insulting; (b) he uses in any public place or at any public meeting words which are threatening, abusive or insulting, being matter or words likely to stir up hatred to that section on grounds of colour, race or ethnic or national origins.' The maximum penalty for this offence was two years' imprisonment and/or a fine of £1,000. The 1965 Race Relations Act was repealed and replaced by a new Race Relations Act in 1976. Sona Osman, 'Should It Be Unlawful To Incite Sexual Violence', in Gail Chester and Julienne Dickey, eds., *Feminism and Censorship* (Bridport, Prism Press, 1988), 156.

7 *ibid.*; Sivanandan, *A Different Hunger*, 17–18.
8 Paul Gilroy, *'There Ain't No Black In The Union Jack'* (London, Hutchinson, 1987), 72–111; Stuart Hall *et al.*, *Policing the Crisis* (London, Macmillan, 1978); Sivanandan, *A Different Hunger*, 23, 27, 32, 33.
9 Quoted in Paul Gilroy, 'Police and Thieves' in Centre for Contemporary Cultural Studies, ed., *The Empire Strikes Back*, 156–7. See also J. Lambert *et al.*, 'Police/Immigrant Relations: A Critique of the Select Committee Report', *New Community*, vol. 3, no. 3, summer 1974, 172–92.
10 Gilroy, 'Police and Thieves', 174. Parmar also argues that the representation of Asian femininity as naturally passive is used to discipline Asian women workers in both South-East Asia and Britain. Pratibha Parmar, 'Gender, Race and Class: Asian Women in Resistance', in Centre for Contemporary Cultural Studies, *The Empire Strikes Back*, 257–63. On the resistances of Asian women in the Indian subcontinent and in Britain, see also Parita Trivedi, 'To Deny Our Fullness: Asian Women in the Making of History', *Feminist Review*, no. 17, autumn 1984, 37–52.
11 Gilroy, *'There Ain't No Black in the Union Jack'*, 58.
12 Douglas Hurd, speech to the Conservative Party Weekend Conference, Wroxton, Oxfordshire, 21 January 1989.
13 Colin Holmes, 'J.A. Hobson and the Jews', in Colin Holmes, ed., *Immigrants and Minorities in British Society* (London, George Allen and Unwin, 1978), 125–58; Nicholas Deakin, 'The Vitality of a Tradition', in *ibid.*, 158–85; Paul Foot, *Immigration and Race in British Politics* (Harmondsworth, Penguin, 1965), 103–23.
14 Douglas Hurd, speech at the Central Mosque, Birmingham, 24 February 1989.
15 Quoted in Gilroy, *'There Ain't No Black in the Union Jack'*, 63.
16 Quoted in Jacqueline Bhabha, Francesca Klug and Sue Shutter, eds., *Worlds Apart: Women Under Immigration and Nationality Law* (London, Pluto, 1985), 85.
17 *ibid.*, 49.
18 According to the 1981 *Labour Force Survey*, the 'economic activity rate' for non-white women is 50 per cent, compared to 47 per cent for white women. Quoted in *ibid.*, 63.
19 Parmar, 'Gender, Race and Class', 241, 245.
20 Stephen Carter, *Reflections of an Affirmative Action Baby* (New York, Basic Books, 1991), 29–30.
21 Judith Butler, *Gender Trouble* (London, Routledge, 1990), 135, 136.
22 The points system ensured that well-educated, English-speaking Chinese applicants aged between 30 and 40 with high incomes would have the best chance of securing a British passport.
23 *The Guardian*, 20 April 1992, 6.
24 Quoted in *The Times*, 21 April 1990, 10.
25 Quoted in *The Guardian*, 20 April 1990, 1. *The Times* dismissed Tebbit's cricket loyalty metaphor as absurd. An editorial pointed out that England's own team on the West Indies tour had two players from South Africa, one from Jamaica, one from Dominica, one from Bar-

bados and a British citizen who had been born in India: 21 April 1990, 11.
26 Quoted in *The Times*, 21 April 1990, 1.
27 *Daily Telegraph*, 5 December 1990, 5.
28 *The Guardian*, 3 December 1990, 1.
29 *Daily Telegraph*, 3 December 1990, 3.
30 *Daily Telegraph*, 7 December 1991, 2.
31 *The Times Saturday Review*, 2 February 1991, 4; *The Guardian*, 3 December 1990, 2.
32 *The Times Saturday Review*, 2 December 1991, 4.
33 *ibid.*, 6.
34 *Daily Telegraph*, 5 December 1991, 1.
35 Winston S. Churchill, speech at the Bolton Conservative Association Dinner, Bolton, 28 May 1993.
36 Winston S. Churchill, 'Immigration: The "No-Go" Area of British Politics', press release, feature article for the *Daily Mail*, 7 June 1993, 4.
37 Winston S. Churchill, 'Brits Back Winston', press release, feature article for the *Sun*, 9 June 1993.
38 Winston S. Churchill, personal correspondence, 11 June 1993.
39 D'Souza, who was born in India and educated at Dartmouth, is the author of *Illiberal Education: The Politics of Race and Sex on Campus* (New York, Free Press, 1991).
40 Gilles Deleuze, *Nietzsche and Philosophy* (New York, Columbia University Press, 1983), 7–8.
41 *ibid.*, 62, 6.
42 Gloria Yamato, 'Something About the Subject Makes It Hard to Name', in Gloria Anzaldúa, ed., *Making Face, Making Soul = Haciendo Caras* (San Francisco, Aunt Lute Foundation Books, 1990), 22.
43 Deleuze, *Nietzsche and Philosophy*, 40.
44 Friedrich Nietzsche, *On the Genealogy of Morals*, trans. Walter Kaufmann (New York, Vintage Books, 1967), 37, 39; Deleuze, *Nietzsche and Philosophy*, 119.
45 Nietzsche, *Genealogy of Morals*, 44–5.
46 *ibid.*, 30.
47 *ibid.*, 41.
48 Etienne Balibar, 'Is There a "Neo-Racism"?', in Balibar and Immanuel Wallerstein, *Race, Nation, Class* (London, Verso, 1991), 20.
49 Conor Cruise O'Brien, *The Siege: The Saga of Israel and Zionism* (New York, Simon and Schuster, 1986), 667, 57, 58.
50 Nietzsche, *Genealogy of Morals*, 62.
51 Nietzsche, *Genealogy of Morals*, 72; Deleuze, *Nietzsche and Philosophy*, 136.
52 Quoted in Gill Seidel, 'The White Discursive Order: The British New Right's Discourse on Cultural Racism With Particular Reference to the Salisbury Review', in I.M. Zavala *et al.*, eds., *Approaches to Discourse, Poetics and Psychiatry* (Amsterdam: Benjamins, 1987), 53–6.
53 *ibid.*, 55–6.
54 Gilroy, *'There Ain't No Black in the Union Jack'*, 61.

55 Deleuze, *Nietzsche and Philosophy*, 61, 139, 34.
56 Nietzsche, *Genealogy of Morals*, 45, 84, 86.
57 *ibid.*, 116.
58 *ibid.*, 134, 127–8.
59 Michel Foucault, *Madness and Civilization* (New York, Vintage Books, 1973), 251, 245, 247.
60 *ibid.*, 184, 189.
61 Michel Foucault, *Discipline and Punish* (New York, Vintage Books, 1979); *The History of Sexuality*, vol. I, An Introduction (New York, Vintage Books, 1980).
62 Foucault, *Discipline and Punish*, 61.
63 Foucault, *History of Sexuality*, vol. I, 137.
64 *ibid.*, 104, 146.
65 Gilroy, *'There Ain't No Black in the Union Jack'*, 107, 104–6.
66 Foucault, *Discipline and Punish*, 27, 203.
67 Michel Foucault, *The Archaeology of Knowledge* (New York, Pantheon, 1972), 47, 72, 108, 109.
68 Michel Foucault, 'Nietzsche, Genealogy, History', in Donald F. Bouchard, ed., *Language, Counter-Memory, Practice* (Ithaca, Cornell University Press, 1977), 151.
69 Foucault, *The History of Sexuality*, vol. I, 26, 54, 119, 149–50.
70 Foucault, 'Nietzsche, Genealogy and History', 145, 147.
71 *ibid.*, 153, 148, 162, 154.
72 *ibid.*, 160.
73 Martin Bernal, *Black Athena: The Afroasiatic Roots of Classical Civilization*, vol. I: *The Fabrication of Ancient Greece, 1785–1985* (London, Free Association Books, 1987).
74 *ibid.*, 2.
75 Foucault, 'Nietzsche, Genealogy, History', 159, 160, 161.
76 *ibid.*, 161.

4 Powellism: the black immigrant as the post-colonial symptom and the phantasmatic re-closure of the British nation

1 Michel Foucault, *The Archaeology of Knowledge* (New York, Pantheon Books, 1972), 47–9.
2 I am appropriating the metropole/periphery metaphor and the supplementary logic of underdevelopment from the 'dependency school' of Latin American political economists such as Andre G. Frank (*Latin-America: Underdevelopment or Revolution* (New York, Monthly Review Press, 1969)) and F.H. Cardoso and E. Faletto (*Dependency and Development in Latin America* (Berkeley, University of California Press, 1979)). Dependency theorists hold that Latin America is not simply a backward region which lags behind the developed countries because of its own internal structures, but that it has been systematically underdeveloped by the developed countries. The term, 'dependency', has a dual function: Latin America's

economic, political and social structures reflect the region's dependent relation with the developed metropole, and the supposedly 'normal' and 'independent' development of the metropole profoundly depends on its exploitation of the supplementary periphery. The totalizing and functionalist aspects of the dependency approach have been widely criticized. See, for example, Ernesto Laclau, 'Feudalism and Capitalism in Latin America', *Politics and Ideology in Marxist Theory* (London, Verso, 1979), 152–50; and Philip O'Brien, 'A Critique of Latin American Theories of Dependency', in I. Oxaal, T. Barnett and D. Booth, eds., *Beyond the Sociology of Development in Latin America and Africa* (London, Routledge, 1975), 7–27.

3 Quoted in Kobena Mercer, 'Powellism: Race, Politics and Discourse', unpublished Ph.D. thesis, Goldsmith's College, University of London, 1990, 136.
4 Enoch Powell, *Freedom and Reality*, J. Wood, ed. (Kingswood, Paperfront, 1969), 190–7.
5 Powell, speech at Trinity College, Dublin, 13 November 1964, in Enoch Powell, *A Nation Not Afraid*, J. Wood, ed. (London, Batsford, 1965), 137, 139.
6 Enoch Powell, speech to the Royal Society of St. George, 22 April 1964, in *Freedom and Reality*, 255.
7 V.G. Kiernan, 'Britons Old and New', in Colin Holmes, ed., *Immigrants and Minorities in British Society* (London, George Allen and Unwin, 1978), 23.
8 Stuart Hall, 'Racism and Reaction', in John Rex *et al.*, *Five Views of Multi-Racial Britain* (London, Commission for Racial Equality, 1978), 25.
9 J. Laplanche and J.-B. Pontalis, *The Language of Psychoanalysis* (New York, W.W. Norton and Co., 1973), 465, 466, 471, 472.
10 Cathy Caruth, 'Introduction', *Psychoanalysis, Culture and Trauma, American Imago*, spring 1991, vol. 28, no. 1, 1–12.
11 James Walvin, *The Black Presence: A Documentary History of the Negro in England, 1555–1869* (New York, Shocken Books, 1972), 8, 11.
12 Beverly Bryan, Stella Dadzie and Suzanne Scafe, *The Heart of the Race: Black Women's Lives in Britain* (London, Virago, 1985), 6.
13 Walvin, *The Black Presence*, 10–11, 12, 15.
14 Hall, 'Racism and Reaction', 25.
15 Quoted in Lauretta Ngcobo, ed., *Let It Be Told: Essays by Black Women Writers in Britain* (London, Virago, 1988), 14–15.
16 Enoch Powell, speech to the Birmingham Conservative Political Centre, 20 April 1968, in *Freedom and Reality*, 216.
17 Laplanche and Pontalis, *The Language of Psychoanalysis*, 317.
18 Slavoj Zizek, *The Sublime Object of Ideology* (London, Verso, 1989), 45, 118, 123.
19 Stuart Hall *et al.*, *Policing the Crisis* (London, Macmillan, 1978), 228.
20 *Birmingham Post*, 26 October 1950, quoted in Mercer, 'Powellism: Race, Politics and Discourse', 132.
21 Mercer, 'Powellism: Race, Politics and Discourse', 111.
22 House of Commons, 3 March 1953, quoted in Paul Foot, *The Rise of Enoch Powell* (London, Cornmarket, 1969), 17–18.

23 Enoch Powell, 'Integration is the Only Way – Over Many Years', *Wolverhampton Express and Star*, 10 October 1964; reproduced in Mercer, 'Powellism: Race, Politics and Discourse', 242.

24 Enoch Powell, Speech to London Rotary Club, Eastbourne, 16 November 1968, *Freedom and Reality*, 227.

25 Quoted in Paul Foot, *Immigration and Race in British Politics* (Harmondsworth, Penguin, 1965), 12.

26 *ibid.*, 31–8.

27 Quoted in *ibid.*, 48.

28 Quoted in Nicholas Deakin, ed., *Colour and the British Electorate, 1964* (London, Pall Mall Press, 1965), 9.

29 Quoted in Paul Rich, *Race and Empire in British Politics* (Cambridge University Press, 1986), 168.

30 Quoted in Deakin, ed., *Colour and the British Electorate, 1964*, 10.

31 Dilip Hiro, *Black British, White British* (London, Eyre and Spottiswoode, 1971), 214.

32 Mercer, 'Powellism: Race, Politics and Discourse', 215, 219, 221.

33 Deakin, *Colour and the British Electorate, 1964*, 11.

34 Mercer, 'Powellism: Race, Politics and Discourse', 222.

35 Hall, 'Racism and Reaction', quoted in *ibid.*, 219.

36 Hall *et al.*, *Policing the Crisis*, 245.

37 Hiro, *Black British, White British*, 318–20.

38 Laplanche and Pontalis, *The Language of Psychoanalysis*, 488.

39 Errol Lawrence, 'Just Plain Common Sense: The "Roots" of Racism', in Centre for Contemporary Cultural Studies, ed., *The Empire Strikes Back* (London, Hutchinson, 1982), 47.

40 Zizek, *The Sublime Object of Ideology*, 48, 78–9, 126.

41 Colin Leys, *Politics in Britain* (London, Verso, 1983), 66–7.

42 *ibid.*, 65, 201.

43 *ibid.*, 70–1, 74, 75.

44 Jeffrey Weeks, *Sex, Politics and Society* (London, Longman, 1981), 259, 275, 254.

45 Hall *et al.*, *Policing the Crisis*, 239.

46 *ibid.*, 245–6.

47 Enoch Powell, speech at the Birmingham Conservative Political Centre, 20 April 1968, in *Freedom and Reality*, 219.

48 *ibid.*, 213–14.

49 Enoch Powell, speech to the London Rotary Club, Eastbourne, 16 November 1968, in *Freedom and Reality*, 227.

50 *ibid.*, 230.

51 Enoch Powell, speech at the Birmingham Conservative Political Centre, 20 April 1968, in *Freedom and Reality*, 217–18.

52 Foot, *The Rise of Enoch Powell*, 114.

53 B. Smithies and P. Fiddick, *Enoch Powell on Immigration* (London, Sphere Books, 1969), 59–60.

54 Enoch Powell, speech at the Birmingham Conservative Political Centre, 20 April 1968, in *Freedom and Reality*, 218.

55 *ibid.*

56 Powell in Smithies and Fiddick, *Enoch Powell on Immigration*, 68.

57 Paul Foot, *The Rise of Enoch Powell*, 113–14.

58 Hiro, *Black British, White British*, 72.
59 Enoch Powell, speech at the Birmingham Conservative Political Centre, 20 April 1968, in *Freedom and Reality*, 218.
60 Powell, speech to London Rotary Club, Eastbourne, 16 November 1968 speech, in *Freedom and Reality*, 230.
61 *ibid.*, 232.
62 *ibid.*, 236, 237.
63 A. Sivanandan, *A Different Hunger* (London, Pluto, 1982), 103.
64 Douglas Schoen, *Enoch Powell and the Powellites* (London, Macmillan, 1977), 33.
65 *ibid.*, 33, 34, 35, 36.
66 See C. Aronsfeld, 'Challenge to Socialist Brotherhood: British Dockers and Coloured Immigration', *Patterns of Prejudice*, Institute of Jewish Affairs, vol. 2, no. 4, July–Aug. 1968, 8–12; and 'Is the Working Class Really Racist?', editorial, *New Statesman*, 2 May 1968, 627.
67 *ibid.*, 37, 39; Andrew Gamble, *The Conservative Nation* (London, Macmillan, 1974), 121.
68 Hiro, *Black British, White British*, 335.
69 *Race Today* analysis of a speech by Richard Crossman, quoted in *ibid.*, 337.
70 Quoted in George Gale, 'The 1970 Election', in John Wood, ed., *Powell and the 1970 Election* (Kingswood, Paperfront, 1970), 61.
71 *ibid.*, 69, 101, 73.
72 Enoch Powell, speech in Northfield, Birmingham, 13 June 1970, *Still to Decide*, ed. J. Wood (London, Batsford, 1972), 26, 26–7, 28.
73 *ibid.*, 28, 31, 29, 30.
74 See Edmund Burke, *Reflections on the Revolution in France* (Indianapolis, Bobbs-Merrill, 1955).
75 Enoch Powell, *No Easy Answers* (London, Sheldon, 1973), 94.
76 Enoch Powell, speech in Northfield, Birmingham, 13 June 1970, in *Still to Decide*, 27, 28.
77 *ibid.*, 28.
78 Henry Louis Gates, Jr., 'Writing "Race" and the Difference It Makes', in Gates, ed., *'Race', Writing and Difference* (University of Chicago Press, 1986), 4, 5.
79 Enoch Powell, *Still to Decide*, 29.
80 Zizek, *The Sublime Object of Ideology*, 98–102.
81 Schoen, *Enoch Powell and the Powellites*, 53.
82 Quoted in Gale, 'The 1970 Election', 79.
83 Quoted in *ibid.*, 80–1.
84 Quoted in 'Stop Press', in Wood, ed., *Powell and the 1970 Election*, 125.
85 Quoted in Schoen, *Enoch Powell and the Powellites*, 59.
86 Diana Spearman, 'Enoch Powell's Election Letters', in Wood, ed., *Powell and the 1970 Election*, 19.
87 Calculated in column inches, Schoen, *Enoch Powell and the Powellites*, 56.
88 Donley Studlar, 'British Public Opinion, Colour Issues and Enoch Powell', *The British Journal of Political Science*, no. 3, 1974, 349.
89 Schoen, *Enoch Powell and the Powellites*, 57.

90 *ibid.*, 115.
91 *ibid.*, 147, 278–9.
92 Hugo Young, *One of Us* (London, Macmillan, 1989), 93.
93 A.H. Lane, *The Alien Menace: A Statement of the Case*, London, Boswell Publishing, 1934, vii.
94 On the 1925 Special Restriction (Coloured Seamen) Order, and Victorian theories of white superiority, see Paul Rich, *Race and Empire in British Politics*, 122–30 and 12–26 respectively.
95 Colin Holmes, 'J.A. Hobson and the Jews', in Colin Holmes, ed., *Immigrants and Minorities in British Society* (London, George Allen and Unwin, 1978), 125–58; Nicholas Deakin, 'The Vitality of a Tradition', in *ibid.*, 158–85.
96 Foot, *Immigration and Race in British Politics*, 103–23.
97 Schoen, *Enoch Powell and the Powellites*, 277.
98 The *Economist*, 26 April 1968, quoted in Hiro, *Black British, White British*, 231.
99 Robert King and Michael Wood, 'The Support for Enoch Powell', in Ivor Crewe, ed., *British Political Sociology Yearbook* (London, Croom Helm, 1975), 244, 247.
100 Schoen, *Enoch Powell and the Powellites*, 227–31, 232–55. See also Diana Spearman's analysis of the letters sent to Powell in 'Enoch Powell's Postbag', *New Society*, 9 May 1968, 667–9.
101 Mercer, 'Powellism: Race, Politics and Discourse', 280.
102 The definition of 'myth' and 'imaginary' is taken from Ernesto Laclau, *New Reflections on the Revolution of Our Time* (London, Verso, 1990), 61–2, 64–5.
103 Andrew Gamble, *The Conservative Nation*, 87–123.
104 Hall, 'Racism and Reaction', 32.
105 *ibid.*
106 Margaret Thatcher, House of Commons, 14 April 1981, quoted in Young, *One of Us*, 234.
107 Quoted in *ibid.*
108 Quoted in Martin Barker, *The New Racism: Conservatives and the Ideology of the Tribe* (London, Junction Books, 1981), 162.
109 Martin Durham, *Sex and Politics* (London, Macmillan, 1991), 61.
110 Schoen, *Enoch Powell and the Powellites*, 239–41; Ken Phillips, 'The Nature of Powellism', in Roger King and Neill Nugent, eds., *The British Right: Conservative and Right Wing Politics in Britain* (Westmead, Saxon House, 1977), 124.
111 Schoen, *Enoch Powell and the Powellites*, 278.
112 Stuart Hall, 'The Great Moving Right Show', in Hall and Martin Jacques, eds., *Thatcherism* (London, Lawrence and Wishart, 1983), 19, 20.
113 Young, *One of Us*, 102–3, 113–16.
114 Thatcher, quoted in Barker, *The New Racism*, 15.
115 *ibid.*, 1.
116 Quoted in *ibid.*
117 Sivanandan, *A Different Hunger*, 111.
118 Hiro, *White British, Black British*, 362–3.

119 Quoted in Frank Reeves, *British Racial Discourse: A Study of British Political Discourse about Race and Race-related Matters* (Cambridge University Press, 1983), 208.

5 Thatcherism's promotion of homosexuality

1 *Out on Tuesday*, Abseil Productions, Channel Four television series, 14 February 1989.
2 Stuart Hall, 'Blue Election, Election Blues', *Hard Road to Renewal* (London, Verso, 1988), 259–67.
3 These estimations are based on an approximate count of Hansard columns devoted to various topics in the debates. The debates were not limited by governmental 'guillotine'.
4 Raymond Williams, quoted in Simon Watney, 'Taking Liberties' in Watney and Erica Carter, eds., *Taking Liberties: AIDS and Cultural Politics* (London, Serpent's Tail, 1989), 25–6.
5 Peter Tatchell, *The Battle for Bermondsey* (London, Heretic Books, 1983), 78.
6 *ibid.*, 130.
7 Quoted in *ibid.*, 139–40.
8 Quoted in Martin Durham, *Sex and Politics: The Family and Morality in the Thatcher Years* (London, Macmillan, 1991), 111–12.
9 *ibid.*, 111–15.
10 *ibid.*, 115.
11 Quoted in *ibid.*, 116.
12 Slavoj Zizek, *The Sublime Object of Ideology* (London, Verso, 1989), 48.
13 *ibid.*
14 *ibid.*, 75.
15 I am using the terms, 'supporters' and 'opposers' to Section 28 to indicate the non-partisan nature of these discourses.
16 Dame Knight, *Official Report*, House of Commons, 8 March 1987, cols. 997–8.
17 Ernesto Laclau, 'Totalitarianism and Moral Indignation', *Diacritics*, vol. 20, no. 3, fall 1990, 91. Laclau is referring to Derrida's analysis of the charges of fascism which have been made against Paul de Man.
18 The first two statistics are from a Harris poll cited by Lord Manson, while the third statistic is from a MORI poll cited by Lord Campbell and Lady Saltoun. *Official Report*, House of Lords, 2 February 1988, col. 999; 1 February 1988, col. 874; and 2 February 1988, col. 1007.
19 Emphasis added, *Official Report*, Standing Committee 'A', 8 December 1987, col. 1220.
20 Pratibha Parmar, 'Rage and Desire: Confronting Pornography', in G. Chester and J. Dickey, eds., *Feminism and Censorship* (Bridport, Prism, 1988), 121.
21 Durham, *Sex and Politics*, 113–14.
22 Cunningham and Grant, *Official Report*, Standing Committee 'A', 8 December 1987, cols. 1211–14 and 1223–4 respectively.
23 Hall argues that the 'traditionalist' Left, which has become hegemonic in the Labour Party, not only refuses to engage with the 'loony

Left' image but actually colludes with it by returning to a 'respect-able, moderate, trade unionist, male-dominated working-class' image in which the traces of the feminist, black and gay struggles are suppressed. 'Blue Election, Election Blues', *Hard Road to Renewal*, 263.

24 The conception of representation as located on the terrain of excess is taken from Simon Watney, *Policing Desire: Pornography, AIDS and the Media* (London, Methuen, 1987).

25 Quoted in Durham, *Sex and Politics*, 122.

26 *Official Report*, House of Commons, 8 March 1987, col. 999. For de-tailed analyses of popular British discourse on AIDS, see Simon Watney, *Policing Desire*, Watney and Carter, eds., *Taking Liberties* and Tessa Boffin and Sunil Gupta, eds., *Ecstatic Antibodies: Resisting the AIDS Mythology* (London, Rivers Oram Press, 1990).

27 Simon Watney, 'Psychoanalysis, Sexuality and AIDS', in Simon Shepherd and Mick Wallis, eds., *Coming On Strong* (London, Unwin Hyman, 1989), 33–7. The New Patriotic Movement held a demon-stration outside the Haringey Civic Centre in 1987: one of its banners read, 'Gay equals AIDS equals Death': Durham, *Sex and Politics*, 114.

28 Kobena Mercer and Isaac Julien, 'Race, Sexual Politics and Black Masculinity', in Rowena Chapman and Jonathan Rutherford, eds., *Male Order* (London, Lawrence and Wishart, 1988), 157; Cindy Patton, *Inventing AIDS* (London, Routledge, 1990), 77–98.

29 Susan Sontag, *AIDS and Its Metaphors* (New York, Farrar, Strauss and Giroux, 1989), 50.

30 Mercer and Julien, 'Race, Sexual Politics and Black Masculinity', 157. A blood donor clinic at the University of Essex in 1988 posted a large sign on its door which read, 'No Homosexuals, No Drug Users, No Africans'.

31 Lord Halsbury, *Official Report*, House of Lords, 16 February 1988, cols. 593–4.

32 Watney, quoted in Boffin and Gupta, *Ecstatic Antibodies*, 10.

33 Quoted in Stonewall, 'Age of Consent Briefing', 1992.

34 *ibid*.

35 Earl of Caithness, *Official Report*, House of Lords, 16 February 1988, col. 611–12.

36 According to the *Oxford English Dictionary* the term 'monster' is derived from the Latin *monstrum*, a divine portent or warning, and from the French *monère*, to warn. 'Monster' was used in seventeenth-century English as a verb, meaning to exhibit as a monster. Foucault discusses the function of the public display of the madman and the tortured body of the accused – the ways in which this regulated exhibition was supposed to demonstrate authority and to demarcate the limit between the rational/not-rational, and the law-abiding/law-breaking – in *Madness and Civilization* (New York, Vintage, 1973) and *Discipline and Punish* (New York, Vintage, 1979).

37 Howard, *Official Report*, House of Commons 15 December 1987, col. 1019.

38 Earl of Caithness, *Official Report*, House of Lords, 1 February 1988, col. 889.

39 Baroness Blatch, *Official Report*, House of Lords, 16 February 1988, col. 599–600.
40 For an account of queer resistances and the debate around 'queerness' in Britain, see Cherry Smyth, *Lesbians Talk Queer Notions* (London, Scarlet Press, 1992).
41 Lord Halsbury, *Official Report*, House of Lords, 18 December 1988, col. 310.
42 Lord Monson, *Official Report*, House of Lords, 16 February 1988, col. 594.
43 Wilshire, *Official Report*, House of Commons, 9 March 1988, col. 406–7.
44 Dickens, *Official Report*, House of Commons, 9 March 1988, col. 406, 417.
45 Lord Campbell, the Earl of Longford and Dame Knight, *Official Report*, House of Lords, 18 December 1986, col. 312, and 18 December 1986, cols. 314–16; and House of Commons, 8 March 1987, col. 998 respectively.
46 Peter Tatchell, 'Gay Men More Likely To Be Found Guilty', *Capital Gay*, 18 January 1991, 4.
47 Patten, *Official Report*, Standing Committee 'A', 18 December 1990, 314–15.
48 Patten, Letter to Robin Squire MP, 8 February 1991, released by the Home Office.
49 My use of a form of the masculine pronoun here is deliberate and will become self-explanatory below.
50 Halsbury, *Official Report*, House of Lords, 18 December 1986, col. 310.
51 *ibid.*
52 Desart, quoted in Jeffrey Weeks, *Coming Out: Homosexual Politics in Britain from the Nineteenth Century to the Present* (London, Quartet, 1977), 106–7.
53 Roger Scruton, *Sexual Desire* (London, Weidenfeld and Nicolson, 1986), 307–8.
54 Maria Maggenti *et al.*, 'A Round Table Discussion: AIDS and Democracy', in Brian Wallis, ed., *Democracy: A Project by Group Material* (Seattle, Bay Press, 1990), 243.
55 Gayle Rubin, 'Thinking Sex' in Carole Vance, ed., *Pleasure and Danger: Exploring Female Sexuality* (New York, Routledge and Kegan Paul, 1984), 267–319.
56 Halsbury, *Official Report*, House of Lords, 18 December 1986, col. 310.
57 Ann Tobin, 'Lesbianism and the Labour Party: The GLC Experience', *Feminist Review*, no. 34, spring 1990, 56–66.
58 *Official Report*, House of Lords, 6 March 1990, col. 1098.
59 *ibid.*, Standing Committee B, 15 May 1990, col. 145.
60 *ibid.*, 147.
61 *ibid.*, cols. 144, 145.
62 Halsbury, *Official Report*, House of Lords, 16 February 1988, 633.
63 Leo Bersani, 'Is the Rectum a Grave?', *October*, no. 43, winter 1987, 204.
64 *ibid.*
65 *ibid.*, 205.

66 Many of these debates originate in the New Right journal, the *Salisbury Review*. See Gill Seidel's analysis in 'The White Discursive Order', in I. Zavala *et al.*, eds., *Approaches to Discourse, Poetics and Psychiatry* (Amsterdam, Benjamins, 1987), 39–66.

67 Beverly Bryan, Stella Dadzie and Suzanne Scafe, *The Heart of the Race: Black Women's Lives in Britain* (London, Virago, 1985), 74, 80. See also Institute of Race Relations, 'Anti-Racist Not Multicultural Education', *Race and Class*, vol. 22, no. 1, 1980, 81–3.

68 Patrick, *Official Report*, Standing Committee 'A', 8 December 1987, cols. 1219–20.

69 Quoted in *Capital Gay*, 30 October 1987, 1.

70 Earl of Caithness, *Official Report*, House of Lords, 1 February 1988, col. 951.

71 *The Guardian*, 11 October 1989, 27.

72 Lord Halsbury, *Official Report*, House of Lords, 18 December 1986, col. 310.

73 Livingston, *Official Report*, House of Commons, 9 March 1988, col. 418.

74 Greenway, *Official Report*, House of Commons, 15 December 1987, cols. 1000, 1002.

75 Jackie Stacey, 'Promoting Normality: Section 28 and the Regulation of Sexuality', in S. Franklin, C. Lury and J. Stacey, eds., *Off-Centre: Feminism and Cultural Studies* (London, Harper Collins, 1991, 284–304).

76 Margaret Thatcher, quoted in Martin Barker, *The New Racism: Conservatives and the Ideology of the Tribe* (London, Junction Books, 1981), 44.

77 Quoted in *Capital Gay*, 30 October 1987, 1.

78 Carmen, Gail, Shaila and Pratibha, 'Becoming Visible: Black Lesbian Discussion', *Feminist Review*, no. 17, autumn 1984, 54; Hazel Carby, 'White Woman Listen! Black Feminism and the Boundaries of Sisterhood', in Centre for Contemporary Cultural Studies, ed., *The Empire Strikes Back*, London, Hutchinson, 1982, 214–17.

79 In constructing this distinction, I am drawing on Laclau and Mouffe's categories, the logic of equivalence and the logic of difference. Ernesto Laclau and Chantal Mouffe, *Hegemony and Socialist Strategy* (London, Verso, 1985).

80 Thatcher, address to the General Assembly of the Church of Scotland, *The Observer*, 22 May 1988, 2.

81 Kellet-Bowman, *Official Report*, House of Commons, 15 December 1987, col. 1009.

82 Fairburn, *Official Report*, House of Commons, 9 March 1988, cols. 372, 382.

83 Baroness Strange, Baroness Blatch, Viscount Buckmaster, *Official Report*, House of Lords, 16 February 1988, cols. 611, 610, 607 respectively.

84 Lord Monson, *Official Report*, House of Lords, 16 February 1988, col. 594.

85 Wilshire, *Official Report*, House of Commons, 15 December 1987, col. 1006. These arguments conform to the 'domino theory of sexual peril' which Rubin identifies in popular, religious, medical and psychiatric

discourse on sexuality. See Gayle Rubin, 'Thinking Sex', in Carole Vance, ed., *Pleasure and Danger*, 282.

86 Wilshire and Lord Ritchie, *Official Report*, House of Commons, 9 March 1988, col. 404 and House of Lords, 16 February 1988, col. 604 respectively.

87 Howard, *Official Report*, House of Commons, 9 March 1988, col. 421.

88 Earl of Caithness, *Official Report*, House of Lords, 16 February 1988, col. 643.

89 Halsbury, *Official Report*, House of Lords, 1 February 1988, col. 874–5.

90 *Capital Gay*, 12 February 1988, 2. All of the letter-writers signed their letters with their full names. I have used initials to identify the authors because it would have been impossible to contact all of them in order to obtain permission for republication of their letters.

91 *Capital Gay*, 12 February 1988, 2.

92 *ibid.*

93 *Capital Gay*, 17 June 1988, 2.

94 Cited in *Capital Gay*, 5 February 1988, 2.

95 Peter Davies, *Capital Gay*, 12 February 1988, 10–11.

96 Quoted in *The Pink Paper*, 13 October 1988, 19.

97 *Capital Gay*, 15 May 1987, 2.

98 *Gay Times*, December 1990, 24.

99 *The Independent*, 18 July 1991, 8.

100 *Capital Gay*, 2 August 1991, 1.

101 *Capital Gay*, 2 August 1991, 2.

102 *The Pink Paper*, 21 April 1988, 15.

103 *Capital Gay*, 6 May 1988, 2.

104 See Mary Fainsod Katzenstein, 'The Spectacle as Political Resistance: Feminist and Gay/Lesbian Politics in the Military', *Minerva: A Quarterly Report on Women and the Military*, vol. 11, no. 1, spring 1993, 1–16.

105 Eric Washington, 'Freedom Rings! The Alliance Between Blacks and Gays is Threatened by Mutual Inscrutability', *The Village Voice*, 29 July 1993, 32.

106 My appropriation of Foucault's conception of the panopticon (Michel Foucault, *Discipline and Punish*) is influenced by Higginbotham's Foucauldian discussion of the tactics of black church women in the United States during the 'Jim Crow' era. Evelyn Brooks Higginbotham, *Righteous Discontent: The Women's Movement in the Black Baptist Church, 1880–1920* (Cambridge, Mass., Harvard University Press, 1993), 187, 196, 221.

107 Marshall Kirk and Hunter Madsen, *After the Ball: How America Will Conquer Its Fear and Hatred of Gays in the '90s* (New York, Doubleday, 1989).

108 Cunningham, *Official Report*, Standing Committee 'A', 8 December 1987, cols. 1211–14.

109 Cunningham, *Official Report*, House of Commons, 15 December 1987, cols. 996–7.

110 Cunningham, *Official Report*, House of Commons, 9 March 1988, col. 373.

111 Roberts, Pike, Hughes, Livingston, Fisher, *Official Report*, Standing Committee 'A', 8 December 1987, col. 1215; House of Commons, 15 December 1987, col. 1014; House of Commons, 9 March 1988, cols. 340, 390; House of Commons, 9 March 1988, col. 417; House of Commons, 9 March 1988, col. 394 respectively.

112 John Marshall, 'Flaunting It: The Challenge of the 1990s', *Gay Times*, January 1989, 12–13.

113 Henry Louis Gates, Jr., 'Writing "Race" and the Difference It Makes', in Gates, ed., *'Race', Writing and Difference* (University of Chicago Press, 1986), 5; Eve Kosofsky Sedgwick, *The Epistemology of the Closet* (Berkeley, University of California Press, 1990), 29, 34, 75. My reading of Sedgwick's text on this point has been influenced by the unpublished papers which were presented by Paisley Currah and Biddy Martin at the Lesbian, Gay and Bisexual Studies Conference, Cornell University, 27 March 1992.

114 Judith Butler, *Gender Trouble: Feminism and the Subversion of Identity* (London, Routledge, 1990).

Conclusion

1 Ashis Nandy, *The Intimate Enemy: Loss and the Recovery of Self under Colonialism* (Delhi, Oxford University Press, 1983).

2 *ibid.*, xi.

3 *ibid.*

4 *ibid.*, xii.

5 *ibid.*, 3.

6 Michel Foucault, *Discipline and Punish* (New York, Vintage Books, 1979) and *The History of Sexuality*, vol. 1 (New York, Vintage Books, 1980).

7 Frantz Fanon, *Black Skin, White Masks* (London, Pluto, 1986).

8 For a critical discussion of Fanon on sexual discourse, see Jonathan Dollimore, *Sexual Dissidence: Augustine to Wilde, Freud to Foucault* (Oxford, Clarendon, 1991), 344–7.

9 Nandy, *The Intimate Enemy*, 18–27.

10 John Mackenzie, *Propaganda and Empire* (Manchester University Press, 1984).

11 Nandy, *The Intimate Enemy*, 32.

Bibliography

Abbagnano, N., 'Psychologism', in Paul Edwards, ed., *Encyclopedia of Philosophy*, London, Collier Macmillan, 1967, 520–1

Alarcón, Norma, 'The Theoretical Subject(s) of *This Bridge Called My Back* and Anglo-American Feminism', in Gloria Anzaldúa, ed., *Making Face, Making Soul = Haciendo Caras: Creative and Critical Perspectives by Women of Color*, San Francisco, Aunt Lute Foundation Books, 1990, 356–69

Allison, David 'Translator's Introduction', in Jacques Derrida, *Speech and Phenomena*, Evanston, Northwestern University Press, 1973, xxxi–xlii

Amos, Valerie and Parmar, Pratibha, 'Challenging Imperial Feminism', *Feminist Review*, no. 17, July 1984, 3–19

Anderson, Benedict, *Imagined Communities: Reflections on the Origin and Spread of Nationalism*, London, Verso, 1983

Appiah, Anthony, 'The Uncompleted Argument: Du Bois and the Illusion of Race', in Henry Louis Gates, Jr., ed., *'Race', Writing and Difference*, University of Chicago Press, 1986, 21–37

Appignanesi, Lisa and Maitland, Sara, *The Rushdie File*, London, Fourth Estate, 1989

Aristotle, *Metaphysics*, Hugh Tredennick, trans., Cambridge, Mass., Harvard University Press, 1933

Aronsfeld, C., 'Challenge to Socialist Brotherhood: British Dockers and Coloured Immigration', *Patterns of Prejudice*, London, Institute of Jewish Affairs, vol. 2, no. 4, July–Aug. 1968, 8–12

Aubenque, P., *Le problème de l'être chez Aristotle*, Paris, Presses Universitaires de France, 1966

Bailey, Cameron, 'Nigger/Lover: The Thin Sheen of Race in "Something Wild"', *Screen*, vol. 29, no. 4, 1988, 12–24

Balibar, Etienne and Wallerstein, Immanuel, *Race, Nation, Class*, London, Verso, 1991

Barker, Martin, *The New Racism: Conservatives and the Ideology of the Tribe*, London, Junction Books, 1981

Barnett, Anthony, 'Fortress Thatcher', in P. Ayrton *et al.*, *World View 1985*, London, Pluto, 1984, 117–20

266

'Iron Britannia', *New Left Review*, no. 134, July–August, 1982, 5–96

Barrett, Leonard, *The Rastafarians: the Dreadlocks of Jamaica*, London, Heinemann, 1977

Barthes, Roland, *Elements of Semiology*, New York, Hill and Wang, 1967
Mythologies, London, Paladin, 1973
S/Z, New York, Hill and Wang, 1974

Berkeley, Humphrey, *The Odyssey of Enoch*, London, Hamish Hamilton, 1977

Bernal, Martin, *Black Athena: The Afroasiatic Roots of Classical Civilization*, vol. 1: *The Fabrication of Ancient Greece, 1785–1985*, London, Free Association Books, 1987

Bersani, Leo, 'Is the Rectum a Grave?', *October*, no. 43, winter 1987, 197–222

Bhabha, Homi, 'The Commitment to Theory', *New Formations*, no. 5, summer 1988, 5–23
'Signs Taken for Wonders: Questions of Ambivalence and Authority under a Tree Outside Delhi, May 1817', in Henry Louis Gates, Jr., ed., *'Race', Writing and Difference*, University of Chicago Press, 1986, 163–84
'The Third Space', interview by Jonathan Rutherford, in Rutherford, ed., *Identity: Community, Culture, Difference*, London, Lawrence and Wishart, 1990, 207–22

Bhabha, Jacqueline, Klug, Francesca and Shutter, Sue, eds., *Worlds Apart: Women Under Immigration and Nationality Law*, London, Pluto, 1985

Bhavnani, Kum-Kum, 'Is Violence Masculine? A Black Feminist Perspective', in Shabnam Grewal *et al.*, eds., *Charting the Journey: Writings by Black and Third World Women*, London, Sheba Feminist Publishers, 1988, 263–8

Boffin, Tessa, and Gupta, Sunil, eds., *Ecstatic Antibodies: Resisting the AIDS Mythology*, London, Rivers Oram Press, 1990
and Fraser, Jean, eds., *Stolen Glances: Lesbians Take Photographs*, London, Pandora, 1991

Bourne, Jenny, 'Cheerleaders and Ombudsmen: The Sociology of Race Relations in Britain', *Race and Class*, vol. 21, no. 4, 1980, 331–52

Boyne, Roy, *Foucault and Derrida*, London, Unwin Hyman, 1990

Brake, Mike, *The Sociology of Youth Culture and Youth Subcultures*, London, Routledge and Kegan Paul, 1980

British Election Study, 1987, Codebook, A. Heath, R. Jowell, Social and Community Planning Research, J.K. Curtice, Principal Investigators; ESRC Data Archive Reference 33066

Bryan, Beverly, Dadzie, Stella and Scafe, Suzanne, *The Heart of the Race: Black Women's Lives in Britain*, London, Virago, 1985

Bulpitt, J., 'Continuity, Autonomy and Peripheralization: The Anatomy of the Centre's Race Statecraft in England', in Zig Layton-Henry and Paul Rich, eds., *Race, Government and Politics in Britain*, London, Macmillan, 1986, 17–44

Burke, Edmund, *Reflections on the Revolution in France*, Indianapolis, Bobbs-Merrill, 1955

Butler, Judith, 'Contingent Foundations: Feminism and the Question of

Bibliography

"Postmodernism"', in Butler and Joan Scott, eds., *Feminists Theorize the Political*, London, Routledge, 1992, 3–21

Gender Trouble: Feminism and the Subversion of Identity, London, Routledge, 1990

Calley, Malcolm, *God's People: West Indian Pentecostal Sects in England*, Oxford University Press, 1965

Campbell, Beatrix, *The Iron Ladies: Why Do Women Vote Tory?*, London, Virago Press, 1987

Campbell, Horace, *Rasta and Resistance: From Marcus Garvey to Walter Rodney*, London, Hansib, 1985

Carby, Hazel V., 'White Woman Listen! Black Feminism and the Boundaries of Sisterhood', in Centre for Contemporary Cultural Studies, ed., *The Empire Strikes Back: Race and Racism in 70s Britain*, London, Hutchinson, 1982, 212–35

Cardoso, F.H. and Faletto, E., *Dependency and Development in Latin America*, Berkeley, University of California Press, 1979

Carmen, Gail, Shaila and Pratibha, 'Becoming Visible: Black Lesbian Discussions', *Feminist Review*, no. 17, autumn 1984, 54–66

Carmichael, Stokely and Hamilton, Charles, *Black Power: The Politics of Liberation in America*, New York, Random House, 1967

Carter, Stephen, *Reflections of an Affirmative Action Baby*, New York, Basic Books, 1991

Caruth, Cathy, 'Introduction', *Psychoanalysis, Culture and Trauma*, *American Imago*, spring 1991, vol. 28, no. 1, 1–12

Cashmore, Ernest, *The Logic of Racism*, London, Allen and Unwin, 1987

Rastaman, London, Unwin, 1984

and Troyna, Barry, eds., *Black Youth in Crisis*, London, Allen and Unwin, 1982

Introduction to Race Relations, London, Routledge and Kegan Paul, 1983

Centre for Contemporary Cultural Studies, eds., *The Empire Strikes Back: Race and Racism in 70s Britain*, London, Hutchinson, 1982

Chauncey, George, 'Christian Brotherhood or Sexual Perversion? Homosexual Identities and the Construction of Sexual Boundaries in the World War I Era', in Martin Duberman, Martha Vicinus and George Chauncey, eds., *Hidden From History: Reclaiming the Gay and Lesbian Past*, New York, Penguin, 1990, 294–317

Churchill, Winston S., 'Brits Back Winston', press release, feature article for the *Sun*, 9 June 1993

'Immigration: The "No-Go" Area of British Politics', press release, feature article for the *Daily Mail*, 7 June 1993

Cohen, G.A., *Karl Marx's Theory of History: A Defence*, Princeton University Press, 1978

Cohen, Stanley, *Folk Devils and Moral Panics*, London, Basil Blackwell, 1980

Copleston, Frederick, *A History of Philosophy*, London, Doubleday, 1985

Cornell, Drucilla, 'Gender, Sex and Equivalent Rights', in Judith Butler and Joan Scott, eds., *Feminists Theorize the Political*, New York, Routledge, 1992, 280–98

Coward, Rosalind, and Ellis, John, *Language and Materialism*, London, Routledge and Kegan Paul, 1977

Crewe, Ivor, 'The Electorate: Partisan Dealignment Ten Years On', in Hugh Berrington, ed., *Change in British Politics*, London, Frank Cass, 1984, 183–215

'Has the Electorate Become Thatcherite?', in Robert Skidelsky, *Thatcherism*, London, Chatto and Windus, 1988, 25–49

'How to Win a Landslide Without Really Trying: Why the Conservatives Won in 1983', in Austin Ranney, ed., *Britain at the Polls: A Study of the General Election*, Durham, Duke University Press, 1985, 155–196

'The Labour Party and the Electorate', in Dennis Kavanagh, ed., *The Politics of the Labour Party*, London, George Allen and Unwin, 1982, 9–49

Cronon, David, 'Black Moses: Marcus Garvey and Garveyism', in Okon Edet Uya, ed., *Black Brotherhood*, Lexington, Heath, 1971, 172–93

Crosby, Christina, 'Dealing With Differences', in Judith Butler and Joan Scott, eds., *Feminists Theorize the Political*, New York, Routledge, 1992, 130–43

Culler, Jonathan, *Ferdinand de Saussure*, Ithaca, Cornell University Press, 1986

Davies, Peter, commentary, *Capital Gay*, 12 February 1988, 10–11

Davison, R.B., *Black British: Immigrants to England*, London, Oxford University Press, 1966

Deakin, Nicholas, *Colour and the British Electorate, 1964*, London, Pall Mall Press, 1965

'The Vitality of a Tradition', in Colin Holmes, ed., *Immigrants and Minorities in British Society*, London, George Allen and Unwin, 1978, 158–85

Deleuze, Gilles, 'Active and Reactive', in David Allison, ed., *The New Nietzsche*, Cambridge, Mass., MIT Press, 1985, 80–106

Nietzsche and Philosophy, New York, Columbia University Press, 1983

'Nomad Thought', in David Allison, ed., *The New Nietzsche*, Cambridge, Mass., MIT Press, 1985, 142–9

Derrida, Jacques, 'But, beyond . . .', in Henry Louis Gates, Jr., ed., *'Race', Writing and Difference*, University of Chicago Press, 1986, 354–69

Edmund Husserl's Origin of Geometry: An Introduction, Stony Brook, Nicolas Hays, 1978

'Letter to a Japanese Friend' in David Wood and Robert Bernasconi, eds., *Derrida and Différance*, Evanston, Northwestern University Press, 1988, 1–6

Limited Inc, Evanston, Northwestern University Press, 1988

Of Grammatology, Baltimore, Johns Hopkins University Press, 1974

'Racism's Last Word', in Henry Louis Gates, Jr., ed., *'Race', Writing and Difference*, University of Chicago Press, 1986, 329–38

Speech and Phenomena, Evanston, Northwestern University Press, 1973

Descombes, Vincent, *Modern French Philosophy*, Cambridge University Press, 1980

Diawara, Manthia, 'Black Spectatorship: Problems of Identification and Resistance', *Screen*, vol. 29, no. 4, 1988, 50–60

Bibliography

Dollimore, Jonathan, *Sexual Dissidence: Augustine to Wilde, Freud to Foucault*, Oxford, Clarendon, 1991

Dreyfus, Hubert, and Rabinow, Paul, *Michel Foucault: Beyond Structuralism and Hermeneutics*, University of Chicago Press, 1983

D'Souza, Dinesh, *Illiberal Education: The Politics of Race and Sex on Campus*, New York, Free Press, 1991

Duffield, Mark, 'New Racism ... New Realism: Two Sides of the Same Coin', *Radical Philosophy*, no. 37, summer 1984, 29–34

Dunleavy, Patrick and Husbands, Christopher, *British Democracy at the Crossroads: Voting and Party Competition in the 1980s*, London, Allen and Unwin, 1985

Durham, Martin, *Sex and Politics: The Family and Morality in the Thatcher Years*, London, Macmillan, 1991

Dyer, Richard, 'White', *Screen*, vol. 29, no. 4, 1988, 26–48

Edgar, David, 'The Free or the Good', in Ruth Levitas, ed., *The Ideology of the New Right*, Oxford, Polity Press, 55–79

Edwards, Adolph, *Marcus Garvey, 1887–1940*, London, New Beacon Books, 1972

Egbuna, Obi, *Destroy This Temple: The Voice of Black Power in Britain*, London, MacGibbon and Kee, 1970

Fanon, Frantz, *Black Skin, White Masks*, London, Pluto, 1986

The Wretched of the Earth, New York, Grove Press, 1968

File, Nigel, *Black Settlers in Britain, 1555–1958*, London, Heinemann, 1981

Foner, Nancy, *Jamaica Farewell: Jamaican Migrants in London*, London, Routledge and Kegan Paul, 1979

Foot, Paul, *Immigration and Race in British Politics*, Harmondsworth, Penguin, 1965

The Rise of Enoch Powell, London, Cornmarket, 1969

Foucault, Michel, *The Archaeology of Knowledge*, New York, Pantheon, 1972

'Body/Power', interview by the editorial collective of *Quel Corps?*, in Colin Gordon, ed., *Power/Knowledge*, New York, Pantheon, 1980, 55–62

'The Confession of the Flesh', interview by Alain Grosrichard *et al.*, in Colin Gordon, ed., *Power/Knowledge*, New York, Pantheon, 1980, 194–228

Discipline and Punish, New York, Vintage Books, 1979

The History of Sexuality, vol. I, New York, Vintage Books, 1980

Madness and Civilization: A History of Insanity in the Age of Reason, New York, Vintage Books, 1973

'Nietzsche, Genealogy, History' in Donald F. Bouchard, ed., *Language, Counter-Memory, Practice*, New York, Cornell University Press, 1977, 139–64

The Order of Things, London, Tavistock, 1970

'Power and Strategies', interview by the editorial collective of *Les révoltes logiques*, in Colin Gordon, ed., *Power/Knowledge*, New York, Pantheon, 1980, 134–45

'Prison Talk', interview by J.J. Brochier, in Colin Gordon, ed., *Power/Knowledge*, New York, Pantheon, 1980, 36–54

'Sex, Power and the Politics of Identity', interview by Bob Gallagher and Alexander Wilson, *The Advocate*, 7 August 1984, 26–30, 58

'Truth and Power', interview by Alessandro Fontana and Pasquale Pasquino in Colin Gordon, ed., *Power/Knowledge*, New York, Pantheon, 1980, 109–33

Frank, Andre G., *Latin-America: Underdevelopment or Revolution*, New York, Monthly Review Press, 1969

Franklin, Mark, *The Decline of Class Voting in Britain*, Oxford, Clarendon Press, 1985

Freud, Sigmund, *The Interpretation of Dreams*, Harmondsworth, Penguin, 1976

Fryer, Peter, *Staying Power: The History of Black People in Britain*, London, Pluto, 1984

Fuss, Diana, *Essentially Speaking: Feminism, Nature, and Difference*, London, Routledge, 1990

Fyfe, Christopher, 'Race, Empire and the Historians', *Race and Class*, vol. 33, no. 4, 1992, 15–30

Gale, George, 'The 1970 Election', in John Wood, ed., *Powell and the 1970 Election*, Kingswood, Paperfront, 1970, 50–83

Gamble, Andrew, *The Conservative Nation*, London, Macmillan, 1974
 The Free Economy and the Strong State: The Politics of Thatcherism, Durham, Duke University Press, 1988

Garrison, Len, *Black Youth, Rastafarianism and the Identity Crisis in Britain*, London, ACER, 1979

Garvey, Amy Jacques, *Black Power in America*, Kingston, United Printers, 1968

Gasché, Rodolphe, *The Tain of the Mirror*, Cambridge, Mass., Harvard University Press, 1986

Gates, Jr., Henry Louis, 'Talkin' That Talk', in Gates, ed., *'Race', Writing and Difference*, University of Chicago Press, 1986, 402–9
 'Writing "Race" and the Difference It Makes', in Gates, ed., *'Race', Writing and Difference*, University of Chicago Press, 1986, 1–20

Gilroy, Paul, 'Managing the "Underclass"', *Race and Class*, vol. 22, no. 1, 1980, 47–61
 'Police and Thieves', in Centre for Contemporary Cultural Studies, ed., *The Empire Strikes Back: Race and Racism in 70s Britain*, London, Hutchinson, 1982, 143–82
 'Steppin' Out of Babylon: Race, Class and Autonomy', in Centre for Contemporary Cultural Studies, ed., *The Empire Strikes Back: Race and Racism in 70s Britain*, London, Hutchinson, 1982, 276–314
 'There Ain't No Black in the Union Jack': The Cultural Politics of Race and Nation, London, Hutchinson, 1987

Gouldbourne, Harry, ed., *Black Politics in Britain*, Aldershot, Avebury, 1990

Gramsci, Antonio, *Selections from the Prison Notebooks of Antonio Gramsci*, Quintin Hoare and Geoffrey Nowell Smith, eds. and trans., London, Lawrence and Wishart, 1971

Greater London Council, *Rastafarianism in Greater London*, London, GLC, 1984

Gupta, Sunil, 'Black, *Brown* and White', in Simon Shepherd and Mick Wallis, eds., *Coming On Strong: Gay Politics and Culture*, London, Unwin Hyman, 1989, 163–79

Hall, Stuart, 'Cultural Identity and Diaspora', in Jonathan Rutherford, ed., *Identity: Community, Culture, Difference*, London, Lawrence and Wishart, 1990, 222–37

The Hard Road to Renewal, London, Verso, 1988

'New Ethnicities', in Kobena Mercer, ed., *Black Film, British Cinema*, London, Institute of Contemporary Arts, 1988, 27–30

'Race, Articulation and Societies Structured in Dominance', in UNESCO, ed., *Sociological Theories: Race and Colonialism*, Paris, UNESCO, 1980, 305–46

'Racism and Reaction', in John Rex *et al.*, *Five Views of Multi-Racial Britain*, London, Commission for Racial Equality, 1978, 23–35

and Critcher, Chas, Jefferson, Tony, Clarke, John and Roberts, Brian, *Policing the Crisis: Mugging, the State, and Law and Order*, London, Macmillan, 1978

and Jacques, Martin, *New Times: The Changing Face of Politics in the 1990s*, London, Lawrence and Wishart, 1989

eds., *The Politics of Thatcherism*, London, Lawrence and Wishart, 1983

and Jefferson, Tony, eds., *Resistance Through Rituals: Youth Sub-cultures in Postwar Britain*, London, Hutchinson, 1976

et al., eds., *Culture, Media, Language: Working Papers in Cultural Studies, 1972–9*, London, Hutchinson, 1980

Haraway, Donna, *Primate Visions: Gender, Race and Nature in the World of Modern Science*, New York, Routledge, 1989

Harrison, Bernard, *An Introduction to the Philosophy of Language*, London, Macmillan, 1979

Heath, Anthony *et al.*, *Understanding Political Change*, Oxford, Pergamon Press, 1991

Hebdige, Dick, *Subculture: The Meaning of Style*, London, Methuen, 1979

Higginbotham, Evelyn Brooks, *Righteous Discontent: The Women's Movement in the Black Baptist Church, 1880–1920*, Cambridge, Mass., Harvard University Press, 1993

Hines, Vince, *Britain, the Black Man and the Future*, London, Zulu Publications, 1972

Hiro, Dilip, *Black British, White British*, London, Eyre and Spottiswoode, 1971

Hirschmann, Nancy, *Rethinking Obligation: A Feminist Method for Political Theory*, Ithaca, Cornell University Press, 1992

Hirst, Paul, *After Thatcher*, London, Collins, 1989

Holmes, Colin, 'J.A. Hobson and the Jews', in Colin Holmes, ed., *Immigrants and Minorities in British Society*, London, George Allen and Unwin, 1978, 125–58

hooks, bell, 'Talking Back', in Gloria Anzaldúa, ed., *Making Face, Making Soul = Haciendo Caras: Creative and Critical Perspectives By Women of Color*, San Francisco, Aunt Lute, 1990, 207–11

Husserl, Edmund, *Cartesian Meditations*, The Hague, Martinus Nijhoff, 1969

Logical Investigations, London, Routledge and Kegan Paul, 1970

Independent Committee of Inquiry, *Policing in Hackney, 1945–84: A Report Commissioned by the Roach Family Support Committee*, London, Karia Press, 1989

Institute of Race Relations, 'Anti-Racist Not Multicultural Education', *Race and Class*, vol. 22, no. 1, 1980, 81–3

'Is the Working Class Really Racist?', editorial, *New Statesman*, 2 May 1968, 627

Jacobs, Brian, *Racism in Britain*, London, Croom Helm, 1988

Jah Bones, 'Language and Rastafari', in David Sutcliffe and Ansel Wong, eds., *The Language of Black Experience: Cultural Expression Through Word and Sound in the Caribbean and Black Britain*, Oxford, Basil Blackwell, 1985

Jenkins, David, *Black Zion: The Return of Afro-Americans and West Indians to Africa*, London, Wildwood, 1975

Jessop, Bob, 'The Transformation of the State in Postwar Britain', in Richard Scase, ed., *The State in Western Europe*, London, Croom Helm, 1980, 23–93

Jessop, Bob, *et al.*, *Thatcherism*, Cambridge, Polity Press, 1988

John, Gus, 'West Indies and the Youth Service', *Race Today*, vol. 3, no. 4, April 1971, 130–1

Johnson, Linton Kwesi, 'The Reggae Rebellion', *New Society*, vol. 35, no. 714, 10 June 1976, 589

'Roots and Rock: The Marley Enigma', *Race Today*, vol. 7, no. 10, October 1975, 237–8

Jordan, June, interview by Pratibha Parmar, in Pratibha Parmar, 'Black Feminism: the Politics of Articulation', in Jonathan Rutherford, ed., *Identity: Community, Culture, Difference*, London, Lawrence and Wishart, 1990, 108–13

Jowell, Roger, Witherspoon, Sharon and Brook, Lindsay, eds., *British Social Attitudes: The Fifth Report*, Aldershot, Gower, 1988

Jowell, Roger, Brook, Lindsay, and Taylor, Bridget, with Prior, Gillian, eds., *British Social Attitudes: The Eighth Report*, Aldershot, Gower, 1991

Julien, Isaac and Mercer, Kobena, 'De Margin and De Centre', *Screen*, vol. 29, no. 4, 1988, 2–10

Kapo, Remi, *A Savage Culture: Racism – A Black-British View*, London, Quartet, 1981

Katzenstein, Mary Fainsod, 'The Spectacle as Political Resistance: Feminist and Gay/Lesbian Politics in the Military', *Minerva: A Quarterly Report on Women and the Military*, vol. 11, no. 1, spring 1993, 1–16

Katznelson, Ira, *Black Man, White Cities: Race, Politics and Migration in the United States, 1900–30 and Britain, 1948–68*, Oxford University Press, 1973

Kavanagh, Dennis, *Thatcherism and British Politics: The End of Consensus?*, Oxford University Press, 1987

Kearney, Richard, *Modern Movements in European Philosophy*, Manchester University Press, 1986

Kiernan, V.G., 'Britons Old and New', in Colin Holmes, ed., *Immigrants*

and Minorities in British Society, London, George Allen and Unwin,
1978, 23–62
King, Anthony, 'Margaret Thatcher as a Political Leader', in Robert
Skidelsky, ed., *Thatcherism*, London, Chatto and Windus, 1988,
51–64
King, Robert and Wood, Michael, 'The Support for Enoch Powell', in
Ivor Crewe, ed., *British Political Sociology Yearbook*, London, Croom
Helm, 1975, 239–63
Kirk, Marshall and Madsen, Hunter, *After the Ball: How America Will
Conquer Its Fear and Hatred of Gays in the '90s*, New York, Doubleday,
1989
Knowles, Caroline, *Race, Discourse and Labourism*, London, Routledge,
1992
Lacan, Jacques, *Ecrits*, London, Tavistock, 1977
Laclau, Ernesto, 'Community and Its Paradoxes: Richard Rorty's
"Liberal Utopia"', unpublished paper
New Reflections on the Revolution of Our Time, London, Verso, 1990
Politics and Ideology in Marxist Theory, London, Verso, 1979
'Totalitarianism and Moral Indignation', *Diacritics*, vol. 20, no. 3, fall
1990, 88–95
and Mouffe, Chantal, *Hegemony and Socialist Strategy*, London, Verso,
1985
Lambert, John *et al.*, 'Police/Immigrant Relations: A Critique of the Select
Committee Report', *New Community*, vol. 3, no. 3, summer 1974,
172–92
Lane, A.H., *The Alien Menace: A Statement of the Case*, London, Boswell
Publishing, 1934
Laplanche, J. and Pontalis, J.-B., *The Language of Psychoanalysis*, New
York, W.W. Norton and Co., 1973
Lawrence, Daniel, *Black Migrants – White Natives: A Study of Race Relations
in Nottingham*, Cambridge University Press, 1974
Lawrence, Errol, '"In the Abundance of Water the Fool is Thirsty":
Sociology and Black "Pathology"', in Centre for Contemporary
Cultural Studies, ed., *The Empire Strikes Back: Race and Racism in 70s
Britain*, London, Hutchinson, 1982, 95–142
'Just Plain Common Sense: The "Roots" of Racism', in Centre for
Contemporary Cultural Studies, ed., *The Empire Strikes Back: Race and
Racism in 70s Britain*, London, Hutchinson, 1982, 47–94
Layton-Henry, Zig, *The Politics of Race in Britain*, London, George Allen
and Unwin, 1984
and Rich, Paul, eds., *Race, Government and Politics in Britain*, London,
Macmillan, 1986
Leapman, Michael, *Kinnock*, London, Unwin Hyman, 1987
Levitas, Ruth, ed., *The Ideology of the New Right*, Cambridge, Polity Press,
1986
Lewis, Gordon, 'Race Relations in Britain: A View From the Caribbean',
Race Today, vol. 1, no. 3, July 1969, 78–80
Lewis, Roy, *Enoch Powell*, London, Cassell, 1979
Leys, Colin, *Politics in Britain*, London, Verso, 1983

Lorde, Audre, interview by Pratibha Parmar and Jackie Kay, 'Frontiers', in Shabnam Grewal *et al.*, eds., *Charting the Journey: Writings by Black and Third World Women*, London, Sheba Feminist Publishers, 1988, 121–31

Mackenzie, John, *Propaganda and Empire*, University Press, 1984

McNeil, Maureen, 'Making and Not Making the Difference: The Gender Politics of Thatcherism', in Sarah Franklin, Celia Lury and Jackie Stacey, eds., *Off-Centre: Feminism and Cultural Studies*, London, Harper Collins, 1991, 221–40

Maggenti, Maria, *et al.*, 'A Round Table Discussion: AIDS and Democracy', in Brian Wallis, ed., *Democracy: A Project by Group Material*, Seattle, Bay Press, 1990, 241–58

Malik, Michael Abdul, *From Michael de Freitas to Michael X*, London, Andre Deutsch, 1968

Mama, Amina, 'Black Women, the Economic Crisis and the British State', *Feminist Review*, no. 17, autumn 1984, 21–36

Marshall, John, 'Flaunting It: The Challenge of the 1990s', *Gay Times*, January 1989, 12–13

Martin, Biddy and Mohanty, Chandra Talpade, 'Feminist Politics: What's Home Got to Do With It?', in Teresa de Lauretis, ed., *Feminist Studies/Critical Studies*, Bloomington, Indiana University Press, 1986, 191–212

Martin, Tony, 'Garvey and Scattered Africa' in Joseph Harris, ed., *Global Dimensions of the African Diaspora*, Washington, Howard University Press, 1982, 243–9

Marx, Karl, 'The Eighteenth Brumaire of Louis Bonaparte', *The Selected Works of Karl Marx and Frederick Engels*, Moscow, Progress Publishers, 1966, vol. I, 394–487

Mercer, Colin, 'Fascist Ideology', in James Donald and Stuart Hall, eds., *Politics and Ideology*, Milton Keynes, Open University Press, 1986, 208–39

Mercer, Kobena, 'Powellism: Race, Politics and Discourse', unpublished Ph.D. thesis, Goldsmith's College, University of London, 1990
'Skin Head Sex Thing: Racial Difference and the Homoerotic Imaginary', *New Formations*, no. 16, spring 1992, 1–23
and Julien, Isaac, 'Race, Sexual Politics and Black Masculinity', in Rowena Chapman and Jonathan Rutherford, eds., *Male Order*, London, Lawrence and Wishart, 1988, 97–164

Midgett, Douglas, 'West Indian Ethnicity in Great Britain', in Helen Safa and Brian du Toit, eds., *Migration and Development*, The Hague, Mouton, 1975, 57–82

Miles, Robert, 'Between Two Cultures? The Case of Rastafarianism', *Working Papers in Ethnic Relations*, Bristol, SSRS Research Unit on Ethnic Relations at the University of Bristol, paper no.10, 1978
'Marxism versus the Sociology of "Race Relations"', *Ethnic and Racial Studies*, vol. 7, no. 2, 1984, 217–37

Minkowitz, Donna, 'Outlawing Gays', *The Nation*, 19 October 1992, 420–1

Mohanty, Chandra Talpade, 'Introduction: Cartographies of Struggle', in Mohanty, Ann Russo and Lourdes Torres, eds., *Third World*

Women and the Politics of Feminism, Bloomington, Indiana University Press, 1991, 1–50

Mouffe, Chantal, ed., *Dimensions of Radical Democracy: Pluralism, Citizenship, Community*, London, Verso, 1992

Mullard, Chris, *Black Britain*, London, Allen and Unwin, 1973

Muller, John and Richardson, William, *Lacan and Language*, New York, International Universities Press Inc., 1982

Mure, Geoffrey, *Introduction to Hegel*, Oxford University Press, 1940

Murray, Nancy, 'Anti-Racists and Other Demons: The Press and Ideology in Thatcher's Britain', *Race and Class*, vol. 27, no. 3, 1986, 1–19

Nairn, Tom, *The Break-Up of Britain: Crisis and Neo-Nationalism*, London, Verso, 1977

'The Crisis of the British State', *New Left Review*, vol. 130, Nov.–Dec. 1981, 37–44

'Enoch Powell: the New Right', *New Left Review*, vol. 61, May–June 1970, 4–11

Nandy, Ashis, *The Intimate Enemy: Loss and the Recovery of Self under Colonialism*, Delhi, Oxford University Press, 1983

Ngcobo, Lauretta, ed., *Let It Be Told: Essays by Black Women Writers in Britain*, London, Virago, 1988

Nietzsche, Friedrich, *On the Genealogy of Morals*, Walter Kaufmann, trans., New York, Vintage Books, 1969

Norris, Katrin, *Jamaica: The Search for Identity*, Oxford University Press, 1962

Norval, Aletta, 'Letter to Ernesto', in Ernesto Laclau, *New Reflections on the Revolution of Our Time*, London, Verso, 1990, 135–58

'Race and Class in South Africa: A Post–Marxist Approach', unpublished paper presented to the Ideology and Discourse Analysis Seminar, University of Essex, 7 December 1988

O'Brien, Conor Cruise, *The Siege: The Saga of Israel and Zionism*, New York, Simon and Schuster, 1986

O'Brien, Philip, 'A Critique of Latin American Theories of Dependency', in I. Oxaal, T. Barnett and D. Booth, eds., *Beyond the Sociology of Development in Latin America and Africa*, London, Routledge and Kegan Paul, 1975, 7–27

Official Report, Hansard Report of the Debates in the House of Commons, the House of Lords and Parliamentary Committees, as noted

Osman, Sona, 'Should It Be Unlawful to Incite Sexual Violence,' in Gail Chester and Julienne Dickey, eds., *Feminism and Censorship*, Bridport, Prism, 1988, 151–60

Ousley, H., et al., *A Different Reality: A Report of the Review Panel on the Handsworth Rebellions*, Handsworth, West Midlands County Council, 1986

Out on Tuesday, Abseil Productions, Channel Four television series, 14 February 1989

Owens, Joseph, *The Doctrine of Being in the Aristotelian Metaphysics*, Toronto, Pontifical Institute of Medieval Studies, 1978

Parmar, Pratibha, 'Gender, Race and Class: Asian Women in Resistance', in Centre for Contemporary Cultural Studies, ed., *The Empire Strikes*

Back: Race and Racism in 70s Britain, London, Hutchinson, 1982, 212–35

'Rage and Desire: Confronting Pornography', in Gail Chester and Julienne Dickey, eds., *Feminism and Censorship*, Bridport, Prism, 1988, 119–132

Parry, Geraint, Moyser, George and Day, Neil, *Political Participation and Democracy in Britain*, Cambridge University Press, 1992

Pathak, Zakia and Rajan, Rajeswari Sunder, '"Shahbano"', in Judith Butler and Joan Scott, eds., *Feminists Theorize the Political*, New York, Routledge, 1992, 257–79

Patton, Cindy, *Inventing AIDS*, London, Routledge, 1990

Peele, Gillian, 'Parties, Pressure Groups and Parliament', in Patrick Dunleavy, Andrew Gamble and Gillian Peele, eds., *Developments in British Politics 3*, New York, St Martin's Press, 1990, 69–95

Phillips, Ken, 'The Nature of Powellism', in Roger King and Neill Nugent, eds., *The British Right: Conservative and Right Wing Politics in Britain*, Westmead, Saxon House, 1977, 99–132

Phoenix, Ann, 'Theories of Gender and Black Families', in T. Lovell, ed., *British Feminist Thought*, Oxford, Basil Blackwell, 1990, 199–33

Plummer, John, *Movement of Jah People*, Birmingham, Press Gang, 1978

Plummer, Ken, ed., *Modern Homosexualities: Fragments of Lesbian and Gay Experience*, London, Routledge, 1992

Pollard, Paul, 'Jamaicans and Trinidadians in North London', *New Community*, vol. 1, no. 5, autumn 1972, 370–7

Porter, Bernard, *The Lion's Share: A Short History of British Imperialism*, London, Longman, 1984

Powell, Enoch, *Freedom and Reality*, John Wood, ed., Kingswood, Paperfront, 1969

A Nation Not Afraid, John Wood, ed., London, Batsford, 1965

A Nation or No Nation? Six Years in British Politics, Richard Ritchie, ed., London, Batsford, 1978

No Easy Answers, London, Sheldon, 1973

Still to Decide, John Wood, ed., London, Batsford, 1972

Pryce, Ken, *Endless Pressure: A Study of West Indian Life-Styles in Britain*, Bristol Classical Press, 1985

Przeworski, Adam, *Capitalism and Social Democracy*, Cambridge University Press, 1985

Racevskis, Karlis, 'Michel Foucault, Rameau's Nephew and the Question of Identity', in James Bernauer and David Rasmussen, eds., *The Final Foucault*, Cambridge, Mass., MIT, 1988, 21–33

Reeves, Frank, *British Racial Discourse: A Study of British Political Discourse about Race and Race-related Matters*, Cambridge University Press, 1983

Rex, John, 'The Problem of the Sociology of Race Relations', in Rex, *Race, Colonialism and the City*, London, Routledge and Kegan Paul, 1973, 193–229

'The Theory of Race Relations: A Weberian Approach', in UNESCO, ed., *Sociological Theories: Race and Colonialism*, Paris, UNESCO, 1980, 117–42

and Tomlinson, Sally, 'Class Analysis and Colonial Immigrants', in Rex

and Tomlinson, *Colonial Immigrants in a British City*, London, Routledge and Kegan Paul, 1979, 1–35
Rich, Paul, 'Conservative Ideology and Race in Modern British Politics', in Zig Layton-Henry and Paul Rich, ed., *Race, Government and Politics in Britain*, London, Macmillan, 1986, 45–72
Race and Empire in British Politics, Cambridge University Press, 1986
Riddell, Peter, *The Thatcher Era and Its Legacy*, Oxford, Basil Blackwell, 1991
Robertson, David, *Class and the British Electorate*, Oxford, Basil Blackwell, 1984
Rose, Richard and McAllister, Ian, *Voters Begin to Choose: From Closed-Class to Open Elections in Britain*, London, Sage, 1986
Rose, Steven and Rose, Hilary, 'Less Than Human Nature: Biology and the New Right', *Race and Class*, vol. 27, no. 3, 1986, 47–66
Ross, William, *Aristotle*, London, Methuen, 1949
Rousseau, Jean Jacques, *The Social Contract and Discourses*, G.D.H. Cole, trans., London, J.M. Dent and Sons, 1973
Rubin, Gayle, 'Thinking Sex' in Carole Vance, ed., *Pleasure and Danger: Exploring Female Sexuality*, New York, Routledge and Kegan Paul, 1984, 267–319
Rushdie, Salman, *Imaginary Homelands*, London, Granta, 1991
The Satanic Verses, London, Penguin, 1988
Said, Edward, *Orientalism*, London, Penguin, 1987
'Orientalism Reconsidered', *Race and Class*, vol. 27, no. 2, 1985, 1–15
Sandoval, Chela, 'Feminism and Racism: A Report on the 1981 National Women's Studies Association Conference', in Gloria Anzaldúa, ed., *Making Face, Making Soul = Haciendo Caras: Creative and Critical Perspectives By Women of Color*, San Francisco, Aunt Lute, 1990, 55–74
de Saussure, Ferdinand, *Course in General Linguistics*, London, McGraw-Hill, 1966
Schmitt, R., 'Phenomenology', in Paul Edwards, ed., *Encyclopedia of Philosophy*, London, Collier Macmillan, 1967, 135–51
Schoen, Douglas, *Enoch Powell and the Powellites*, London, Macmillan, 1977
Schwarz, Bill, 'Conservatism, Nationalism and Imperialism' in James Donald and Stuart Hall, eds., *Politics and Ideology*, Milton Keynes, Open University Press, 1986, 154–87
Scott, James, *Domination and the Arts of Resistance: Hidden Transcripts*, New Haven, Yale University Press, 1990
Scott, Joan, 'Experience', in Judith Butler and Scott, eds., *Feminists Theorize the Political*, New York, Routledge, 1992, 22–40
Scruton, Roger, *Sexual Desire*, London, Weidenfeld and Nicolson, 1986
Sedgwick, Eve Kosofsky, *The Epistemology of the Closet*, Berkeley, University of California Press, 1990
Seidel, Gill, 'The Concept of Culture, "Race" and Nation in the British and French New Right', in Ruth Levitas, ed., *The Ideology of the New Right*, London, Polity Press, 1986, 107–35
'The White Discursive Order: the British New Right's Discourse on Cultural Racism with Particular Reference to the *Salisbury Review*',

in I. Zavala *et al.*, eds., *Approaches to Discourse, Poetics and Psychiatry*, Amsterdam, Benjamins, 1987, 39–66

Shyllon, Folarin, 'Blacks in Britain', in Joseph Harris, ed., *Global Dimensions of the African Diaspora*, Washington, Howard University Press, 1982, 170–94

Silverman, David, and Torode, Brian, *The Material Word: Some Theories of Language and Its Limits*, London, Routledge and Kegan Paul, 1980

Sivanandan, A., *A Different Hunger: Writings on Black Resistance*, London, Pluto, 1982

Skidelsky, Robert, ed., *Thatcherism*, London, Chatto and Windus, 1988

Smith, M.G., Augier, Roy and Nettleford, Rex, 'The Ras Tafari Movement in Kingston, Jamaica', *Social and Economic Studies*, vol. 9, no. 3, 1960, supplement

Smithies, Bill, and Fiddick, Peter, *Enoch Powell on Immigration*, London, Sphere Books, 1969

Smyth, Cherry, *Lesbians Talk Queer Notions*, London, Scarlet Press, 1992

Solomos, John *et al.*, 'The Organic Crisis of British Capitalism and Race: The Experience of the Seventies', in Centre for Contemporary Cultural Studies, *The Empire Strikes Back: Race and Racism in 70s Britain*, London, Hutchinson, 1982, 9–46

Sontag, Susan, *AIDS and Its Metaphors*, New York, Farrar, Strauss and Giroux, 1989

Spearman, Diana, 'Enoch Powell's Postbag', *New Society*, 9 May 1968, 667–9

'Enoch Powell's Election Letters', in John Wood, ed., *Powell and the 1970 Election*, Kingswood, Paperfront, 1970, 19–50

Spivak, Gayatri Chakravorty, *In Other Worlds*, New York, Routledge, 1987

'Translator's Preface', in Jacques Derrida, *Of Grammatology*, London, Johns Hopkins University Press, 1976, ix–lxxxvii

Stacey, Jackie, 'Promoting Normality: Section 28 and the Regulation of Sexuality', in Sarah Franklin, Celia Lury and Jackie Stacey, eds., *Off-Centre: Feminism and Cultural Studies*, London, Harper Collins, 1991, 284–304

Stacey, Tom, *Immigration and Enoch Powell*, London, Tom Stacey, 1970

Staten, Henry, *Wittgenstein and Derrida*, Lincoln, University of Nebraska Press, 1984

Stevenson, Dennis and Wallis, Peter, 'Second Generation West Indians: A Study in Alienation', *Race Today*, vol. 2, no. 8, August 1970, 278–80

Studlar, Donley, 'British Public Opinion, Colour Issues and Enoch Powell', *The British Journal of Political Science*, no. 3, July 1974, 371–81

Swilling, Mark, 'The United Democratic Front and Township Revolt in South Africa', unpublished paper presented at the Eighteenth Annual Congress of the Association for Sociology in Southern Africa, University of the Western Cape, Cape Town, 29 June – 2 July 1987

Tatchell, Peter, *The Battle for Bermondsey*, London, Heretic Books, 1983

'Gay Men More Likely To Be Found Guilty', *Capital Gay*, 18 January 1991, 4

Taylor, Clyde, 'The Master Text and the Jeddi Doctrine', *Screen*, vol. 29, no. 4, 1988, 62–70

Thatcher, Margaret, address to the General Assembly of the Church of Scotland, *The Observer*, 22 May 1988, 2

  The Revival of Britain: Speeches on Home and European Affairs, 1975–1988, London, Aurum Press, 1989

Tobin, Ann, 'Lesbianism and the Labour Party: The GLC Experience', *Feminist Review*, no. 34, spring 1990, 56–66

Trivedi, Parita, 'To Deny Our Fullness: Asian Women in the Making of History', *Feminist Review*, no. 17, autumn 1984, 37–52

Utley, T.E., *Enoch Powell: The Man and His Thinking*, London, William Kimber, 1968

Vincent, Theodore, *Black Power and the Garvey Movement*, San Francisco, Ramparts, 1976

Walvin, James, *The Black Presence: A Documentary History of the Negro in England, 1555–1860*, New York, Schocken Books, 1972

Washington, Eric, 'Freedom Rings! The Alliance Between Blacks and Gays is Threatened by Mutual Inscrutability', *The Village Voice*, 29 July 1993, 25, 31–3

Watney, Simon, *Policing Desire: Pornography, AIDS and the Media*, London, Methuen, 1987

  'Psychoanalysis, Sexuality and AIDS' in Simon Shepherd and Mick Wallis, eds., *Coming On Strong: Gays, Politics and Culture*, London, Unwin Hyman, 1989, 22–38

  and Carter, Erica, eds., *Taking Liberties: AIDS and Cultural Politics*, London, Serpent's Tail, 1989

Webster, Wendy, *Not a Man to Match Her*, London, The Women's Press, 1990

Weeks, Jeffrey, *Coming Out: Homosexual Politics in Britain from the Nineteenth Century to the Present*, London, Quartet, 1977

  Sex, Politics and Society: The Regulation of Sexuality Since 1800, London, Longman, 1981

Willetts, David, 'The Family', in Dennis Kavanagh and Anthony Seldon, eds., *The Thatcher Effect*, Oxford, Clarendon Press, 1989, 262–73

Williams, Patricia J., *The Alchemy of Race and Rights*, Cambridge, Harvard University Press, 1991

  'Lani, We Hardly Knew Ye', *The Village Voice*, 15 June 1993, 27, 28

Willis, Paul, *Learning to Labour: How Working Class Kids Get Working Class Jobs*, Farnborough, Saxon House, 1977

Wittgenstein, Ludwig, *Philosophical Investigations*, Oxford, Basil Blackwell, 1958

Wolpe, Harold, *Race, Class and the Apartheid State*, London, James Currey, 1988

Yamato, Gloria, 'Something About the Subject Makes It Hard to Name', in Gloria Anzaldúa, ed., *Making Face, Making Soul = Haciendo Caras*, San Francisco, Aunt Lute Foundation Books, 1990, 20–4

Young, Hugo, *One of Us: A Biography of Margaret Thatcher*, London, Macmillan, 1989

Zinn, Maxine Baca, *et al.*, 'The Costs of Exclusionary Practices in

Women's Studies', in Gloria Anzaldúa, ed., *Making Face, Making Soul = Haciendo Caras: Creative and Critical Perspectives By Women of Color*, San Francisco, Aunt Lute Foundation Books, 1990, 29–41

Zizek, Slavoj, *The Sublime Object of Ideology*, London, Verso, 1989

Index